37.94

796.01

Applying Educational Psychology in Coaching Athletes

Jeffrey J. Huber, PhD

Human Kinetics

Library of Congress Cataloging-in-Publication Data

Huber, Jeffrey J., 1953-
  Applying educational psychology in coaching athletes / Jeffrey J. Huber.
    p. cm.
  Includes bibliographical references and index.
  1. Coaching (Athletics)--Psychological aspects. 2. Educational psychology. I. Title
  GV711.H74 2012
  796.077--dc23

                            2012014408

ISBN-10: 0-7360-7981-5
ISBN-13: 978-0-7360-7981-5

The web addresses cited in this text were current as of May 2012, unless otherwise noted.

Acquisitions Editor: Myles Schrag; **Developmental Editor:** Kevin Matz; **Assistant Editor:** Susan Huls; **Copyeditor:** Joanna Hatzopoulos Portman; **Indexer:** Susan Danzi Hernandez; **Permissions Manager:** Dalene Reeder; **Graphic Designer:** Joe Buck; **Graphic Artist:** Kathleen Boudreau-Fuoss; **Cover Designers:** Robert Reuther and Keith Blomberg; **Photographer (cover):** KenSeet/Corbis RF; **Photo Production Manager:** Jason Allen, **Art Manager:** Kelly Hendren; **Associate Art Manager:** Alan L. Wilborn; **Illustrations:** © Human Kinetics; **Printer:** Edwards Brothers Malloy

Printed in the United States of America   10   9   8   7   6   5   4   3   2   1

The paper in this book is certified under a sustainable forestry program.

Human Kinetics
Website: www.HumanKinetics.com

United States: Human Kinetics
P.O. Box 5076
Champaign, IL 61825-5076
800-747-4457
e-mail: humank@hkusa.com

Canada: Human Kinetics
475 Devonshire Road Unit 100
Windsor, ON N8Y 2L5
800-465-7301 (in Canada only)
e-mail: info@hkcanada.com

Europe: Human Kinetics
107 Bradford Road
Stanningley
Leeds LS28 6AT, United Kingdom
+44 (0) 113 255 5665
e-mail: hk@hkeurope.com

Australia: Human Kinetics
57A Price Avenue
Lower Mitcham, South Australia 5062
08 8372 0999
e-mail: info@hkaustralia.com

New Zealand: Human Kinetics
P.O. Box 80
Torrens Park, South Australia 5062
0800 222 062
e-mail: info@hknewzealand.com

E4700

To my wife, Lesa, and our children,
Julia and David. Thanks for your love,
support, and understanding
during my coaching career.
You were always on my mind
and in my heart
and you are the most important
people in my life.

And to all those wonderful athletes
who gave me their heart, trust, and devotion.
Many of your stories are in this book.

CONTENTS

Part III Athletes and Theories of Cognitivism 149

Part V Developing Your Coaching Skills and Philosophy   339

PREFACE

If my coaching career were an Aesop's fable, it would have to be *The Tortoise and the Hare*. I would be the tortoise and Michael the hare.

About the time when I began coaching, Michael, a very successful former athlete, also began coaching. He was a multiple-time U.S. national champion and U.S. Olympian, so naturally he attracted some of the best recruits in the country. He knew the sport well and was successful right out of the chute. In contrast, I attracted zero top recruits and, frankly, I had much to learn about the sport and about coaching. While he won quickly and won big, I stayed home, plodding along and reading about his athletes' exploits. After a few years, Michael left the sport to pursue a business venture. During his absence I earned a doctorate in educational psychology with an emphasis in cognition and motor learning. Educational psychology is the study of applying principles of psychology to the teaching and learning process. My wife also earned her doctorate and we then loaded up the car with our two very young children, cat, and dog and drove to Bloomington, Indiana.

For the first 6 years at Indiana University, I taught classes on educational psychology for teachers, preparing students to apply principles of psychology to the teaching and learning process in their future classrooms. I also coached the men's and women's diving teams. This point in my life reminds me of Robert Frost's poem "The Road Not Taken."

> . . . I shall be telling this with a sigh
> Somewhere ages and ages hence:
> Two roads diverged in a wood, and I—
> I took the one less traveled by,
> And that has made all the difference.
> [Robert Frost, "The Road Not Taken," 1920]

In my mind, I had found two diverging roads in the wood—coaching and teaching—and I intended to take both. But at some point things became blurry. I couldn't see a difference anymore between teaching and coaching or between students and athletes. It all seemed to be the same thing. Theories, concepts, paradigms, principles, laws, and research data that influence teaching and student learning in the classroom seemed equally effective for influencing coaching and athlete learning in the practice setting. Factors that make for effective teaching seemed to me to also make for effective coaching. Teachers of excellence and coaches of excellence essentially do the same things. Instead of traveling two separate roads, I had in fact been traveling the same road. Being a teacher and being a coach are the same thing.

Eight years after he left, Michael returned to the sport. And things had changed. Or, rather, *I* had changed. Since his departure I had become a more effective coach by better understanding how athletes learn and how coaches teach. At the NCAA championship that year he walked up to me, smiled, and good-naturedly asked, "What happened?" What he meant was "How did you become so successful as a coach since I last saw you?" The previous year I had been named U.S. Olympic coach for a second Olympic Games and—I'm not going to lie—at that NCAA championship I had a dominant team, so much so that I was voted NCAA Coach of the Year. It may have taken over two decades but the tortoise had finally victoriously crossed the finish line.

My reason for coaching, however, had nothing to do with any personal motivation for becoming an Olympic coach or an NCAA Coach of the Year. It had everything to do with Jimmy. Our paths fortuitously crossed when I volunteered to coach at Cypress College in Southern California. I was pursuing a master's degree in English at the time but felt compelled to repay the sport that I had recently retired from and that had generously given me so much. Cypress College didn't pay me anything to coach their men's and women's teams but I was provided the opportunity to run an age group program for free. In other words, I wouldn't be charged pool rent. I really didn't want or have the time to run an age group program because I was attending graduate school full-time and working for Hank—my dad—on the side but, of course, when I heard the words *for free,* I couldn't resist. That wasn't such a lucrative idea. The most money I ever made in one month was $200. But in hindsight it turned out to be a brilliant idea for finding a career path.

Two months after I launched (instead of ocean liner think row boat) my age-group program, two 14-year-old boys wandered into the pool—Brian and Jimmy. Brian was a good-looking and physically talented boy while Jimmy was a gangly, acne-faced, uncoordinated, and physically awkward lad. Immediately I had visions of grandeur for Brian. He was going to be my first superstar and Jimmy—well, Jimmy was going to be a nonentity on the team and most likely eventually fade away.

I couldn't have been more wrong.

I will never forget Jimmy's first day of practice—an inauspicious beginning for sure. He attempted to climb onto the trampoline and in the process somehow put his foot through the springs, fell backward, and almost did a back dive onto the gymnasium floor. For a moment I thought he was going to kill himself. I wanted to teach him how to dive and eventually learn a back dive, but that wasn't what I had in mind! In contrast to Jimmy, everything came more easily for Brian. But despite my preconceived notions and biased expectations, Jimmy prevailed and it was Brian who eventually faded away.

Through sport Jimmy found something he needed in his life, something he couldn't find anywhere else. Sport became his manna, his lifeline, his necessity—a way for him to find self-esteem, pride, belongingness, and salvation. He far exceeded my expectations of what I thought he could achieve and he reminded me of the superiority of motivation over talent and the power of the human spirit. He was just so determined at that precise moment in his adolescent life to accomplish something noteworthy, to overcome some obstacle, to meet some challenge—to prove to himself that he was a competent and capable human being after all. Every practice was a triumph over the impossible. Within 6 months Jimmy was performing a full list of dives on the 1-meter springboard and several dives on the 3-meter springboard. I learned to believe in the unbelievable.

When I discovered Jimmy would have to quit the team because his parents couldn't afford the monthly $20 club fee, I told him he could wash and wax my car each month and in return I would coach him. You see, I needed Jimmy as much as Jimmy needed sport. I wanted to pay back the sport but I wasn't prepared for what the sport continued to give back to me. I loved coaching that kid. *He* had become *my* manna, *my* lifeline, *my* necessity. Watching him come to practice every day and accomplish the impossible stirred my coaching soul and made each practice a gift. And, I had a very clean car.

I lost track of Jimmy so I can't say for sure, but I think—hope—I made a difference in his life to some degree just as several of my coaches made a difference in mine. I know Jimmy made a difference in my life. He taught me the power of hope and determination. Coaching is an amazingly rewarding profession. I don't think any greater profession exists where you can affect the lives of others and at the same time receive such deep and lasting intrinsic reward.

THE BECOMING COACH

This book is not about *being* a coach, it is about *becoming* one. It is about you becoming the kind of coach you dream of becoming—the effective, successful, and unforgettable coach, the coach who knows how to teach, the coach who positively affects the athletic careers and lives of young athletes, the coach kids never forget. Becoming this coach in part means understanding the different learning theories, principles, paradigms, and practices that lead to successful coaching.

This book, then, is about applying principles of psychology to the motor learning and coaching process, just as I did early in my coaching career, to understand not *what* athletes learn and *what* coaches teach but, rather, *how* athletes learn and *how* coaches teach. A number of principles helped guide the writing of this book.

Teaching a motor skill is similar to teaching a subject in a classroom setting. Therefore, principles of psychology that apply to teaching and learning in a classroom also apply to coaching and motor learning in a practice setting.

Cognition plays a role in motor learning just as it does in classroom learning. Learning a motor skill and learning a classroom subject require many of the same cognitive skills. Consequently, many of the cognitive implications associated with classroom teaching and learning apply to coaching and motor learning.

Coaching and learning are about making connections. Rumelhart and Norman (1981) suggest that learning occurs through the formation of analogies. In other words, the process of learning something new involves connecting it with something already known. Each theory in this book examines connections important for effective coaching and athlete learning. For example, respondent (classical conditioning) learning theory examines the connection between positive neutral stimuli and your sport. Operant conditioning learning theory looks at the connection between a behavior and its consequences. Motivation learning theory looks at connections such as the one between internal locus of control and effort.

Effective coaching accelerates motor learning. Any coach will tell you that there is no shortcut to success. Chase and Simon (1973) famously suggested that it takes approximately 10 years or 10,000 hours to achieve expertise in sport and nonsport domains. Whether it is chess, music, mathematics, tennis, or swimming, achieving expertise takes a prerequisite amount of time and, while it may or may not be possible to shorten this time parameter, it is certainly possible to lengthen it through ineffective coaching. On the other hand, effective coaching is like the straight line between two points: the shortest distance. When you understand how athletes learn and how coaches teach, you can help your athletes rapidly improve, getting from point A to point B in the least time.

Effective coaching involves developing athletes' physical, mental, and emotional abilities. Athletes bring three abilities to their sport: physical ability, mental ability, and emotional ability. It doesn't do you much good to develop athletes' physical ability if you don't concomitantly develop their mental and emotional abilities. And, in truth, it may not be possible to teach an athlete without considering all three abilities.

Effective coaching involves developing psychologically healthy, competent, and confident athletes who have a sense of self-worth. This development positively affects their motor learning and performance and their lives after sport. At the center of the teaching process is the individual. As Buscaglia (1984) says, "You don't teach subjects; you teach people." Consequently, one goal as a coach should be to help players grow as human beings and not simply as athletes. The nice thing about such a goal is that it comes back twofold to positively affect motor learning and performance. Individuals who possess a healthy psychological perspective, competence, confidence, and a sense of self-worth tend to be better learners (Brunson & Vogt, 1996) and achievers (Kohn, 1993).

Coaching is both an art and a science. I had the good fortune to work with some amazing athletes who were also amazing human beings. I thank them for their faith in me and their dedication to the program and for acting as guinea pigs during my "longitudinal study" of coaching and motor learning. Although I taught these athletes, they taught me and one of the things I learned from them is that coaching is both an art and a science. While scientific approaches to coaching and training are necessary for coaching effectiveness and athlete success, they neglect an athlete's humanity. Scientific approaches tend to dehumanize athletes and overlook issues such as feelings, personal values, personal growth, emotions, and communication, all of which are important to human beings. Therefore, a successful approach to coaching includes both art and science. As Eisner (1982) suggests, every successful teaching experience is a result of both art and science. Some coaches believe that the art of coaching cannot be described or quantified; I disagree. Throughout the book I provide specific examples of the artful coach in action.

So, this book is about art—understanding principles of psychology that affect unscientific and less quantifiable factors such as emotions, motivation, expectations, self-worth, and relationships like the one I established with Jimmy years ago. And this book is about science—applying principles of psychology to the motor learning and coaching process, just as I did early in my coaching career, to more fully understand *how* athletes learn and *how* coaches teach.

To be of value, learning theories must have direct application for coaching athletes. Theories don't mean much to coaches unless they lead to specific applications for coaching athletes. Therefore, throughout the text I provide these applications. For example, in discussing humanism I provide guidelines for coaches to follow when applying the nondirective model of coaching. To be even more specific, I provide a mock dialogue between athlete and coach that uses these guidelines. In discussing practice management and discipline, I provide guidelines for creating an atmosphere that engenders appropriate behavior and then give examples of how these guidelines can be applied in a practice setting.

The processes of how athletes learn and how coaches teach are inseparable. Every discussion in this book about the athlete and athlete learning is also a discussion about the coach and coach teaching because both athlete and coach are the dancers and learning and teaching are the dance.

> Oh chestnut-tree, great-rooted blossomer,
> Are you the leaf, the blossom or the hole?
> O body swayed to music, O brightening glance,
> How can we know the dancer from the dance?
> — *Among School Children, by William Butler Yeats*

It was the summer before my freshman year in college and I was lifeguarding at a private club. Paul was small for his age. His mother contracted German measles (rubella) during pregnancy and Paul was born blind and deaf. He first attracted my attention because of his love for the water. I think it was the most wonderful thing to him in his world and I wonder how many of us have something in our lives that excites us as much as Paul enjoyed being in the water. He would spend those summer days in the baby pool wading, kneeling, putting his face in the water, running in water circles, slapping the water— and laughing. He liked to lie in the water, look up toward the sky, and rapidly wave his right hand in front of his face. I think he did it because it created a kaleidoscope-like effect for what little eyesight he had. He would wave his hand and laugh and I asked myself if there was anything comparably simple in my life that I enjoyed nearly so much.

Paul's mother was a warm and loving woman who knew how important the water was to him, but she also worried about his safety, as did I. One day I approached her and asked if I could teach him to swim. She was surprised. I don't think she thought he was capable of learning to swim, especially at such a young age. With her permission I set up a time each morning before the pool opened when Paul and I could work together. That first morning I took his tiny hand and together we waded into the shallow end of the *big boy* pool. It was the beginning of our first dance.

Paul did indeed learn to swim that summer. I refused to accept any money from his mother because my reward was watching him jump into the deep end and swim safely to the side—no more wading pool for this guy. His world just got a lot bigger. It was my joy to see the smile on his face and the sense of accomplishment I imagined he must be feeling. Did I unexpectedly discover something I enjoyed almost as much as Paul enjoyed playing in the water and waving his hand in front of his face? I think so. My freshman year of college I decided to become a teacher.

There is no dance without the dancer. There is no coach if there is no athlete. There is no teaching if there is no learning. And how do we know the dancer from the dance? We don't. The chapters in this book are about both athlete and coach and about both teaching and learning and how, when everything magically comes together, coach and athlete and teaching and learning dissolve into one to create a beautiful and ineffable waltz-like experience.

CHAPTER STRUCTURE

Each chapter begins with a story about an athlete or coach that highlights the significance of the theory under consideration. The introduction is followed by a chapter overview and then the theory is clearly defined and carefully outlined. Perhaps most important, each chapter offers specific applications of the learning theory for coaching athletes. Each chapter concludes with a composite picture of the athlete and the coach and sections titled Your Coaching Toolbox, The Scientific and Artful Coach, and If You Remember Only Three Things. Suggested readings are also provided.

CONCLUSION

I am convinced that coaches can develop into elite coaches just as athletes can develop into elite athletes. This book is written for coaches yearning to reach their greatest coaching potential and be the elite coach they dream of becoming. I hope the information contained in this book contributes to their growth and success as much as it did mine.

The Becoming Coach

Key Terms

active participants

cognitive skill

empowering

games approach

motor learning

motor performance

motor skill

psychology

reflective coaching

target behaviors

target context

target skills

task analysis

Second semester was always a long stretch of road. Dual meets, championships, and international competitions put me on the road and kept me out of the classroom. I was gone so many days that I only taught first semester each academic year. I have no doubt that I did my best coaching during those semesters when I taught the course *Educational Psychology for Teachers*. It was an invigorating and inspiring semester. I was reading and thinking about learning theories at night. I was talking about these theories and their applications and creating classroom scenarios to actively engage students in the morning. Then I was coaching and trying to practice what I preached in the afternoon. I was conscious that I was a more effective coach when I was teaching educational psychology than when I wasn't. It wasn't something I had to recall later—I knew then that I was at my coaching best. Second semester would come and I wondered how I could hold on to the coaching magic I experienced the previous semester.

This book exists because of my desire to recapture that magic. Because I was traveling to so many national and international competitions, it was hard to stay grounded. To keep my sanity, maintain my focus, and find a coaching edge I quietly began reading and writing in my hotel room about educational psychology for coaches. I had no intention of publishing a book; I simply wanted to keep the magic rolling and be an effective coach. You could say I wrote this book for a selfish reason: to make myself a better coach. And that is probably true—at least in the beginning.

Reading about respondent conditioning learning theory at night inspired me to create a positive learning environment in the morning. Pairing positive experiences that engendered success and happiness helped me create the *salivating athlete*, the athlete who couldn't wait to practice. Over a 5-year period, 16 of my athletes made the U.S. national team and reached lifelong goals. Studying cognitive learning theory helped me better understand how athletes think and how cognition plays an important role in motor learning and performance. I found myself asking athletes, "What were you thinking before and during your last performance?" Their responses informed my teaching, accelerated their learning, and helped me shape the *supercomputing athlete*. Understanding emotion theory helped me see the connection between thoughts, emotions, and performance. Besides asking my athletes what they were thinking about, I found myself asking the *emotional athlete* what he or she was feeling before and during performance, particularly competition performance.

Like those second semesters, my coaching career was a long stretch of road—over 37 years. Eventually my reason for writing this book changed. Once I decided to publish it, it was no longer just for me; it became a book for coaches—fellow coaches, colleagues, brothers and sisters working in the trenches just like me. I don't profess to be a great coach; many coaches are far more successful than I. But I know what it's like to be the underdog coach and what it means to fight and scrap your way to success. I wanted to write something for those coaches who are trying to find a coaching advantage, become better coaches, and achieve a slice of coaching success.

Each semester I taught, I increasingly included the perspective of the coach and athlete in my curriculum because some of my students were music education majors and prospective teachers who planned to also coach. I wanted to offer those students an experience that would prepare them to work with the aspiring musician and the eager athlete. I wondered why no textbook was available for them. I thought a book on educational psychology for coaches should exist. And now it does.

EDUCATIONAL PSYCHOLOGY

Educational psychology is the field of study in which principles of psychology are applied to the teaching and learning process. **Psychology** is a branch of science that concerns itself with human behavior and thinking. Psychology studies human behavior and thinking by means of scientific methods that rely on consistency, accuracy, precision, and objective methods of measurement. A scientific approach uses procedures and research designs that attempt to eliminate subjectivity, bias, and random factors that might unduly influence the real meaning or significance of a study.

THEORIES

A **theory** is an attempt to summarize and explain what scientists observe. For example, when Pavlov noticed that the dogs in his laboratory began salivating before they could see or smell their food, he eventually formulated his theory of classical conditioning to summarize, explain, and predict the type of behavior he observed. Classical conditioning is but one of many learning theories. Once after a lecture regarding different learning theories, a student asked, "What is the one correct theory for learning?" It would be nice if such a theory existed—a single unifying learning theory that completely explained all human learning and provided a lockstep approach to teaching. Unfortunately, no such theory exists for several reasons.

One reason is that human learning rarely involves invariants as do chemical compounds. When you combine two chemicals, the result is usually predictable. However, when you take two athletes and use the same learning approach, you might get two different results in learning. Athletes are human beings and human beings are notoriously unpredictable, individually unique, and idiosyncratic in their responses. If you take two people to a movie, one might love it and the other might hate it.

Another reason there is no all-encompassing learning theory is that human beings are difficult to examine. For example, if you are a physicist and you want to know more about the internal makeup of an atom, you might use an accelerator, smash a few atoms, and see what particles appear. If you are an auto mechanic and have a problem with an engine, you simply open the hood, examine the engine, and take apart some of the pieces. The study of human beings is not so straightforward. You can neither smash human beings to see what is inside them nor open the hood to see how they run.

Having said this, you might ask, "Well, then, what good are learning theories? What useful purpose do they serve?" Theories are important because even if they cannot be as certain as laws they help explain, predict, and influence human behavior. Consequently, it is useful to view the different learning theories outlined in this book as tools in your coaching toolbox: Use one tool as an effective coaching approach for one athlete or specific learning situation and use another tool for a different athlete or learning situation. Much like the skilled auto mechanic, you select the appropriate theoretical learning tool from your coaching toolbox to fix the problem—finding a way to effectively teach your athletes.

MOTOR SKILL

Schmidt and Wrisberg (2008) define **motor skill** as "A skill for which the primary determinant of success is the quality of the movement that the performer produces" (p. 4). With regard to motor skill, the primary importance is the quality of the movement itself rather than the quality of the perceptual and decision-making aspects of the movement. For example, a weightlifter competing in the clean and jerk focuses on the correct movement to maximize the amount of weight being lifted.

In contrast to motor skill, a **cognitive skill** is one in which the main emphasis is on knowing what to do as opposed to doing what you are supposed to do. Playing chess is an example of a mainly cognitive skill. Few skills are one or the other; most skills are somewhere in between completely motor and completely cognitive on the continuum and require both motor skill and cognitive skill (see table I.1).

Even in events such as high jumping, weightlifting, and archery, especially at the elite level where performance may be mainly automatic, a certain amount of cognitive skill is involved. As Schmidt and Wrisberg (2008) write, "Rarely, however, do either cognitive or motor elements become entirely unimportant to performance. Even highly skilled athletes must think about what they need to do, such as the split-second tactical decisions that sailors in the America's Cup yacht race must make" (pp. 7-8).

MOTOR LEARNING

Learning, whether it involves teaching mathematics, science, or English in the classroom, or teaching motor skill and performance on the field of play (e.g., weight room, ice rink, tennis court, soccer field, basketball court, diving well, swimming pool, baseball or softball field) is about one thing: change. **Motor learning** can be defined as "the changes, associated with practice or experience, in internal processes that determine a person's capability for producing a motor skill" (Schmidt & Wrisberg, 2008, p. 11). One could add to the end of this definition the words "…that persist over time." Change that is impermanent is not really change. For example, athletes who make a change one day but resort to the same familiar bad habit the next day have not really made a change; therefore, real learning has not occurred.

The goal of the effective and successful coach is to facilitate lasting changes within athletes. Basketball coaches want their players to become better defenders, protect the ball, and perceive and exploit defensive miscues. Strength coaches want their athletes to improve lifting techniques, break through limiting self-expectations, and fatigue. Hockey coaches want their athletes to learn better skating technique, improve puck control, and quicken recognition and response time for defensive and offensive setups. Swimming coaches want their athletes to change their stroke techniques and learn mental strategies for dealing with fatigue and pain. Baseball and softball coaches want their

Table I.1 Motor-Cognitive Continuum

MOTOR SKILLS ←		→ COGNITIVE SKILLS
Minimum decision making	**Some decision making**	**Maximum decision making**
Maximum motor skill	**Some decision making**	**Minimum motor skill**
High jumping	Quarterbacking	Playing chess
Weightlifting	Race car driving	Playing bridge
Archery	Point guard	Coaching a sport

Adapted, by permission, from R.A. Schmidt and C.A. Wrisberg. 2008, *Motor learning and performance*, 4th ed. (Champaign, IL: Human Kinetics), 8.

athletes to learn better pitch recognition and swing technique and improve reaction time to pitches, hits, and steals. All of these goals demand the same thing: change in athlete behaviors, which is part of motor learning.

MOTOR PERFORMANCE

Motor performance is the external and therefore observable attempt by an individual to produce a voluntary action that is susceptible to influences such as motivation, attentional focus, fatigue, and physical condition (Schmidt & Wrisberg, 2008). Motor performance is the external manifestation of an athlete's internal process for motor learning. An athlete can't learn a motor task without performance attempts or practice. The performance may vary due to influencing factors, but through practice the athlete's capabilities for producing the action improve. This improvement is assumed to be motor learning. Motor learning is certainly occurring when relatively stable repetitions of proficient performance occur, especially if they occur under different sets of circumstances (Schmidt & Wrisberg, 2008).

WHAT IS COACHING?

It is important to ask this question because as a coach you need to know what you are expected to do, what your responsibilities are, and what you should expect from yourself. It might be easier to first consider what coaching is not: Eggen and Kauchak (2008) cite three common misconceptions about teaching and learning to teach that apply to coaches, too.

1. *Coaching is the process of transmitting knowledge to athletes.* Some aspiring coaches erroneously believe that coaching is simply the process of telling athletes what to do. These coaches perceive themselves as the all-knowing dispensers of information. Although coaches do transmit knowledge to their athletes, the coach's job is really to facilitate learning. From a cognitive learning theory perspective, the athlete is the one who ultimately finds the meaning inherent in new information and this meaning is most often connected to something the athlete already knows. For example, in the **games approach** that Martens (2004) outlines, athletes discover through experience what the game is all about, what to do, and what they need to learn.

2. *Playing the sport provides all the knowledge needed to coach the sport.* Some coaches believe that if they were athletes in a particular sport then they are knowledgeable enough to coach the sport. This misconception is pervasive both in the classroom and on the practice field. It is ironic that the best athletes do not always make the best coaches. As Leonard (1992) writes, "John McEnroe might turn up in later years as a superb tennis coach—but he might not. The teaching tactics of a Nobel laureate could turn out to be poison for the mind of a neophyte physicist. It's particularly challenging, in fact, for a top performer to become

a first-rate teacher. Instruction demands a certain humility; at best, the teacher takes delight in being surpassed by his or her students" (pp. 56-57).

Simply being a former athlete of the sport is insufficient preparation for becoming a successful coach. Sternberg and Horvath (1995) identify three areas in which expert teachers share common characteristics: knowledge, efficiency in problem solving, and insight into solving educational problems. In my experience, expert coaches share these same characteristics. They know a lot about their sport and about teaching and learning, and they are good problem solvers.

3. *To learn to coach, experience in the practice setting is all that is necessary.* Some coaches also mistakenly believe that if they were in a practice setting as athletes, then that is all that is necessary for them to be effective coaches. Or, if they have observed other coaches, that is sufficient for learning how to coach. As Eggen and Kauchak (2008) point out, there are two problems with not having direct teaching experience. One problem is that you won't always observe effective teaching. The other problem is that you may not know what to look for when trying to identify good teaching.

Now, return to the original question: What is coaching? For one thing, coaching is decision making.

Coaching as Decision Making

To a great extent, coaching is about decision making and you are the person in charge, the captain steering the ship. You have the autonomy to make decisions that affect you, your program, and your athletes. Every day you are called upon to make decisions regarding a variety of different matters. Through your coaching experience you learn to be an effective decision maker; when you continually make good decisions you provide your program with stability and continuity and guide your athletes in the right direction, making the crooked path straight, helping your athletes go from good to great in the shortest amount of time possible.

A simple but useful paradigm for understanding decision making during the coaching process is to consider before, during, and after coaching.

Before Coaching

Before coaching is the decision-making process of deciding the who, what, where, when, and how of coaching.

• *Who—the individual athlete*: Before coaching, consider who you will be coaching and the individual differences among athletes. These differences include age, ability level, experience level, motivational level, emotional level, cognitive development, social and personality development, physical maturation, moral development, and level of attentional focus.

- *What—the task*: Before coaching, consider what is to be taught. The *what* process means identifying the demands of the task. According to Schmidt and Wrisberg (2008) these task demands are accurate sensory perception, decision making, and movement execution. For example, the racquetball player must perceive the speed and direction of the ball coming off the wall, decide where to return the ball, and be able to execute the correct racket swing.

To understand the *what* of a motor performance it is useful to conduct a **task analysis**, which is the two-part process of identifying the components of the task and the underlying abilities for task performance. Task analysis helps you identify target skills and target behaviors. **Target skills** are the actual tasks an athlete wishes to successfully perform, such as pinch a backhand shot into the corner in racquetball. **Target behaviors** are the observable actions athletes must produce to successfully perform target skills, such as the positioning of the feet and bringing the racket back high before initiating the backhand swing to pinch the ball into the corner.

- *Where—the target context*: **Target context** is the environment in which the motor skill is going to be performed. It is one thing to drop a ball and hit a backhand in practice but an entirely different thing to chase the ball during a hotly contested racquetball game and hit a backhand.

- *When—the time of season*: Your decision making is affected by where you are at in your season. For example, if it is early in the season, you may decide to change the mechanics of your golfer's stroke but most likely decide to not attempt to make any change late in the season heading into the championship.

- *How—the coaching strategy*: The *how* has to do with the decisions you make to create an environment conducive for motor learning and performance. Part of this process is to use different coaching strategies outlined in this book such as behavioral, cognitivistic, and humanistic coaching strategies. The *how* also has to do with selecting drills and presentation techniques such as guidance, demonstrations, rehearsal, peer coaching, transfer of learning, and direct instruction.

Coaching

Once you have done your preparatory decision making, it is time to implement your coaching plan and strategies. During coaching, you monitor athlete safety and maintain an ongoing assessment of the effectiveness of your practice plan and strategies. Based on your assessment during the coaching phase, you may decide to alter your practice plan. Nothing is set in stone. If what you are doing isn't working, then change course. During this time you also maintain effective practice management and discipline so that you create and maintain an atmosphere conducive for effective coaching and learning.

After Coaching

After coaching you assess the effectiveness of practice. Did you reach your goals? What worked well? What didn't? In other words, you reflect on whether or not goals were attained, reevaluate athlete readiness, and begin preparing a practice plan for your next coaching session. This stage of the instructional process is important because without reflective evaluation, you may continue down the same instructional path even though it does not lead to improved athlete performance. A good rule of thumb is if it works, keep it; if it doesn't work, throw it out. Some of the things you want to consider in your assessment are the products of practice: knowledge of concepts, control and coordination, muscles being used, movement efficiency, attention, and error detection and correction.

Coaching as Reflection

In many ways, coaching is a reflective activity. Reflective teaching is the process of thinking about teaching activities (Moallem, 1997). **Reflective coaching** involves thinking about the consequences of your actions, the beliefs you hold that affect your behavior, and your coaching methods and styles. It also is about acquiring new information and improving your coaching effectiveness (Eby, 1998). So, reflective coaching can be regarded as a proactive process in which you assume more responsibility for planning, implementing, and evaluating what you do and how you can do it better. The coach of excellence is always evaluating and looking for ways to improve. What you did last year was great, but how can you do it better this year? You know your competition is working hard to improve and beat you, so you need to improve on last year, last semester, last month, last week. Improving your coaching effectiveness results in better training, improved athlete performances, and increased competitive success.

Effective and successful coaches take the time to examine all aspects of their coaching life. They reflect on things such as their well-being ("Am I growing as a person and a coach?"), reasons for coaching ("Am I coaching for the right reasons?"), goals ("Am I moving away or toward my goals? Am I helping my athletes reach their goals?"), dreams and aspirations ("Am I where I thought I would be in my career?"), personal life ("Do I have balance in my life? Is my personal life positively or negatively affecting my coaching effectiveness?"), and coaching methods ("Are the drills I'm using effective or could I be using different drills? Is my approach in working with my athletes effective or should I use a different approach?").

Coaching as Coaching

Coaching is about exhibiting effective coaching behaviors. In other words, if you act like a successful coach, you more than likely will become a successful coach. A benefit of coaching is that you learn exemplary behaviors that make you an effective leader and worthy role model. Effective coaching requires effective behaviors.

After a review of research on effective teaching, MacKay (1982) identified 28 behaviors that effective teachers exhibit while teaching. The following lists these behaviors translated from in-class teaching behaviors to in-practice coaching behaviors.

Recommended Effective Coaching Behaviors

- Use a system of rules dealing with personal and procedural issues.
- Prevent inappropriate behavior from continuing.
- Direct disciplinary action accurately.
- Frequently move around the practice area and monitor athlete on-task training behaviors.
- Handle disruptive behavior in a subtle manner.
- Make sure that drills and practice assignments are interesting and worthwhile, especially when young athletes work independently.
- Use a system of rules and guidelines that allow athletes to practice skills and drills with a minimum of direction.
- Optimize practice time. Athletes should be actively involved and productively engaged in drills and skills that result in improved motor learning and performance.
- Use a standard signal to gain athletes' attention.
- Begin speaking to the team only when everyone's attention is focused on you.
- Use a variety of coaching techniques that accommodate an athlete's particular learning needs.
- Use a system for checking back with athletes. For example, if you ask an athlete to review and rewrite some practice goals, then you should follow up and see that the request was completed.
- Relate all drills to the main concept being taught and the purpose of the drill.
- Employ techniques that provide for the gradual transition from concrete to more abstract activities. For example, begin by teaching a specific skill and then introduce the concept of generalization and explain how the concrete skill can be applied to other similar motor movement situations.
- Use a mixture of low and high order questions. Asking questions causes athletes to think and it is useful to ask them simple questions and then follow up with more complex questions. For example, you might ask an athlete, "What are you supposed to do on this drill?" and then ask, "What is the ultimate purpose of this drill?"

- Be aware of everything occurring during practice.
- Be able to attend to more than one issue at a time.
- Manage a smooth but quick transition from one practice activity to another.
- Maintain the pace of practice.
- Be clear when presenting ideas to the team.
- Be able to motivate athletes.
- Communicate clearly and provide evidence of caring, accepting, and valuing your athletes.
- Be sensitive and responsive to athletes' statements, feelings, experiences, and obvious and subtle mannerisms and meanings.
- Pay attention to all athletes, not just the elite athletes or the athletes you prefer to coach.
- Use techniques such as rephrasing, providing clues, or asking a new question when athletes don't understand and can't answer the question correctly.
- Use praise to reward outstanding performance and encourage underperforming athletes who aren't able to perform at that level.
- Use mild criticism occasionally to communicate expectations to more able athletes.
- Try to integrate athlete-initiated interactions, such as questions, comments, ideas, and suggestions into the practice plan.

Adapted from A. MacKay, 1982, *Project quest: Teaching strategies and pupil achievement.* Occasional Paper Series (Alberta, Canada: Centre for Research in Teaching, Faculty of Education, University of Alberta).

To further understand the behaviors for highly effective and successful coaching, the United States Olympic Committee (USOC) surveyed America's elite national team coaches and asked them a number of questions. One question was what traits or qualities they thought personified a successful coach (Sellers, 2008). Some of the traits or qualities they ranked as important were knowledge, communication, listening, commitment, dedication, perseverance, leadership, passion, open-mindedness, flexibility, creativity, patience, and drive. Their answers also revealed these additional insights regarding successful coaching.

Traits and Qualities of Successful Elite Coaches

- Ability to instill belief, trust, or confidence in athletes
- Big vision, balanced by ability to set and adjust goals
- Caring about others more than self
- Perseverance and a sense of humor

- Attention to skills development of athletes; tailored to athlete needs
- Precise training techniques and coaching on a daily basis
- Ability to filter
- Problem-solving orientation
- Ability to observe without judgment
- Desire to improve through knowledge
- Quality decision makers under pressure
- High level of integrity and fairness
- Ability to multitask with equal amounts of high energy
- Knowledgeable and with an ability to transfer knowledge simplistically
- Being focused on the process
- Being creative and open-minded to new ideas and approaches
- Having thick skin
- Being flexible, but decisive
- Having excellent instructional skills, ability to deliver message
- Understanding critical zone training

Coaching as Problem Solving

Coaching is also about engaging in effective problem solving. Through your coaching experience you learn to be an adept problem solver who is capable of finding skillful, sensitive, and sometimes pragmatic approaches to solving often complex problems that have no obvious, simple, or easy recipe for resolution attainment. For example, you may be called upon to solve problems such as resolving disagreements between athletes, disciplining athlete misbehaviors, enhancing athlete self-esteem, expanding athlete expectations, restoring team morale, or setting higher standards.

Problem solving is a great challenge of coaching, but it is also very rewarding. As the saying goes, if it were easy, everyone would do it. There is no better feeling at the end of the season than to stand back and watch all the pieces fall into place for a successful championship. You remember all the pitfalls, obstacles, and setbacks that befell your team throughout the season, yet here you are at the pinnacle of the moment. Your problem solving resolved all contretemps and assured a successful season's end. You kept the ship on course, guiding your athletes and program through turbulent times, providing the stability and continuity necessary for eventual smooth sailing and reaching the shores of success. It is no wonder that troubled businesses often turn to coaches for advice.

Coaching as Empowering Athletes

Coaching also is about the intrinsically rewarding opportunity of making a difference in the lives of your athletes by empowering them. **Empowering** athletes means increasing their feelings of uniqueness, self-confidence, and self-competency. Empowered athletes believe they can accomplish goals through personal effort and responsibility. One way to empower athletes is to allow them to be **active participants** in the learning process. You can facilitate active participation by including athletes in the decision-making process. Decision making empowers athletes just as it empowers coaches. Allowing athletes to set personal and team goals, soliciting athlete input, letting athletes help design practices, and asking athletes questions such as "What do you think?" are all ways of involving athletes as active participants. Active participation helps athletes assume greater responsibility and feel that they are in control of their careers and have the autonomy to control their destiny.

Kohn (1993) suggests that when people become active participants the sense of empowerment they experience can have a noticeably positive effect on their achievement, behavior, values, and sense of well-being. Moreover, Brunson and Vogt (1996) suggest that these learners also become more tolerant, more trusting, and better learners. When you teach motor skill and performance, also teach athlete empowerment.

Coaching as Science

Coaching is about science. You can't be an effective coach or conduct yourself as a truly professional coach without an understanding of the science of coaching and the science of your sport. A scientific knowledge base allows you to make objective, educated, and informed decisions and solve problems based on technical skills, scientific data, laws, principles, paradigms, and learning theories grounded in solid research. These theories allow you to explain human learning and, more importantly, predict and impact change in human behavior.

Former Indiana University and International Swimming Hall of Fame diving coach Hobie Billingsley once commented that a significant turning point in his coaching career came when he was introduced to Sir Isaac Newton and his three laws of motion. An understanding of Newton's laws, particularly his third law of motion (for every action there is an equal, opposite reaction), profoundly influenced Hobie's understanding and teaching of the sport of diving.

Coaching as Art

Coaching is about art, too. A purely scientific approach to coaching doesn't lead to coaching effectiveness because it overlooks humanistic aspects of the athlete, the coach–athlete relationship, and the motor learning process. Science without art may get the facts right but it lacks meaning or lasting value. The coach who is purely scientific lacks the depth and sensitivity to genuinely understand, communicate, and connect with athletes. As Leonard (1992) writes, "Knowledge, expertise, technical skill, and credentials are important, but without the patience and empathy that go with teaching beginners, these merits are as nothing" (p. 58).

The converse is true, too: A purely artful approach to coaching won't lead to coaching success either. Art without science has sentimental emotion, but no real substance. As Faulkner (1950) might say, it does not have " . . . the old universal truths lacking which any story is ephemeral and doomed . . . ." Coaches who try to get by without an understanding of the *universal truths* of their sport—biomechanics, physics, physiology, and pedagogy—ultimately lose the respect, admiration, and control of their athletes because they are soon perceived as incompetent.

Once when I was in college, after performing well at the conference championship, a teammate and I decided to celebrate by buying two cigars after the meet had concluded. Neither one of us smoked, but we thought it would be fun to celebrate. In fact, we decided to just chomp on them rather than light them. As we were walking down the hotel stairs, our swimming coach saw us and angrily told us, "Throw those things out!" A few minutes later, he came back, put his hands on our shoulders, and said, "Boys, I'm sorry. You go ahead and have some fun. You earned it." Sometimes a small gesture and the touch of a hand makes a point and creates an emotional connection. Although he was known to the sporting community as a technician and scientific coach, that night and in that brief moment he proved to be an artful coach as well. If you want to become an effective and successful coach, become both a scientific and an artful coach.

Coaching as a Profession

Coaching is a noble profession. The best coaches also happen to be the most professional ones, too. What does it mean for a coach to become a professional? Lortie (1975) suggests several factors that determine whether or not an individual is a professional.

• *Becoming a professional coach involves acquiring specialized schooling.* If you were an athlete in the sport you now coach, you may draw upon that experience to guide your coaching, but your athletic experience alone isn't sufficient for becoming a professional coach. To become a true professional you need specialized schooling, which in part means acquiring the knowledge (e.g., biomechanics, psychology, and physiology) associated with your sport. Highly successful coaches tend to be well read and well informed not just about their sport but about a great many things. Basketball coach John Wooden was a high school English teacher and continued to read and write throughout his life. Football coach Bill Walsh was a cerebral coach nicknamed *The Genius* for his innovations and creativity. Football coach Woody Hayes was an avid reader of history and swimming coach Doc Counsilman (1968) wrote *The Science of Swimming,* which applied principles of fluid mechanics to swimming strokes.

- *Becoming a professional coach involves experiencing a formal apprenticeship.* An apprenticeship is an opportunity to study under a successful coach. Many successful coaches were once assistant coaches to other successful coaches. Duke University coach Mike Krzyzewski played under Bobby Knight at Army and then was a graduate assistant for him at Indiana University. Bo Schemblechler coached under Woody Hayes at Miami University of Ohio. NFL head football coach Bill Belichick has had more than a dozen assistant coaches go on to become head coaches in the NFL or collegiate level. Apprenticing under a successful coach is one of the best ways to become a professional coach.

- *Becoming a professional coach involves having autonomy.* Autonomy means that as a coach you have the independence and freedom to make all types of decisions when it comes to working with athletes. State and federal laws govern how you discipline athletes and bylaws and codes are mandated by your sport's national governing body, but much of what you do is up to you. As a professional coach, *you* draw up practices and game plans, *you* select appropriate skills and drills, *you* evaluate athlete readiness, *you* determine seasonal training, *you* establish team rules, and *you* discipline athletes.

Some might argue that coaches lack a prerequisite amount of autonomy to be considered true professionals. However, the amount of autonomy you retain is in most cases really up to you. Many young coaches make the mistake of abdicating authority and responsibility for their programs for a variety of reasons. Perhaps they feel unprepared to assume total responsibility for running their programs or maybe they are too lazy to do the extra work that comes with the territory of being a coach. Truly professional coaches retain their autonomy.

- *Becoming a professional coach includes high reward.* At the professional level the monetary reward can be more than adequate and even desirable. Professional football, basketball, and baseball coaches generally have substantial contracts. At the collegiate level, the coaching salaries for these sports also are very lucrative. For other sports and other competitive levels (e.g., primary and secondary education), the monetary reward is less than lucrative. Coaching for all sports and for all levels does, however, offer high intrinsic reward through experiences such as helping athletes achieve athletic goals, increase self-competency, conquer fear, overcome self-doubt, master skills, experience success, and make dreams come true.

Coaching as a Journey—The Becoming Coach

Coaching is a journey. The athletes, the personal challenges, the camaraderie, the esprit de corps, the development of character, the self-discipline, the fatigue, the victories, and, yes, even the defeats are all part of the journey. As Faulkner (1939) wrote in *The Wild Palms*, "If I were to choose between pain and nothing, I would always choose pain." If nothing else, coaching reminds you that you are indeed alive. It is better to feel the agony of defeat than nothing at all . . . but wait until next season and the thrill of victory.

You have much to experience and learn on your journey toward becoming an effective and successful coach. In fact, it is a lifelong process. To paraphrase Japanese swordmaster Yamaoka Tesshu:

Do not think that
This is all there is.
More and more
Wonderful teachings exist—

The [*coaching profession*] is unfathomable.

I wish you the best of luck on your coaching journey and hope this book helps you along the way.

SUGGESTED READINGS

HBO. (2010). *HBO sports documentary: Lombardi.* HBO Entertainment.

[Vince Lombardi was simply a great teacher in the classroom and football field. He took a basketball team and made them into a champion team, even though he didn't know much about basketball. It is interesting to follow his coaching journey toward becoming a legendary coach.]

Leonard, G. (1992). *Mastery: The keys to success and long-term fulfillment.* New York: Penguin Books.

[Leonard has a wonderful take on life, success, and fulfillment for us as coaches and human beings.]

Martens, R. (2012). *Successful coaching* (4th ed.). Champaign, IL: Human Kinetics.

[Martens offers some great tips for becoming a successful coach.]

PART I

Athletes and Theories of Motivation

This book begins with theories of motivation. As some of the stories in part I suggest, when all things are equal, motivation is the difference maker. Motivation may be the greatest determining factor for athlete success. It helps athletes reach their goals and make their dreams come true. It also is the factor that makes for great coaching. Simply put, effective coaches know how to motivate their athletes.

In part I you are introduced to the *unstoppable athlete* and the *resilient athlete* and applicable theories for helping you create these driven athletes. Theories of behaviorism, cognitivism, and humanism help you understand and learn how to push the motivation button for your players. You influence athlete motivation through the reinforcements you provide, the feedback you give, the practice environment you create, the behaviors you model, the way you communicate, the expectations you hold, and the basic and metaneeds you fulfill.

Don't limit these theories of motivation to just your athletes. It is equally important to understand how to motivate yourself. After all, the coach is the motivational role model for the team. As the coach goes, so goes the team. As you read through these theories, consider how they can apply to you and how you can become the unstoppable, resilient coach—the motivational leader of your team.

CHAPTER 1

The Unstoppable Athlete

Applying Motivation Theory

Key Terms

additive principle
aesthetic needs
arousal
arousal theory
attainment value
attitude or belief change
autotelic experience
basic needs
behavioral change
belongingness and love
  needs
coaching efficacy
cognitive dissonance
  theory
cognitive evaluation
  theory
cognitive needs
collective self-efficacy
compartmentalization
competence motivation
competence motivation
  theory
constructivism
controlling aspect
cost

deficiency needs
discovery learning
emotive influence
enactive influence
expectancy
expectancy–value theory
exposure to or recall of
  information
extrinsic motivation
flow
imaginal influence
informational aspect
informational feedback
inquiry approach
instructional scaffolding
interest
intrinsic motivation
intrinsic value
Jonah complex
metaneeds
motivated behavior
motivating feedback
motivation
multiplicative principle

need–drive theory
pain–pleasure principle
peak experiences
perceptual distortion
persuasory influence
physiological needs
pressing
psychological hedonism
psychological needs
ripple effect
safety needs
self-actualization
self-discipline
self-efficacy
self-esteem
self-esteem needs
self-talk
teacher efficacy
unstoppable athlete
unstoppable coach
utility value
value
vicarious influence

> **"** *You see things; and you say, 'Why?' But I dream things that never were; and I say, 'Why not?'* **"**
>
> *George Bernard Shaw, Back to Methuselah*

Kimberly had a dream. And she had the motivation to persevere and reach that dream. She wasn't very good, but she believed she could become so. During her sophomore year she sent her recruiting tape to the top collegiate programs in the country. Every coach who saw the tape said, "No, thanks." In truth, her tape was awful. Despite the poor review of the tape, one collegiate coach looked at her college transcript and noticed she was a straight-A student. The coach thought, *If she can work that hard in the classroom, maybe she can work that hard in practice. And if she is that smart with her subjects, maybe she is smart enough to learn quickly, which she will need to do if transferring after her sophomore year in college.*

That coach decided to take a chance on Kimberly and he invited her to train with him for the summer. He told her that he wanted to get to know her and her to get to know him before making a commitment. After all, they might find they didn't like each other or couldn't get along or couldn't forge a solid athlete–coach relationship. After a few days, the coach had a gut feeling about Kimberly. He not only invited her to join the team but he also offered her a partial scholarship. His colleagues said he was nuts to waste valuable scholarship money on an unproven athlete, especially when so many experienced high school recruits were available to be immediately competitive, and they would have 4 years of eligibility instead of 2.

The coach carefully considered the pros and cons and thought long and hard about all the facts. In the end he did as he always did: He followed his heart, which told him to take on Kimberly. So, the coach and athlete set to work, beginning the long journey that was taking them somewhere—they just didn't know where quite yet.

In the beginning, it was more challenging than he had expected. She had a long way to go to become competitive. However, he had been right about one thing: She could work. She was fierce in practice and she was a quick learner. As time passed, she steadily improved. Her motivation to become the best grew until it was unsurpassed by any collegiate athlete in her conference and in the country. Although she and her coach were filled with great expectation, her junior year ended lackluster with less-than-hoped-for results. One year was down with nothing noteworthy to report except a lot of hard work, determination, and tears. Every setback, disappointment, and failure of her junior year was like a drop of fuel on a fire, flaming her passion and motivating her to work even harder.

Her senior year began with a few minor victories but the conference championship was a disaster. With tears streaming down her cheeks, she sat in the stands watching the final—a final *she* should have been in—watching other women whom she knew she could beat. She had failed to make the finals in her senior year. How could this be? She had worked harder than any athlete in the field. She had prepared more than any athlete, wanted it more than any athlete, and demanded more from herself than any athlete. The heartache was almost unbearable. Still, her motivation was unmatched; it kept her in the game, kept her coming back. She went home after that debacle and vowed to work even harder. At the NCAA qualifying meet she performed slightly better than she had at the conference championship and managed to eke out a qualifying spot for the NCAA championship. This would be the first national championship of her short career.

Indeed, her career *was* short: She switched sports her senior year in high school. She had fewer than 4 years of experience in her new sport, which is not a lot of time to get good at a sport contested by hundreds of elite collegiate athletes across the country. No female athlete in her sport had ever come in as a first-timer with so little experience and won an NCAA championship. She didn't even make the finals at her conference championship, so it was unlikely that she would come close.

However, the highly motivated athlete is an unstoppable force, a body in motion that mystifyingly wills itself to even greater motion. In the preliminary competition she was suddenly consumed by the thought *I'm going to make the finals of the NCAA championship!* Thinking about making the finals instead of performing well enough to qualify for the finals was a mental sidetrack. In the blink of an eye, she dropped out of first place but somehow she stayed in the pack as the last-place qualifier. Before the finals, her coach made her promise to think only about performance, like a mountain climber, hand over hand, inching ever closer to the summit. She kept her promise by giving her best physical, mental, and emotional effort, making the most of the performance moment. She wanted to know about her final performance: "Coach, how was that?" she said. With a smile he responded, "You can forget about it now. Look up at the scoreboard." And there it was, like an afterthought: NCAA national champion!

Kimberly wasn't the most talented athlete in the contest that night and she certainly wasn't the most experienced, but she was without a doubt the most motivated. She repeatedly shook off defeat and disappointment throughout the season and she willed herself to victory because she wanted it so badly. She was the unstoppable force who, upon meeting the immovable object… moved it. If there were a hundred athletes and I could only choose one, I would always choose the highly motivated athlete. This chapter is the story about the unstoppable athlete and how you can use motivation theory to facilitate high motivation in your athletes to help them reach their greatest athletic potential.

CHAPTER OVERVIEW

Human motivation does not have one overarching theory. Just as with human learning, many theories exist for motivation. A successful coach once said that he tried to find the right buttons to push to motivate his athletes. This comment implies that many ways exist to motivate athletes and you need to use different methods for motivating each athlete. What are these so-called buttons and how do you *push* them? In other words, what are the methods for motivating athletes and how do you apply them to turn athletes into unstoppable forces like Kimberly?

Theories of motivation are derived from four general learning theories: behaviorism, cognitivism, social cognitive learning, and humanism. This chapter examines motivational theories associated with each general learning theory and the application of these motivational theories for increasing athlete motivation.

The chapter begins with behaviorism, looking briefly at reinforcement, praise, external and internal feedback, and respondent conditioning. Next is an overview of cognitive theories: arousal theory, cognitive evaluation theory, cognitive dissonance theory, and self-efficacy theory. Then, the chapter examines social cognitive learning theory and the influence of observational learning on increasing athlete motivation, and then expectancy–value theory. It concludes with a discussion of humanistic theories: Maslow's hierarchy of needs theory, flow theory, competence motivation theory, and Rogerian theory.

BEHAVIORISM AND MOTIVATION

According to the concept of **psychological hedonism** and the **pain–pleasure principle**, people are motivated to obtain pleasure and avoid pain. This simple explanation for human motivation, however, seems incongruous with the picture of the hard-working athlete training through extremely demanding and often painful (*not* pleasurable) conditions to achieve a long-range goal. How do you account for this type of athlete motivation? According to behaviorism, you would argue that somehow athlete motivation to train under such grueling circumstances is being reinforced. A reinforcer increases the probability that a response will reoccur. When a rat receives a food pellet (reinforcer) for feverishly pressing a lever in the Skinner box, the rat is more likely to press the lever again.

Reinforcement and Praise

When used according to the principles of operant conditioning, reinforcement can have a significant impact on motivation and human behavior. Consider the successful coach who always seems to have upbeat and motivated athletes willing to charge through a brick wall for their coach. Unfortunately, the example of the unsuccessful coach whose athletes always seem to be downcast, downtrodden, and unmotivated also exists. One factor that separates the successful coach from the unsuccessful coach is the use of positive reinforcers, in particular, praise. Although the use of praise is discussed in detail in chapter 10, several rules about the use of praise (*pushing the praise button*) are worth repeating here.

Praise provides information to athletes not only about performance but also about notion of self. In other words, it tells athletes about the quality of their motor performance, but it often also tells them about their self-worth and competence. For example, when you say, "Jerome, way to think. That's the way to make the correction the first time!" you are letting him know about his improved performance and also, and more important, about his intelligence, effort, and capacity for change. Contrast this coaching comment with the droll and uninspired "Okay. Go on to the next drill." Often, just a few precisely put words make a significant and long-lasting difference in an athlete's notion of self and motivation.

Praise should be used judiciously. It is easy to use praise too often so that it becomes meaningless to athletes or too infrequently so that it is ineffective in influencing behavior. Young coaches in particular often use praise too frequently. Successful coaches find the right balance for dishing out praise so that when they do use praise, it has real punch and positively affects athlete motivation.

Praise should include specific, constructive encouragement to build self-esteem (Hitz & Driscoll, 1994). Encouraging comments should be clear and specific rather than vague and general. Athletes want to know not only the *what* but also the *why*. If they aren't doing something correctly, they want to know why it is wrong and why a different approach is better. At the same time, they also want to be encouraged for their effort and ability to succeed with future attempts. For example, the type of praise in the following statement increases self-esteem and motivation while it concomitantly provides constructive encouragement: "Maria, you took the race out too fast but I admire your determination, adventurousness, and fearlessness! Those are qualities you should be proud of and will serve you well in the future. However, you need to pace yourself and run your own race next time."

Praise should be sincere. Sincere praise not only provides reinforcement, but it also sends an emotional message that says you genuinely care for your athletes and want to see them succeed. Athletes who perceive that their coaches care for them are motivated to give even greater effort in practice. Conversely, insincere praise, besides being ineffective, communicates to athletes that you have little regard for them and their performances. Sincere praise builds the athlete–coach relationship while insincere praise undermines it. Which type of praise do you give your athletes?

Praising effort is important, particularly for young athletes. Children who are praised for their efforts are more apt to develop a view of ability as something they can control and something that can change (Mueller & Dweck, 1998). Consequently, these athletes are more apt to be motivated to train hard and expect results based on personal effort. In contrast, people who are praised for their talent tend to view ability as fixed and unchanging. Consequently, when these athletes experience failure, they are less motivated to train hard.

External Feedback as Reinforcement

Like praise, external feedback can serve as a reinforcer for athlete behaviors. For example, in the game of hot and cold, people shout out "hotter" and "colder" to express how close the player is to reaching the goal. The hotter game players get (i.e., the closer they get to their achievement goal) the more motivated they become to keep going. In this regard, both knowledge of results (KR) and knowledge of performance (KP) act as reinforcers. Two specific external feedback properties that athletes find motivating are the aptly named motivating feedback and informational feedback.

Motivating feedback is defined as feedback about an individual's progress toward goal achievement that energizes and directs behavior. For example, consider a runner who is on the second to last lap and her coach tells her she is on pace for a personal best time. When athletes believe they are improving and moving toward their goals, they become increasingly motivated in their pursuit of goal achievement.

Informational feedback is defined as feedback that provides performers with error correction information, either descriptive (what happened) or prescriptive (what needs to happen). This type of feedback is motivating to all athletes, but it is particularly motivating for athletes engaged in deliberate practice (i.e., setting specific goals for everything they do in practice). For these athletes, informational feedback is like food to a hungry traveler; they devour it. They want to improve with each practice and informational feedback helps temporarily satisfy their craving for knowledge about their progress toward improved performance.

Extrinsic and Intrinsic Motivation

Some people engage in specific behaviors because they have **extrinsic motivation**: They engage in the behaviors because they anticipate certain external rewards. For example, some athletes try out for a team because they anticipate earning a varsity letter, a trophy, a college scholarship, and so on. Other people have **intrinsic motivation**: They engage in athletics because they respond well to internal sources of reinforcement such as personal satisfaction and sense of accomplishment. These athletes derive internal reinforcement from achievements such as throwing a perfect pass, performing a great gymnastics routine, swishing a 3-point shot, running a perfect race, and so on. The beauty of sport is that this list is virtually endless.

Research suggests that people who respond to intrinsic motives are more committed, enjoy their activities more, and are more persistent when they confront failure (Agbor-Baiyee, 1997). While this research examined student behavior, research examining athletes found similar results (Vallerand & Losier, 1999). Close to intrinsic motivation is a concept called **interest** (Wigfield, Eccles, & Rodriguez, 1998). People who engage in activities simply for the fact that they like doing it and expect no external reward can be said to have an interest in that activity. A primary objective for all coaches should be to encourage athletes to develop a genuine interest in their sport.

Keep in mind, however, that external rewards can be useful for facilitating interest and intrinsic motivation. For example, when I was learning to dive, our coach purchased gold (it was actually yellow, but it looked like gold to my teammates and me) diving suits like the one reigning Olympic champion Bernie Wrightson wore when he won the gold medal. We all aspired to become gold medalists like Bernie, but we could not buy the suit. We could only acquire the suit by earning it, by learning a full list of high-degree-of-difficulty dives on the 3-meter springboard. We wanted to earn that suit so badly that we would do almost anything, including learning scary and difficult new dives that no one our age was performing back then. The suit became a symbol of courage, effort, determination, and noteworthy accomplishment. We did not remain in the sport simply because of the suit, but it sure captured our interest and ignited our intrinsic motivation.

Conditioned Responses

Athletes who associate positive physiological responses, such as relaxation and appropriate arousal level, and enhancing emotions, such as joy and satisfaction, are more likely to love their sport and come to practice highly motivated to train. Therefore, to increase motivation, coaches need to condition their athletes to respond positively to not only their sport but the many aspects of their sport, such as training, stretching, conditioning, drill and skill work, and competing. For many athletes, especially young ones, a positive conditioned response is what brings them back each day, each week, each month, and each season. Because conditioning is so important to the motor learning process and athlete success, chapter 3 examines it in detail (see The Salivating Athlete).

Applying Behaviorism to Increase Athlete Motivation

Based on the theory of behaviorism, coaches can push a number of "behavioral buttons" to increase athletes' motivation.

Follow the guidelines for the effective use of praise. Although praise is an effective reinforcer, it can be misused. Know when, what, and how to use it. Successful coaches are masters at effectively using praise to motivate their athletes.

Use external feedback as you would other types of reinforcers. External feedback for all athletes, but particularly elite athletes, is highly reinforcing. The more accurate the external feedback, the more reinforcing it becomes for them.

Years ago when I first began working with an elite athlete, who already was a NCAA champion and world champion, I learned two things rather quickly: Remember what correction you give him and give him accurate feedback about whether or not he made the correction on the subsequent attempt. If I forgot the correction or my feedback was inaccurate, he kindly let me know about it! Highly effective coaches provide accurate and timely external feedback.

Recognize individual differences. No two athletes are exactly alike. It is important to keep these differences in mind when using reinforcement to influence motivation. What is reinforcing for one athlete might not be reinforcing to another athlete. Knowing how to push their buttons in part means knowing what is reinforcing to them. For example, some athletes hate being pulled aside and lectured while other athletes take it as a compliment and a sign that you care about them and their goals.

Reinforce effort in order to encourage intrinsic motivation. In the long run, athletes train harder and longer and persevere in their sport when they are intrinsically motivated. For this reason, reinforce effort. Athletes who associate ability and achievement with effort are more likely to be motivated to train and maintain their motivation during difficult training cycles.

Condition athletes to have a positive physiological response to their sport. Athletes who have an interest and love for their sport (training and competition) will be engaged and motivated. You can facilitate a positive response by continually pairing positive conditioned stimuli with positive unconditioned stimuli. A significant way to create a positive response is to facilitate success and mastery during practice, make practice and competition fun, and focus on effort.

Use external reinforcers. Sometimes external reinforcers can be effective for kick starting or augmenting an athlete's internal motivation. In the case of the gold diving suit, it is interesting to note that every diver on the team did indeed earn a suit. Most went on to successful high school careers and a number of us went on to compete collegiately and nationally. One athlete even made the U.S. Olympic team, and one stayed around long enough to coach collegiate diving for over 37 years. Sometimes, a seemingly small external reward can go a long way toward intrinsically motivating athletes. It is funny how after all these years grown men still occasionally gather and talk about "the suit" and how they cherish it and have it stored away like a rare artifact, precious and immeasurably valuable, a tangible reminder of the intangible rewards they received from their memorable experience in sport. I am sure that athletes in all sports have similar stories and memories.

COGNITIVISM AND MOTIVATION

A coach shows a young gymnast a new move on parallel bars. Without any prompting on the coach's part, the young girl immediately begins practicing the movement over and over on her own. She spends the remainder of practice on the routine and the next day works equally hard on the routine until she performs it competently. How do we explain this girl's motivated behavior? Behaviorism might suggest that she is being reinforced, but no immediate or overt reinforcement is being administered. Perhaps the best explanation for her motivated behavior comes from cognitive-based theories.

Although reinforcement is useful in promoting motivation, athletes are more than rats and motivated by more than simple reinforcers. According to cognitive theory, athlete motivation is explained by the very human (as opposed to rodent) need and ability to process (understand) information, anticipate distant outcomes, delay gratification, add meaningfulness to goals, establish beliefs about personal competence, and make attributions for success and failure. From a cognitive perspective, one would say that the young gymnast's motivated behavior is influenced by her need to understand how to generate the movement and desire to attribute success to her ability and effort.

The following section examines this perspective in greater detail. It introduces cognitive theories of motivation and some coaching applications for increasing motivation in your athletes.

Arousal Theory

Arousal has to do with the psychological and physiological activation of the athlete. From a cognitive perspective, **arousal theory** is important because it reminds you that psychological arousal is necessary in order for athletes to attend to incoming stimuli, whether it is your coaching feedback, the position of players on the court, or other vital cues related to successful motor performance. With too little arousal they don't attend to your comments and their performance cues. Nor do they attend to your comments and their performance cues with too much arousal. Consequently, motivation according to arousal theory can be defined as the appropriate psychological and physiological activation of the athlete to attend to incoming stimuli. So, learn how to press the *attention button* to increase athlete motivation. For capturing athlete attention, see chapter 6.

Once your athletes are cognitively alert and ready to attend to incoming information, what do they actually do with this information? This question most concerns cognitive theorists. Once the rat receives the pellet, not much else happens in its tiny brain (okay, even this little creature engages in the simple cognitive process of mapping) but athletes actually do a lot with incoming information. The following section returns to a behavioral concept (external reward) and looks at it from a cognitive perspective.

Cognitive Evaluation Theory

Research in the area of attribution theory suggests that external rewards can diminish a young athlete's intrinsic motivation (Deci, Koestner, & Ryan, 2001). On the other hand, the **additive principle** posits that external rewards help increase, or add to, intrinsic motivation. In other words, the young athlete who lacks motivation to participate in an achievement situation is more likely to participate if given an external reward. So, which position is correct? Is it good or bad to use external rewards? The relationship between external rewards and intrinsic motivation is not that simple. The **multiplicative principle** suggests that the interaction between intrinsic and extrinsic reinforcement can either add to or detract from intrinsic motivation. What may mediate this process is cognitive evaluation.

Cognitive evaluation theory (Deci & Ryan, 1985) suggests that the effect of external rewards on an individual has to do with how the individual perceives the reward. When people perceive that external forces control their behavior, intrinsic motivation is likely to decrease. Athletes with this perception become like puppets; external forces seem to control them. This effect is called the **controlling aspect** of extrinsic motivation. For example, when a young athlete is given money to participate in a sport, he may lose interest and quit competing when the money is no longer available. In this case, the perception is *Since the reward no longer exists, participation should cease.*

However, when people perceive external rewards as informational feedback confirming competence and self-determination, intrinsic motivation is likely to increase. Athletes with this perception perceive themselves to be in control. This situation is known as the **informational aspect** of extrinsic motivation. For example, when a young athlete receives an external reward of a newspaper article or recognition at a year-end banquet, he may perceive this information as confirmation of competence and self-determination. In this case, the perceived information confirms ability and effort and increases intrinsic motivation. When I learned a full list of difficult optional dives on the 3-meter springboard and received the gold suit, the suit was external validation and confirmation of my ability, courage, and hard work; I earned it through my own competence and self-determining behavior.

The message here is simple: When you push the *reward button* to motivate your athletes, connect the reward you provide to motivated behaviors such as effort, competence, and self-determination.

Cognitive Dissonance Theory

Athletes behave on the basis of their information and beliefs. But what happens when they receive information that conflicts with their current information and beliefs? **Cognitive dissonance theory** (Festinger, 1957, 1962) suggests that when an individual simultaneously holds two contradictory units of information (the defining feature of cognitive dissonance) the individual will be motivated to reduce or eliminate the contradiction. When you confront athletes—particularly those entrenched in negative beliefs and self-limiting attitudes, perceptions, and behaviors—with contradictory information, you motivate them to reduce or eliminate their dissonance.

So, how do you push the *dissonance button* to motivate your athletes and make them unstoppable forces of nature? You can reduce cognitive dissonance in five ways: attitude or belief change, compartmentalization, exposure to or recall of information, behavioral change, and perceptual distortion.

The following section examines these five means for helping athletes reduce cognitive dissonance. Consider an athlete who is reluctant to believe she can become conference champion even though her past performances say otherwise.

Attitude or belief change: The athlete who doesn't believe she can become conference champion is most likely to *not* become conference champion simply because she doesn't have faith in herself. Therefore, for her to become the athlete you know she can become, she must change her self-belief. It's not a technical issue, not an ability issue, and not a training issue. It is simply a matter of belief. Changing her belief enables her to reduce her dissonance and reach her athletic potential. But how do you help her change her belief? One way is through the process of compartmentalization.

Compartmentalization: This is the process of placing certain beliefs and attitudes into different or special *compartments*. For example, assume that the athlete under consideration had two rather poor performances during the season and she has been focusing on those two performances. If you help her see the big picture (i.e., the whole season) and the fact that those performances were aberrations from her normal performance level, you can help her compartmentalize them and reduce dissonance. You might point out that those two performances came during bouts of intense training and that the discrepancy between her ability to become conference champion and her performance in those two competitions was simply due to overtraining or some other intervening but temporary variable.

Exposure to or recall of information: To further change her self-belief, you confront her with confirmatory evidence for why she can become conference champion. You show her all she has accomplished and all she is capable of achieving. You show her practice results, competition results, and any other type of information that loudly and clearly proclaims she can be conference champion. You encourage her to recall past successes and challenge her to change her self-belief. By exposing her to information that clearly indicates she is capable of becoming conference champion, she is motivated to change her belief and thereby reduce dissonance.

Behavioral change: The change in self-belief is likely to result in a change in behavior. An athlete who now believes she is capable of becoming a conference champion begins behaving like a conference champion. Her training habits, demeanor, confidence, composure, body language, and so on are all likely to change due to her change in self-belief. For a coach, it is one of the most pleasurable, satisfying, and rewarding experiences to watch athletes morph into new people. When this change happens, you know that truly great things are about to follow.

Sometimes, however, a change in behavior needs to precede a change in self-belief. In other words, it is effective to have your athletes behave like champions even though they aren't quite ready—yet—to believe they will become champions. External behaviors have a way of influencing internal beliefs and attitudes. When athletes change behaviors, they change self-beliefs and attitudes, thereby eliminating dissonance. By acting (and training) like a conference champion, your athlete eventually comes to believe she can become a conference champion.

Perceptual distortion: This has to do with how athletes alter the information at hand. Sometimes perceptual distortion is a good thing and sometimes it isn't. For example, when an athlete has 2 poor performances out of 20, like the athlete you have been considering, she needs to distort that information of the 2 poor performances so that it doesn't reflect badly on her self-belief. Elite level athletes seem to be good at this type of distortion. Hit the net three consecutive times and the elite tennis player still believes the next shot is going to be perfect. Miss four consecutive 3-point attempts and the elite basketball player still believes the next shot is going downtown. By distorting the few poor performances, successful athletes maintain positive self-belief.

On the other hand, unsuccessful athletes tend to be less discriminating and perhaps less honest in their use of perceptual distortion. They use perceptual distortion to hide weaknesses, cloak lack of effort, and cover up self-doubt and disbelief. For example, they may possess two contradictory pieces of information: dissonance between how hard they believe they are training and their actual level of effort in practice. These athletes are likely to distort how hard they actually train unless you give them objective data that clearly indicate they could be giving more effort.

Exceptionally effective coaches are masters at using the concept of dissonance theory to motivate athletes. They have an uncanny ability to cognitively shock and awe athletes in ways that force them to adopt new attitudes, perceptions, and behaviors. In a sense, they are able to help athletes reinvent themselves so that they perceive themselves as capable instead of incapable, powerful instead of powerless, participants instead of spectators, finalists instead of semifinalists, champions instead of runner-ups, and believers instead of disbelievers.

This is perhaps the greatest challenge coaches confront: changing athlete attitudes and self-beliefs. For many athletes, the most formidable opponents they are likely to confront during their athletic careers are ultimately themselves and their self-imposed limiting self-perceptions. When you create cognitive dissonance and help them resolve this dissonance, you encourage your athletes to adopt new attitudes, beliefs, behaviors, perceptions, and expectations that lead to highly motivated behaviors. Some reluctant athletes find it difficult to change long-held attitudes and beliefs so you may need to take a more aggressive approach (push, cajole, demand) in getting them to elevate their attitudes and beliefs. Of these new attitudes and beliefs, perhaps none is more important or has greater implications for athlete motivation than self-efficacy.

Self-Efficacy Theory

According to Bandura (1997), **self-efficacy** is "beliefs in one's capabilities to organize and execute the courses of action required to produce given attainments" (p. 3). Self-efficacy embodies two components. The first component has to do with the actual skills (competencies) required to achieve attainment. The second has to do with the individual's personal estimate of competence. Athletes with high self-efficacy believe that in certain situations they have the necessary skills to meet the challenge and perform well. Athletes with low self-efficacy believe the opposite. Athletes with high self-efficacy are motivated to confront challenges because they are confident they will do well. Athletes with low self-efficacy tend to avoid challenges.

Bandura distinguishes between self-esteem and self-efficacy, which are often confused. **Self-esteem** has to do with the perception of personal self-worth, while self-efficacy has to do with self-competency. Bandura uses the example of ballroom dancing to distinguish between self-esteem and self-efficacy. Some people might perceive themselves as having a great deal of self-worth, but concomitantly perceive themselves as having very little competence or ability to ballroom dance.

Effects of Self-Efficacy on Motivation

Bandura (1993) suggests that efficacy belief influences thoughts, emotions, behavior, and motivation. Efficacy belief also influences what people choose to do and not do and sometimes where they choose to do it. Some athletes choose to perform certain athletic feats in practice but are reluctant to do them in front of a crowd because they judge themselves to be less than competent, even though they perform quite well in practice. A basketball player who can hit a 3-point shot during practice may lack the self-efficacy to risk taking the shot during a game.

Efficacy belief also influences the amount of effort athletes will put forth when faced with difficulties. An athlete with a strong perception of efficacy is likely to persist longer and expend more effort to succeed than an athlete with a weak perception of efficacy. When faced with a difficult situation, the athlete with low self-efficacy is likely to give up or not attempt the endeavor at all.

People who judge themselves as having high self-efficacy also are willing to accept risks and seek challenges. Because they believe in their competence, these people are not afraid to try new things and go beyond past personal best performances. It is not surprising that these people are motivated to set high goals that match their high level of perceived efficacy. Athletes who judge themselves as having high self-efficacy are likely to set goals such as winning a state championship, setting a record, achieving a personal best, and so on. In contrast, athletes with low self-efficacy are likely to set more modest goals.

When you help your athletes establish greater self-efficacy you increase their motivation to accept risk and seek more challenging goals.

According to Bandura (1986) goals are important because they establish the criteria for success or failure. Goals are highly motivating because people are motivated to achieve success and avoid failure. Because goals are associated with success and failure, they also are associated with emotional reactions: satisfaction, joy, and contentment with success and sadness, depression, and disappointment with failure. This connection with significant emotions makes goals powerful sources of motivation.

Judgments of self-efficacy also influence thoughts and emotions to motivate behavior. Athletes who judge themselves as having low competency are more likely to generally evaluate themselves negatively. These negative thoughts lead to low self-esteem and negative emotions, which lead to inaction and lethargy. Evidence shows that people with high self-esteem are both physically and psychologically healthier than people with low self-esteem (Bandura, 1997). According to Bandura (1997), high self-efficacy gives people the confidence and ability to handle life's stressors. This advantage is significant for athletes and coaches since sport and the demands of training and competition mirror many of life's stressors. The athlete with high self-efficacy is more likely to adequately handle stressors such as fear, fatigue, soreness, injury, defeat, and competition.

Not every individual will have the face of the athlete with high self-efficacy. Therefore, an important task for coaches is to develop high self-efficacy and a corresponding sense of self-confidence in athletes. How are personal judgments of self-efficacy developed? How can coaches help build positive self-efficacy in their athletes? These two questions are profoundly important for you to answer if you want to develop confident athletes who are willing to take risks, seek challenges, persevere in the face of adversity, and perform at a high level, particularly when it matters most.

Development of Self-Efficacy Judgments

Bandura (1997) suggests that four sources influence self-efficacy development: enactive (actual) experiences, vicarious (secondhand) experiences, persuasory (persuasion) experiences, and emotive (arousal or emotional states) experiences.

Enactive influence is the actual performance outcomes that people experience as a direct result of their own actions. The success or failure of one's actions, especially if it is continual success or failure, has an influence on the positive or negative evaluation of self-efficacy. People who rarely experience success are likely to have negative evaluations of self-efficacy. People who experience a high rate of success are likely to form positive evaluations of self-efficacy. However, as is shown later with attribution theory, it is not necessarily the case that success always produces positive self-efficacy. Some people attribute their experience of success to luck or some other external factor over which they have no control, not to their own competence and effort.

Vicarious influence is also referred to as secondhand influence because it has to do with observing the performances of others. Comparative information helps people make judgments about self-worth and personal competence. Athletes who see teammates habitually perform worse than them may use this comparative information to develop a high evaluation of their own athletic competence. Similarly, athletes who typically see teammates perform better than them may develop a low evaluation of their own athletic competence. Bandura (1981) suggests that the most important comparisons children use for establishing personal competence are those derived from comparisons with their peers, particularly in a competitive setting.

Persuasory influence is the act of verbally persuading an individual into doing something. When coaches use verbal persuasion, they implicitly convey to their athletes a positive judgment regarding the athletes' competency. For example, a coach says, "Come on, Suzy. You can make this next set of sprints!" This comment communicates to the athlete that the coach believes she has the competence to meet the challenge. People form notions of self based in part on feedback from significant others. Therefore, when a coach expresses belief in an athlete's competency, it goes a long way toward helping the athlete develop and sustain high self-efficacy.

Emotive influence has to do with the emotions and physiological state (arousal) that athletes experience with their sport. Specific emotional responses lead to specific and often dramatic physiological changes and different levels of activation or excitement of the central nervous system. Bandura (1997) suggests that emotions, such as high arousal, can affect self-judgments and personal efficacy. For example, a high level of fear can lead to judgments of low personal competence. The baseball player in the batter's box who is overcome with fear is likely to decide that he is incapable of making good contact with the ball.

Imaginal influence occurs when athletes form efficacy beliefs by imagining themselves or others performing successfully (or unsuccessfully) in anticipated competition situations. For this reason, imaginal influence is considered another source of efficacy information (Maddux, 1995). Imagining being victorious over an opponent can raise efficacy judgment and endurance performance (Feltz & Riessinger, 1990). Additionally, mental rehearsal strategies appear to enhance competition efficacy belief and competitive performance (Callow, Hardy, & Hall, 2001; Garza & Feltz, 1998; Short, Bruggeman, et al., 2002).

If creating high self-efficacy is important for motivation, how do you push the *self-efficacy button*? The following section addresses this question.

Building Self-Efficacy to Increase Athlete Motivation

How do you build self-efficacy in your athletes to make them confident and unstoppable forces? Use the following guidelines to help you.

Increase athlete awareness of the self-efficacy concept. Don't underestimate the importance of self-efficacy for creating competent, confident, and motivated athletes. Share the concept of self-efficacy with your athletes, parents, and staff. Discuss how positive self-efficacy is developed and how it is diminished. Make self-efficacy part of your coaching curriculum.

Model self-efficacy. Research on self-efficacy has identified a specific type of self-efficacy called teacher efficacy (Woolfolk & Hoy, 1990; Woolfolk, Rosoff, & Hoy, 1990). **Teacher efficacy** is a teacher's belief that he or she can positively influence all students, even difficult students, and help them learn. A teacher's perception of self-efficacy is one of the few personal teacher characteristics that correlate with student achievement (Ashton & Webb, 1986). Another body of research (Feltz et al., 1999) indicates the importance of **coaching efficacy**—a coach's belief that he has the ability to affect the learning and motor performance of his athletes. Performance in this sense extends as well to the psychological, attitudinal, and teamwork skills of the athletes (Feltz, Short, & Sullivan, 2008). Self-efficacious coaches believe in their coaching competency and their ability to bring forth the unseen potential in all their athletes. Therefore, they are more likely to work harder and persist longer when working with athletes. Modeling self-efficacy motivates their athletes to imitate similar self-efficacious behavior.

Several studies suggest that formal education programs play a role in developing coaching efficacy (Lee, Malete, & Feltz, 2002; Malete & Feltz, 2000). As Feltz, Short, and Sullivan (2008) write, "however, an effective, well-designed coaching education program should enhance the level of one's coaching efficacy if it increases one's knowledge about the skills of coaching" (p. 162). This book should help increase your knowledge of coaching skills and your coaching efficacy.

Create a learning environment in which athletes experience success and mastery. As Bandura (1997) points out, successful performance is a positive enactive (actual outcome) influence that promotes self-efficacy. Rather than reduce athlete expectations and decrease task difficulty to achieve success, create ways for athletes to attain success such as providing ample time to achieve mastery, breaking up tasks into smaller units, using group cooperation, using peer coaching (a team member coaches another team member), and so on.

Monitor peer comparisons. In some situations peer comparison can be informative and helpful for encouraging young athletes to elevate their expectations, effort, and performances. For example, a swimmer who doesn't think he can make a particularly grueling set of practice swims might think differently when he sees three of his buddies complete the set. He will most likely try harder, make the sets, and thereby elevate his evaluation of his competency. However, in other cases peer comparison isn't helpful because some athletes are not very good at making accurate peer comparisons. For example, a young and late-maturing athlete might compare herself to a teammate who is the same age but more physically mature. Often it is best if you have your athletes focus on their own training, goals, and performances rather than on other athletes and things over which they have no control.

Emphasize athlete cooperation and team success rather than just individual success. In cooperative settings, comparison with peers is not nearly as important to people as it is in competitive settings. You can foster a cooperative practice environment in many ways, such as setting team goals and not just individual goals, encouraging teammates to provide feedback to each other in addition to the coach's feedback, having older athletes mentor younger athletes, asking an athlete to work with a teammate on a particular skill, and so on.

Develop team self-efficacy. The positive effects of self-efficacy are not limited to the individual athlete. Groups that collectively demonstrate high self-efficacy tend to outperform groups that exhibit low self-efficacy (George & Feltz, 1995). **Collective self-efficacy** occurs when all team members have confidence in the team. They believe in one another and their ability as a group to rise to the occasion and perform successfully in demanding situations. As Hall of Fame basketball player Michael Jordan (1994) put it, "But when we stepped in between the lines, we knew what we were capable of doing. When a pressure situation presented itself, we were plugged into one another as a cohesive unit" (p.23). Feltz, Short, and Sullivan (2008) identify 14 techniques for enhancing and maintaining collective efficacy:

- Defining success in mastery terms
- Mastery climate
- Team goal setting
- Modifying the task
- Simulation
- Manipulating the schedule
- Shifting the focus off the score
- Positive team talk
- Building team cohesion
- Team attributions
- Videotaping success
- Coach modeling confidence
- Controlling group size
- Verbal persuasion

Use verbal persuasion to develop positive notions of athlete competency. Effective coaches are exceptional salespeople. They are masters at selling new merchandise. In this case, *new merchandise* refers to new techniques, new training regimens, new risks, new challenges, new goals, and even new perceptions of competency. For example, you can go a long way toward improving an athlete's notion of self-efficacy when you sit down with her and say, "Listen, I have had many conference champions, so I can tell you from experience that you have all the physical, mental, and emotional tools to become our next champion! Now, here's our plan . . . ." This type of statement has a powerful effect of elevating athlete self-efficacy.

Communicate expectations of competency through your actions. Verbal persuasion is effective, but in the long run words don't mean much if you don't back them up with actions that corroborate your verbalizations. One way to demonstrate your belief in your athletes' competency (and thereby increase their self-efficacy) is to encourage them to take risks and accept challenges. When you encourage athletes to step outside their comfort zones and attempt more challenging performance tasks, you tacitly communicate your belief in their competency. Encouraging them to set higher and more difficult goals is a way to indirectly tell them they are competent athletes capable of attaining a higher level of performance.

Teach athletes to use self-talk and self-affirmation statements. Thoughts affect emotions, which then affect performance (Zinsser, Bunker, & Williams, 2001).

Theodorakis, Weinberg, Natsis, Douma, and Kazakas (2000) have reviewed research that supports the use of self-talk as a means of promoting and maintaining positive thoughts, confidence (feelings of competency), and high-level performance. Maintaining a feeling of competency is particularly important during those critical seconds when keeping one's composure and confidence is the difference between success and failure. The basketball player who tells herself she can hit the shot before she attempts her free throw with only a second remaining in the game; the swimmer who tells himself to relax, focus, and stay in control on the final lap; and the quarterback who in the final seconds of the game tells himself to be the eye of the storm and finds the open receiver for the winning touchdown are all examples of self-talk helping athletes maintain self-confidence and a belief that they can competently meet the challenge.

Because self-talk is extremely helpful in establishing athlete self-efficacy, the following two sections discuss this concept in greater detail.

Categories of Self-Talk Positive **self-talk** comes in the form of words uttered aloud to oneself or in the form of private mental thoughts. Athletes are always talking to themselves, even if they aren't always aware of it. Therefore, it is important that they become conscious of their self-talk, monitor it, and keep it positive. Positive self-talk enhances performance and negative self-talk impairs performance. Every coach has had an athlete who always seems to talk negatively to teammates and self. Negative self-talk is self-destructive and debilitating to individual and team performance.

Landin and Herbert (1999) have identified three types of self-talk that positively affect emotions and performance: task-specific statements relating to technique, encouragement and effort, and mood words. These kinds of self-talk can help athletes develop a positive mental attitude, instill self-confidence, and increase motivated behavior.

Task-specific statements relating to technique. This category involves the use of self-talk that reinforces specific technique used during performance. For example, the basketball player getting ready to shoot a free throw might use the words "Relax the wrist and follow through with the fingers" as a reminder for correct shooting form.

Encouragement and effort. This type of self-talk uses words of self-encouragement to persevere and try hard. For example, the cross country runner who is slightly behind in a race might say, "Hang in there; you can do it. Make your move now."

Mood words. This category of self-talk employs words that favorably affect an athlete's mood or arousal level. For example, the athlete looking to increase arousal might say, "aggressive!" In contrast, the athlete looking to remain calm might say, "patience" depending on the type of performance and the particular stage in the performance routine.

Self-talk is more effective when the statements are

- brief and phonetically simple to utter,
- logically associated with the actual performance, and
- appropriate and connected to the sequential timing of the performance (Landin & Herbert, 1999).

Using Self-Talk to Build Self-Confidence   Self-talk is a powerful tool for athlete motivation. Athletes can use it directly or indirectly to enhance self-confidence and maintain self-efficacy. When athletes push the *self-talk button* (e.g., say, "You can do it." "Hang in there." "You've got it. Keep going."), they are capable of motivating themselves and maintaining their unstoppable momentum. Zinsser et al. (2001) have identified five specific uses of self-talk: building and developing self-efficacy, acquiring new skills, creating and changing mood, controlling effort, and focusing attention or concentration. They are discussed next.

Building and developing self-efficacy. Self-talk can positively affect thoughts and emotions which in turn help engender a belief in personal self-competency and ability to perform well, particularly at critical moments. Athletes listen to many voices—the voices of their peers, parents, coaches, and teammates—but the voice they listen to most is their internal voice. When this voice speaks, they listen. When it tells them they are competent and able to meet the challenges of the moment, they believe it.

Acquiring new skills. Self-talk can enhance self-confidence during the skill acquisition phase in several ways. Self-talk can remind the learner of improvements being made during the learning process, encourage the learner to continue persevering during trying moments of the learning process, and help the learner focus on appropriate actions, particularly during the associative stage of learning when learning is more conscious than automatic.

Creating and changing mood. Self-talk can help set an appropriate mood state for learning and performance or change an inappropriate mood state into an appropriate one. As mentioned earlier, words have a powerful impact on emotions, which in turn have an impact on performance. Sometimes, as simple of a statement such as "Relax and be patient" is enough to help athletes avoid getting frustrated.

Controlling effort. Self-talk can help athletes maintain an appropriate level of physical effort throughout a competition, lengthy practice, or challenging moment. Self-talk can help elevate effort level when the task demands greater effort or when effort level has dropped and needs elevating. Examples of self-talk that help control effort level include "Pick up the pace," "Get going," "Stay on target," and "Reenergize."

Focusing attention or concentration. Self-talk also can help athletes maintain an appropriate level of psychological arousal (mental focus and concentration). Phrases such as "Focus" and "Eyes on the prize" help athletes maintain or regain focus and concentration. For more information on emotion and performance, see chapter 9.

SOCIAL COGNITIVE LEARNING AND MOTIVATION

So far this chapter has examined behavioral and cognitive theories related to motivation. This section considers theories of motivation that are both behavioral and cognitive in nature.

A young basketball player attends her first professional basketball game. She is awestruck at what she sees: an enthusiastic crowd; a massive arena, an electric atmosphere; and amazingly talented, dedicated, and godlike athletes reinventing what she thought she knew was the game of basketball. The next day she tries out for her junior high basketball team and spends every afternoon and most evenings in the gym. She practices for hours, imitating the basketball players she observed and she dedicates herself to someday becoming a professional basketball player.

How do you explain this young girl's behavior, her quest to become a great basketball player? In behavioral terms, this young athlete's behavior doesn't appear to receive any immediate reinforcement. In cognitive terms, she doesn't seem to be motivated by a need to understand, make assessment of competence, or establish attributions for success and failure. The best explanation for her motivated behavior comes from Bandura's social cognitive learning theory.

Social cognitive theory (Bandura, 1986) emphasizes learning through observation of others. Through observational learning, people simply watch and imitate others, modeling changes in behavior, thinking, and emotions. Bandura's theory is behavioristic because it uses principles of operant conditioning to explain why people imitate and don't imitate certain observed behaviors. For instance, an athlete who observes the team captain receiving reinforcement for paying attention and speaking politely to the coach imitates a similar behavior and also receives reinforcement.

But how does this explain the young girl's behavior of imitating the professional basketball player? She receives no apparent reinforcement for her imitative behavior. Social cognitive theory is cognitivistic because it recognizes the cognitive activities inherent in observational learning. People symbolize, imagine, consider cause–effect relationships, and anticipate the outcomes of their behaviors. From a social cognitive perspective then, the young girl imagines being a professional basketball player, understands that many years of hard work are necessary to become one, and anticipates the reinforcement she will receive in the distant future once she becomes a professional player.

Expectancy–Value Theory

With social cognitive theory, as well as with other cognitive-based theories (particularly self-efficacy), people's choice of actions, as well as their persistence and performance are mediated by their expectations for success and failure and the value placed on their choice of actions (Eccles & Wigfield, 2002). According to **expectancy–value theory** of motivation, people perform cognitive operations to establish expectancy and value. **Expectancy**, much like self-efficacy, is "individuals' beliefs about how well they will do on upcoming tasks, either in the immediate or long-term future" (Eccles & Wigfield, 2002, p. 119). **Value** is the worth or value of their choice. For example, the young basketball player believes she has the competency to become a professional basketball player in the long-term future and determines that her goal is valuable enough to put in much work to accomplish it. Value has four components: attainment value, intrinsic value, utility value, and cost.

Attainment value is the importance the individual gives to the choice. Among other things, attainment value is influenced by how well the choice fits into an athlete's plan and how it reflects self-image. For example, the young basketball player sees herself as an outstanding athlete and so her self-image fits with her plan to become a professional athlete.

Intrinsic value refers to the intrinsic enjoyment and satisfaction the athlete derives from an activity. The young basketball player finds playing basketball intrinsically motivating and looks forward to the many long hours of practice.

Utility value has to do with how well the choice coordinates with present and future goals. The young basketball player loves the game and looks forward to playing competitively in junior high school, high school, college, and in a professional league. Basketball has high utility value for her because it coordinates with her present and future goals.

Cost of an option has to do with negative possibilities such as failure, stress and anxiety, effort expended, conflicting options, injury, monetary loss, and so on. When making choices, cost is a critical factor for athletes to consider. In pursuing her dream of becoming a professional basketball player, the young girl will give up social time, lose touch with good friends who don't play basketball, perhaps tear a knee ligament, sprain an ankle, and so on. Is her experience worth the cost? She believes it is.

Social cognitive theory, as well as other cognitive theories such as self-efficacy, can be characterized as *expectancy × value theories*. In other words, **motivation** is the product of two main factors: the individual's expectation of success and the value or meaningfulness of the goal. If either of these two values is zero, then motivation will be absent and no effort will be made to achieve the goal. If both values are high, motivation will be high.

$$\text{Expectancy of success} \times \text{Value of goal} = \text{Level of motivation}$$

Social cognitive learning theory helps explain the young basketball player's behavior. She observes the professional basketball players receiving reinforcement (attention, notoriety, fame, and so on) and vicariously shares their reinforcement. She believes she has the competency to someday become a professional player (expectancy) and is willing to sacrifice whatever is necessary (value) to reach her goal. Consequently, she is highly motivated to imitate the behavior of the professional players.

Now, consider a different athlete who attends a professional game, observes athletes being reinforced for their behaviors but has little expectancy of success because he is not tall enough or good enough to play basketball. Because he doesn't derive a great deal of satisfaction from playing basketball (low intrinsic value), prefers to play racquetball in the future (low utility value), and doesn't want to give up spare time to practice (cost), the value factor would be low. Because both expectancy and value factors would be low, he would be unmotivated to imitate the behaviors of the professional basketball players.

Expectancy–value theory also is useful for understanding coach motivation and interaction with athletes. Considerable research (e.g., Solomon, Striegel, Eliot, Heon, Maas, & Wayda, 1996; Solomon, 1998) indicates that a coach's expectancy (belief) of how well an athlete will do on upcoming and future tasks influences the level of motivation and type and quality of feedback the coach provides. In other words, a coach's perception of an athlete's ability and improvement potential acts as a self-fulfilling prophecy and ultimately influences the athlete's level of performance.

Martinek (1981) has proposed a four-step model for understanding how a coach's expectations can influence an athlete's behavior and performance:

1. The coach develops expectations for an athlete early in the season.
2. The expectations affect the coach's interaction (feedback) with the athlete.
3. The feedback the athlete receives from the coach influences the athlete's self-perceptions, motivation, and learning opportunities.
4. The athlete's performance conforms to the coach's initial expectations.

What coach would have expected Kimberly from the story at the beginning of this chapter to have become a national champion, not just in 2 years, but ever? Coach expectancies are important and the good news is that they can change. For example, Horn (1984) found that a coach's perceptions of an athlete can be modified over the course of a season as information concerning the athlete's performance becomes available.

Applying Social Cognitive Learning Theory to Increase Athlete Motivation

It is important for athletes to learn many types of behaviors, such as social behaviors, learning behaviors, champion behaviors, and motor behaviors. How do you push the *imitation button* to increase motivation in your athletes to imitate these behaviors? The following text offers some guidelines.

Increase expectancy and value. Motivation is the product of expectancy (self-belief) of success and value (meaningfulness) of the goal. Therefore, increasing both expectancy and value increases motivation. Athletes won't be motivated to imitate if they don't believe (expect) they have the ability to imitate the observed behaviors. Consequently, create situations for your athletes to successfully perform actual outcomes (enactive influence) that closely resemble the observed behaviors to be imitated. Persuade (persuasory influence) your athletes that they are capable of imitating the observed behaviors. Have athletes watch (vicarious influence) teammates imitating observed behaviors so that they say to themselves, "Well, if she can do it, so can I!" Increase expectancy by helping your athletes attribute success to stable causes and failure to unstable causes.

To increase value, emphasize the meaningfulness of the goal. Sometimes athletes only understand after the fact how valuable it is to do something. Help them see the value of imitating a behavior beforehand: "This drill may seem boring or unimportant, but in reality it is extremely important for laying a foundation for your future success. All great athletes in your sport practice this drill. That is how they became great!" Also, emphasize the emotional and physiological (emotive influence) benefits associated with imitating the behavior. For example, say, "This is going to be so cool! You will love it. Let's go for it!"

Use direct reinforcement to increase motivation. Directly reinforce appropriate behaviors athletes imitate. Because social cognitive theory uses principles of operant conditioning, direct reinforcement motivates athletes to repeat these behaviors.

Use vicarious reinforcement to increase motivation. Recall that vicarious reinforcement is reinforcement that results from observing someone else receive reinforcement. Research has shown that the administration of reward (or punishment) to a model has a similar effect on the behavior of the observer (Bandura, 1962). Consequently, when your team is watching, look for opportunities to reinforce significant role models (e.g., team captain, most liked player, best player) on the team for modeling appropriate behaviors. Other team members will be motivated to imitate behaviors such as proper technique and correct motor performance.

Reinforce modeled motivated behavior. **Motivated behavior** includes athlete actions that personify motivation. Examples of motivated behavior are being energetic, excited, and eager before and during practice, arriving early for practice, staying after practice to get in extra training, and giving high effort. Returning to the preceding section, you can use vicarious reinforcement to reinforce a team role model for finishing strong on a tough set of wind sprints, for example. Other players are likely to be equally motivated to finish strong on the wind sprints. Now, let's say the same role model eagerly arrives early to practice and excitedly says, "I can't wait to start training. Give me a tough practice coach!" These motivated behaviors also can be vicariously reinforced so that other players arrive early to practice and display a similar upbeat, positive, and motivated attitude towards practice. Reinforcing a model creates a **ripple effect** (Kounin, 1970) that acts like a stone dropped into a pond with the ripple emanating throughout the team to the behavior of others.

Reinforce imitated motivated behaviors. Besides reinforcing the model, you also can reinforce the observer. When you see your athletes imitate motivated behavior, use *direct reinforcement* to encourage them to continue these behaviors. Similarly, when you see athletes imitate unmotivated behavior, discourage these behaviors with some type of acceptable punishment.

Inhibit modeled unmotivated behaviors. Punishing team role models for unmotivated behavior inhibits other athletes from imitating similar unmotivated behaviors. Punishing an athlete for habitually arriving late to practice and being sluggish, disinterested, and reluctant to practice discourages other team members from imitating similar unmotivated behavior. For example, when I first started coaching, I inherited a program in which the number one goal of the athletes seemed to be to do as little work as possible. Athletes would stroll in late, chit chat, move slowly, and ask when practice would be over. On my first day I explained my team rules and policies. On the second day I kicked my best athlete out of practice for arriving late. Send a clear message to your athletes: If they want to exhibit unmotivated behavior they should find another program.

Model the behaviors you hope to see in your athletes. There is a prayer that goes something like this: *What we hope to see in others may we see in ourselves.* If you want to see motivated behavior in your athletes, then model motivated behavior. If you come to practice highly motivated, radiate hopefulness and optimism, work even harder after failure, take responsibility for the team's or an athlete's failure, never shirk responsibility, and attribute success to effort and ability and failure to lack of effort, your athletes will observe and imitate similar behaviors.

Unfortunately, coaches can model unmotivated behavior that their athletes observe and imitate. If you come to practice unprepared, tired, lethargic, disinterested, and unmotivated, don't expect your athletes to be emotionally charged and ready to give 100% effort either. Your behaviors and attitudes set the pace, tone, intensity, and expectations for your practices and program. As goes the coach, so goes the team. It is an honor but also a privilege and responsibility to be a coach. What type of motivational behavior do you model?

Maintain flexibility in your perceptions about your athletes. Be conscious of the expectations you have for your athletes. Avoid pigeonholing athletes through your expectations and be open to new information about athletes' progress and ability. You may have A-level, B-level, and C-level athletes on your team, but don't assume that C-level athletes will never become A-level athletes. Some coaches have the attitude of "This person is a C-level athlete and always will be a C-level athlete." This limiting expectation can be easily and nonverbally communicated to athletes and undermine their motivation. Sometimes athletes make surprisingly huge strides in their performances by making one change: finding another coach. What changed for the athlete? The new coach's expectancy of what the athlete could accomplish. What are *your* expectancies for your athletes?

HUMANISM AND MOTIVATION

Why does an athlete choose to dedicate many years and countless hours in the pursuit of excellence? For example, a high school sophomore boy comes home from school one day and tells his parents that he is going to dedicate himself to his sport and see how far he can go and how good he can become. What motivates an athlete to set off on such a journey? In most cases it is for neither money nor fame but, rather, something deeper and more personal: an inner desire to strive to reach one's greatest potential, much like the mountain climber and the challenge of reaching the summit. How high is it possible to climb?

In behavioral terms, one might say this high school boy is somehow being reinforced for his goals and behavior. In cognitive terms, one might say he has a need to understand or an internal locus of control or high self-efficacy. In social cognitive learning terms, one might say he is imitating an observed behavior and has formed a logical expectation about reward and success. But none of these theoretical explanations seems to get to the heart of the matter. In fact, *heart* seems to be the appropriate word here because some human behaviors can only be explained when you understand the human heart. The best explanation for this boy's motivation comes from the learning theory of humanism.

The humanistic view was developed in the 1940s as a reaction to behaviorism and Freudian psychology. For this reason it is sometimes referred to as the *third force psychology*. Psychologists such as Abraham Maslow and Carl

Rogers believed that neither Skinner's behaviorism nor Freud's psychology adequately explained many aspects of human behavior and human motivation. The same also can be true about cognitivism. The cognitive perspective falls short of fully explaining human motivation and behavior, particularly when it comes to matters of the heart.

The humanistic view of motivation emphasizes a unique intrinsic source of motivation that humanists describe as the need for **self-actualization** (Maslow, 1970, 1968), the innate process of becoming more fully human (Rogers & Freiberg, 1994), and the need for self-determination (Deci, Vallerand, Pelletier, & Ryan, 1991). All of these perspectives share the belief that human beings have an innate desire to continually strive to become more than they currently are—to strive to reach their greatest human potential.

One reason I continually came back to coaching year after year was the amazing potential of individual athletes and the challenge of helping them reach their greatest potential not only as athletes but also as human beings. As a coach, how do you use humanistic learning theory to increase athlete motivation to help your athletes reach their greatest potential? Following is a look at Abraham Maslow's well-known hierarchy of needs theory, which incorporates the concept of self-actualization.

Maslow's Hierarchy of Needs Theory

According to **need–drive theory**, human behavior is motivated on the basis of needs and the drive to fulfill these needs. *Needs* are the states of deficiency or lack within an individual. Those needs cause *drives,* which are the energies, tendencies, or urges to act. Maslow suggests that human behavior is motivated by seven categories of needs and he divides these needs into two groups: basic needs (also termed deficiency needs) and metaneeds (also termed growth needs). These groups of needs are outlined in Maslow's hierarchy of needs in figure 1.1.

These needs are considered hierarchical because lower-level needs must first be met before higher-level needs can be satisfied. These lower-level needs, called **basic needs**, also are termed **deficiency needs** because they motivate human behavior whenever the needs are deficient (lacking). For example, the need for food causes a hunger drive, which results in the individual taking action to eat and thereby reduce the hunger drive. This process is called *drive reduction.* The following section outlines the basic needs.

Basic Needs

According to need–drive theory, needs may be divided into two broad categories: physiological needs and psychological needs. **Physiological needs** are basic biological needs, such as food, water, temperature regulation, sleep, rest, and so on. Athletes can accomplish very little in practice if some of these basic physiological needs are unmet. For example, an athlete who hasn't eaten all day is more motivated to find a meal than train.

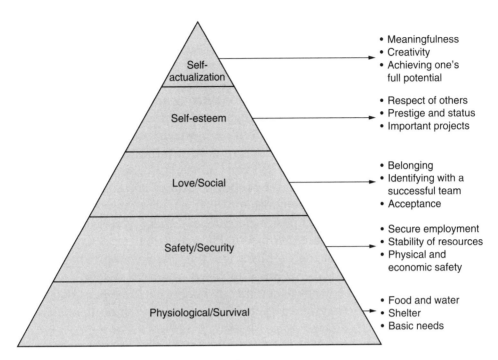

Figure 1.1   Maslow's hierarchy of needs.

Reprinted, by permission, from G. Fried, 2010, *Managing sport facilities,* 2nd ed. (Champaign, IL: Human Kinetics), 48.

Safety needs include physical security and psychological safety. For example, athletes who are fearful for their physical well-being at practice (e.g., afraid of being beat up after practice or being physically injured in practice because of lack of readiness) are likely to be unmotivated to attend practice and train. In contrast, athletes who trust their coach and teammates and feel secure in practice look forward to practice and are motivated to train.

Psychological needs are equally important, even at the most basic level. **Psychological needs** include the need for affection, belonging, achievement, independence, social recognition, and self-esteem. Athletes can have psychological safety when offered an environment in which they are treated with respect, receive positive and constructive criticism, feel welcomed and accepted, and so on. Athletes who have their psychological needs met in your program come to practice motivated to train.

Belongingness and love needs are also basic needs and include such things as affiliation, acceptance, and affection. To satisfy these needs, athletes do things such as seek to develop relationships involving reciprocal affection or identify themselves as members of a group. Athletes can fulfill these needs in part when they have accepting and supportive teammates. Do you encourage your athletes to be accepting and supportive? These needs are fulfilled also when they have a coach who genuinely cares about them, demonstrates this affection, and seeks to establish meaningful coach–athlete relationships. What type of relationship do you have with your athletes? How far do you go in helping your athletes fulfill these basic needs?

According to Maslow, the final and highest basic need is self-esteem. **Self-esteem needs** include the need to cultivate and maintain a high self-opinion and to develop feelings of adequacy, self-confidence, self-worth, and competency. According to Rowan (1998), self-esteem needs can be separated into two different needs. One self-esteem need is for athletes to hold a high opinion of themselves. The other self-esteem need is for significant others to hold the athletes in high esteem; they reflect a positive opinion of the athletes and give them approval and recognition. When you provide positive feedback to your athletes and you hold positive opinions of them, you help build their self-esteem and you motivate them from a humanistic perspective. Coaches who talk negatively about their athletes and hold negative opinions of them ultimately lower athlete self-esteem. Which type of coach are you?

Once these basic needs have been met and continue to be reasonably sustained, the athlete can begin satisfying metaneeds (growth needs).

Metaneeds

Metaneeds are called *growth needs* because, unlike the basic needs that result from deficiencies, the metaneeds arise from the natural and innate human motivation to strive toward personal growth. The metaneeds include **cognitive needs** and **aesthetic needs**—the search for truth and goodness; the acquisition of knowledge; and the appreciation of beauty, order, and symmetry.

The highest growth need in Maslow's hierarchy of needs is **self-actualization**—the innate desire within all individuals to continually strive toward reaching their greatest human potential. This need can never be fully met. People cannot reach their fullest potential because they can never reach perfection, but they strive nevertheless. Self-actualization is an ongoing process rather than a permanent, achievable state of being.

Helping Athletes Meet Basic Needs

It is exciting to note how many of the basic needs and metaneeds can be satisfied through an individual's participation in sport. Take, for example, the *physiological need* for food. Athletes who come to practice hungry typically run out of gas physically, mentally, and emotionally. They become lethargic and cognitively unresponsive. While you can't necessarily feed everyone, you can teach athletes the importance of good nutritional habits. It may take them a year or two to make significant changes, but it will happen and it will have a positive impact on their training and performance and a positive impact on the quality of their life after athletics. And as their coach, it is important that you be a role model for good nutrition. Don't be hypocritical; practice good nutrition yourself.

You also can help satisfy some of your athletes' safety needs. You have a responsibility to establish a safe training environment. This safety refers to both physical safety and psychological safety. *Physical safety* means that athletes are not subjected to physical punishment by either the coach or teammates. It also means that athletes are not confronted with excessive physical harm beyond the normal demands of the sport. For example, asking athletes to attempt difficult skills or tasks they are unprepared to complete and that will result in physical pain and failure not only creates an unsafe training environment but also creates an atmosphere of fear and anxiety.

Psychological safety means that athletes are not subjected to ridicule, public embarrassment, hazing, or other forms of psychological punishment by either the coach or teammates. To provide a psychologically safe training environment, set guidelines and rules for athlete interaction and overtly communicate specific ways in which athletes can support their teammates. You have a responsibility to provide physical and psychological safety for your athletes. You also have a responsibility to provide physical and psychological safety in your methods of communicating, disciplining, and motivating your athletes. I once observed a coach who thought it necessary to repeatedly thump an athlete on the chest when he wanted to make a point. It scared the daylights out of the young boy.

You can help athletes fulfill their *belongingness and love needs* through their participation in sport in several ways. Genuinely caring about your athletes, wanting to see them do well, and demonstrating a genuine affection for them goes a long way in helping your athletes feel loved and accepted not only as athletes but as human beings. This attitude also helps them feel that they truly belong to the team. You can also facilitate perceived team affiliation when including athletes in the decision making process, asking them to participate in goal setting, and expecting them to be responsible for not only themselves but also to some degree for the team and program.

Athletes can also satisfy the need for heightened *self-esteem* through their participation in sport. Take the time to recognize your athletes and their accomplishments. Also, based on the notion of attribution theory (see chapter 2), take the time to recognize your athletes' efforts and competencies and demonstrate through word and deed your acceptance of them.

Once the basic needs have been adequately fulfilled, athletes can turn their attention and motivation to the metaneeds.

Helping Athletes Meet Metaneeds

There is something noble, inspiring, and hopeful about the picture of humanity that Maslow draws when he discusses his view of growth needs. He depicts human beings as motivated people who seek knowledge, truth, beauty, and goodness and who desire to become better human beings, continually striving to exploit their talents, capacities, potentialities, and so on (Maslow, 1970). You can help your athletes fulfill their *cognitive needs* when you urge them to become students of the sport. Encourage them to seek deeper knowledge of their sport and themselves and provide them with information about all aspects of their sport, such as strength and conditioning, nutrition, mental training, laws of physics, periodization, sport psychology, and stretching. To help them satisfy *aesthetic needs,* emphasize the higher-order concepts of sport such as the beauty of athletic performance, purity of sport, sporting behavior that transcends winning, and peak experiences.

From observation it seems that human beings do not always appear to behave according to Maslow's theory; thus, it has been criticized. Even Maslow (1971) in a book published posthumously lamented the fact that relatively few truly self-actualized individuals appear to exist. Perhaps one reason for the dearth of self-actualized human beings is that the process of self-actualization requires self-sacrifice, effort, determination, and self-discipline. As Maslow himself observed, many human beings suffer from the **Jonah complex**. Like the biblical character Jonah, people fear their greatness and avoid personal growth and fulfillment of their talents—thus the necessity for sport. Through sport and the facilitative efforts of coaches, athletes can acquire the attributes of self-sacrifice, effort, determination, and self-discipline necessary for personal growth.

To help athletes strive toward *self-actualization,* you can emphasize that the process of self-actualization is an ongoing pursuit with changing goals. For example, one criticism of Maslow's hierarchy is that it suggests the existence of an end point to self-actualization, that human beings can reach a point at which they have achieved their greatest potential (Rowan, 1998). Rather than a pyramid with a defined apex, Rowan (1998) suggests that a ladder with no end point better represents the self-actualization journey. Explain the concept of self-actualization to your athletes as a never-ending process of self-actualization and encourage them to engage in a lifelong pursuit of excellence in all aspects of their lives. Challenge them to accept their potential greatness and their responsibility to nurture and develop their greatness.

One area of sport in which athletes can experience self-actualization is what Maslow calls **peak experiences**. He suggests that these vivid, memorable, and profoundly moving experiences come close to representing self-actualization. Peak experiences are a justification for and validation of not only the value of sport, but also its uniqueness. Few endeavors in life offer such a unique and valued growth experience. Toward the end of his career, Maslow recognizes the possibility and importance of peak experiences not only in life experiences but also in even childhood experiences (Hoffman, 1998). Maslow suggests that we can discover peak experiences throughout our lives: in the memorable experiences of scenic grandeur, resolved crises, near-death occurrences, and, hopefully, unique moments in sport.

Flow Theory

Mihaly Csikszentmihalyi (pronounced cheeks-sent-me-high) has coined the term *flow* to describe what Maslow referred to as peak experiences. **Flow** is a conceptual representation of a seemingly effortless and intrinsically joyful activity in which an individual engages for no external reward or expectation of future benefit but simply because the activity itself is found rewarding. Csikszentmihalyi calls this type of experience an **autotelic experience**. Susan Jackson has taken the concept of flow and applied it to exercise and sport. In this context, Jackson (1995) says, "Flow is a state of optimal experiencing involving total absorption in a task, and creating a state of consciousness where optimal levels of functioning often occur" (p.138).

According to Csikszentmihalyi (1990), the flow experience has nine characteristics, which are all worth noting for coaches:

1. Balance between challenge and skill level
2. Merging of action and cognition: moving in a way that is automatic, spontaneous, unconscious
3. Clearly defined goals
4. Clear, unambiguous feedback
5. Total concentration on the skill being performed
6. Paradox of control: a sense of being in control without trying to be in control
7. Loss of self-awareness: becoming one with the activity being performed
8. Loss of time awareness
9. Autotelic experience: the end result when the preceding eight characteristics have been achieved

Experiencing Flow in Sport

More recently, in their book *Flow in Sports* (1999), Jackson and Csikszentmihalyi describe flow as "a harmonious experience where mind and body are working together effortlessly, leaving the person feeling that something special has just occurred" (p. 5). They go on to write, "This is because flow lifts experiences from the ordinary to the optimal, and it is in those moments that we feel truly alive and in tune with what we are doing" (p. 5). They also add *transformation of time* to the list of characteristics that describe flow.

Factors that Facilitate or Inhibit Flow for Athletes

Jackson (1992, 1995) has identified some factors that facilitate flow and factors that inhibit flow. These factors are apparent in many successful athletes and are well worth reviewing.

The following factors facilitate flow:

Motivation to perform. Athletes who are motivated to perform, both in practice and in competition, are more likely to achieve flow and perform exceptionally well.

Optimal arousal level prior to performance. It is a great challenge to help athletes find that precarious balance between being psyched but not overly psyched, calm but not overly calm, nervous but not overly nervous. Chapter 9 addresses this challenge.

Maintaining appropriate focus. It is an even greater challenge to help athletes maintain the right focus, pay attention to the process and not the outcome, focus on themselves and their own performance rather than their competitors and their performances. It is so easy for athletes to lose focus prior to competition.

Precompetition and competition plan and preparation. Simply put, successful athletes have a precompetition and competition plan and preparations and they follow their plans. A plan really isn't a plan if it isn't adhered to, right? Without a preparation plan it is ridiculously easy for athletes to fall off the wagon—to lose motivation and focus and become over- or underaroused. Having a plan is a critical aspect for achieving flow. A plan facilitates an athlete becoming absorbed in the process and achieving flow.

Physical preparation and readiness. This factor is the most important aspect for achieving flow and having a plan comes second. Without physical preparation and readiness an athlete can forget about achieving flow. I have never played the piano, but I am certain that if I sat at the keyboard I could not achieve a flowlike experience trying to tickle the ivories because I have absolutely no physical preparation or readiness.

Optimal environmental and situational conditions. Optimal conditions, such as good weather and great facilities, are conducive for achieving flow. These factors are often outside an athlete's control. However, successful athletes can learn how to adjust to maintain flow (see p. 53).

Unity with teammates and coach. Positive interactions and open communication, sharing a common goal and purpose, and maintaining a sense of trust and cohesiveness facilitate a strong connection between athlete and teammates or athlete and coach.

Confidence and positive mental attitude. Confidence can be defined as the athlete's belief that he possesses the ability to meet the upcoming challenges. Confidence isn't something an athlete simply has; it is something an athlete earns through hard work, discipline, and preparation. As Indiana University basketball coach Bobby Knight used to say, *The will to succeed is important, but what's more important is the will to prepare.* But even if the preparation is there, it is important for athletes to maintain their confidence and a positive mental attitude before and during the battle. They need to forcefully remind themselves of their hard work and preparation so that when it comes time to jump out of the plane, they trust themselves and know they are ready to pull the chute.

Feeling good about performance during contest. When things feel good and effortless, athletes are experiencing flow. Which comes first, feeling good or experiencing flow? It is hard to say because each feeds off the other. To facilitate feeling good about performance, athletes can be patient—let the performance just happen, and avoid pressing. **Pressing** refers to the act of trying too hard (i.e., harder than usual or necessary) and using muscles disassociated with the actual movement. For example, a baseball hitter might tense up the face and neck muscles immediately before swinging the bat, which will result in slower bat speed.

The following factors inhibit flow:

Lack of physical preparation and readiness. As previously mentioned, physical preparation and readiness are important for facilitating flow. Consequently, a lack of these two factors inhibits flow. For example, if an athlete suddenly fatigues because of a lack of physical conditioning, maintaining flow becomes a losing struggle. At the 2011 Pan American Games several water polo teams lost because in the final period they simply ran out of gas. Watching an opponent race down unguarded and score a goal is a buzz kill for any athlete's flow experience.

Inability to maintain appropriate focus. Again, maintaining focus is critical for staying motivated and in a flowlike state. Overthinking (sometimes called *paralysis through analysis*) and carrying emotional baggage such as worry, frustration, and doubt inhibit flow. Athletes need to let it all go, grip it and rip it, swing for the fences, and not worry about the outcome.

Negative mental attitude. Dwelling on negative thoughts, self-doubts, and uncontrollable factors clouds the mind, impedes performance, and inhibits flow.

Negative team play and interactions. Negative talk between teammates, poor teammate performance, and feeling disconnected from teammates inhibits flow.

Poor performance. When things suddenly turn ugly—unforced errors, unexpected slips or misses, poor technique, or changes in plan occur—losing flow is easy.

Inappropriate arousal level before competition. Emotionally flat, emotionally sky high, and overly anxious are all inhibitory influences on flow.

Lack of motivation. Perceived lack of challenge, no specific performance goals, and other factors can cause lack of motivation, which inhibits flow.

Problem with precompetitive preparation. Sometimes prior to competition things just go haywire for athletes and they come to the erroneous conclusion that they won't perform well. And then in competition they don't perform well.

Nonoptimal environmental or situational conditions. At the 1968 Olympic Games, as USA diver Keith Russell stepped on to the 10-meter platform, the entire audience began booing because if he hit his dive, Mexican diver Alvaro Gaxiola would not win an Olympic medal. Officials waited for the noise to subside, but the crowd never quieted. The antagonistic environment inhibited Keith from experiencing flow. He badly missed his last dive. Alvaro won the silver medal, and Keith finished fourth, 1.59 points behind third and 2.15 points away from second.

Mismatch between skill level and challenge difficulty. Several researchers have suggested that the flow experience is really an interaction between skill level and challenge difficulty (Kimiecik & Stein, 1992; Stein, Kimiecik, Daniels & Jackson, 1995). If the athlete has a high skill level and the task is challenging, the athlete is likely to experience flow. If the athlete has a high skill level and the task is not challenging, the athlete is likely to experience boredom. If the athlete has a low skill level and the task is challenging, the athlete is likely to experience anxiety, but if the task is not challenging, the athlete is likely to experience apathy.

Applying Flow Theory to Increase Athlete Motivation

Flow is the motivational state from which great performances emanate. Highly successful athletes learn how to optimize factors that facilitate flow and deal with factors that inhibit flow. These athletes learn how, as one former athlete of mine once said, "to go to that 'place' I need to be at in order to perform well."

So, what can you do to push the *flow button* to motivate your athletes to have peak experiences? The following guidelines can help.

Ensure optimal physical preparation and readiness. First and foremost, prepare your athletes to be physically ready to perform well. Flow cannot just magically occur without physical preparation and readiness. Your athletes must be able to demonstrate the same level of stamina, strength, flexibility, consistency, and skill in their practice performances that they demonstrate in their competition performances. For example, athletes who run out of gas in the final period will step outside their flow state and be outperformed by the opposing team.

Recognize and emphasize factors that facilitate flow. If you are building a program and can't decide what to emphasize in your coaching, this is a good place to start: Within your curriculum, include the factors that facilitate flow. After all, one major purpose of sport is to provide an opportunity for athletes to experience harmonious, uplifting, and transformative experiences. Another way to emphasize flow is to explain the concept of flow to your athletes.

Help athletes develop and maintain a positive mental attitude. As Charles Swindoll wrote, "The longer I live, the more I realize the impact of attitude on life. I am convinced that life is 10% what happens to me and 90% how I react to it." Teams with a positive mental attitude are more cohesive and train in a more productive and optimistic training environment that facilitates high motivation and flowlike experiences.

Some athletes are naturally upbeat and positive while others often tend to be sulky or in a funk. Perhaps the difference is because of trait personality differences. Help athletes who bring a negative vibe to your team see the positive correlation between a positive mental attitude and a positive motor learning and performance experience. Help them become more positive by having them set a personal goal to do so, learn how to monitor and redirect their thoughts, and change their self-talk to more positive statements. You can pair an athlete with another athlete who has a positive mental attitude or find an athlete or former athlete who can serve as a mentor. Set the importance of a positive mental attitude as a core value of your program. Set team rules that encourage a positive mental attitude and penalize a negative mental attitude.

Encourage positive emotions and mental attitude before and during competition. Before leaving the United States for the 2008 FINA Diving World Cup in Beijing, China, I told my athlete I would not attend the competition unless she promised to maintain a positive mental attitude during the camp and at the World Cup. Although she usually maintained a positive attitude, this competition would be her first World Cup and athletes can sometimes react strangely to high-level competition. So, I made this request because it is impossible to have a flowlike competitive experience if athletes don't have a positive mental attitude before and during competition. She had an amazing performance and missed the bronze medal by less than 2 points. Maintaining a positive attitude in that competition helped her get to fourth in the world.

Some athletes train hard and prepare themselves physically, but not mentally for competition. They may have a positive attitude toward training but a negative attitude toward competition. These athletes arrive at a competition with a negative attitude and immediately experience debilitating thoughts and negative emotions such as foreboding, anxiety, and dread. Help these athletes cognitively restructure their thinking so that they can view competition with a new perspective. Teach them that competition is an opportunity to succeed, not an opportunity to fail; it is an opportunity to be aggressive and attacking, not a situation in which to be fearful and timid; and so on. A positive mental attitude is no guarantee that athletes will experience flow, but a negative mental attitude surely guarantees poor performance.

Model a positive mental attitude. Perhaps the most effective means of encouraging your athletes to maintain a positive mental attitude is to maintain one yourself. Coaches who model a positive mental attitude typically have teams with a positive outlook. Similarly, coaches who model a negative mental attitude usually have teams with a negative outlook. What is *your* mental attitude? What we hope to see in our athletes, may we see in the coach. If you want your athletes to have a positive mental attitude, then have one yourself.

Teach athletes to deal with factors that inhibit flow. A few years ago I had the opportunity to witness a fascinating presentation Olympic diver Scott Donie gave at a training camp for promising junior athletes. He talked about how he took all the things he most hated about the sport of diving and made them the things he most liked. He specifically talked about windy weather (environment) and a bad takeoff and competitive stress (situation) and how he learned to embrace them. No wonder Scott was an Olympic silver medalist and a member of two U.S. Olympic teams.

Rarely does everything go smoothly in a competition. There are always some bumps along the competitive road but successful athletes know how to traverse this road to maintain flow. Teach your athletes how to deal with inhibitory flow factors. For example, teach them how to do such things as refocus after a making an error, eliminate negative thoughts and debilitating doubts, recapture a positive attitude and positive self-talk, deal with nonopti-mal environmental and situational conditions, and discard negative emotions. Help your athletes understand that a poor warm-up doesn't mean they will perform poorly in competition.

Match skill level with challenge difficulty. When you give athletes a chal-lenging but reasonably attainable task, you can promote a flow experience for them. Consequently, carefully consider an athlete's current individual skill level before assigning practice tasks.

Competence Motivation Theory

Even though Maslow's theory adds significantly to the body of knowledge related to motivation, it omits a very human motive: the need to feel competent (Rowan, 1998). R.W. White (1959) argues that **competence motivation**— the innate need to achieve competence and feel competent—is one of people's most important intrinsic needs. When my son David was young and I would try to help him tie his shoes, he would repeatedly push my hands away and say, "I can do it myself!" In more than 37 years of coaching, I have witnessed that human beings have a powerful innate desire to do things for themselves, to prove to themselves that they are capable and competent. Such an outlook explains why without prompting, young athletes practice a skill repeatedly until they get it right: They want to achieve competency.

Based on the concept of competence motivation, Harter (1978) has devel-oped **competence motivation theory**. According to the theory, an innate need to be competent motivates athletes to attempt mastery to satisfy the need. Successful attempts at mastery promote self-efficacy and feelings of personal competence that lead to increased competence motivation and fur-ther mastery attempts. Failed mastery attempts result in negative emotions, low competence motivation, fewer mastery attempts, and possibly youth sport dropout. Because competence motivation involves growth and develop-ment of the individual, it can be considered one aspect of self-actualization (Lefrançois, 2000).

Applying Competence Motivation Theory to Increase Athlete Motivation

Promote successful mastery attempts. When you promote successful mastery attempts, you indirectly increase an athlete's competence motivation. Accord-ing to Harter's theory, successful mastery attempts lead to increased self-efficacy, positive emotions, and feelings of competence, which lead to increased competence motivation and further mastery attempts.

Avoid serving as the external driving force for athlete motivation. Sometimes athletes need a motivational push in the right direction. Done in the right situ-ation and in the right way, a push can be effective, but it is rarely as effective as letting the push come from the athlete. Athletes are intrinsically motivated to do things themselves and achieve competence not only in sport but, according to Harter (1978), in all domains of human achievement. For many athletes, then, the button to push to motivate them is the *competence button*. In this case, at least for the coach, no button exists. You simply lay a foundation for learning and then step back and give athletes the freedom and support to push their own *competence button* and pursue competency. Sometimes coaches can get in the way of athlete learning and motivation. Don't *over* coach; get out of the way of the unstoppable athlete.

Trust the concept of competence motivation in your coaching. It may not seem true sometimes, but athletes do want to feel competent and demonstrate competence. Trust this concept, be patient, and wait for your athletes to get in touch with their inner desire for competence. Some athletes, especially those with overbearing parents or pushy former coaches, may have been externally pushed from the beginning of their careers and they sometimes lose touch with their desire to be competent. They momentarily forget what they felt and demonstrated naturally at a very young age, namely, the attitude of *I can do it myself.* Give them time, support, and patience in letting them rediscover their own *competence button*.

How do you back away but still encourage your athletes to take responsibility for their motivation? One way to help athletes push their *competence button* is to take a Rogerian approach to coaching, which is discussed in the next section.

Rogerian Theory

Carl Rogers was a psychotherapist whose findings, thoughts, and writings influenced psychotherapy, counseling, and teaching. His book *Freedom to Learn* (Rogers & Freiberg, 1994) influenced generations of teachers (including me) and led to new concepts such as the open classroom and the nondirective model of teaching. Much of his writings are based on his experiences with clients and his keen interest in answering questions concerning individual perceptions, perceived relationships with others, and what conditions are most facilitative for personal change and growth. While the concept of the open classroom has faded from popularity, Rogers' theory still provides teachers with a unique and effective way of interacting and communicating with students—and facilitating student motivation. His theory also has relevance for coaches and athletes—and athlete motivation.

Rogers believed that people are intrinsically motivated to seek growth, develop their natural abilities, self-determine, and become autonomous. Inherent in Rogers' belief is the idea that people are capable of controlling their own destiny but sometimes they need a little help getting there. This help, suggests Rogers, comes in the form of nondirective facilitation. Another way to describe nondirective facilitation is *helping athletes help themselves.* The following section outlines some suggestions Rogers offers for helping people help themselves.

Applying Rogerian Theory to Increase Athlete Motivation

Rogers never provided explicit details concerning how teachers might help students strive toward self-actualization. He did, however, provide some key concepts that help guide the teaching and learning process. These concepts lead to some interesting and effective coaching applications for increasing athlete motivation.

Act as facilitator rather than director of the coaching and learning process. Using a Rogerian approach to coaching means stepping back and being nondirective, allowing athletes to take the lead. One nondirective coaching tool is the **inquiry approach**, which involves asking athletes questions that challenge them to consider new ideas, possibilities, and approaches. For example, when an athlete approaches you and asks what corrections need to be made, you might respond by saying, "What corrections do you think need to be made and why?"

A nondirective approach isn't appropriate for every situation. For example, young beginning athletes most likely would be startled or unnerved to receive a nondirective response to their novice question and would certainly be incapable of providing a substantive answer. However, in many situations the nondirective approach is an effective coaching tool for encouraging thought, responsibility, and autonomy. The nondirective approach changes the coach's role from director to facilitator of learning and engages athletes in the coaching and learning process and encourages them to be self-motivated. Coaches should become increasingly facilitative as athletes become increasingly proficient and seasoned performers.

Use a constructivistic approach to coaching. This is another way to use a less direct instructional method (i.e., be nondirective). **Constructivism** is a philosophical and psychological position that suggests that much of what an individual learns and understands is constructed by the individual. Therefore, *constructivistic approaches* are instructional methods that are athlete-centered much like **discovery learning**, which is the acquisition of new information as a result of the learner's efforts. Associated with a constructivistic approach is the concept of **instructional scaffolding**, in which the coach provides athletes with selective assistance (e.g., by asking questions, directing attention, giving hints about possible strategies) to help them accomplish things they could not otherwise completely accomplish on their own.

Act as an active participant fundamental to the coaching and learning process. This means that you invite athletes into the decision-making process as much as possible so that together you and your athletes participate in the learning experience. You can accomplish this when you ask athletes to do things such as establish season and daily practice goals, assist in writing up workouts, provide self-assessment, peer coach, and offer ideas and suggestions. I learn something new at every practice, and many times this learning comes from my athletes.

Develop self-discipline within athletes. Rogers (Rogers & Freiberg, 1994) believed student self-discipline is a clear goal for the humanistic teacher. For your athletes to develop self-discipline, they must be given and must accept personal responsibility. They also need to be held accountable for that which they are responsible. Besides accepting responsibility, your athletes need to understand the meaning of self-discipline and see it as something to be followed every day. **Self-discipline** is doing what you know you should do and doing it all the time, even when no one is looking. Self-discipline is necessary for personal growth and self-actualization. Athletes who lack self-discipline lack the ability to consistently attend practice motivated to train. These athletes will never reach their greatest athletic potential.

Respect and develop autonomy within athletes. Rogers argued that people should be helped to become autonomous. Athletes have the right to make decisions that personally affect their lives, their practices, and their athletic careers. This does not mean that athletes make all the decisions, but it does mean that as a coach you seek, respect, value, and weigh their input. Some coaches have trouble with this type of coach–athlete relationship because they mistakenly think it undermines their authority and control. Just the opposite is true. When you give athletes the freedom to be autonomous, you demonstrate strength of character and confidence in yourself and in your athlete's ability to self-govern.

Create an environment of unconditional acceptance. In an environment of unconditional acceptance, you foster trust, warmth, acceptance, and growth. In this environment, you also value individual athletes for who they are and place athletes at the center of the learning environment. Rogers called this type of learning place a student-centered school. You can create an athlete-centered sport program to some extent in a practice environment. Much of the onus for creating this environment falls on your shoulders. While the athletes assume more responsibility and control for their own learning, you demonstrate unconditional acceptance.

Perceive athletes as self-motivated and encourage them to act in accordance with this perception. Athletes form notion of self in part from feedback from significant others, particularly their coach. When you reflect a belief that your athletes are self-motivated, you encourage them to establish such an attitude and act in accordance with it. You also can achieve the opposite result if you believe that they aren't self-motivated. What belief do you have about your athletes?

Use facilitative and nondirective techniques and language to shape athlete attitudes and behaviors. Following are some techniques:

- *Be reflective.* When athletes talk, genuinely listen, reflect their statements, and encourage them to think about their thoughts. When an athlete says something, listen and paraphrase back what you thought was said and then ask, "What I hear you saying is _____. What do you think you should do?"

- *Be supportive.* Communicate unconditional regard and support. This means that whatever the athlete says, you will give it genuine consideration, respect, and thought.
- *Encourage self-assessment.* Ask questions such as "What do you think you can do to improve that aspect of your performance or training?"
- *Encourage responsibility.* Ask questions such as "What do *you* need to do?"

THE UNSTOPPABLE ATHLETE

The **unstoppable athlete** is someone who loves the sport, is reinforced for effort and not place of finish, and is intrinsically motivated but occasionally receives external rewards. It is someone with a positive notion of self, formed by positive feedback from significant others. It is someone who is cognitively alert and engaged, uses positive self-talk, has a strong sense of competence and confidence, and more than likely works with a coach with high self-efficacy. It is someone with a positive mental attitude who more than likely learned it from observing a coach or significant others. The unstoppable athlete is self-determined, autonomous, and unafraid to dream and strive to make those dreams become reality.

Isn't sport wonderful? Think about it for a moment or, if you prefer, think about it for a career. Sport is a place for children, adolescents, and adults to experience success, joy, and flow; confront challenges, take risks, and achieve mastery; acquire confidence, competency, and autonomy; fulfill basic, meta, and intrinsic needs; develop hopefulness, optimism, and a positive mental attitude; and increase self-esteem, self-determination, and self-motivation. And you have the privilege of playing a critical role in determining the quality of all these experiences.

THE UNSTOPPABLE COACH

The unstoppable athlete needs the **unstoppable coach**. If you want to play a critical role in shaping experiences that create the highly motivated athlete, you need to be equally motivated yourself. You have to set the motivational intensity for your team and program. Think of the coach or teacher you disliked. More likely than not it will be easy for you to become that person by being lazy, negative, cognitively disengaged, and extrinsically motivated. Now think of the coach or teacher you liked, the one who made a lasting impression on you, the one who instilled a love of the game in you, the one who inspired you so much that you decided to coach. It didn't happen by accident. That person was energetic, cognitively engaged, positive, risk-taking, determined, and intrinsically motivated about the game and the players. Be the unstoppable coach.

YOUR COACHING TOOLBOX

Here is your first theory for your coaching toolbox and perhaps the most important tool in the box: When you use different motivational theories in your coaching, you become The Great Motivator, The Wizard of Coaching. You push all the right buttons to create unstoppable monsters ready to destroy any obstacle in their path. Some coaches use dubious motivational techniques they learned from their former coach, witnessed another coach use, worked once for them when they were athletes, or invented themselves. While some of these techniques may indeed increase athlete motivation, very often these homemade motivational remedies are patently ineffective and inappropriate. Let your approach to motivating your athletes be guided by sound motivation theory grounded in behaviorism, cognitivism, social cognitive learning, and humanism.

THE SCIENTIFIC AND ARTFUL COACH

From a behavioral perspective, the scientific coach understands the appropriate use of reinforcement and external feedback and encourage intrinsic motivation. The artful coach will sense what type of rewards each athlete finds reinforcing, when to offer rewards and when to withhold them, and how to create an environment that conditions athletes to love their sport and everything connected to it.

From a cognitive perspective, the scientific coach connects external rewards to behaviors such as effort and competence, presents contradictory evidence that forces athletes to adopt more positive attitudes and self-beliefs, models self-efficacious behaviors, creates an environment in which athletes experience success and mastery, and teaches athletes positive self-talk. The artful coach sells athletes new perceptions of attitudes and self-belief, persuades them they are capable of high achievement, and determines appropriate task difficulty so that practice is challenging but attainable (particularly for young athletes).

From a social cognitive perspective, the scientific coach reinforces athletes for imitating appropriate behaviors and significant others for modeling appropriate behavior. The scientific coach also reinforces motivated behavior and develops practice plans that culminate with successful athlete mastery attempts. The artful coach is sensitive to personal behavior, making sure he or she is modeling appropriate behaviors that athletes observe.

From a humanistic perspective, the scientific coach understands the significance of third force psychology, looks beyond the Xs and Os, and increases motivation by appealing to athletes' intrinsic motivation to achieve competency and actualize potential. The scientific coach also looks for ways to satisfy athletes' basic and metaneeds. The artful coach senses when to be directive and when to be nondirective, uses constructivistic approaches to coaching, respects the autonomy of the individual, offers unconditional acceptance, and takes a facilitative approach to helping athletes.

IF YOU REMEMBER ONLY THREE THINGS

1. *Remember to avail yourself of the different theoretical approaches for increasing athlete motivation.* Many motivation theories exist and all of them are useful tools in your coaching toolbox. One theoretical tool may be effective for some athletes and situations while other tools are more effective for other athletes and situations. Each motivational tool has something unique to contribute to increasing athlete motivation. Don't get stuck on one approach to increasing athlete motivation. For example, consider a humanistic approach to increasing motivation. When researchers (Agne, Greenwood, & Miller, 1994) examined differences between teachers who had been selected Teacher of the Year and in-service teachers, the former were rated significantly more humanistic than the latter. If you want your athletes to hold you in high esteem, perceive you as Coach of the Year material in their eyes, and consider you a great motivator, use humanism theory as one of your approaches to increasing athlete motivation.

2. *Remember the influential role you play in influencing athlete motivation.* You are one of the lead characters in a play called *Motivating Athletes.* When you consider all the motivation theories discussed in this chapter, you play a starring role, along with your athletes, in pretty much every scene. Briefly consider, if you will, some of your many roles in *Motivating Athletes:*

   • *Disseminator* of reinforcement in the form of praise, rewards, and feedback

   • *Creator* of a learning environment that conditions athletes to love the sport

   • *Role model* for hopefulness, optimism, positive mental attitude, motivated behavior, responsibility taking, and effort

   • *Determiner* of difficult but attainable goals

   • *Conveyor* of a belief that athletes are competent and capable

   • *Proponent* of effort, mastery, task (rather than ego) involvement, challenges, risk taking, and positive self-talk

   • *Fulfiller* of many of the basic needs and metaneeds

   • *Facilitator* of nondirective and constructivistic models of coaching

   You do all this and more to increase athlete motivation and create a masterpiece, a tour de force, a Broadway hit—the unstoppable athlete. Bravo, coach! Take a bow.

3. *Remember that motivation may be the single most important factor in coach effectiveness and athlete achievement.* Coaches who understand motivation theories know how to push the right buttons to motivate their athletes. And highly motivated athletes are forces of nature that won't be denied and can't be stopped. Motivation is the unknown quantity, the X factor, the difference maker, the determinate of achievement. It is the difference between mediocrity and excellence. It is the indomitable force that fears no defeat, overcomes fatigue, answers self-doubt, responds to adversity, conquers fear, rebuffs discouragement, and even heals injury. The highly motivated athlete is the unstoppable force moving the immovable object.

SUGGESTED READING

Jackson, S.A., & Csikszentmihalyi, M. (1999). *Flow in sports: The keys to optimal experiences and performances.* Champaign, IL: Human Kinetics.

[The authors nicely apply Csikszentmihalyi's beautiful concept of flow to sports. I still remember practices and competitions in which I was experiencing (as many athletes have experienced) something I couldn't at the time put a name to—*flow.*]

Joyce, B., Weil, M., & Calhoun, E. (2009). *Models of teaching.* Boston: Allyn & Bacon.

[Several of the teaching models in this book I found fascinating and readily adaptable and useful for coaching and increasing athlete motivation.]

Rogers, C.R. & Freiberg, H.J. (1994). *Freedom to learn.* New York: Macmillan.

[The ideas in this book turned me on to teaching and inspired me to become a teacher. It offers a Rogerian perspective on teaching and learning.]

Weinberg, R.S. & Gould, D. (2011). *Foundations of sport and exercise psychology* (5th ed.). Champaign, IL: Human Kinetics.

[I asked our sport psychologist at the Olympic Games to recommend a book and this is the one he cited. Nice choice and well worth the read. It covers so much material.]

CHAPTER 2

The Resilient Athlete
Applying Attribution Theory

Key Terms

amotivation
attribution-dependent
attribution-free
attribution theory
attributions
competitive climate
covariation principle
ego-enhancing strategy
ego-involved learners
ego-protecting strategy
entity view
failure-accepting athletes
failure-avoiding athletes

functional attribution
   strategy
helplessness
hopefulness
hopelessness
incremental view
learning goal
locus of causality
locus of control
logical attribution
maladaptive attributional
   pattern
mastery climate

mastery-oriented
   athletes
performance climate
performance goal
personal responsibility
resilience
resilient athlete
resilient coach
self-determination
   theory
stable
unstable

> **"** *Would you like me to give you a formula for success? It's quite simple, really. Double your rate of failure. You are thinking of failure as the enemy of success. But it isn't at all. You can be discouraged by failure or you can learn from it. So go ahead and make mistakes. Make all you can. Because remember that's where you will find success.* **"**
>
> *Thomas J. Watson*

The *120th damn place, the 120th damn place.* That's all he could think about as he stood alone in the locker room, his jaw clamped shut and a lump in his throat the size of his fist that was clenched as if he was trying to compress a piece of coal into a diamond. There were many reasons to rationalize his poor performance: He was a relative beginner in the sport, he was not really prepared for the competition, and so on. Anyone in his position would have finished just as poorly. But 120th place? That's all he could think about. It was the only qualifying meet for advancing to the U.S. national championship, and out of 120 competitors he finished dead last. He had a truckload of emotions: anger—no, make that rage—or perhaps fury is more accurate, embarrassment, shame, bludgeoned ego, and damaged pride. He wished that truckload of emotions could be taken away like trash being hauled to the garbage dump. But fortunately for him the emotions weren't going away anytime soon.

Fortunately? It's funny how differently athletes respond to failure. Some allow it to psychologically crush them and they become hopeless while others use it as fuel for their motivational fire and they remain hopeful and resilient. In his case, 120th place ignited a raging motivational fire that could only be extinguished by sweet redemption, by returning to the same meet next year and performing better. Nothing else would do. And he knew the only way to taste a piece of his redemption pie was to give more effort—way more effort—and improve his athletic ability. He couldn't guarantee qualifying for the national championship, but he didn't really care about qualifying. He just wanted to prove to himself—and to others—that he was capable and to dump those agonizing, burning emotions, to trade them in for a new set of emotional clothes: pride, competency, and satisfaction. He went to his parents and told them he was dedicating himself 100% to his sport and asked for 100% of their support. They agreed. Then he met with his coach and told him the same thing. He also petitioned his coach to come in on their only day off of the week and train him for a brief practice. His coach agreed to his requests.

One year later he returned to the scene of the crime—the qualifying meet. He didn't dominate and win. He did, however, finish in the top four and qualify for the national championship; he went from 120th place to 4th place. That truckload of emotions had finally been emptied and new emotions stowed onboard. That lump of coal of an athlete had nearly transformed himself into a shimmering diamond. It was one of the most satisfying and memorable experiences of his life. And he had done it by accepting personal responsibility, giving more effort, and improving his ability.

In November 2011 the *New York Times* published an article about a promising young baseball player who fell into a depressive state after a personal setback in his life (Atkins, 2011). He lost hope and relinquished his baseball dream. He looked back several years later and wondered what he could have accomplished had circumstances been different.

When confronted with adversity and failure, why do some athletes maintain hope and bounce back and why do others become devastated by it? As Thomas J. Watson, former president of IBM, suggests in the quote at the beginning of this chapter, failure is part of the becoming process. This concept especially applies to improving as an athlete or coach and achieving athletic success. There isn't a scientist, inventor, business person, artist, athlete, or coach who hasn't experienced the bitter taste of failure before enjoying the sweet taste of success. Failure is something to be embraced. It is an experience from which to learn, grow, and succeed. Still, many athletes perceive failure as something to be avoided and find the experience of failure to be something they can't adjust to, recover from, or overcome.

Resilience is the ability to recover or adjust quickly to misfortune or change. This chapter is the story of the **resilient athlete** and how you can help athletes establish an attributional mindset so that they maintain hopefulness, recover or adjust quickly to misfortune, and discover athletic success.

CHAPTER OVERVIEW

The chapter begins with an outline of the attribution theory and the three dimensions for making attributions: locus of control (causality), personal responsibility (controllability), and stability. Then it examines the belief about ability (whether or not it is changeable), emotional responses to perceived locus of control, and mastery orientation. The chapter concludes with several applications of attribution theory for increasing athlete resiliency.

ATTRIBUTION THEORY

An athlete serves well and her team wins the volleyball game. Oddly, she doesn't appear overly excited or seem to feel much sense of satisfaction. She says afterward that her performance was more luck than anything else. How do you explain this unmotivated type of behavior? According to self-efficacy theory, success and failure provide feedback about athlete competency, so why doesn't she experience feelings of competency and satisfaction? Well, athletes aren't always so predictable. They don't react to their successes and failures the way we might predict. When athletes perform well, some believe they did well because they have athletic ability and worked hard, while others believe success resulted from luck or the contributions of other teammates or some other external cause. What mediates these beliefs are the causal explanations (**attributions**) athletes make for the events that take place in their lives.

Attribution theory is a cognitive motivation theory concerned with the predictable consistencies in what people interpret to be the causes to the outcomes of their behaviors. According to attribution theory, the intent of every person is to explain his or her behaviors in terms of perceived causes. In other words, people ask *Why?* in their attempts to understand their successes and failures: "Why did I play golf so well today?" "Why did I serve so well in volleyball?" "Why did I lose that race?" "Why did I miss that routine?" "Why did I blow that assignment?" Based on work by Heider (1944, 1958), Weiner (1972) suggested two main causal dimensions for attributions:

locus of control and stability. Later, Weiner (1985) suggested that three factors help to explain the achievement-driven behavior and non-achievement behavior of individuals. These three factors, shown in figure 2.1, are locus of control (which he referred to as locus of causality), controllability (personal responsibility), and stability.

Locus of Control (Causality)

The attributions we make depend to a large degree on one aspect of our personality: locus (place) of control (Weiner, 1994). **Locus of control** (also known as **locus of causality**) is a person's consistent tendency to attribute behavioral outcomes to specific causes over which the person either does or does not have control. According to Weiner, some people are internally oriented and some are externally oriented. Those who are *internally oriented* attribute their successes and failures to ability, effort, or a combination of both. These attributes are within the person's control. Athletes who perform well in a competition and have an internal locus of control attribute success to physical talent (ability) or hard work (effort). In contrast, athletes who are *externally oriented* are more likely to attribute success and failure to factors outside their control, such as luck and task difficulty. Athletes who perform well in a competition and have an external locus of control attribute success to luck (as in the example of the volleyball player), and when they perform poorly they attribute failure to task difficulty.

Personal Responsibility (Controllability)

An internal or external orientation also determines an athlete's sense of **personal responsibility** and feeling of controllability. Athletes with an external locus of control perceive the causes of their successes and failures as being

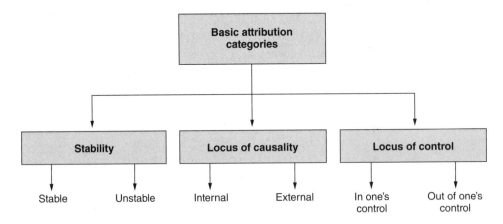

Figure 2.1 Weiner's (1985) three-dimensional model of casual attribution.

Adapted, by permission, from R.S. Weinberg and D. Gould, 2011, *Foundations of sport and exercise psychology,* 5th ed. (Champaign, IL: Human Kinetics), 64.

outside their control. Consequently, they assume no personal responsibility for the outcomes of their behaviors. In contrast, athletes with an internal locus of control perceive the cause of their successes and failures as being within their control and, consequently, they accept personal responsibility for the outcomes of their behaviors. For example, athletes with an external locus of control see the *external* negative influence of friends who don't support their athletic goals as something uncontrollable. However, athletes with an internal locus of control see this as something controllable, accept responsibility, and then do something about it such as re-educate their friends, disassociate from their friends, make new friends, or ignore their friends.

Personal responsibility also extends to *internal* influences, such as effort. Athletes with an external locus of control perceive effort as something outside their control and therefore not their responsibility. In contrast, athletes with an internal locus of control perceive effort as something they control and therefore take personal responsibility. So, for instance, after a poor performance, athletes with an external locus of control attribute poor performance to an off day, bad luck, or other factors outside their control and therefore accept little responsibility for the outcome of their behavior. In contrast, athletes with an internal locus of control attribute poor performance to lack of effort and then work harder in practice to better prepare for the next competition.

Another internal influence is ability. This topic is interesting because athletes and coaches can view ability as either fixed or adaptable. Athletes with an external locus of control perceive ability as fixed and uncontrollable and therefore reject responsibility for changing it. On the other hand, internally oriented athletes see ability—much like the athlete who placed 120th in the chapter-opening story—as something adaptable and controllable and they accept responsibility for maximizing their talent. As the next section explains, athletes' views of causes such as ability depend on whether or not they view them as stable and unchanging or unstable and modifiable.

Stability and Instability of Causes

The causes that athletes attribute for the outcome of their performances can be seen as highly stable and unchanging or unstable and changeable. **Stable** causes include ability and task difficulty and **unstable** causes are effort and luck. For example, if athletes attribute failure to ability, they attribute their poor performance to an internal and stable cause and therefore won't expect to perform any better in the future. On the other hand, if they attribute failure to effort, they *might* attribute their poor performance to an internal and unstable cause and are likely to try harder and attempt to perform better in the future.

The word *might* is important to use here because ability may be perceived as either stable or unstable depending on the athlete's belief about the nature of ability. This belief is an important point to remember for coaches hoping to influence athletes' attributions for success and failure. The next section explores this concept in greater detail.

BELIEFS ABOUT ABILITY

Athletes can operate with two views of ability: entity and incremental. An **entity view** of ability sees ability as stable and uncontrollable, as a characteristic that one is born with and cannot be changed. According to this perspective, some athletes have more ability than others and the amount of ability each person has is set. In contrast, an athlete who adopts an **incremental view** of ability sees ability as unstable and controllable, as a characteristic that can be changed, expanded, and enhanced through effort.

Athletes who have an entity view of physical ability tend to use the strategy of setting easily attainable performance goals. They avoid challenge and risk taking. Instead, they look for situations that make them appear competent and protect their self-esteem. They tend to keep doing what they do best, never giving too much effort or risking failure because if they work hard and fail it means they have low ability, which would in turn diminish their self-esteem. These athletes are the ones who never seem to take chances, push themselves, or set lofty goals. They also tend to be undermotivated in practice.

Athletes who hold an entity view also use the strategies of procrastination and not trying hard. In this situation, they might accept a challenge but then not try hard, reasoning thus: "If I don't try and then fail, no one will think I don't have ability." These athletes might reduce training before a competition so that they have an excuse: "I really didn't train much for this competition, so I'm not very prepared." Such a statement gives them an out if they perform poorly. It also lowers the standard for success: "Well, I only made the first cut, but that is great considering how little training I have done." While such a strategy reduces anxiety and the negative self-implications of failure, it also significantly reduces athlete motivation and, subsequently, the level of training, learning, and motor performance.

In contrast, athletes who hold an incremental view of ability tend to set difficult performance goals. They seek challenge and risk taking. They look for challenging practice situations that test their competency, improve their ability, and make them better athletes. These athletes are not afraid to risk or fail. To them, failure does not mean lowered self-esteem or ability; rather, it means learning something new, increasing effort and ability, and ultimately, attaining success much like Thomas J. Watson indicated in his quote at the outset of this chapter.

PERCEIVED CAUSALITY AND EMOTIONAL RESPONSE

According to Weiner (1992), what motivates behavior is not the attribution to one cause or another; it is the emotion that occurs in response to the attribution. In other words, athletes' emotional responses to the attributions they make motivate future behavior. Two types of emotional responses are related to athletic outcomes: attribution free and attribution dependent. **Attribution-free** emotional responses occur without the athlete first determining the cause of the outcome. In this case, the athlete simply reacts naturally to the outcome of events. The athlete is happy when success occurs and sad or disappointed when failure occurs.

Attribution-dependent emotional responses occur in direct response to causal attributions made regarding the perceived cause of the outcomes. In this situation, an athlete might be sad after a successful competition if she perceives the victory as meaningless because the outcome resulted from an external cause such as luck or lack of competition. Conversely, an athlete might experience hopefulness after a loss if he perceives the loss as meaningful because the outcome resulted from an unstable cause such as poor officiating. Figure 2.2 (Weiner, 1985) identifies the types of affective responses athletes might elicit depending on their perceived attributions within the three dimensions of locus of causality, controllability, and stability.

When athletes with an internal locus of causality succeed, they attribute the outcome to an internal cause such as ability and therefore they feel pride, self-esteem, and satisfaction. On the other hand, when these same athletes fail, they experience reduced feelings of pride, self-esteem, and satisfaction because they attribute the failure to an internal cause. In other words, it was their fault. If, however, these athletes attribute success or failure to an external cause, then they have little if any emotional response because they attribute the outcome to some outside influence.

For the controllability dimension, emotional responses to success or failure to a large extent depend on the athlete's perception of who is in control of the outcome. If the athlete perceives herself in control and failure occurs, the emotional response can include shame, guilt, or depression. If success occurs, the emotional response can be confidence and a feeling of competence. On the other hand, if the athlete perceives others to be in control, failure can result in feelings of anger, surprise, or astonishment. If success occurs, the emotional response can be gratitude or pity for opponents.

For the stability dimension, athletes tend to feel either hopeful or hopeless about future success depending on the perceived attribution. A perception of a stable attribution leads to the emotions of hopefulness for success and hopelessness for failure. For instance, the athlete who attributes success or failure to ability (a stable cause) feels hopefulness after several successes but hopelessness after several losses. ("What's the use? I just don't have the ability and I will always lose.") On the other hand, the perception of an unstable attribution leads to the emotions of uncertainty for success and hopefulness for failure. For example, if the athlete perceives ability to be unstable ("Through effort I can gain greater ability."), the athlete experiences uncertainty with success ("Well, I think I can succeed again next

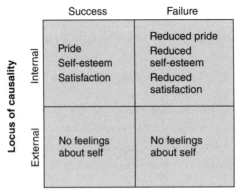

Figure 2.2 Emotional responses associated with various combinations of outcomes and attributions.

Reprinted, by permission, from R.H. Cox, 2002, *Sport psychology: Concepts and applications* (Dubuque, IA: Wm. C. Brown Publishers), 60. ©The McGraw-Hill Companies.

time!") and hopefulness with failure ("Well, with more work and improved ability, I can succeed!").

ATTRIBUTIONS, ACHIEVEMENT MOTIVATION, AND SELF-WORTH

Covington (Covington, 1984; Covington & Omelich, 1984, 1987) suggests that a connection exists between need for achievement, attributions for success and failure, beliefs about ability, self-efficacy, and self-worth. These variables combine to make three types of motivational sets: mastery oriented, failure avoiding, and failure accepting.

Mastery-oriented athletes tend to value achievement and see ability as something on which they can improve (incremental view). Consequently, these athletes tend to focus on learning goals that will help them increase their skills, ability, and motor performance. A **learning goal** is defined as a personal intention to improve abilities and learn regardless of how many mistakes are made or how awkward the individual may look during this learning process. Rather than focus on the outcome of competition, such as place of finish and who they beat, they focus on their own individual performance and look for ways to improve performance, much like the expert who engages in deliberate practice, always setting personal practice goals and finding ways to master every aspect of his domain.

Failure-avoiding athletes in contrast see ability as fixed (entity view) and tend to set performance goals. A **performance goal** is defined as a personal intention to appear competent or perform well in front of others. These athletes are labeled **ego-involved learners** because they focus on how well they are performing and how others judge them. They lack a strong sense of self-competency and self-worth separate from their athletic performances. In other words, their ego is connected to their performances (usually their most current performance), and they tend to feel as athletically competent as their last competition. Consequently, they fail to ever develop a truly stable sense of self-efficacy. To feel confident, these athletes protect their self-image at all cost by avoiding failure, using strategies such as avoiding risk taking, procrastinating, giving little effort, setting easily attainable (or totally unattainable) goals, and claiming not to care.

These strategies reduce training, learning, motor performance, and motivation, which ultimately leads to the failure the athletes hoped to avoid. If failure persists, as it most certainly does if they continue using the same strategies, the athletes eventually decide they are incompetent. Once this occurs, their egos are crushed and their sense of self-worth and self-efficacy deteriorates to the point where they accept failure and give up. In other words, they become failure-accepting athletes.

Failure-accepting athletes attribute their failures to low ability and believe they have no control over changing this fact. These athletes have given up and are likely to become depressed, apathetic, hopeless, and helpless. As a coach, you do not want to develop failure-accepting athletes. Everything that sport is about is contrary to the image of failure-accepting athletes. I have had the privilege of working with such athletes and facilitating their transformation into mastery-orientated athletes. How is this metamorphosis possible? How do you push the *attribution button* to create highly motivated, resilient athletes? The next section offers some suggestions to help you.

APPLYING ATTRIBUTION THEORY TO INCREASE ATHLETE MOTIVATION

Help athletes establish an internal rather than external locus of causality (control). It is important that athletes perceive themselves as in control of their own destiny. To paraphrase Sir Francis Bacon, *The mold of an athlete's fortune is in his or her own hands.* Accepting credit for success and accepting responsibility for failure rather than crediting success or failure to an uncontrollable cause is psychologically empowering for athletes. Athletes who take responsibility for their failures but feel they can control their destiny can learn from their mistakes, make changes, and work harder in the future. When accepting responsibility for failure it is important, especially for young athletes, to attribute the failure to something they can change so that they believe future results will be different rather than inevitable.

Use attributional training to alter athlete attribution orientation. While an internal locus of causality is a mature psychological orientation, research suggests that children tend to operate with an external orientation but become more internally oriented with age (Rotter, 1971). Participation in sports can help children move to an internal orientation (Duke, Johnson, & Nowicki, 1977) as can attributional training, which research suggests can positively influence a child's future expectations and performance (Rudisill, 1988). Attributional training involves the coach creating planned interventions to alter athlete perceptions and performance and teach athletes a functional attribution strategy.

Functional attribution strategy occurs when athletes learn to explain the cause of failure outcomes as controllable and unstable. In contrast, underperforming athletes often operate with a maladaptive attributional pattern. A **maladaptive attributional pattern** occurs when athletes attribute failure to a cause that is internal, stable, uncontrollable, and global (Prapavessis & Carron, 1988). In other words, an athlete with a maladaptive attributional pattern attributes failure to causes that are personal (internal), unchanging (unstable), and uncontrollable. This athlete also tends to apply this orientation to everything in life (global). As Cox (2002) puts it,

> For an example, an athlete with low self-esteem with a history of failure might explain a recent failure thus: "I am just no good at this." This explanation, correctly interpreted, may tell the coach

that this young person believes that he is responsible for the failure, there is no likelihood for change in the future, he has no control over the situation, and he is likely to experience failure in most athletic mastery attempts.

Reprinted, by permission from R.H. Cox, 2002, *Sport psychology: Concepts and applications* (Dubuque, IA: Wm. C. Brown Publishers), 65. ©The McGraw-Hill Company.

Before beginning attributional training, it is helpful to objectively determine the types of attributions your athletes give for their performance outcomes. Athletes can take several diagnostic tests to determine the types of attributions they make, such as the Causal Dimension Scale (CDS) and the Causal Dimension Scale II (CDSII). However, simply asking athletes why they succeeded or failed can reveal some of these attributions. Once you have identified the maladaptive attribution pattern, counsel your athletes so that you can help them structure a more productive and facilitative orientation. Cox provides an excellent example of this interaction (2002, p. 65):

Coach: Sally, it appears that you feel that your failure to return serve in your last match as due to lack of skill.

Sally: Not just skill. I really don't have what it takes to be a good tennis player. I'm just not coordinated and never will be.

Coach: Actually, I've known lots of good tennis players who felt that way when they first started. I'm sure you are no different.

Sally: Do you really think so?

Coach: Yes, I do. You have a whole week before your next match. I'll work with you on your footwork. I'm sure you will do better next time. Practice really helps, but it does take time.

In this case, the athlete is unlikely to immediately change her orientation since the attribution pattern has most likely been in operation for some time. Cox (2002, p. 65) recommends the following steps to help athletes form more suitable attributions:

1. Record and classify attributions that athletes make for successful and unsuccessful outcomes.

2. For each outcome, discuss with the athlete causes or attributions that might lead to a greater expectancy for success and increased effort.

3. Provide an attributional training program for athletes who consistently give attributions that lead to negative implications for future outcomes.

4. For best results, combine planned goal setting with attributional manipulation.

The process of identifying attributions and changing attributions may seem difficult, but it is not. Individuals create perceptions of themselves based in part on feedback from others; in this case the feedback from a respected and trusted coach can greatly influence athlete attributions. For example, consider the following situation where a coach and athlete meet and the coach first attempts to identify the athlete's attributions (based on past experiences with the athlete, the coach probably already has an idea of these attributions) and then proceeds to help the athlete alter perception of attributions.

Coach: Taylor, I can see that you are disappointed and maybe even a little discouraged about your performance yesterday.

Taylor: Yeah. I feel pretty bad about it. It's the same old thing again. I just don't have what it takes. I don't have the physical ability or the mental ability to perform well in competition.

Coach: Taylor, you may feel like you don't have the talent to perform well or the ability to put it all together in competition, but I completely disagree with you. I think you have what it takes. What other causes do you think might be holding you back?

Taylor: I don't know. I am trying to pattern my approach to the sport just like Marc but maybe Marc is just more talented than me.

Coach: Listen, Taylor, Marc doesn't have any more talent than you do. In fact, he probably has less! But what Marc does have is determination and faith that the harder he works the better he is going to get.

Taylor: I have seen Marc work pretty hard.

Coach: Taylor, working hard is something you have complete control over, if you want to. The harder you work, the more you are going to maximize your physical ability.

Taylor: I guess I didn't perform well in the last competition because I didn't train hard enough, not because I don't have the talent. I am going to set a goal to do more in practice each day.

Coach: That is great, but don't forget the other things. Marc competes well because he buys into everything we do. You can't become a champion by doing just some of the things. You have to do them all. So besides working harder in practice, you need to work harder in the weight room, set more challenging learning goals, meet with our sport psychologist, keep a journal, practice relaxation and visualization, and use better self-talk.

Taylor: You bet, Coach. Those are all things I control!

Coach: Exactly! Your destiny is in your own hands, but only if you choose to accept responsibility, work harder, and do everything necessary to reach your goals.

The preceding meeting between coach and athlete actually occurred with one of my athletes. The preceding season, Taylor did not make top 16 at the conference championship. The next season, however, he bought into everything, changed his attributional orientation, and finished as conference champion. It was an especially gratifying victory, not only because of how far he had come as an athlete, but because he entered finals as the number one seed, handled the pressure, and nailed his last dive to win by 2 points. It is exciting to see what our athletes can accomplish when they take personal responsibility, assume control, work hard, and have faith in their ability.

Remember that comparison to others is part of forming attributions. The **covariation principle** occurs when athletes compare their performances to the performances of others. When the performance of others agrees (covaries) with the athlete's performance, attributions are external. When the performance of others disagrees with the athlete's performance, attributions are internal. For example, if an athlete beats a highly ranked golfer whom no one has beaten, the athlete is likely to attribute success to the internal causes of ability and effort ("Gee, almost no one ever beats her; I must be pretty good and my hard work is paying off!"). However, if the athlete beats an unranked golfer whom everyone has beaten (i.e., covaries), the athlete is likely to attribute success to the external cause of task difficulty. ("It wasn't that difficult; everyone beats her.")

The covariation principle also can apply to the past performances of others. Athletes can compare themselves to former athletes by viewing video replay or looking at past results. The best thing I ever did for our program was invest in a record board. Once school records were posted, the records began to tumble. Athletes would look up at the record board and think, "You know, I am really close to breaking that record. I must be pretty good. I bet I have the ability to set a new record!"

Help athletes form logical attributions. For example, when athletes decide that they have ability because they beat someone that most athletes lose to, they are using logic and forming a **logical attribution** for success. But athletes aren't always so logical. Sometimes they miss the point; they overlook the obvious. Athletes form illogical attributions in two worst-case scenarios. In the first, athlete A performs really well (e.g., personal best) but still loses to athlete B. Now, maybe athlete B normally loses to everyone, but not this time because athlete B had a great performance. It happens. Everyone has her day. But athlete A misses the point. Rather than look at the personal best performance, athlete A illogically concludes "Well, everyone beats B and I didn't, so I must not have ability." In this situation, the coach needs to point out the obvious to athlete A: "You had a great day, a personal best, and it is because of your increased ability and high effort. Keep up the hard work. You are getting better and on the right track!"

In worst-case scenario two, athlete A performs really poorly but still beats athlete B. Now, normally no one beats athlete B, but that day B stood for *Bad*. Everyone has an off day. But athlete A misses the obvious: Athlete B just wasn't the same athlete that day (maybe B decided to be athlete C—as in *can't win today*), and illogically concludes, "Well, no one beats B, but I did, so I must be working hard enough in practice." In this situation, the coach may need to make the point with athlete A: "Listen, you really haven't been training that hard. You just got lucky today. Don't get me wrong, you have the ability to succeed, but you need to take more responsibility for your training and get your butt in gear and give more effort. It is all within your control!"

Consider playing a tough competition schedule. Logical attribution also has significance when it comes to strength of competitive schedule. Some coaches choose to set a soft competitive schedule in the early season because they think a number of victories will boost athlete confidence heading into conference play. However, athletes know when they are playing soft teams and are likely to attribute their successes to the external cause of lack of task difficulty rather than the internal cause of ability. In this scenario, the team mentality is "Everybody beats this team, not just us (covariation). We won because it was easy, not because we are good (logical attribution)."

Based on the concepts of covariation and logical attribution, athletes are better served when they play teams as good as or better than themselves. In this case a win or a loss is beneficial. If they win, they attribute success to effort and ability. If they lose, it is possible to see their loss as a moral victory and attribute it to effort and ability. For example, after a close loss to the top ranked golf team the coach might say, "Look, ladies, we just played the number one ranked team in our district and we narrowly lost to them. We played them almost even and at some points we even outplayed them. With hard work and maximizing our abilities, I can't wait to play them again in the championship tournament." Either way it is a win–win situation for the team if the coach helps the athletes form logical attributions.

Help athletes avoid making attributions influenced by egocentrism. Athletes do not always use logic in making causal attributions because sometimes their egos influence their thinking. When athletes attribute all successes to internal causes it is called **ego-enhancing strategy**. When athletes attribute all failures to external causes, it is called **ego-protecting strategy**. Both of these strategies are considered illogical models of attribution while the strategy of covariation is considered a logical model.

Perhaps no athlete, especially a highly motivated and successful athlete, ever uses a completely logical approach to the attributional process. For example, the up-and-coming athlete hungry to conquer the world, beat the defending champion, and become the next champion looks for any sign to confirm ability and effort and establish an internal locus of causality. Unfortunately, some athletes are never willing to attribute failure to an internal locus of causality and therefore are never willing to accept personal responsibility because they are too busy protecting their fragile egos.

A fine line exists between protecting ego and accepting responsibility for failure, particularly for elite athletes. Athletes need to accept responsibility, but do so in a way that maintains their self-confidence. When failure occurs, it is important that you help your athletes perceive the causes of failure as due to controllable and unstable attributes that can change over time. Let your athletes know that they failed because they did not work hard enough but also that they can and will work harder. Let them know they failed because they lacked the necessary physical skills but also that they can refine and improve those skills over time.

Help your athletes develop a sense of hopefulness. Giving athletes impossible tasks to master and continually setting them up for failure can lead to an orientation of stable and external causes and what Weiner (1985) calls hopelessness and what Seligman (1995) calls learned helplessness. Both terms refer to the emotional response to failure that people connect to a stable cause. **Hopelessness** is the expectation that failure will continue because it is associated with a stable cause. Learned **helplessness** is the perception that no matter what a person does it will not make a difference, so there is no use in trying. Seligman defines this concept in terms of the phrase *giving up without even trying.*

Your coaching philosophy should include the goal of empowering athletes so that they perceive themselves as competent, confident, responsible, and capable; they believe they have the ability and can give the effort to control their destiny; and they never give up trying. When confronted with success or failure these athletes are more likely to respond with hopefulness. Recall from the beginning of the chapter that **hopefulness** is the expectation that success will continue and failure will soon cease. This chapter essentially has been all about creating the hopeful athlete. You can foster hopefulness in several ways. Encourage your athletes to be optimists and have a positive mental attitude. Encourage them to attribute failure to unstable ("Failure is only temporary.") and internal ("If I try harder I can succeed.") causes (Grove & Pargman, 1986). Give your athletes tasks that are difficult but attainable—challenging activities, goals, drills, practice sets, and so on that they can master through sustained effort and increased ability. Encourage your athletes to take personal responsibility; let them participate in goal setting, decision making, and self-evaluation.

Use emotional responses to gauge your athletes' attributional orientations. As indicated earlier in this section, certain emotions are associated with various outcomes and attributions. For example, an internal locus of causality and the outcome of success are associated with the emotions of pride, self-esteem, and satisfaction while an external locus of causality results in no feelings about the self for success or failure. A coach might deduce that an athlete who expresses little if any emotion after failure is making a logical attribution that failure was external; it resulted from some outside factor that had nothing to do with the athlete. This might be the case; perhaps the weather was a deciding factor. However, if the athlete's actions actually caused the outcome, you need to let the athlete know that greater personal responsibility, effort, and dedication are necessary.

If you notice that many of your athletes are experiencing negative emotions such as hopelessness, shame, guilt, depression, or anger, it is a signal that you are establishing excessively high performance standards for which they are unprepared to achieve. In this case, you immediately need to reevaluate your program and coaching effectiveness and make changes.

Help young athletes make appropriate attributions for success and failure. Young athletes are in the process of forming attributional orientations. Consequently, when they succeed, they should be encouraged to perceive their success as stable and internal. An internal attribution encourages them to feel pride in their accomplishment and believe that success is likely to occur again (stable) because they were responsible for the success. On the other hand, when young athletes experience repeated failure, they should be encouraged to select unstable and internal attributions. An unstable attribution helps them believe that success is an option in the future. ("Well, I am just learning this sport and still don't have the skill level, but I soon will!") An internal attribution encourages them to take responsibility for the loss ("I didn't perform correctly; I need to practice more and improve my ability.") rather than attribute the failure to some external cause such as bad luck. Helping young athletes make appropriate attributions for success and failure promotes feelings of self-efficacy and self-confidence (Cox, 2002).

Rehabilitate failure-avoiding and failure-accepting athletes. Most coaches believe in the power of sport to build up human beings, so it is important to them to recognize and rehabilitate failure-avoiding athletes and failure-accepting athletes. These types of athletes benefit from attributional training. Help them set new, realistic, and attainable goals. Create opportunities for them to experience success and encourage them to attribute their success to effort and ability. Help them disassociate their ego, self-esteem, and self-worth from their athletic performances. Who they are as human beings has nothing to do with how well or poorly they perform. Also, help failure-accepting athletes recognize the signs of depression and helplessness and teach them strategies for dealing with these symptoms.

Develop mastery-oriented athletes. Finally, develop a mastery climate in practice to encourage athletes to take a mastery orientation toward their sport. In a **mastery climate**, you reinforce your athletes for working hard, demonstrating improvement, helping others through cooperation, and believing that each player's contribution is worthwhile. This climate is much different than a **competitive climate** (also referred to as **performance climate**) in which athletes perceive that poor performance and mistakes will be punished, high-ability athletes will receive preferential attention and recognition, and the coach encourages competition between players.

To develop a mastery climate, you can manipulate practice conditions following the guidelines in the acronym TARGET (Epstein, 1989). These suggestions are particularly helpful for coaches who work with youth sport participants.

T: *Task*—Use tasks that involve variety and diversity to increase motivation in learning and task involvement.

A: *Authority*—Give athletes opportunities to participate actively in the learning process. Involve them in decision making and monitoring their personal growth.

R: *Reward*—Administer rewards based on individual gains and improvements rather than on social comparison.

G: *Grouping*—Place athletes in groups so that they can work on similar skills in a cooperative learning environment.

E: *Evaluation*—Allow athletes to use numerous self-tests that focus on effort and personal improvement.

T: *Timing*—Make sure that the interactions of the preceding conditions are timed in such a way to be effective.

SELF-DETERMINATION THEORY

Perhaps the best way to understand the theories discussed in chapters 1 and 2 is to consider a general theory of motivation outlined by Deci and Ryan (1985, 2000). **Self-determination theory** suggests that all individuals are motivated to satisfy three basic needs: competence, autonomy, and relatedness (i.e., belongingness). For example, an athlete may be motivated to train hard in cross country to fulfill a need to feel competent. ("I am capable of running under a six-minute mile pace.") Another athlete might be motivated to play tennis to fulfill a need to feel autonomous. ("I like the ability to select serves and shots that outfox my opponent.") And another athlete might be motivated to play water polo to fulfill a need to feel social connectedness or belongingness. ("I love being a part of a team and get as much pleasure from assisting on a goal as I do scoring a goal.") Some athletes may be motivated to fulfill all three needs.

To what extent these needs (motives) are fulfilled in each athlete leads to a continuum of motivated behavior as depicted in figure 2.3.

The more a coach can facilitate athletes fulfilling these needs, the more these athletes move from extrinsic motivation to intrinsic motivation and, consequently, from low self-determination to high self-determination. Research, investigating sustained motivation of elite athletes (Mallett & Hanrahan, 2004) indicates that these elite athletes were intrinsically motivated (e.g., personal goals and achievement) rather than extrinsically motivated (e.g., financial incentives). In general, then, intrinsic motivation leads to greater self-determination while extrinsic motivation leads to lower self-determination.

Based on self-determination theory, there appear to be different types of influences that motivate behavior as motivation becomes increasingly more self-determining as it moves from extrinsic to intrinsic motivation. At the highest level, self-determined athletes are engaged (i.e., intrinsically motivated) in

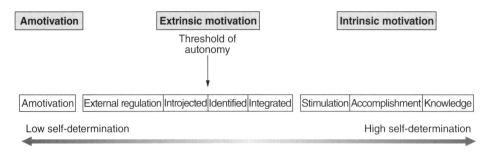

Figure 2.3 Continuum of extrinsic to intrinsic motivation.

Adapted, by permission, from R.S. Weinberg and D. Gould, 2011, *Foundations of sport and exercise psychology*, 5th ed. (Champaign, IL: Human Kinetics), 140.

an activity for reasons of knowledge, accomplishment, and stimulation. Less self-determined athletes are engaged (i.e., extrinsically motivated) in an activity for somewhat less intrinsic reasons (e.g., outcomes and external rewards). At the furthest end of the continuum is **amotivation**, in which the individual is neither intrinsically nor extrinsically motivated and therefore experiences feelings of incompetence and lack of regulation (i.e., lack of self-determination).

Extrinsic and Intrinsic Motivational Influences Associated With Different Degrees of Self-Determined Behavior

Intrinsic Motivation—High Self-Determination

- *Knowledge*—The athlete finds pleasure and satisfaction from learning something new such as the value of nutrition to performance, the importance of a new training cycle or strategy, or the role of self-talk for motor performance.

- *Accomplishment*—The athlete finds pleasure and satisfaction from mastering something new such as a new wrestling move, new personal best score or time, or new backhand tennis swing.

- *Stimulation*—The athlete finds pleasure and satisfaction from the sheer engagement in the activity.

Extrinsic Motivation—Moderate Self-Determination

- *Integrated regulation*—The athlete is motivated because the outcome is valued and therefore it is personally important. For example, an athlete decides to climb a mountain because she thinks the challenge and completion of the climb are valued outcomes. Integrated regulation is considered the most developmentally advanced form of extrinsic motivation.

- *Identified regulation*—The athlete may not find the activity pleasurable but he engages in it anyway because he recognizes (identifies) that the activity has worth. For example, an athlete participates in a sport because he knows he will gain personal growth, insight, and development. Integrated and identified regulation, like the three influences for intrinsic motivation, leads to a feeling of *want* rather than *ought* and has been found to positively connect to affective, cognitive, and behavioral outcomes (Vallerand 1997; Vallerand & Rousseau, 2001).

- *Introjected regulation*—The athlete is motivated by some internal influences but generally is regulated by external contingencies. For example, an athlete may participate in a sport to please her parents.

- *External regulation*—The athlete is motivated completely by external influences such as rewards and constraints. For example, an athlete participates in a sport so that his parents will buy him a car.

Amotivation—Low Self-Determination

- *Amotivation*—The athlete is neither extrinsically nor intrinsically motivated. For example, an athlete shows up late for practice, leaves as early as possible, and has no personal goals or motivation to train. This athlete is simply physically present at practice and, unfortunately, experiences feelings of incompetence, lack of personal control, and boredom.

The general theory of self-determination helps coaches better understand the other theories examined in chapters 1 and 2. For example, consider attribution theory. Athletes who develop an internal locus of control believe they ultimately control their performance outcomes. Consequently, they have a greater feeling of self-determination and are more intrinsically motivated than those athletes who maintain an external locus of control and believe that things are outside of their control.

THE RESILIENT ATHLETE

The **resilient athlete** firmly believes that no matter how many times he or she fails success is lurking just around the next corner. The resilient athlete sees the silver lining in every dark cloud, the stars in the nighttime sky, the potential in every challenging situation, the ugly lump of coal that can become a shimmering diamond. This athlete has an internal locus of control, takes personal responsibility for success and failure, and believes that more effort results in greater achievement and that ability can be improved.

The resilient athlete has a high sense of self-efficacy and isn't afraid of failure, since failure does not threaten his or her self-esteem, self-worth, or ego. The resilient athlete's motivational attitude allows him or her to set moderately difficult goals, take risks, psychologically deal with failure in a healthy way, attribute success to effort, assume personal responsibility for motor learning and performance, focus on learning (performance) goals, and quickly bounce back from adversity.

THE RESILIENT COACH

Much of what this book discusses is as germane to coaches as it is to athletes. Often little distinction exists between coach and athlete. Just as a motor performance is intimately and intricately connected to the performer, so much so that it is almost impossible to separate the two, coach teaching is equally connected to athlete learning. The **resilient coach** possesses a high sense of self-efficacy. The resilient coach, like the resilient athlete, possesses high self-determination, is intrinsically motivated, and is an effective teacher because she continually seeks competence, autonomy, and relatedness. The resilient coach works extra hard to prove coaching competency, takes charge, calls the shots, and, motivated by a desire to relate to others, connects well with athletes.

All of these needs translate into a successful teaching and learning environment. The resilient coach is motivated by a need for stimulation (i.e., loves coaching), accomplishment (i.e., loves seeing athletes learn and succeed), and knowledge (i.e., loves to know more about the sport and how coaches teach and how athletes learn). In sum, the resilient and highly self-determined coach provides a teaching and learning environment comparable to her motivational orientation. In contrast, the coach with low self-determination is extrinsically motivated or even amotivated. This coach does the bare minimum, is physically but not emotionally present at practice, and experiences feelings of incompetence and lack of control. What is *your* motivational orientation? What is *your* teaching and learning environment?

YOUR COACHING TOOLBOX

Here is your second coaching tool: Attribution theory helps coaches better understand their athletes—why some athletes when faced with failure remain hopeful and resilient and others do not, why some athletes fear and avoid failure and others fear it not, why athletes explain their successes and failures for much different reasons. The theory also provides coaches with some specific applications for helping athletes establish attributional perspectives that bolster their athletes' ability to remain resilient during the trials and tribulations of motor learning, performance, and competition.

THE SCIENTIFIC AND ARTFUL COACH

The scientific coach uses attribution theory to understand, explain, predict, and alter athlete attributions for success and failure. The scientific coach uses the concept of attribution theory to help athletes self-evaluate their attributional orientations and develop new orientations where necessary.

The artful coach is sensitive to the durability of athletes when it comes to perseverance and attributional toughness. For example, some athletes can endure more failure, greater risks, and more difficult tasks than others. Some athletes have resilient egos, some have fragile egos. Some athletes can accept more personal responsibility than others. Some athletes are more honest with themselves about the reasons they attribute for success and failure. Some athletes can maintain a greater sense of hopefulness than others. It is important to build up each athlete's attributional orientation, but degrees of difference always exist among athletes.

IF YOU REMEMBER ONLY THREE THINGS

1. *Remember to establish a mastery climate in your practices*. A mastery climate is one in which athletes are reinforced for working hard, demonstrating improvement, helping others through cooperation, and believing that each player's contribution is worthwhile. In a mastery climate, athletes are given challenging but attainable tasks. What is the climate like at your practices?

2. *Remember to encourage your athletes to take personal responsibility*. When they assume personal responsibility for their training and outcomes, they establish an internal locus of control. They perceive their successes and failures as things within their control, not some external and uncontrollable factor. If they fail, they take responsibility for it, try harder, and work to enhance their ability.

3. *Remember that athlete attribution orientation can be altered*. It is easy for coaches to sometimes form impressions of athletes: This athlete has an internal locus of control, this athlete doesn't. This athlete avoids failure, this one doesn't. This athlete takes responsibility, this one doesn't. Of course, these impressions are true to some extent. Athlete attribution transformations, however, do occur; athletes do change—through experience in sport, mastery climate, and coach intervention. Every coach adores the resilient athlete, but these athletes don't come to you readymade. It is up to you to facilitate the transformation.

SUGGESTED READINGS

Deci, E.L. & Ryan, R.M. (1985). *Intrinsic motivation and self-determination in human behavior*. New York: Plenum Press.

[A good read for any coach interested in athlete motivation and self-determination.]

Stallone, S. (1976). *Rocky*.

[Why do we love this Oscar-winning, rags-to-riches movie? Because it embodies the quintessential resilient athlete, the athlete who perseveres against all odds and self-determines destiny. More than 30 years later, athletes still watch this movie to get psyched for training and competition. The universal truths of sport never change.]

Weinberg, R.S. & Gould, D. (2011). *Foundations of sport and exercise psychology* (5th ed.). Champaign, IL: Human Kinetics.

[A book that covers so much material. This book should be in every coach's library.]

Athletes and Theories of Behaviorism

The two chapters in part II examine several learning theories based on behaviorism. *Behaviorism* is a general term for theories of learning primarily concerned with the observable components of behavior. Specifically, behavioristic scientists look at conditions called *stimuli*, which cause organisms to elicit certain behaviors, called *responses*. These scientists then try to develop rules that explain the relationships and interactions between stimuli and responses. These relationships are known as the rules of *conditioning*. For this reason, these theories are often labeled *stimulus–response (S–R) theories* or *behavioristic theories*.

Behavioristic scientists restrict their experiments to that which can be directly observed, predicted, manipulated, and evaluated. This is in stark contrast to another type of learning approach we will examine later in the book called cognitivism. Cognitivism considers that which is incapable of being directly observed: the intellectual or mental processes of learning. The first chapter—chapter 3—in part II examines a rather famous but often misunderstood and little used (at least for motor learning) theory developed by Russian scientist Ivan Pavlov—respondent conditioning theory. The chapter outlines the theory, introduces the salivating athlete, and explains why it might well be the most important learning theory discussed in this book. We next look at a somewhat similar theory postulated by Edward Thorndike—connectionism theory.

In chapter 4 we consider a theory developed by B.F. Skinner known as operant conditioning theory. Operant conditioning theory is behavioristic but quite different from respondent conditioning. Skinner makes the case that individuals don't simply respond to their environment but, rather, operate within and on it. The chapter examines a number of different operant conditioning tools available to coaches for influencing athlete behaviors and introduces the athlete in the Skinner box. Both chapter 3 and 4 provide specific suggestions for applying respondent and operant conditioning theories for positively affecting how athletes learn and how coaches teach.

The Salivating Athlete

Applying Respondent Conditioning Theory

Key Terms

bonds
cognitive restructuring
connectionism
contiguity
deconditioning
generalization

gradual stimulus
  presentation
hidden curriculum
law of effect
law of set

prepotent
reinforcement
respondent conditioning
salivating athlete
salivating coach

" *It is amazing what human beings can accomplish when they are filled with a sense of passion.* "

About 5 years before my father passed away, I decided to take him hunting. He loved to hunt more than anything in life; it was his passion. My brother and I had always secretly hoped that when it was the old man's time to go he would keel over in a field or duck blind with his shotgun in his arms and his beloved hunting dog by his side. I arranged for him to hunt a small parcel of untilled, wooded land called a slew on a farm that my best friend's father owned in northern Nebraska. My dad no longer had a hunting dog; Mister, an English springer spaniel and his best friend, had passed away a few years back. So I decided to bring my dog Jackson, a buff-colored cocker spaniel that had never been trained a lick in how to hunt. In fact, the most outdoor activity he had experienced was some fierce squirrel chasing at a park near our home. But he was a robust and energetic dog with good endurance and probably the pick of the litter.

The day of the hunt was magnificent; the sky was clear and the weather was brisk but comfortable. It was a good day to walk the field. We were looking for pheasants and I was hopeful. But right before the hunt I began to have misgivings. What was I thinking after all? My dad could barely walk; he was in an advanced stage of Parkinson's disease. He could barely hold a gun, let alone raise it to his shoulder, aim, and fire. Before the hunt I asked him to show me if he could raise the gun. He complied and made a feeble attempt at raising the gun to his shoulder. What was I thinking? And Jackson didn't know a thing about hunting. He was never trained to hunt, had no hunting experience, and was basically a house dog. Here we were in farming country hunting this little slew. There couldn't possibly be any pheasants here today and, even if there were, there was no way my dad was going to shoot one. If we did find one, I would have to shoot it, which would be a miracle in itself since I was a bad shot.

We began the hunt, my dad on one side of the slew and I on the other with Jackson between us. At the outset I noticed my dad's pace no longer seemed to be that of a person with Parkinson's. He was more nimble; his feet moved with a steady pace I had not seen in years. And then my dad called out, "That's what a hunting dog is supposed to do," and I noticed that Jackson was methodically working back and forth from one side of the slew to the other. Eventually we came near the end of the slew and I thought, *Oh, great. I knew there wouldn't be any birds in here.* At that point, we reached the end and Jackson took one last sweep across the slew.

To my surprise, Jackson flushed the one and only pheasant! At the end of the slew was an open field and that pheasant had no place to hide. He had to make a move and suddenly the bird took flight. I raised my gun and pulled the trigger, but nothing happened. I had forgotten to take off the safety. But I heard a shot and saw the bird plummet to the ground. In one clean move, my dad had raised his gun and winged the pheasant with one shot. Although it was winged and couldn't fly, the bird could run, and run it did. It took off as soon as it hit the ground. The only way to get the bird now was with a hunting dog.

The next thing I saw was Jackson bolt after the bird, running as fast as his four paws could carry him. In all his canine glory, Jackson tracked it down, grabbed it with his mouth, brought it back, and dropped it at my dad's feet. Jackson glanced up at my dad with a look that said he had found his passion and genetic mission in life. Never had a dog looked more blissful in this earthly realm than Jackson did at that moment. My dad had a look on his face as though he had just died and gone to hunter's heaven. I stood there with my mouth agape and eyes wide open. It is awe inspiring to be in the presence of such passion.

Thinking back on that day I am struck by the fact that human beings (and, yes, canines) who are filled with passion can accomplish almost anything. This chapter is a tale about the passionate athlete—or what I call the salivating athlete—and how coaches can create an environment that engenders in their athletes an abiding love and deep passion for the game.

CHAPTER OVERVIEW

This chapter examines two behavioral theories that influence learning. The first theory is known as respondent conditioning, also called classical or Pavlovian conditioning. Although it is often overlooked in coaching and motor learning texts, respondent conditioning is perhaps the single most important learning theory discussed in this book. This theory helps explain the learning that occurs when stimuli are repeatedly paired with each other. The second theory covered in this chapter is Thorndike's connectionism, which serves as a transition from respondent conditioning to operant conditioning examined in chapter 4. **Connectionism** suggests that learning is the formation of connections between stimuli and responses. Perhaps most important to coaches are the laws of learning that Thorndike outlines for helping learners form connections or what he refers to as bonds. The chapter provides some simple but effective methods of applying these theories in coaching athletes.

PAVLOV'S CLASSICAL (RESPONDENT) CONDITIONING

Ivan Pavlov, the Russian physiologist whose name has become a synonym for classical (respondent) conditioning, discovered his noteworthy observation by accident. He was researching digestion in dogs and in 1904 he was even awarded a Nobel Prize in medicine and physiology for his work on digestion. During the course of this work, he noticed that the dogs in his laboratory began to salivate when they were about to be fed, even before they could see or smell the food. He noticed that the dogs seemed to begin salivating at the sight of their keepers or even when they heard footsteps.

These observations encouraged Pavlov to conduct a series of experiments that are now well known. In one experiment, he rang a bell or sounded a buzzer—neither of which generally led to salivation—and then immediately presented the dogs with their food, a stimulus that usually led to salivation. Pavlov discovered that if this pairing of food with the bell or buzzer was repeated often enough, the bell or buzzer alone began to elicit salivation from the dogs.

In Pavlov's experiments, the bell or buzzer is referred to as a conditioned stimulus (CS), the food is an unconditioned stimulus (US), salivation in response to the food is an unconditioned response (UR), and salivation in response to the bell or buzzer is a conditioned response (CR). A neutral stimulus (NS) is any stimulus that does not normally lead to a response. In the case of Pavlov and his dogs, the bell and buzzer initially were neutral stimuli. The classical conditioning paradigm is outlined in figure 3.1.

Classical conditioning also is known as **respondent conditioning** because the individual responds to stimuli in the environment. These stimuli, such as food, elicit a response from the individual. To better understand the process of classical conditioning with athletes, it might be helpful to examine scenario 1.

Before conditioning

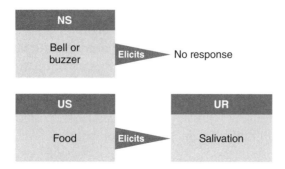

Conditioning process

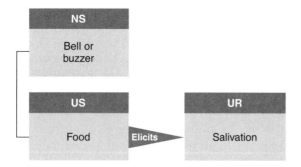

In this process, the NS (bell or buzzer) is repeatedly paired with the US (food).

After conditioning

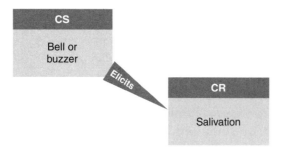

Figure 3.1 The classical conditioning paradigm.

Scenario 1

A diver who has dived springboard for approximately 6 years is pushed to learn a platform list that is an entirely new task. He must develop new skills within about 2 weeks, which is a relatively short period. The diver learns a list of dives during this time but he experiences several crashes (rough landings on the water surface) in the process. He develops a high level of anxiety and fear and he begins to evidence maladjusted behaviors such as repeated balking, nervous twitching, and avoidance behavior toward the platform.

Figure 3.2 outlines the respondent conditioning paradigm for scenario 1.

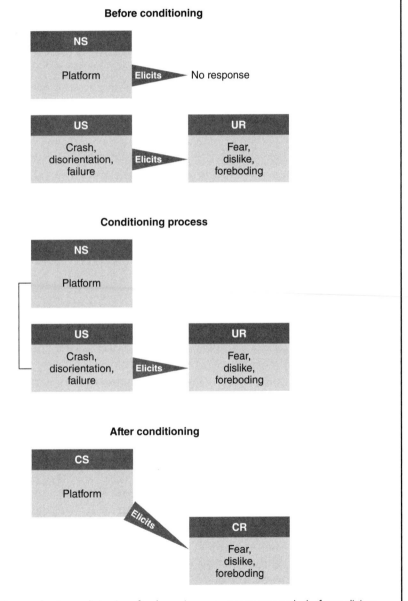

Figure 3.2 Respondent conditioning for learning responses toward platform diving.

Before the conditioning process, assuming the diver had no prior platform experience, platform presumably elicited no response and, therefore it can be considered a neutral stimulus. During the conditioning process, because of the diver's lack of experience, insufficient time, and readiness, platform (NS) was paired with the unconditioned stimuli of crashing, disorientation (maybe he got lost in the dive), and failure, which in turn automatically elicited the unconditioned responses of pain, fear, dislike, and foreboding.

After the conditioning process, the NS (platform) has now become the conditioned stimulus (CS) and automatically elicits the conditioned responses (CR) pain, fear, dislike, and foreboding. Over time the CS (platform) begins to elicit from the athlete maladaptive behaviors, such as repeated balking, nervous twitching, and avoidance behavior. For example, the diver may feign sickness and miss practice on platform days or develop a mysterious injury or exaggerate a minor injury that would preclude diving platform.

A similar and all-too-familiar example to further illustrate negative respondent conditioning is the coach in scenario 2 or the physical education teacher who uses running as punishment for misbehavior (figure 3.3). In addition to teaching a sport or a skill, the teacher unwittingly teaches the student to hate running. Teaching a hatred for running was never meant to be one of the track coach's goals or part of the physical education teacher's curriculum. Nonetheless, it becomes so through the process of respondent conditioning.

Scenario 2

A high school freshman decides to try out for the track team. Having never run competitively before, the whole experience is new to her. She arrives late for practice the first week and as punishment the coach makes her run extra laps after practice. The following week, she decides to try a different sport.

Respondent conditioning can occur also in a classroom setting, such as in a mathematics class. Mathematics is presumably a neutral stimulus that initially evokes little emotional response, but through repeated pairing with negative unconditioned stimuli, such as an unfriendly teacher and failure, many students develop a negative conditioned response to the subject.

Recall scenario 1. The diver was asked to do too much too soon; experienced pain, disorientation, and failure; and very quickly learned to associate platform with the conditioned responses of fear, dislike, and foreboding. In turn, these emotional and physiological responses engendered maladaptive behaviors, such as nervous twitching and avoiding practice. Even though the coach did not intentionally intend to teach such associations or

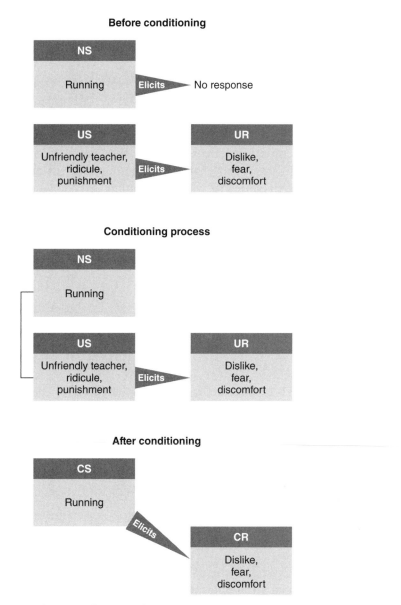

Figure 3.3   Respondent conditioning for running.

negative responses, they occurred because of the structure of the learning experience.

One might summarize the respondent conditioning discussion to this point with the question "What good does it do for coaches to teach a skill and for athletes to learn a skill if at the same time these same athletes are unconsciously learning negative emotional and physiological responses that result in maladaptive behaviors toward the sport?" The answer, of course, is that it does very little good.

POSITIVE RESPONDENT CONDITIONING EXAMPLES

The goal of every coach should be to create a program that engenders positive emotional, physiological, and behavioral responses in athletes. Such responses are important for creating an enjoyable athletic experience, developing athletes as healthy human beings, and promoting high-level performance and competitive success. So far the chapter has examined several negative examples of respondent conditioning. Fortunately, many positive examples exist that you will want to emulate in your coaching and sport program.

In scenario 3 the baseball coach creates a positive, memorable experience of youth sport. He creates an environment in which praise, acceptance, fun, excitement, learning, success, and a love for the game are bundled into one unforgettable experience. Figure 3.4 outlines the respondent conditioning process for scenario 3.

Scenario 3

A middle school boy tries out for the local youth baseball team. The first week of practice is chaotic; players are running around, trying different positions, laughing, and generally having a great deal of fun. The coach loves baseball and is eager to start practice and even engages in many of the drills himself. He is friendly, kind, willing to help every player on the team, and quick to praise and encourage the athletes. The young boys respect and admire him. They adopt the coach's infectious love for the game and continue to participate in the sport after they leave his program.

At this point, you may be asking, "What does respondent conditioning have to do with coaching and motor learning and why is it so important?" It is a fair question to ask.

Given the scenarios just presented, the reason that respondent conditioning is so important in coaching is because conditioning athletes to love their sport may be the most important factor for athlete success. This statement is true no matter how you as a coach define success. If success means kids become excited, engaged, enamored, and devoted to your sport, then respondent conditioning is important. If success means achieving performance excellence, then the theory also is important because athletes who are passionate about their sport tend to be highly motivated , which means they work hard in practice, set daily goals, exert a high level of effort, and continually search for ways to improve, thus increasing likelihood of success.

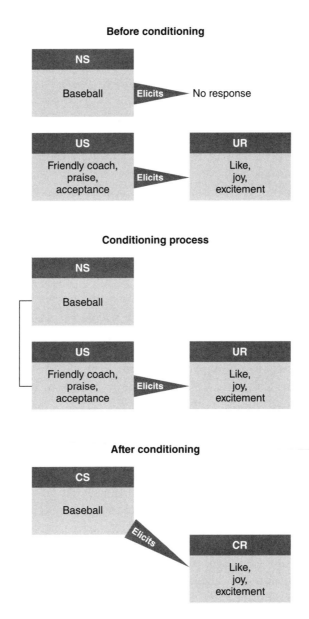

Figure 3.4 Respondent conditioning for learning to play baseball.

As you will see in the section Characteristics of Deliberate Practice in chapter 7, one factor differentiating the elite from the nonelite performer is a willingness to practice at a much higher level of intensity, focus, and effort on a daily basis. This willingness emanates in part from a high level of motivation and passion nurtured earlier in an athlete's career by repeated pairing of positive unconditioned stimuli with the athlete's particular sport.

The United States Olympic Committee conducted a notable study called *The Path to Excellence: A Comprehensive View of Development of U.S. Olympians*

Who Competed from 1984-1998 (Gibbons, Hill, McConnell, Forster, & Moore, 2002). In this study, 816 former Olympians who attended the Winter and Summer Olympic Games from 1984 through 1998 completed a questionnaire providing information about their training and development. In a follow-up to this document, entitled *Reflections on Success: U.S. Olympians Describe the Success Factors and Obstacles that Most Influenced their Olympic Development* (Gibbons, McConnell, Forster, Tuffy, Riewald, & Peterson, 2003), these athletes indicated that one of the top 10 factors for their success was a love of their sport.

Also worth noting is Bloom's (1985) research where he found that individuals who achieved excellence, such as Olympic athletes, artists, musicians, and scientists, first developed a love of the activity during their early years. Bloom found that the people most responsible for helping to engender this love were the initial coaches and teachers. Coupled with the theory of respondent conditioning, this finding leads to several significant coaching applications.

APPLYING RESPONDENT CONDITIONING THEORY IN COACHING ATHLETES

So how do you apply respondent conditioning to coaching your athletes? Interestingly, there are classroom-related instructional applications (LeFrancois, 2000) of respondent conditioning that can be applied to coaching athletes as well as applications specifically related to coaching athletes (Smith & Smoll, 2001; Thompson, 2003). Following are some specific guidelines for applying respondent conditioning for creating the salivating athlete.

Maximize the frequency, distinctiveness, and potency of pleasant unconditioned stimuli. After reading this chapter so far, this application is probably obvious to you, but it is less obvious to many coaches and physical education teachers (e.g., think of scenario 2). Create environments that offer many positive unconditioned stimuli, particularly for young athletes. Keep in mind scenario 3 in which the young baseball players are learning about baseball and trying different positions on the field while also experiencing success, fun, acceptance, support, and nurturing. Sure, practice might be chaotic and could be run more efficiently, but practice is fun, the coach is warm and inviting, and his exuberance for the sport rubs off on his players. How many of these young players are likely to learn to love the sport and choose to continue playing?

The salivating athlete is the athlete who can't wait to get to practice, the player who shows up early and stays late for practice, the kid who dreams about the sport at night and wants to practice even on a day off. This is the type of athlete coaches should want to develop.

From my own experience I know how important a coach can be at that optimal time in an athlete's life. When I was a young diver, I had some terrible coaches. One coach threw a chair in the water at me for not learning a new dive—a dive he had neither prepared me to learn nor understood himself how to teach. I had such a miserable experience that at the age of 12 I quit the sport.

Later, as a high school freshman I decided that to be cool in school I needed to go out for a sport. I decided to give springboard diving one more try. By chance a truly gifted coach named Morry Arbini happened to move into the area where I lived just as I decided to resume my diving career. He came my freshman year of high school and left after my senior year. What a stroke of luck.

Coach Arbini was the toughest coach I ever dived for. He was demanding, resolute in what he expected, and gave no quarter. If he asked you to do something, you were expected to do it without question. Despite his toughness, he had something that I had never seen in another coach: He cared about you as a person and was emotionally involved in your diving and what you wanted to accomplish. He was genuinely excited when you learned a new dive and quick to congratulate you and spend time talking about your practice. He wasn't afraid to show his emotions. If you did something he liked, it was usually followed by a smile, clap of the hands, pat on the back, or even a bear hug. What he may have lacked in technical expertise he compensated for with a passion for the sport, a love for his athletes, and the ability to create a positive learning environment that engendered responses of joy, passion, excitement, and love for the sport.

Practice was challenging, but rewarding; and it was demanding, but fun. Seriousness was balanced with humor and the shear enjoyment of the sport. I still recall a number of my practices, my first back 2 1/2 somersault, my first triple twisting 1 1/2 somersault, and all my first dives off the 10-meter platform. It was one of the scariest, most challenging, most rewarding, and most enjoyable times of my life.

To this day I am deeply grateful for the opportunity to have learned from him. I am sure that I became a coach because of him. After I retired from diving and began my coaching career, I took three of the six most important awards I earned during my career and mailed them to him. In the enclosed letter I wrote, "Without you, I would never have achieved so much. These are as much yours as they are mine. Thanks for giving me your time, your experience, your wisdom, and your heart and soul. I can never truly repay you, but I can pass on what you gave me to other athletes." During the 4 short years he coached me, he developed divers who eventually went on to win national and conference championships, high school and collegiate All-American honors, and divers who became age group and collegiate coaches.

If you want to turn on your athletes to your sport, be a coach like Morry.

Minimize the unpleasant and negative unconditioned stimuli. Consider scenario 4 in which the coach maximizes rather than minimizes unpleasant stimuli of seriousness, rigidity, inflexibility, and intolerance. It is important, especially for young athletes, to minimize unpleasant and negative stimuli and promote pleasant and positive stimuli that condition athletes to love their sport.

Scenario 4

A high school freshman decides to try out for the cross country team. The coach is extremely serious; no laughing, joking, or fooling around is permitted during practices. The same serious atmosphere exists at team functions and little team camaraderie exists. The athlete wants to continue running but also has an interest in soccer and would like to try both sports. However, the coach gives him an ultimatum; he tells the athlete that he must choose only one of the two sports. The athlete chooses soccer.

Scenario 4 is something I witnessed a young boy experience his freshman year of high school. He loved running in middle school and hoped to continue running for his high school track team. He also was interested in soccer, mainly because many of his friends played, but he wanted to continue running as well. Under different circumstances, I think the boy would have run all 4 years of high school. The coach likely was unaware of the learning atmosphere he created; many coaches are. Be conscious of and eliminate the unpleasant and negative stimuli in your program.

No matter what level you coach at, endeavor to keep the sport experience fun. Sure, the higher you rise in a sport, the more demanding it becomes and the more difficult it becomes to attain the next level. Some amount of seriousness and intolerance are necessary at certain levels of athletic competitiveness, but these demands have to be balanced with a healthy perspective and approach to the sport. Athletes have to work hard, work smart, *and* work at having fun. Athletes who have fun while they work hard are ultimately more successful than athletes who just work hard. It is well known that after a grueling set, International Swimming Hall of Fame coach Doc Counsilman from Indiana University used to reward his swimmers with jelly beans. Some of the best swimmers in the world were working themselves to their edge in practice just for a few jelly beans. The beans themselves didn't mean much to the athletes, but they had a lot of fun earning them.

Athletes need to enjoy their sport at any level. Even at the Olympic Games, athletes need to remember to enjoy the entire Olympic Games experience and have fun. They need to remember that they got into the sport because they enjoyed doing it and that they should continue to enjoy the process and everything that comes with it. Whether or not they would attain an Olympic medal, they should be able to look back and know they gave their best effort. As the Olympic creed states, "The most important thing in the Olympic Games is not to win but to take part, just as the most important thing in life is not the triumph but the struggle. The essential thing is not to have conquered but to have fought well."

What do the words *best effort, the struggle,* and *fought well* mean? They mean in part that athletes should commit to clear process goals, be immersed in the performance process (not immersed in a competitor's performance process), focus on relevant cues, and find enjoyment in the performance process. These aspects of motor performance help put athletes into the flow of performance. The saying that learning should be fun has a lot more meaning when understood from a classical conditioning perspective. The coach who makes athletes laugh and smile while they are doing drills is pairing positive stimuli (laughter and smiling) with an unconditioned stimulus (drills) and may succeed in teaching athletes the following:

1. To smile, laugh, and have fun

2. To associate important drills with athletic performance

3. To like their sport, practice time, the coach, the smell of chlorine, locker room, wrestling mat, gymnasium, and anything else associated with their experiences for their particular sport

Athletes who learn these responses can grow beyond just liking their sport to eventually loving it. When a coach yells and screams at athletes and makes them suffer miserably through practice, what do athletes learn?

Monitor yourself to make sure you are a source of pleasant and positive stimuli. Are you a source of pleasant and positive stimuli or a source of unpleasant and negative stimuli? For example, you may perceive yourself as using a cooperative coaching style (Martens, 2004), where you allow your athletes to take responsibility and share in decision making, but in reality your athletes perceive you as using a command coaching style where you make all the decisions and tend to be hard-nosed and dictatorial. Or, you may think you offer your athletes friendliness, praise, and acceptance like the coach in scenario 3, whereas your athletes think you are unfriendly and interpret many of your remarks as sarcastic and full of ridicule instead of praise.

Coaches are human beings just like athletes; they are not immune to the stresses and demands of the coaching profession. Who you think you are or how you think you act and relate to your athletes may change over time. It might be a result of stress during the season, burnout, personal matters outside of practice, time constraints, or other issues affecting your coaching performance. The point is that you have to carefully monitor and evaluate yourself so that you are a source of pleasant and positive stimuli for your athletes.

Be aware of and eliminate the hidden curriculum. The **hidden curriculum** means the things that coaches teach and the things athletes learn that are not part of the overt curriculum. Often coaches teach these things unintentionally, unconsciously, and randomly. This chapter has already mentioned negative examples of the hidden curriculum: the track coach and gym teacher who unconsciously teach a hatred for running, the mathematics teacher who unintentionally teaches a dislike for mathematics, and the diving coach who unintentionally teaches an aversion to platform diving. Certainly, these leaders did not intend to teach such negative emotional reactions; nonetheless, they did.

Fortunately, positive examples exist of coaches providing pleasant and positive stimuli that elicit athlete responses of like, joy, excitement, and love for their sport. They include Morry Arbini coaching diving, the baseball coach in scenario 3, the coaches cited by the former Olympians, and the coaches and teachers cited in Bloom's study. These positive examples of respondent conditioning are not part of a hidden curriculum, but part of an overt curriculum that highly effective coaches purposely designed to help athletes ignite a passion and love for their sport. Eliminate the hidden curriculum.

Use respondent conditioning to decondition negative physiological and behavioral responses. Respondent conditioning is an involuntary and unconscious process for learning physiological and emotional responses that negatively or positively affect athlete performance. Little, if any cognition occurs. Like one of Pavlov's salivating dogs that involuntarily reacted to the bell or buzzer, the salivating athlete responds to a particular stimulus without much thought process. For example, in scenario 5 the gymnast who suddenly freezes and can't perform a particular movement is eliciting not so much a cognitive problem as a learned physiological response brought about through the repeated pairing of a neutral stimulus (the motor skill) with some type of negative unconditioned stimulus, such as disorientation, injury, pain, or failure, which elicits the conditioned response. In this case the response is perhaps fear and a feeling that the muscles are frozen. Often, the athlete reports that he or she wants to perform the movement but simply can't get the body to do it.

Scenario 5

Slowly over time a gymnast becomes increasingly anxious about performing her beam routine. On a number of occasions when she was younger she experienced some falls and injuries while practicing on the beam. Suddenly at one practice she freezes and can't perform the more difficult part of her routine. The next day she has trouble performing more of the routine. This continues until one day she freezes every time she tries to begin her routine.

This learned response is similar to, say, a snake phobia, where the presentation of a snake automatically elicits responses of fear, anxiety, and avoidance. The person does not have to consciously think about the snake; he simply reacts automatically with minimal cognitive processing (stimulus recognition) to the presentation of the snake. Similarly, the likelihood of having to do the gymnastics movement, even the mere thought of doing the movement or visualizing the movement, can automatically elicit the negative emotions associated with the response and the conditioned response of freezing. The gymnast's physiological response in scenario 5 was likely caused in part by her past experiences of trauma (Grand & Goldberg, 2011). To promote positive and healthy responses to your sport, ensure as much as possible that athletes practice in a safe training environment, avoid traumatic injury, and master one skill before progressing to a more difficult skill.

Through a process called *deconditioning*, it is possible to alter athletes' conditioned negative responses so that they learn to relax and enjoy those motor movements that once elicited responses such as fear, freezing, and avoidance. **Deconditioning** uses progressive relaxation, mental imagery, self-talk, cognitive restructuring, and stimulus presentation to help athletes gradually learn to control their physiological responses in the presence of the conditioned negative stimulus. For example, the gymnast who freezes when she attempts her beam routine can begin deconditioning by standing next to the beam, visualizing her routine, and trying to remain relaxed and calm.

Deconditioning has been an effective strategy for many athletes, including my own. At the 2007 U.S. National Indoor Championship, platform diver Cassandra Cardinell experienced a *freeze* moment on an inward 3 1/2 somersault from the 10-meter platform. At the World Trials a few months earlier, she missed a leg when she tried to grab her tuck and crashed into the water. Subsequently, when she would initiate the somersaulting action off the platform she would tense up, resulting in her having trouble rotating fast enough to make the dive. The more this situation persisted, the greater her anxiety became and the worse the dive became. Like many talented and successful athletes, she made the mistake of hiding this situation from me, fearing that if she showed a sign of weakness I would think less of her. Finally, I asked her how she was feeling about the dive and suddenly the dam broke loose and tears began to fall.

After she told me her story, I surprised her by saying that the problem wasn't mental. With a startled look on her face, she asked me what, then, was the problem. I told her that the problem was her physiological response to her traumatic crash at the World Trials (as well as another similar episode with the dive at a meet in China after the World Trials) and then I explained the theory of respondent conditioning. Immediately she had a relieved look on her face. She was a tough athlete and competitor, and an intelligent person. Besides being an NCAA champion, she was an NCAA postgraduate scholarship recipient. Because she is all of these things, she assumed that she was simply not being mentally tough enough and therefore, she was reluctant to meet with me and reveal her problem.

Because she didn't understand the nature of her problem, she became increasingly agitated and emotionally upset that she couldn't fix it. This increased agitation only exacerbated the problem. She had gotten to the point where even doing a simple lead-up, which she had done hundreds of times in preparation for performing her inward 3 1/2, caused her to experience fear, foreboding, and anxiety. This is generally the case where the conditioned response begins to spread to other areas of the athlete's sport. For this reason it is important to deal with the situation as soon as possible. The longer it lingers, the worse it gets.

The concept of respondent conditioning is helpful for athletes because it gives them a reason to understand and explain why they are not handling these types of situations. It isn't because they are mentally weak and it isn't because of something they consciously learned. It's simply because of a pairing of one stimulus with another. Fortunately, the theory of respondent conditioning also provides a remedy to the situation, discussed next—deconditioning.

Step 1: *Make sure the problem is not technical in nature.* One of the first things I did when we worked on overcoming her problem was to make sure the problem was not incorrect technique. If a technical problem was causing her to miss her leg in the somersault, I wanted to make sure that we corrected it so that it would never happen again. Upon review, some slight technical errors did exist and we corrected them. These corrections bolstered her confidence and motivation to regain proficiency on the dive. However, they didn't completely solve the problem because the errors weren't really the cause of the problem.

Step 2: *Identify the type of problem.* A problem is much easier to solve when you know what type of problem it is because identifying the problem leads to selecting the right solution. In Cassandra's case, the problem was physiological in nature, so I explained the concept of respondent conditioning. I let her know that the problem was more physiological than mental, but that cognition would play a role in helping her overcome her problem.

Step 3: *Confront past trauma.* Athletes tend to suppress past traumatic experiences; they ignore them as if they never happened. These suppressed experiences, however, are not forgotten and over time can build up and boil over. It is cathartic for athletes to recall these traumatic experiences, put them in perspective, and recognize how these experiences contributed to their debilitating physiological response and current problem. It was healing for Cassandra to talk about the instances when she crashed, particularly the ones when I was not present, such as the one in China.

Step 4: *Use cognitive restructuring.* **Cognitive restructuring** involves challenging and changing negative thoughts, false beliefs, and erroneous rationalizations. In Cassandra's case, there was no reason for her to buy into the thought that she couldn't do the dive well. ("Okay, you have done this dive well hundreds of times in the past. You nailed it to win the NCAA Championship, so you know you can perform it safely and proficiently in the future.") I asked her to list all the reasons why she could safely perform the dive—and there were many. I also asked her to list the negative things she was afraid of and how she could deal with those issues. I encouraged her to create a plan of attack, a counteroffensive for dealing with the enemy—negative thoughts, false beliefs, and inaccurate rationalizations.

Step 5: *Use self-talk.* Self-talk can change thoughts, emotions, and physiology. For Cassandra, who was by nature a positive person, she needed to recapture her optimism by using forceful and positive self-talk that directed her thoughts to positive statements that in turn helped create positive emotions and a more relaxed body state. It is important, however, for an athlete to not adopt an adversarial relationship with negative thoughts (Grand & Goldberg, 2011). Negative thoughts are often the body's natural defense system warning an athlete of potential harm. Therefore, athletes should perceive them as part of the "team," as friendly suggestions to be unemotionally acknowledged and responded to in a curious and relaxed manner.

Step 6: *Use mental imagery and relaxation with gradual stimulus presentation.* **Gradual stimulus presentation** is the bit-by-bit introduction of the conditioned stimulus. Both mental imagery and relaxation are helpful in reducing anxiety by reducing muscular tension. Cassandra began step 6 by trying to relax while viewing past performances of her performing the dive well (she had many video clips). She then worked on relaxing while visualizing herself performing the dive. Then she took baby steps in learning to relax; she simply stood backwards on the lower platform and worked on relaxing. Next, she worked on relaxing on an inward somersault off the side of the pool and then progressed to an inward 1 1/2 off the 3-meter platform, then an inward double off the 3-meter platform, and then an inward 2 1/2 off the 5-meter platform.

Eventually Cassandra made it back to the 10-meter platform and performed the dive safely and proficiently. At the 2008 U.S. Olympic Trials it was her best dive. She scored 7.5s and 8.0s the three times she performed it. Although she narrowly missed making the second Olympic team, she did win the U.S. National Championship that summer, beating the winner of the Olympic Trials (and 2000 Olympic gold medalist) in the process. She certainly came a long way: from not being able to think about the dive without being emotionally devastated to performing it extremely well in the Olympic Trials and later that summer at the national championship. In the last national championship (and the last dive of the last event) of her career, she nailed a back 2 1/2 somersault with 1 1/2 twists to win the gold medal.

For serious problems athletes should consult a professional. The preceding 6 steps worked well for a number of my athletes over the years. However, I don't profess to be a licensed sport psychologist or counselor and neither should you. If your athlete has a more serious problem, the best thing you can do is immediately refer the athlete to a certified and trained professional who has experience in dealing with those types of problems. Furthermore, if your athlete is a minor, it is important to discuss the problem with the parents.

Remember that conditioning doesn't always require much repeated pairing of a neutral stimulus with a negative or positive stimulus. For example, a young baseball player doesn't have to get hit in the face with a baseball more than once to develop a negative conditioned response. And Thompson (2003) writes about the young athlete who tries out for wrestling, is physically pummeled the first day of practice, and never wrestles again. Be acutely aware of the stimuli you pair with the athlete experience.

THORNDIKE'S CONNECTIONISM THEORY

Through careful and scientific observation of animal behavior Edward L. Thorndike (1898) postulated a theory of connectionism that explains learning as the formation of **bonds** (connections) between stimuli and responses. Thorndike's theory of human learning states that a person makes a variety of responses (trial and error) until a response leads to a solution, or what Thorndike called a "satisfying state of affairs." That response is then learned. To use Thorndike's words, the response is "stamped in." Thus, learning is simply a matter of *stamping in* connections between stimuli and responses.

Pavlov and others believed that these bonds are formed through simple **contiguity**, the simultaneous occurrence of stimuli. In contrast, Thorndike believed that what better explains learning (the formation of bonds) is **reinforcement**; in other words, the consequence of a response leads to the response being learned or unlearned. This concept of reinforcement is a nice transition to chapter 4, which looks at B. F. Skinner and his operant conditioning theory. But before turning to that chapter it is useful to look briefly at some laws of learning that Thorndike postulated based on his theory of connectionism.

In developing his theory of connectionism, Thorndike postulated several laws: the law of effect, the law of readiness, the law of exercise, and several subsidiary laws (the law of multiple responses, the law of set or attitude, the law of prepotency of elements, and the law of response by analogy). Perhaps of most interest is Thorndike's **law of effect**, which states that any action producing a satisfying effect will be repeated in similar situations. This law is a bridge between respondent conditioning and operant conditioning. It recognizes the connection between a pleasant stimulus and a response (respondent conditioning) and also the connection between a voluntary goal-directed behavior (operant) and the consequence for emitting that behavior (operant conditioning). Thorndike was interested in applying his research and writing to education; consequently, you can use a number of instructional applications of connectionism to become a more effective coach. Those applications are discussed next.

APPLYING CONNECTIONISM THEORY IN COACHING ATHLETES

Reward correct trials. Thorndike believed that learning occurs by rewarding correct trials (behavioral responses), which leads to a satisfying state of affairs. Consequently, it is important that coaches not only provide athletes with the opportunity to emit a variety of responses and reward the correct responses, but also shape the learning experience in such a way that correct responses are more likely to occur. For example, the coach who asks athletes to perform skills they are not ready to execute is unlikely to see the correct response. Consequently, these athletes rarely, if ever, receive any intrinsic or extrinsic reward. They feel dissatisfaction with their sport and are likely to look for another sport or other endeavors.

Establish athlete readiness. Learner readiness, then, is important for determining the learning tasks and for achieving success, rewards, and a satisfying state. It is important that athletes experience success during the learning process. Too much failure can result in displeasure, dislike, avoidance behavior, and a feeling of helplessness. Consequently, it is important that the coach establish athlete readiness. This determination is no easy task and takes experience, knowledge, education, understanding, and sensitivity. Remember, coaching is both an art and a science. The artful and scientific coach takes into consideration a number of factors, such as level of physical, intellectual, and emotional maturation; skill proficiency and skill progression; motivation; psychological stability; and individual differences. This book is an effort to help prepare coaches to be able to make many of these determinations.

Establish athlete learning attitudes. According to Thorndike's **law of set** or attitude, people often respond to novel situations in terms of predetermined sets, or attitudes, that they possess. Since respondent conditioning is a nearly unconscious and automatic learning process, coaches and athletes need to be aware of positive and negative attitudes, then work toward accentuating positive attitudes and avoiding negative ones. Because they exercise considerable influence in determining athlete attitudes, coaches in particular should endeavor to encourage positive attitudes that contribute to a healthy training atmosphere and an appropriate perspective toward motor learning, competition, and sport. For example, coaches can encourage athletes to develop attitudes such as placing a high value on effort and performance rather than place of finish, making creative changes in practice rather than performing the status quo, supporting teammates instead of undermining them, achieving personal bests rather than social comparison, and taking responsibility for their development rather than relying solely on their coach.

Attract athlete attention. According to Thorndike's subsidiary law of prepotency of elements, people tend to react to the most significant, or **prepotent**, elements of a situation rather than the entire situation. This means that coaches must be careful to stress, or make prepotent, important aspects of the learning situation. For example, when teaching a new skill, stress one or two main points rather than inundate your athletes with too many of the finer details. A detailed analysis can wait until later.

Teach generalization. **Generalization** occurs when a previously learned response is transferred to a different but somewhat similar situation. In other words, when a new stimulus is presented, the individual reacts to it as though it were the familiar old stimulus already encountered. Consequently, after an athlete has learned a new motor skill, it is important that you point out how the skill might be applicable to other similar situations. For example, when connecting into a backward somersault on springboard and platform dives the diver can apply the same action to reverse somersaulting dives. Another example of generalization is the similarity of the backhand to the forehand in tennis, squash, or racquetball. Successful coaches are proficient at pointing out generalizations and elite-level athletes are able to recognize and apply these generalizations to other situations.

Generalization extends to respondent conditioning and the responses associated with the sport that athletes learn. Athletes who respond positively to their sport can generalize a similar positive response to other aspects of their sport such as stretching, conditioning, grueling practices, video review, early morning practices, and so on.

CONCLUSION

What is more important, particularly in the early stage of skill acquisition for young athletes: to teach the motor skill or to teach a love for the sport? Although both are necessary and important, think about adherence to an activity in terms of respondent conditioning. For example, consider the teacher who is adroit at turning on kids to reading. Maybe some of the students leave the class as not the best readers, but because of their love for reading, they continue to read on their own, frequent the library, borrow books, ask their parents to buy books for their birthday, and eventually become competent lifelong readers.

A similar response occurs when coaches turn on kids to their sport; these young athletes persist in the sport and eagerly pursue opportunities to practice, learn, and compete. In the long run, teaching a love for the sport is more important than teaching a motor skill. Many people cite a positive experience as the reason or time in their lives when they decided to follow a certain path or career. Because of my classroom experiences with two remarkable high school English teachers, I planned to become an English teacher and not a coach. In fact, my undergraduate degree was English education.

Over the years, many of my divers learned difficult dives off the 10-meter platform. In fact, some years every athlete on my team competed on platform; one year I had as many as 14 platform divers, which is unusual for most diving teams. These divers were kids who decided to climb 33 feet in the air, throw their bodies off a platform as tall as a three-story building, and hit the water at a speed of about 35 miles per hour. When introducing divers to platform, I tried to follow one rule: Create a learning environment in which athletes develop a positive physiological response to platform diving. In other words, my goal was to help them relax, have fun, and learn to love diving platform.

It is exciting to help athletes learn to relax and ultimately enjoy something they once feared or found unpleasant. For example, a college freshman diver named Al Burns refused to stand backward on the 10-meter platform because he was so nervous he was afraid his shaking legs would buckle. During his freshman and sophomore years, I never set a timetable for him learning a platform list. I simply created practices where he experienced fun, success, and relaxation. One morning 3 years later, he decided to throw a backward 3 1/2 somersault (one of the most difficult dives on platform) *cold turkey* (which means without any warm-up preparation other than adequately stretching and doing some dry-land rehearsal drills) off the 10-meter platform for morning practice. He nailed the dive. Al is a prime example of how you can change a conditioned response in your athletes. He moved from fear and trepidation to excitement and risk taking. I told him afterward that anyone who could do what he did could accomplish anything in life.

THE SALIVATING ATHLETE

Like Pavlov's salivating dogs, the **salivating athlete** learns physiological responses through the repeated pairing of conditioned stimuli with unconditioned stimuli. This pairing conditions your athlete to become the salivating athlete, the passionate athlete, the athlete who loves the sport and everything connected to it, the athlete who persists because of sheer joy, the athlete who quite possibly goes on to inspire other athletes or one day become an Olympian.

Remember that respondent conditioning occurs virtually all the time, regardless of the learning situation or ancillary learning that might simultaneously occur. This is because respondent conditioning is an unconscious and automatic learning process that occurs whether or not you want it to occur and that teaches involuntary emotional responses such as like or dislike, excitement or ennui, and pleasure or fear. It also teaches (induces) physiological responses such as anxiety or relaxation, and nervousness or calmness. And these responses lead to either adaptive or maladaptive athlete behaviors. Through this process you can condition your athletes to become like Al, who learned to love platform diving, or you can condition them to become like the novice runner in scenario 2, who learned to dislike running and try a different sport. The choice is yours.

THE SALIVATING COACH

Like my dog Jackson and like my father Hank (and perhaps like that doomed pheasant Jackson snared that glorious morning—we will never know!), the most passionate athletes are the most successful athletes. The same is true for coaches: The most passionate coaches are the most successful coaches. The **salivating coach** is the coach who is passionate about the sport and working with athletes, the coach who turns kids on to the sport, the coach like Morry, the coach who creates the perfect respondent conditioning environment for learning, the coach who engenders in athletes a lasting love of the sport. Without the salivating coach it is unlikely there is the salivating athlete. The dancer and dance are inseparable.

YOUR COACHING TOOLBOX

The third tool in your coaching toolbox, respondent conditioning theory, helps you gain perspective on your athletes: why they develop certain physiological, emotional, and behavioral responses to your sport; what types of responses they can or will form; and how you can control your practice environment to ensure your athletes develop healthy, positive, and appropriate responses. When you turn on your athletes to your sport, you tap into a wellspring of emotion, energy, enthusiasm, passion, and love—and create the salivating athlete.

THE SCIENTIFIC AND ARTFUL COACH

As a scientific coach, you understand the theory of respondent conditioning and its influence on the learning environment and athlete development. With this knowledge, you, the empowered scientific coach, design a program in which you maximize pleasant unconditioned stimuli and minimize unpleasant unconditioned stimuli. You evaluate athlete readiness so that success and satisfaction are likely to occur. You establish an athlete learning attitude that emphasizes effort, change, and performance. And you act as a source of pleasant stimuli. This atmosphere is not created accidentally, but rather through conscious, careful, and deliberate scientific planning. Little if any hidden curriculum exists in your program.

As an artful coach, on the other hand, you create a program in which your athletes pair fun, joy, and excitement with your sport. You do this in part by providing praise, warmth, humor, encouragement, and acceptance. You also model behaviors that you hope to see in your athletes. You arrive at practice excited, you have fun at practice, and you find joy in your sport and in working with young people. Your behaviors imbue your practices with pleasant unconditioned stimuli that encourage your athletes to experience positive unconditioned responses and pair these responses with your sport.

The importance of the artful coach in action cannot be understated. Take, for example, the warm, personable, and encouraging coach who has that magic touch for challenging kids, creating teachable moments, and turning kids on to a sport at an early age. The artful coach is keenly attuned to the type of stimuli he or she is pairing with the sport and works untiringly to monitor and maintain a learning environment that creates the salivating athlete, the athlete who loves the sport and can't wait for the next practice.

Love is not a very scientific term. It is neither easily defined nor readily available for observation and scientific study. However, we know it when we experience it. For example, Coach Arbini (see p. 97) had a genuine love for his sport and his athletes, and he created an atmosphere that encouraged his young athletes also to love the sport and to love everything associated with it: early morning practices, hard work, teammates, the competition both within the team and between other teams, learning new dives, the smell of chlorine, and much more. I don't think it is possible to observe or measure the love that the artful coach brings to his sport, but athletes recognize, experience, and cherish it nonetheless.

IF YOU REMEMBER ONLY THREE THINGS

1. *Remember to help athletes, particularly young athletes, learn to love what they do.* Through the use of respondent conditioning, you influence your athletes' emotions, physiological responses, desires, and motivation. Like the teacher who turns on kids to reading, turn on your athletes to your sport. By creating the salivating athlete, you create the persistent athlete who is likely to remain a part of your sport forever; and you create the passionate athlete, the athlete who can accomplish nearly anything.

2. *Remember to avoid the hidden curriculum.* Be diligent so that little, if any, learning within your program goes unnoticed or happens by chance. Consciously control the pairing of neutral stimuli with unconditioned stimuli so that you create a learning environment that results in not only the learning of appropriate motor skills and performance, but also the learning of positive emotional and physiological responses.

3. *Remember to minimize unpleasant stimuli and maximize pleasant stimuli.* This may sound like a simple request but it isn't always so simple. When the season isn't going so well, when your job might be on the line, when you have suffered successive defeats, or when you are as tired as your athletes and no hope seems in sight, you still must manage to keep a smile, be upbeat, and remain a source of pleasant stimuli for your athletes. You avoid taking out your frustration and discouragement on your athletes, you continue to be the calm in the midst of the storm, and, most importantly, you endeavor to keep it fun.

SUGGESTED READINGS

Bloom, B.S. (1985). *Developing talent in young people.* New York: Ballantine Books.

[Bloom's book is a wonderful read on working with gifted young people and offers great insights and suggestions for coaches working with youth.]

Fried, R.L. (2001). *The passionate teacher: A practical guide.* Boston: Beacon Press.

[What better title for the aspiring salivating coach? Books like this help us rekindle the fire for being the passionate coach.]

Gibbons, T., Hill, R., McConnell, A., Forster, T., & Moore, J. (2002). *The path to excellence: A comprehensive view of development of U.S. Olympians who competed from 1984-1998.* Results of the Talent Identification and Development Questionnaire to U.S. Olympians. A USOC 2002 publication.

Gibbons, T., McConnell, A., Forster, T., Tuffey-Riewald, S., and Peterson, K. (2003). *Reflections on success: U.S. Olympians describe the success factors and obstacles that most influenced their Olympic development.* Results of the Talent Identification and Development Questionnaire to U.S. Olympians. A USOC 2003 publication.

[Both of these articles are interesting, but if you read only one, read the second one. It lists some factors and obstacles that coaches should be aware of. For example, one factor that athletes list is having a coach who has tactical and skill knowledge. It behooves all coaches to continually improve their knowledge of skills and tactics and thus improve their effectiveness.]

Lewis, M. (2005). *Coach: Lessons on the game of life.* New York: Norton.

[An extremely short and simple but emotionally moving read about an author who looks back 30 years to his high school baseball coach and the lessons his coach taught him about life. It's worth the 60 minutes to read.]

Shaara, M. (1999). *For love of the game.* New York: Ballentine Books.

[This is a book that was turned into a movie starring Kevin Costner as Billy Chapel and Kelly Preston as Jane Aubrey. It reminds coaches and athletes about the love of playing sports and why athletes play and why coaches teach.]

CHAPTER 4

The Athlete in the Skinner Box

Applying Operant Conditioning Theory

Key Terms

athlete in the Skinner box

champion behavior

coach in the Skinner box

combined schedule

continuous reinforcement

delayed feedback

discrimination

exclusion

extinction

extinction rate

extrinsic feedback

fixed schedule

generalization

generalized reinforcer

informational feedback

instantaneous feedback

intermittent reinforcement

interval schedule

intrinsic feedback

isolation

knowledge of performance

knowledge of results

motivating feedback

negative reinforcement

negative reinforcer

nonexclusion

operant

operant conditioning

perceptual trace

positive reinforcement

positive reinforcer

prepractice reference

presentation punishment

primary reinforcer

random schedule

ratio schedule

reference of correctness

reinforcement

reinforcer

removal punishment

reprimands

respondent conditioning

response cost

schedule of reinforcement

shaping

Skinner box

summary feedback

time-outs

variable schedule

Not long ago, Marc, a former diver of mine, called to ask me some questions for a documentary on the sport of diving he was contemplating making. He asked me a surprisingly simple question, a question I had never asked myself. "When did you know you were hooked on the sport?" How had I been associated with the sport as an athlete and coach for nearly 50 years and never considered this question? And now, in the twilight of my coaching career, I confronted it. With little hesitation I visualized the color yellow. *Why the color yellow?* I asked myself. After all these years, I had nearly forgotten about the medal—the medal that hooked me.

I was 11 years old, and my family and I were vacating in northern California. My father noticed there was a diving competition nearby and suggested I enter it even though I was a novice diver. Prior to Marc's question and my ensuing moment of recollection, I never realized how much I had in common with Jimmy, the young boy I worked with those many years ago at Cypress College when I began my coaching career. I wasn't gangly or awkward like Jimmy, but I was small for my age, self-conscious and, like Jimmy, desperately in need of self-affirmation, of achieving something to cure my deep-seated case of insecurity blues and to prove my competency and self-worth. At that northern California competition, I miraculously earned, for the first time in my adolescent life, a medal. Not a flimsy ribbon like the kiddy ribbons I had won in the past. This was the real deal, big-time hardware, something solid I could bite into, something I could get my hands firmly around, something that screamed achievement, competency, and success. I decided that day to become a diver. Thank goodness they gave medals down to fifth place. The ribbon attached to that beautiful bronze medal was yellow.

Over the years I safeguarded the medal, ensconcing it in a handmade wooden box with a glass top, lovingly placed next to other precious keepsakes. A fifth place medal from a 12-and-under age group invitational meet nestled next to commemorative medals from Olympic Games, world championships, Pan American Games, and other noteworthy competitions. The medal meant that much to me. I would like to say I still have that medal, but I don't. Someone else is its caretaker now.

I recognized *the look* on Oliver's face the first time I met him; the same look I had seen on Jimmy's face that first day of practice at Cypress College many years ago; and the same look that must have been on my eleven-year-old face. A look that said, "I need to prove something to myself." A look that asked, "Am I a person of worth?" Nature doesn't distribute genes uniformly or, for that matter, fairly. Like grass seed tossed and scattered wildly into the wind on a spring day, genes haphazardly spread by some random force of nature I don't understand. Oliver's brother received the classroom learning genes while Oliver inherited the motor learning genes. His brother matriculated to Cambridge College and after graduation accepted a prestigious job with the internet company Google in their London office. Oliver was a bright child; he just learned differently from his brother and often more slowly than his classmates. Like other young students with similar learning disabilities, Oliver simultaneously could become frustrated, furious, forlorn, fractious, and forgetful, especially when it came time to do his homework. He found refuge from these emotions and his classroom failures in sport.

Sport was his safe haven, his classroom where he was the straight-A performer, his kingdom where he was lord and master, overseer of sweet success and a sense of competency and self-worth. Although he was only twelve when I first met him, our connection was instantaneous, I guess because we shared *the look*. He trained at my camp for a few weeks that summer and then returned home to Great Britain. Although he had left, he remained in my thoughts and not long after his departure I sat down and penned him a letter. At the conclusion of the letter I wrote, "And I hope the enclosed medal brings you as much luck and success as it did me." So Oliver is the new owner of the fifth place bronze medal with the yellow ribbon. I am not sure where he keeps it, but I hope it has a place of honor. I like to think it's resting comfortably now next to the gold medal he won several years later when he became the youngest national champion in the history of Great Britain diving.

The consequences of our behaviors have an indelible effect on our future behaviors. Consider the following story.

Some time ago, I recruited a young man named Jon who came from a private school in Baltimore, Maryland. He wasn't the best student in his high school (it was very competitive) but he was a good student nonetheless. He made an official recruiting visit. After getting to know him, I decided that I absolutely had to have him on my team. He was a phenomenal kid who loved Indiana University (IU) and wanted more than anything to be a part of my program. The only catch was getting him into school. Our admissions director at the time thought that because Jon was ranked rather low in his class, he should not be admitted because Indiana University had already declined admission to several other students at Jon's high school who were ranked above him.

I tried to have him admitted as a sponsored student. This sponsorship process took way too long. I can remember Jon calling me as he was packing his car and getting ready to drive with his parents to Bloomington—in late August—and asking me if he thought he would be admitted. At that point I still had not received confirmation about his admittance and I couldn't tell him for sure that he had been or would be admitted. Still, I told him I believed very strongly he would be admitted. Imagine: Jon was going to travel hundreds of miles to Indiana University on blind faith; he had no guarantee of being admitted.

That day I promised him I would never forget his devotion to me and the IU program and that if he did get into school I would give him my heart and soul. So, he and his parents left Baltimore and drove all the way to Bloomington, Indiana without any tacit assurance that he would matriculate to Indiana University. Of course, I wouldn't be telling this story if he had not been admitted. He did get into school. And every day at practice I gave him my heart and soul. And I praised him for his loyalty, devotion, effort, and determination. When we won our first men's national team title, he voluntarily threw a list of dives on the 10-meter platform, even though he wasn't much of a platform diver. He nearly wiped out on one dive, but his effort scored team points and helped us win that title. He was the ultimate team player.

It has been a decade since he graduated but I regularly receive a call from him, just checking in with me to see how my family is doing and how the program is progressing. My wife Lesa and I attended his wedding in Baltimore. When I think of Jon, I think not only of a man of great character but also of how much reinforcement coaches receive in return when they reinforce the behaviors they want to see in their athletes. Athlete behaviors reinforce coach behaviors. A week didn't go by without my thanking him for his faith in me and in *our* program. I would shake his hand or pat him on the back after practice for his effort that day and praise him for his continual improvement . I appointed him team captain his senior year, presented him with the award for most improved athlete, and hugged him after we won our first national team championship. Jon was never the best diver on our team, but he was the heart and soul of our team. And he represented the best of what our team could and did become as both athletes and human beings.

Athletes ultimately practice and perform for the love of the sport, for the sheer pleasure of it, for the flow-like experience. But don't discount the immense and immeasurable effectiveness a well-timed, aptly chosen, and meaningful simple reward such as a fifth place medal with a yellow ribbon can have in reinforcing and shaping athlete behavior. Using the tools of operant conditioning theory, such as reinforcement, an athlete's behavior can be shaped much like B.F. Skinner shaped the behavior of rats in his controlled environment known as the Skinner box. This chapter is the story of the athlete in the Skinner box and how you can use principle of operant conditioning theory to shape the behavior of your athletes. This chapter also is the story of the coach in the Skinner box and how principles of operant conditioning shape our behavior much like Jon shaped my behavior.

CHAPTER OVERVIEW

The chapter begins with a brief discussion about the difference between respondent and operant conditioning. How exactly does operant conditioning work? The chapter examines the operant conditioning paradigm and plugs in some specific real-life examples of athlete behaviors. Next is reinforcement and how it functions to shape behavior. Then it examines eight operant conditioning coaching tools for influencing your athletes' behaviors and considers different types of schedules of reinforcement. A section describes four types of athlete behaviors to consider when using operant conditioning: social, learning, motor, and champion. Finally, it offers some specific applications of operant conditioning for coaching effectiveness.

SKINNER'S OPERANT CONDITIONING THEORY

While Pavlov was influential in the introduction of respondent conditioning, B.F. Skinner, one of the most influential psychologists of the 20th century, is the originator and main spokesperson for the theory of operant conditioning.

As mentioned in chapter 3, Thorndike (i.e., his law of effect) was a precursor to operant conditioning theory but Skinner was among the first psychologists to distinguish between two types of behavior. In one condition, many responses can be engendered by a stimulus and can become conditioned to other stimuli through the process Pavlov described. Skinner referred to these responses as elicited responses and he labeled the behavior *respondent* because it occurs in response to a stimulus. However, Skinner claimed that another condition or class of behaviors exist that are not elicited by any known stimuli. Rather, they are emitted responses. Skinner labeled them **operant** responses because they are operations the individual performs. To clarify, in the case of **respondent conditioning**, the individual reacts to the environment, whereas in the case of **operant conditioning**, the individual acts upon the environment. Another difference between the two behaviors is that, as mentioned earlier, respondents are primarily involuntary, whereas operants are more voluntary.

As noted in chapter 3, responses such as fear, anxiety, foreboding, joy, and pleasure are all largely automatic, involuntary, and mainly conditioned responses to specific situations and specific conditioned stimuli. In contrast, operants, such as solving a mathematics problem, running, shooting a basketball, and hitting a baseball are deliberate, intentional, and voluntary responses brought about not by conditioned stimuli but by personally controlled actions rather than reactions.

While Thorndike believed that the effect of reinforcement is to strengthen the bond between the stimulus and the response, Skinner stated that the stimulus is often unknown and, in any case, irrelevant to learning. The most important link or bond formed is between the response and the reinforcement, not between the stimulus and the response. According to Skinner's operant conditioning theory, when an emitted response is reinforced, the probability increases that the response will be repeated.

Operant Conditioning Paradigm

To understand more about operant conditioning, Skinner studied animals. In a typical Skinnerian experiment, a rat is placed in a **Skinner box** (a small, controlled environment constructed to ensure that certain responses are likely to be made), responses are measured, and the responses are either rewarded or punished. For a typical Skinner experiment the box consists of a lever, a light, an electric floor grid, and a food tray. Training a rat to depress the lever is simple. When the rat depresses the lever, the light illuminates and a food pellet drops into the tray. Very quickly most rats learn to depress the lever to receive food. They continue to depress the lever for a while even if they no longer receive a food pellet. Training a rat to not depress the lever also is simple. When the rat depresses the lever, the floor grid conducts a mild electric current. A rat also can be trained to depress the lever if doing so turns off the electric current.

You can learn most of what you need to know about Skinner's operant conditioning theory from observations of the Skinner box. The rat's behavior of depressing the lever is an operant (an almost random behavior that is emitted by the rat rather than elicited by a specific stimulus). The food pellet is the reinforcer that serves to increase the probability that the rat's action of pressing the lever will reoccur. The mild electric current is the punishment that serves to decrease the probability that the rat's action is likely to reoccur. Figure 4.1 outlines Skinner's operant conditioning paradigm.

Although the rat emits a number of responses, only the lever pressing action is rewarded. Consequently, through operant conditioning the probability increases that the rat will press the lever again. Additionally, operant conditioning theory posits that whatever discriminative stimuli (SD) were present during the time of reinforcement are stimuli that after learning may bring about the operant. In the case of the rat and the Skinner box, the sight of the box may function as an SD for a lever-pressing response. Skinner would

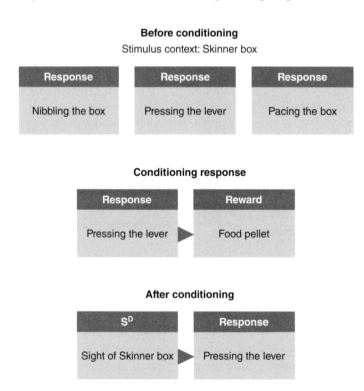

Figure 4.1 Skinner's operant conditioning paradigm.

argue that SDs function as signals indicating that a certain behavior may lead to a specific reinforcement.

Now, examine the operant conditioning paradigm while considering scenario 1, in which the athlete arrives early to practice and immediately begins stretching. Figure 4.2 outlines the conditioning process.

Scenario 1

An athlete arrives early for practice and immediately begins stretching. While stretching, her coach spends time talking with her, giving her extra attention, and praising her for her eagerness, promptness, and desire. The athlete continues to arrive early for practice throughout the remainder of the season.

It is important to notice that in scenario 1 the athlete is being reinforced not merely for arriving early to practice but for arriving early and beginning to stretch. How often have you seen athletes arrive early, waste time fooling around, and then be the last ones to begin practice? Although it is important for athletes to enjoy camaraderie and a certain amount of jesting creates a

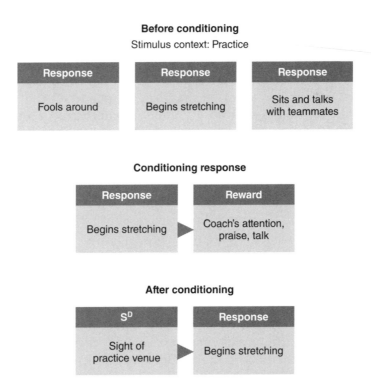

Figure 4.2 Operant conditioning for an athlete arriving early to practice.

relaxed and jovial atmosphere conducive for learning, practice time is precious and not to be squandered. One of my athletes exhibited this bad behavior. However, when I applied principles of respondent conditioning, by the end of first semester she started arriving early and getting immediately into her warm-up routine just like the athlete in scenario 1. Do you have athletes that might respond similarly?

Reinforcement and Reinforcer

Two terms associated with operant conditioning are *reinforcer* and *reinforcement*. According to Skinner, a **reinforcer** is a stimulus that causes reinforcement; **reinforcement** is the process of using this stimulus. In the example of the rat in the Skinner box, the pellet is the reinforcer and the dispensing of the pellet after the lever is press is the reinforcement.

The accepted definition of a reinforcer is *any stimulus that increases the probability that a response will occur.* In other words, the effect of a stimulus determines whether or not it is reinforcing. For example, an athlete singled out at a team meeting and reprimanded for loud behavior may find the attention reinforcing and be likely to repeat the undesirable behavior at the next team meeting. In another situation, an athlete may be praised in front of the team for exemplary behavior but find the attention embarrassing and not reinforcing. The point is that a stimulus might be highly reinforcing for one athlete but not for another. Consequently, it is important for the artful coach to be sensitive to each learning situation and to differences between athletes and what they find reinforcing.

Two types of reinforcers exist: primary and generalized. A **primary reinforcer** is a stimulus that is naturally reinforcing (i.e., the individual does not have to learn reinforcing). Primary reinforcers are generally related to an unlearned need or drive, such as food, drink, or sex. These stimuli tend to be highly reinforcing and are referred to as positive stimuli. A **generalized reinforcer** is a previously neutral stimulus that, through repeated pairing with other reinforcers in different contexts, has become generally reinforcing. For example, success, prestige, notoriety, and money are examples of powerful generalized reinforcers. The importance of success is discussed in greater depth later in this chapter.

Reinforcers can be either positive or negative. A **positive reinforcer** is a stimulus that increases the probability that a response will occur when added to the learning situation. Positive reinforcers tend to be pleasant stimuli. A **negative reinforcer** is a stimulus that increases the probability that a response will occur when the stimulus is removed from the situation. Negative reinforcers tend to be aversive stimuli such as the mild electric shock the rat receives in the Skinner box. The electric shock acts as a negative reinforcer if it is only turned off when the rat makes the correct response of depressing the lever. In other words, once the rat depresses the lever, it is rewarded with no longer receiving the electric shock. Obviously athletes do not need such terrible negative reinforcers; they may experience a few less odious types of negative reinforcers such as glares and disapproval.

Imagine that you want to have the rat cease depressing the lever. In this case, if you administer a shock every time it depresses the lever, the shock acts as a form of punishment and the behavior is likely to cease. The two types of punishment are **presentation punishment** (sometimes referred to as *castigation*, *positive*, or *type I punishment*) and **removal punishment** (sometimes referred to as *penalty*, *negative*, or *type II punishment*)The next section examines in more detail the two types of reinforcement and then the two types of punishment and the process of extinction.

Positive Reinforcement (Reward)

Positive reinforcement is the presentation of a pleasant stimulus that acts as a reward and increases the probability that a response will reoccur. Examples of positive reinforcers in coaching include smiles, praise, attention, and compliments, to name a few. Feedback also can be a form of positive reinforcement. Examples of positive reinforcement available to athletes include reaching goals, winning medals, positive statements from teammates, and feedback from coaches (e.g., "Nice job, Raj! The racket placement on your backhand was perfect!").

Consider scenario 2, in which the golfer continually uses a slow backswing. Instead of criticizing her slow speed, you might decide to wait until her swing speeds up, even if only slightly, and praise her for the correction. Or, you might have her set a goal of performing the correct club speed five consecutive times and then praise her when she meets that goal.

Scenario 2

Your sophomore athlete on the high school golf team continues to bring her golf club back too slowly in her backswing. You are at the point where you are tired of continually telling her to bring the club back faster. It is early in the season and a good time to make swing changes.

Numerous examples of positive reinforcement exist, but coaches do not use them as often as they should. Perhaps coaches are always looking for the mistakes in motor performance and trying to correct these mistakes. In their zeal to help athletes improve and reach their goals, coaches often overlook and fail to recognize the good things athletes do and the corrections they make to improve their performances.

Negative Reinforcement (Relief)

Negative reinforcement is the relief (removal) of an aversive stimulus that increases the probability that a response will occur. Implicit or explicit threats of punishment, failure, detention, ridicule, anger, and evil stare are all examples of negative reinforcement if they are removed after the appropriate behavior is demonstrated. As mentioned earlier, an example of a negative reinforcer is the electric current running through the floor grid. If the current could be turned off only by pressing the lever, then the current would act as a negative reinforcer. Negative and maladaptive behaviors can occur with the zealous use of negative reinforcement. In general, most, but not all, types of negative reinforcement are inappropriate and unacceptable coaching tools.

Since you can't use electric shock as a negative reinforcer for your athletes, a more appropriate (and humane) example would be the use of a glare. Consider scenario 3 in which two athletes are talking while you are talking to your team. In this scenario, you might glare at the two athletes until they cease talking. A glare also might be useful in encouraging athletes to perform the correct movement. For example, you might use a glare when an athlete repeatedly makes the same mistake. Instead of saying anything, you simply look at him. Once he has performed the correct movement, you remove your gaze.

Scenario 3

It is early in the season and you are talking about an important topic: mental preparation for competing in the championship at the end of the season. It is important because a number of your athletes choked at last season's championship and you don't want to see them choke again. While you are talking to the entire team, two athletes continue talking to each other and ignoring your talk. This is not only distracting to the other athletes but rude behavior directed at you.

Presentation Punishment

Presentation punishment (castigation) involves the presentation of an aversive stimulus after a response is emitted in an attempt to eliminate the response. Most often, presentation punishment refers to physical punishment. A number of objections and negative side effects are associated with negative punishment. However, sometimes it becomes necessary to administer punishment and some less harsh, more acceptable forms of punishment other than physical punishment are available. These forms of punishment include reprimand, time-out, and response cost.

Reprimands are censures or reproofs that let athletes know their behaviors are inappropriate and must cease. Reprimands can be mild or harsh and can be verbal or nonverbal, such as shaking your finger at an athlete. Verbal reprimands are effective if they identify the inappropriate behavior and provide specific rationales for why the behavior is inappropriate (Van Houten & Doleys, 1983). For example, when an athlete makes an inappropriate joke about another athlete on the team, it is more effective to say, "Terrell, don't say things like that because those types of comments about teammates are inappropriate and harm team unity and team spirit," rather than to simply say, "Terrell, don't say that."

Reprimands are best administered softly and at a close distance. In one study, Van Houten, Nau, MacKenzie-Keating, Sameoto, and Colavecchia (1982) found that the most effective reprimands were from a distance of 1 meter. Also, reprimands should be simple and unobtrusive so that practice activity continues uninterrupted.

Time-outs involve removing athletes from a situation in which they would normally receive reinforcement and placing them in a situation in which they do not receive reinforcement. Brantner and Doherty (1983) identify three types of time-outs that classroom teachers can use, and therefore coaches can use them, too. The first time-out is isolation. **Isolation** involves removing the athlete from the practice environment. For example, the athlete might be told to sit in the locker room. The second time-out procedure is **exclusion**. With this type of time-out the athlete is excluded from the ongoing activity and is not allowed to participate or watch. The mildest form of time-out is called **nonexclusion**. In this time-out procedure, the athlete is allowed to watch practice but not allowed to participate.

The final type of effective punishment is response cost. **Response cost** occurs when athletes lose reinforcers for inappropriate behavior. For example, you might set up a point system where your athletes receive points for good behavior but lose points for misbehavior. Such a system is similar to token reinforcement, which is used in classrooms. One advantage of response cost is that it does not remove the athlete from the learning environment. Another advantage of response cost is that it is associated with a reinforcement procedure. As previously discussed, using reinforcement has many benefits.

Consider scenario 4, in which the athlete continually forgets his coach's instructions. Some forgetfulness is understandable and part of human nature, but when it happens repeatedly, team members can perceive it as a sign of disrespect toward the coach and program. It also can negatively affect the practice atmosphere and learning environment. It is best to confront the athlete privately, but if it continues to persist, you will need to address it publicly and administer a reprimand so that the offending athlete and other team members know exactly where you stand on the issue and what type of learning behavior you expect from each of your players. Without taking a stand, you may lose the respect and control of your team and program.

In one sense, scenario 4 is a discipline problem. In another sense, it is a motor learning issue and an operant conditioning issue. Without demonstrating appropriate learning behavior (i.e., paying attention to your coaching comments), your athletes are likely to learn much less during practice than they are capable of learning. So, to eliminate inappropriate behavior and improve your practice learning atmosphere, you administer the operant conditioning

---

Scenario 4

One of your athletes continually forgets to do what you tell him to do. His forgetfulness borders on rudeness and lack of respect toward the coach. His behavior is affecting the practice and learning environment because your other athletes observe the rude behavior and are put off by it. Some of the younger athletes wonder why they have to follow your instructions but the offending athlete does not.

---

tool of presentation punishment. I use scenario 4 because it is a situation I once faced. The athlete was extremely talented and a nice person, but somewhat obstinate and set in his learning patterns.

In this case, immediately after he performed a dive I asked the diver, "What was the correction you were supposed to make on that dive?" If he responded, "I don't remember," I would reprimand him in front of the other athletes for failing to accomplish such a simple request that other team members easily mastered. Usually, I don't care for public reprimand, but in this case I needed to let the other athletes know that I would not tolerate forgetting my comments. Also, I didn't want the other athletes to think I was playing favorites. They had to remember my comments, so why shouldn't he? It's a simple process: I provide instruction and they remember that instruction and give every effort to make the correction. If the diver in scenario 4 forgot my corrections more than three times, I dismissed him from practice. He was a good kid at heart and sincerely wanted to become a good diver, so not being allowed to practice was punishment.

After some time, his ability to remember my comments improved and so did his diving. I am happy to report that 2 years later he was Big Ten champion on both 1-meter and 3-meter springboard and NCAA All-American in those events as well.

Removal Punishment

Removal punishment (penalty) involves the removal (loss) of a positive stimulus following a behavior (penalty). It is referred to as removal because a positive stimulus is taken away (lost), unlike presentation punishment where an aversive stimulus is presented. An example of removal punishment would be the removal (loss) of playing a game or fun drill after practice because a player misbehaved or fooled around and didn't finish the designed workout. The player is permitted to engage in the game after finishing the workout.

Many athletes respond well to this type of punishment. You ask them to raise their level of expectation, behavior, and performance to a height you know they can attain. If they fall short of this level, then they endure a penalty which in this case is the removal of a positive stimulus (privilege). In a sense, their fate lies in their own hands. Giving a greater physical, emotional, and mental effort helps them avoid the penalty. It is important to remind your athletes that practice is a *privilege,* not a right, and certainly not something they have to do. If my athletes ever said, "I have to practice," I reminded them that in fact they do not *have* to practice; they *get* to practice, and if they didn't want to practice, they could take the day off, and the week off, and, actually, the whole year off. My point is that it is a privilege to attend practice, and as coach you should see it that way and so should your athletes. This is one reason, among many, why you should never use practice as punishment. Some considerations with regard to administering punishment are discussed next.

Considerations Regarding Punishment

In summary, coaches must remember several points with regard to reinforcement and punishment. First, remember that you can use both positive (pleasant) and negative (aversive) stimuli for both reinforcement and punishment. Second, remember that whether or not a stimulus is reinforcing depends on the effect it has on the person's behavior. If the stimulus causes the behavior to reoccur, then it is reinforcing. Third, remember that even though punishment is effective in affecting behavior, a case can be made against punishment, particularly physical punishment:

• Ethical and humanitarian considerations exist against the use of physical punishment. Moreover, legal considerations make physical punishment an undesirable tool for shaping behavior. Physical punishment is against national governing body rules, most school codes for teacher and coach conduct and student rights, and, as it should be against a coach's philosophy for working with athletes, particularly young athletes.

• Punishment draws attention to inappropriate behavior but generally does not illustrate appropriate behavior. However, note that punishment avoids this negative outcome when used along with reasoning and other corrective actions.

• Punishment is often accompanied by highly undesirable emotional side effects such as hatred, fear, and anxiety that can be associated with the punisher rather than the punished behavior. These side effects can disrupt the bond between athlete and coach.

• Punishment does not always eliminate inappropriate behavior but simply the suppression of the behavior. Consequently, because it is suppressed but not forgotten, the inappropriate behavior can reappear under the right conditions. For example, in one study (McFadden et al., 1992) that looked at the use of punishment in nine Florida schools, punishment seemed to have little effect on recidivism, which is the repetition of offenses. In other words, punishment simply was not achieving the desired goal of eliminating misbehavior.

• Punishment can cause frustration on the part of the athlete and lead to additional undesirable or maladaptive behaviors, such as avoidance and acting out. Avoidance learning (learning to avoid unpleasant stimulus contexts) and escape learning (learning to escape from unpleasant stimulus contexts) are both potential results from using punishment.

• A coach who punishes violent behavior with violence provides a model of aggressive behavior for athletes. Using violence as punishment may suggest to the athlete that aggressive behavior is appropriate at certain times.

Sometimes circumstances occur in which punishment has to be administered for the good of the misbehaving athlete and for the betterment of the team and program. However, because of the overwhelmingly negative aspects of punishment, it should be administered sparingly and wisely. Administered unwisely, it can lead to some sad results. Consider the coach who withholds water breaks as a form of punishment on a hot and humid day for a football or basketball practice and some of the athletes become sick and have to be taken to the hospital.

For whatever reason, some coaches think that dishing out punishment is a big part of coaching—which it isn't—and that punishment leads to greater discipline and respect—which it doesn't. Coaches of excellence know how to administer punishment, but they are much more interested in commanding respect and instilling discipline using a more subtle and artful approach. When I think of great coaches, legendary basketball coach John Wooden comes to mind. I see him sitting quietly and patiently on the bench during a basketball game with his rolled up game program in one hand and his other hand gesturing like a maestro gently swaying his baton as he instructs his players where to position themselves.

As Thorndike (1931) pointed out, pleasure is much more potent in stamping in responses than pain is in stamping them out. So, use pleasure as often as possible to reinforce good behaviors.

Extinction

Extinction is the cessation of a response as a result of the withdrawal of reinforcement. Since reinforcement maintains a response, removing the reinforcement over time will cause the response to disappear. The time between the removal of reinforcement and the cessation of the behavior is called the **extinction rate**.

The use of extinction is quite common, probably because it is effective and is perhaps the easiest operant conditioning technique to apply. Often its application involves nothing more difficult than the withdrawal of an obvious reinforcement, such as attention in the case of an attention-seeking athlete. Sometimes, however, it may be difficult to identify the source of the reinforcement because the reinforcement is less obvious or in some cases unknown. For example, take the athlete who continually shows off and acts condescendingly toward teammates. What reinforcement maintains this behavior? It could be a number of potential reinforcers, such as peer attention or rebellion.

Extinction also may be difficult to use because withholding reinforcement may not be possible. For example, consider athletes who continually use poor technique but because of variables, such as natural talent or early maturation, are still capable of receiving decent results in competition. Their competition results could be even better with better technique, but the technique remains the same because the athletes continue to outperform their competitors (reinforcement). How do coaches use extinction in this situation? Ask the judges to give their athletes lower marks? Ask your athletes' competitors to run or swim faster? Ask the opposing pitcher to throw tougher pitches to your player? Of course, the answer is that these types of athletes need to be encouraged to focus on performance goals rather than competition goals. "Yes, you ran a good time, but you could run even faster if you worked on your start and running mechanics."

In general, though, extinction is an extremely useful tool because of its effectiveness and ease of application. For example, going back to scenario 2, in which the golfer's backswing is too slow, you might decide to simply ignore her slow swing because every time she was slow, she received your attention, which she found reinforcing. It may sound funny, but it can be quite true: The athlete craves the coach's attention and perhaps unknowingly makes the same mistake to attract attention. Why? Well, some coaches only look for the bad. So, on those occasions when she does demonstrate the correct speed on her backswing, her coach might not say anything to her. By withholding attention for incorrect backswing speed (extinction) and providing attention for correct backswing speed (reinforcement), you may extinguish the incorrect speed and stamp in the correct speed.

Shaping

Recall the rat in the Skinner box. Once the rat emitted the operant response of depressing the lever, it was rewarded with a pellet. But what if the rat never actually makes the response? Of course, in the Skinner box there isn't much for the rat to do, so eventually it gets around to depressing the lever. But in real life, responses sometimes aren't always emitted. In this case, behavior can be affected through the operant conditioning principle of shaping.

Shaping is the differential reinforcement of successive approximations. Shaping is a technique for teaching individuals complex behaviors that were not previously in their repertoires. The technique involves reinforcing responses that become increasingly closer approximations of the final desired behavior. For example, consider scenario 5, in which you want one of your athletes to make eye contact when you provide feedback. In this case, you might wait until the athlete glances in your direction before providing feedback (remember that feedback is a form of reinforcement). Next, you might withhold feedback until the athlete looks at you for at least 2 seconds and then you provide feedback. Next, you might wait until the athlete looks at you for a significant period of time before providing feedback as well as praise. Then, you can say, "Connie, your form was terrific that time and I like the way you looked at me while I was talking. Thank you!"

Besides being used to shape learning behavior, shaping also is useful for facilitating changes in motor movement behavior. For example, you might be working on getting athletes to grab lower on their tucks in somersaulting dives. On their first attempts, they might grab only slightly lower. Although this is not the desired final behavior, it is a response in the right direction, so you would reinforce the response by saying something such as this: "Well, that was a tiny bit lower. Good job. Let's see if you can grab *lower* on the next one." If on the next attempt the grab is not lower, you might simply withhold feedback or say, "No, that wasn't any lower. Try again." If on the next attempt the grab is lower than the first attempt, then you might reinforce that response. You continue this process until the desired low grab is achieved.

Another example of shaping is the weightlifter who doesn't lift up her head high enough on a squat. On her first attempt, she might place her head slightly higher and you say, "Good job. That was higher." On subsequent attempts, you delay positive reinforcement until the head moves even higher and closer to the correct head position on the downward movement of the squat.

Generalization and Discrimination

As a coach you are trying to reinforce all kinds of behaviors. These behaviors include a wide variety of responses, such as motor movements, social interactions, and emotional reactions. It is not possible to reinforce every response for every situation. However, people do seem to make the right responses, at least sometimes, under new situations. They do this through the processes of generalization and discrimination. **Generalization** is the process of transferring a response from one situation to another similar but never-before-encountered situation. As an example of generalization, consider the previous situation of learning to grab lower on a tuck. Say that the diver learned to grab lower on a forward somersaulting dive. Without any prompting from the coach, the diver transfers (generalizes) this response of grabbing lower to an inward somersaulting dive in the tuck position. In the case of the weightlifter performing squats, she might generalize lifting up her head when performing cleans just as she does when performing squats.

Table 4.1 Operant Conditioning Coaching Tools

Tool	Cue words	Explanation
Positive reinforcement	Reward	Presentation of positive stimulus
Negative reinforcement	Relief or removal	Removal of aversive stimulus
Presentation punishment	Presentation, castigation, positive, or Type I	Presentation of aversive stimulus
Removal punishment	Removal, penalty, negative, or Type II	Removal of positive stimulus
Shaping	Successive approximation	Reinforcing partial responses
Generalization	Similar	Responding in similar situation
Discrimination	Dissimilar	Not responding in dissimilar situation
Extinction	Withdrawal of reinforcement	Cessation of response

Discrimination is somewhat the opposite response of generalization. **Discrimination** involves refraining from making a response because the situation is dissimilar and the response would therefore be inappropriate. An example of discrimination would be when a quarterback is confronted with a defensive formation that is somewhat different from the formation he saw the opposing team use in its last game. Is it similar enough to generalize and call the play (make the response) or dissimilar enough to discriminate and not call that particular play (refrain from making the response)? In a sense, the defensive team's goal is to mask or hide its formation, making it difficult for the quarterback and other offensive players to identify the correct situation and appropriate response. This confusion on the part of the defense causes longer cognitive processing and slower reaction time on the part of the quarterback.

Table 4.1 provides a summary of the various operant conditioning coaching tools.

TYPES OF REINFORCEMENT SCHEDULES

Reinforcement can be useful in encouraging athletes to repeat a behavior in the future. However, it is important to understand the correct use of reinforcement. Consider the coach who constantly praises his athletes for everything they do. After a while, the coach's praise loses its potency and no longer acts as a reinforcer. There is a relationship between behavior and how reinforcement is administered, which is referred to as schedule of reinforcement.

Schedule of reinforcement is the time and frequency of presenting reinforcement to the athlete. In other words, when reinforcement is presented and how often it is presented has an effect on the behavior being reinforced. Recall, for example, the concept of extinction (p. 124). When reinforcement is withdrawn, the behavior eventually ceases to be emitted. On the other hand, Skinner noted that even a small reward will lead to the repetition of a behavior and the maintenance of that behavior over time. Too much reward (satiation), however, can lead to the cessation of that behavior, particularly when the reward is removed.

Reinforcement schedule matters because it influences the frequency and duration of a response being emitted. The following section discusses the various types of reinforcement schedules and their effects on behavior.

Continuous reinforcement is a reinforcement schedule in which every correct response is followed by a reinforcer. Research suggests that in the early stages of learning, continuous reinforcement is most effective. This fact suggests that initial learning, particularly for very young children, should involve a greater frequency of reinforcement than for later learning (Lee & Belfiore, 1997). This makes sense when you think of an athlete in the early stages of learning a new skill. It would be confusing and learning would progress more slowly if only some of the correct early responses were reinforced.

Although continuous reinforcement often leads to more rapid learning, it does not lead to longer retention. Moreover, when continuous reinforcement is removed the rate of extinction is much faster than for those behaviors that receive intermittent reinforcement. It is as though the athlete has become dependent upon the reinforcer and, once the reinforcer is removed, motivation to elicit the response is removed and the athlete ceases to emit the response. Continuous reinforcement creates external motivation rather than internal motivation.

Intermittent reinforcement is a schedule of reinforcement in which only some correct responses are reinforced. Also called *partial reinforcement,* intermittent reinforcement does not reinforce all correct responses. You can use several types of intermittent reinforcement schedules: ratio schedule, interval schedule, fixed schedule, random schedule, and combined schedule (see table 4.2).

A **ratio schedule** is an intermittent schedule of reinforcement that only reinforces a certain proportion of responses. For example, only every fourth correct response is reinforced.

An **interval schedule** is an intermittent schedule of reinforcement based on time. For example, a correct response is reinforced every 5 minutes.

A **fixed schedule** is an intermittent schedule of reinforcement in which reinforcement is provided at a fixed interval of time (an interval schedule) or after a specific number of responses (ratio schedule).

A **random schedule,** also known as *variable schedule,* is an intermittent schedule in which reinforcement is provided after an unpredictable amount of time (interval) or amount of responses (ratio).

Table 4.2 Different Types of Reinforcement Schedules

Type of reinforcement schedule	Reinforcement
Continuous	Every correct response is reinforced.
Intermittent	Only some correct responses are reinforced.
Ratio	Proportion of correct responses
Interval	Passage of certain amount of time
Fixed	Specific time or number of responses
Random	Unpredictable time or number of responses
Variable	Fixed interval and no correct response required
Combined intermittent schedules	**Reinforcement**
Fixed-ratio	Fixed proportion of correct responses
Fixed-interval	Fixed amount of time
Variable-ratio	Varying proportion of correct responses
Variable-interval	Varying amount of time

A **combined schedule** involves the use of a variety of different types of reinforcement schedules. For example, you could use a random-ratio schedule of reinforcement in which you provide reinforcement after a certain number of responses, but at unpredictable times.

The main point to remember about schedule of reinforcement is that it is best to begin with continuous reinforcement during early learning and then move to some type of intermittent schedule of reinforcement.

EXTRINSIC FEEDBACK AS REINFORCEMENT

Extrinsic feedback (EF) can be defined as sensory information provided to a learner by an outside source, such as a coach's comments, video replay, a judge's score, and so on. For the purpose of this chapter, extrinsic feedback most often refers to a coach's comments. Extrinsic feedback is information about the outcome of a movement and is in addition to intrinsic feedback, which is the sensory information that comes from outside the body (exteroception) or inside the body (proprioception). Two types of extrinsic feedback are available to you: knowledge of results (KR) and knowledge of performance (KP).

Knowledge of results is external, usually verbal or at least verbalizable, information that informs individuals about the success of their actions with regard to the intended goal. For example, a coach might tell an athlete, "You hooked that last shot with your five iron." In many cases, but not all cases, KR is redundant because often it is identical to intrinsic information. The golfer who hooks his five iron probably can see the shot hook. And the diver who enters the water very short of vertical on a reverse 2 ½ somersault probably (but not always) knows it via intrinsic feedback: "Coach, I know I went way short of vertical. I could feel the water hit the back of my legs."

However, some types of KR are not redundant with intrinsic feedback. For example, gymnasts must wait until the conclusion of their routines to receive their scores and know precisely how the judges evaluated their performances. In this case, KR is feedback about the overall execution and value of the routine, something the gymnasts might not be able to determine solely using intrinsic feedback.

Another case where KR is valuable is when the athlete is sensing incorrect or diminished intrinsic feedback. For example, a golfer who repeatedly does not bring the club back far enough in the backswing simply may not be feeling the incorrect movement: "Well, Coach, it feels like I am bringing it back far enough."

Knowledge of performance (KP) is feedback that provides the individual with information about the quality of the movement. KP also is sometimes referred to as *kinematic feedback* because it provides feedback about the displacement, velocity, acceleration, and other aspects of the movement. For example, consider the softball player who is working on her swing. Her coach might provide KP by saying, "Your bat speed is a little slow. Speed it up by 10% and keep your swing level to the ground." These comments are examples of KP because they contain information about the kinematics (in this case the velocity and movement pattern) of the movement. KP informs people about the quality of their movements, whereas KR provides information about the level of goal achievement.

So, how and when do coaches use extrinsic feedback in an operant conditioning paradigm? The following text explains.

APPLYING EXTRINSIC FEEDBACK USING OPERANT CONDITIONING IN COACHING ATHLETES

Use extrinsic feedback to reinforce movement. Reinforcement increases the probability that the individual will repeat the response. So, if you like what you see, then reinforce it with positive extrinsic feedback. Consider the golf coach who has been stressing to one of her golfers the importance of getting the club farther back on her backswing. The coach finally sees what she wants to see from her golfer and immediately reinforces the behavior with praise and positive feedback: "Great job, Jenny! That's the way to get that club back farther. Keep doing it!" A less effective coach might miss that opportunity to reinforce the behavior, perhaps focusing on another aspect of the swing that was deficient.

Research indicates that in the early stage of learning, particularly for very young children, continuous reinforcement is most effective (Lee & Belfiore, 1997). Continuous reinforcement in the form of praise and KR encourages error-free learning and maintains motivation. When KR is given for each trial (i.e., a relative frequency of 100%) it is helpful to performance because of temporary factors such as guidance and because of motivational and energizing properties (Schmidt & Lee, 2011). After the early stage of motor learning, however, it is better to reduce the relative frequency of KR (i.e., extrinsic feedback) as athletes becomes more proficient; otherwise, they become dependent on this information and fail to process feedback information in a way that helps them permanently learn the task. In other words, they use KR as a crutch (Schmidt & Lee, 2011).

Use motivating extrinsic feedback. **Motivating feedback** is defined as feedback about an individual's progress toward goal achievement that energizes and directs behavior. Because motivating feedback can translate into greater athlete effort, it is important to provide it immediately. Without this type of feedback, athletes can become discouraged and ineffective in practice. However, if you forget to comment on a noticeable improvement, do not despair. You can always remind athletes about their improvement before the next practice. For example, you might forget to compliment a swimmer on his improved breaststroke technique but at the start of the next practice you say, "David, I didn't get a chance to compliment you on your new and improved breaststroke action. It is really getting much better. It is almost what we want!"

Sometimes, athletes are doing the right things in practice but fail to see the improvement in the overall result. For example, the swimmer who changes his stroke pattern might initially swim slower until his new stroke becomes smooth and automatic. It is important, therefore, to remind your athletes that they are getting closer to their goals, even when the results might suggest otherwise. In a sense, using motivating feedback is like playing the game of hot and cold. As athletes get closer to their movement goals, your extrinsic feedback lets them know they are getting warmer. In other words, they are getting closer to their goals.

Research indicates that people who are given motivating feedback during practice report that they enjoy practice more, try harder, and practice longer (Duda & Treasure, 2006; Schmidt & Wrisberg, 2008). As was evident with the salivating athlete, a pleasurable experience paired with practice conditions athletes to associate a positive physiological response to their sport. Consequently, it is important for coaches, particularly coaches who work with youth, to provide motivating feedback during practice.

Use informational extrinsic feedback. **Informational feedback** is defined as feedback that provides performers with either descriptive or prescriptive error correction information. You can supply a great deal of information at any given moment. The coach of excellence, however, is capable of rapidly selecting the most pertinent information, distilling the information into a succinct and detailed form, and expeditiously providing it to the athlete so that the athlete can make corrections. Athletes, particularly elite-level athletes, find informational feedback to be highly motivating. They want to know what is wrong with their performance and how they can improve it.

Provide extrinsic feedback when requested. In a study by Janelle et al. (1997), subjects were asked to learn the task of throwing a tennis ball with their nondominant hand. One group of subjects received no feedback, one group received feedback after each group of five throws, and one group received feedback only when they requested it. Results of the study indicated that the two groups receiving feedback were more accurate and had better form than the group that received no feedback. Moreover, the group that received feedback only when requested performed better than the group that received feedback after each group of five throws. This means that the best time to provide feedback is when the learner requests feedback. Of course, coaches will provide external feedback when they deem it necessary, but perhaps coaches can provide feedback less often, yet more effectively.

Use summary extrinsic feedback. Allowing athletes to make a number of attempts before providing **summary feedback** can be superior to providing immediate feedback 100% of the time. Lavery (1962) conducted a series of experiments that indicated the benefits of summary feedback. Lavery found that compared with giving feedback after every practice attempt, summary feedback produced poorer performances during practice but better performance later on, when the extrinsic feedback was withdrawn.

Why would less feedback contribute to increased learning and better performance later on? One possible answer is that subjects who received instruction less often were less dependent on extrinsic feedback and relied more on intrinsic feedback and information processing activities. This is exactly what coaches hope to see in their athletes—athletes thinking on their own and taking responsibility for their learning. It is difficult to learn how to think as an athlete if the coach is doing all the thinking. Under constant feedback conditions athletes can become dependent on their coaches to do their thinking for them.

It is interesting to note that the group in Lavery's study that received both immediate feedback and summary feedback during practice performed as poorly when feedback was withdrawn as the group that received immediate feedback only. Presumably this group ignored the summary feedback and simply relied on the immediate dependency-producing feedback. Results from Lavery's study suggest that when given a choice, athletes often take the cognitively easy dependency-producing route instead of using their full cognitive abilities and taking ownership of their learning and performances. Coaches need to be aware of this tendency and help athletes become more autonomous and responsible; allow them to make several attempts before providing feedback.

Delay extrinsic feedback when possible. **Instantaneous feedback** is when feedback is provided immediately after performance. In contrast, **delayed feedback** is when feedback is provided to learners several seconds or more following performance. Laboratory research suggests that when extrinsic feedback is given immediately after performance, rather than delaying it a few seconds, learning is diminished (Swinnen, 1990). In other words, extrinsic feedback is more effective when the presentation is delayed after performance, even if the delay is only a few seconds.

INTRINSIC FEEDBACK AS REINFORCEMENT

Intrinsic feedback (IF) can be highly reinforcing. It is defined as the sensory information the athlete senses both inside (i.e., how it feels) and outside (i.e., sight, and sound) the body. Like extrinsic feedback, intrinsic feedback can be highly informative and reinforcing. To better understand the role of intrinsic feedback in motor performance, it is useful to consider a closed-loop theory of motor learning outlined by Adams.

Adams' Closed-Loop Theory of Motor Learning

A closed-loop system essentially means that feedback is coming from within the system, not outside it. According to Adams' (1971) theory, movements are made by comparing the ongoing feedback from the limbs during the motion to an internal (*within the system*) **perceptual trace** that is learned through practice. When an individual makes a positioning movement, intrinsic feedback stimuli are produced that represent the particular locations of the limbs in space. Through practice these stimuli leave a perceptual trace in the central nervous system and memory.

The perceptual trace acts as a **reference of correctness** that includes the feedback qualities associated with correct movement. For positioning responses, for which the individual must learn to locate the limbs at a proper position in space, the actual feedback qualities (muscle, movement, and environmental sensations) are compared with the reference of correctness. The process of minimizing the difference between the feedback received and the reference of correctness results in the limbs being brought to the correct position by a closed-loop process.

Intrinsic feedback can be a powerful source of reinforcement, which is sometimes good and sometimes not so good. For example, consider confident, self-assured, and talented athletes. They fully trust themselves and their intrinsic feedback, which is great unless they have established an imperfect perceptual trace. In this case, their bodies tell them their movements are correct, even though their coaches tell them otherwise. Consequently, the athletes continue to make the same incorrect movements because they are being reinforced by their intrinsic feedback. This explanation helps you comprehend in part why athletes at any level might continue to make the same mistake.

I have worked with many athletes who honestly felt that their arms were in the correct position in their hurdle (i.e., straight up over the head) even though their arms were too low. Obviously, a mechanical reason can explain why the arms are not up high enough, such as leaning back in the last step or lack of flexibility. However, when I had them stand on the ground and I guided their arms into the correct position, most of them reported feeling that the arms were too far back. It is interesting to note that even when these athletes watched their hurdles on video replay and could visually confirm that their arms were indeed in the wrong position, they sometimes reported, "There must be something wrong with the angle of the camera." Intrinsic feedback is indeed a powerful reinforcer.

The Athlete's Perspective

So, what does this all mean for the athlete? When considering intrinsic feedback as a source of reinforcement, several specific suggestions guide the learning process.

Athletes shouldn't always trust what they feel. If athletes could feel everything they did, they wouldn't need coaches and they certainly wouldn't need all of the replay systems and cameras many athletes rely on today. Most of the time their intrinsic feedback is spot on, but not always which explains why they perform some movements incorrectly.

Athletes need to be willing to relearn. In other words, they shouldn't be afraid to tweak. Just because they have done it one way for a long time doesn't mean it is correct. And just because it feels comfortable to them certainly doesn't mean they should continue doing it that way. Here is where an understanding of Adams' theory can motivate them to journey out of their comfort zone and make changes: They must refuse the intrinsic *candy* (i.e., reinforcing intrinsic feedback) and change the movement, even if the new intrinsic feedback feels incorrect and, therefore, not reinforcing.

Athletes should learn it right the first time. Relearning is unnecessary if athletes and coach take the time, trouble, and toil to learn it correctly the first time. Here is where patience is certainly a virtue. Take the time to learn the fundamentals. It is much easier and much less time consuming to learn it right in the beginning than it is to go through the much more difficult and time-intensive process of discarding bad habits and donning new habits.

The Coach's Perspective

From an operant conditioning perspective, what are the implications of Adams' theory for guiding the teaching process for coaches?

Make early learning as error free as possible. According to Adams, the perceptual trace is the most important part of motor learning and the accuracy of any response depends on the quality of the trace. Therefore, the structure of practice becomes extremely important because it affects the shaping and eventual quality of all perceptual traces. Adams believed that feedback in the form of knowledge of results (KR) is not just a positive reinforcement; it provides information about errors, which the athlete uses to solve the motor problem. Contrary to some motor learning theories, Adams believed that any errors produced during the course of practice are harmful to learning because they degrade the perceptual trace. Consequently, in the early stages of learning

Adams believed that errors should be avoided when at all possible and that KR should be maintained until the trace is well established.

Establish a prepractice reference of correctness. You can enhance error-free learning by establishing a pre-practice reference of correctness. A **prepractice reference** is a perceptual trace ingrained before performing the actual movements. You can establish the prepractice reference by providing athletes with detailed intrinsic feedback in the form of verbal reports, instant replay, and delayed replay such as videotapes and DVDs. Research suggests that replay feedback display systems are perhaps most effective when the coach directs or cues athletes to examine salient aspects of the display (Rothstein & Arnold, 1976; Kernodle & Carlton, 1992).

Now that you understand the operant conditioning paradigm and the different types of stimuli that influence athlete behavior, the question to ask yourself is "What are different behaviors I should influence?" As a coach you are a powerful source for influencing athlete behaviors. But what behaviors should you choose to influence? The next section examines four types of athlete behaviors to consider.

FOUR TYPES OF ATHLETE BEHAVIOR WORTH CONDITIONING

This chapter has provided examples of different types of behaviors and how to influence these behaviors using the principles of operant conditioning. It is important coaches do not limit their focus to just motor movement behaviors. When you observe your athletes, you want to observe all types of behaviors that they emit. You want to see the whole picture and shape the development of the athlete as a whole person. Therefore, you will want to consider at least four types of behavior. These types of behavior are social behavior, learning behavior, motor behavior, and what I call champion behavior.

Social Behavior

Social behavior refers to the interaction of athletes with their teammates, coaching staff, opponents, trainers, and others associated with the sport and program. Why is social behavior important?

Part of the sport experience should include the personal growth and maturation of the athlete as a human being, which includes developing appropriate social behavior. A way to encourage athlete growth and maturation is to help them learn to become supportive and trusted teammates. If athletes want to have trusted and supportive teammates, then they need to be trustworthy and supportive to their teammates. Remind them that if they want a friend, then they need to be a friend.

Another way to encourage good social behavior is to reinforce athletes when they demonstrate respect toward teammates, coaches, trainers, and others associated with your program. You want your athletes to become good students, good citizens, good teammates, good role models, and, along the way, good athletes, too. When I first began coaching at Indiana University, I was under pressure to produce champions. Taking over for International Swimming Hall of Fame coach Hobie Billingsley was not easy. Those first few years, I made some mistakes of which I am not proud. One mistake was letting one of my athletes say derogatory remarks about his mother in front of the team. I wish I could go back in time and do things differently. Instead of calling him on the spot and admonishing him for speaking negatively about his mother, who would and did do everything in her power to promote and support her son, I said nothing. To this day it bothers me. What good does it do to develop an athlete who as a human being can't publicly show respect for his mother? And what lesson did I convey to other members of the team that day?

Many years later, one of my athletes spoke disparagingly about his father. I quickly said, "Randy, I don't want to hear you talk about your father like that again. He has done a lot to support you and your career and he deserves your respect and appreciation. Please meet with me in my office this afternoon after practice." In the meeting we discussed the topic of respect and the importance of not belittling parents, teammates, and other significant people in his life. Randy went on to become a good team leader and role model.

Another reason good social behavior is important is that it enhances team chemistry and the training environment. All great programs, whether they are individual sports or team sports, have great team chemistry, which is the result of every athlete contributing to the training atmosphere. Part of this contribution is good social behavior. Social behaviors already mentioned are support, trust, respect, and contribution. Other behaviors include setting a good example, being other-person oriented, and showing sensitivity to others. For the Olympic Games in Beijing, our team had been together for 4 weeks. Part of the glue that held our team together was good social behaviors shown among team members.

How does this happen? How do you get your athletes to demonstrate good social behavior, create team chemistry, and maintain a positive training environment? It does not happen by accident; it takes a conscious effort and some operant conditioning on the part of the coach.

People often remarked that my teams were a hard-working and fun-loving group of athletes who got along and supported each other. This didn't happen by accident. We began each season by setting team goals. Those goals, of course, included outcome goals, such as winning a team championship. But they also included how we wanted to treat each other and support one another inside and outside of practice and competition. Each team member was reminded that every athlete either added to or subtracted from the team environment through his or her contribution and part of this contribution included appropriate social behavior. During team meetings, you can talk about a standard of decorum you want your athletes to follow. You also can provide specific examples and outline specific behaviors within your team rules. Even more important, you need to monitor your athletes, then reinforce appropriate social behavior and punish inappropriate social behavior.

Consider scenario 6. This is a scenario I faced one season with one of my freshmen. This particular athlete was the star athlete on his high school team. Unbeknownst to me, he had a habit of denigrating female members on the university team. After several female athletes talked to me, I sat down with the athlete and reprimanded him privately. I penalized him by kicking him out of practice; he could not return until he had personally apologized to the two women. He came back 2 days later and said he had spoken with both women. Before permitting him to practice again, I spoke with both women. He had only apologized to one. For his lack of honesty, I banned him from another practice and required him to speak with the other woman. About 2 weeks later, I observed him speaking in a friendly manner with one of the women and complimented him.

Scenario 6

One of your male freshman collegiate athletes, unbeknownst to you, behaves disrespectfully to some of your female athletes. Eventually, your female athletes approach you and complain about his inappropriate behavior.

In this scenario, it was important to talk with the athlete privately for several reasons. For one, it showed respect for the athlete by not publicly embarrassing him. Consequently, in our meeting he was less defensive and more open to accepting criticism and direction. Meeting privately also respected the rights of the women who wanted to avoid being singled out publicly in front of the team. And, finally, the private meeting was an opportunity to use reason and logic to explain to the offending athlete why his behavior was inappropriate and why it needed to immediately desist.

The lesson of this story is that you need to monitor your athletes and be prepared to reinforce appropriate social behavior and reprimand inappropriate behavior. Even though this athlete knew of our team goals and code of conduct, he acted inappropriately and I had to take action to suppress inappropriate social behavior and stamp in appropriate behavior. This situation may seem small to some coaches, but if left unchecked it could have escalated into something much greater and caused team disharmony.

Many coaches overlook the fact that the team concept is important even with individual sports. Teaching good social behavior to develop team chemistry leads to a positive training environment, which ultimately leads to improved individual performances. In other words, when they help others, your athletes ultimately help themselves.

Learning Behavior

You can also apply principles of respondent conditioning to encourage behavior that leads to successful learning. Some of these behaviors are discussed next.

Work closely with the coach. This includes being attentive, remembering instruction, and following instruction. Basically, these behaviors contribute to a high level of learning. Recall scenario 4 in which the athlete forgets the coach's comments. It is nearly impossible to achieve the desired goal if the athlete can't remember what the goal is in the first place. The following dialogue is perhaps the worst-case scenario for any coach.

Coach: "What did I ask you to do?"

Athlete: "I don't remember."

Take the sport home. Successful athletes take their sport home with them. They go home and think about that day's practice. They set goals for the following day's practice. They watch video of their practice or video of great athletes in their sport. They attempt to understand their strengths and establish a game plan for eliminating their weaknesses. When you see your athletes display these learning behaviors, reinforce them.

Arrive at practice ready to learn. Ready to learn means showing up to practice on time, getting enough rest, keeping up with class studies and assignments, eating right, having specific practice goals, establishing a learning attitude, and so on. You can facilitate this readiness to learn by explaining to your athletes the importance of arriving on time, taking care of their bodies, avoiding stress by keeping up with their studies, setting practice goals, and creating a mindset conducive for learning. Remind them that the more ready they are to learn the more productive they will be and the quicker they will achieve their goals.

Maintain emotional control. Learning can be frustrating at times for any athlete, even the best. As athletes train and seek improvements, they attempt to move closer and closer to perfection, which can never truly be attained. So, from time to time frustration, discouragement, anger, and a host of other emotions can well up inside athletes. Once this happens, athletes lose emotional control and the emotions act as a wall between the athlete and the learning goal. So, a good learning behavior is maintaining emotional equilibrium. This equilibrium is as important for coaches as it is for athletes.

All of the aforementioned behaviors can be influenced through the principles of respondent conditioning. The athlete who fails to make eye contact with the coach can be shaped to change that behavior. The athlete who forgets to do what you ask can be reinforced when she does remember what you asked her to do. The athlete who shows up to practice unprepared to learn can be reprimanded and penalized for those actions either by the coach or the natural consequences of those behaviors. And the athlete who loses emotional control can be reinforced when he or she maintains emotional control or penalized (e.g., time-out) when emotional control is lost.

Motor Behavior

Teaching new motor behavior (movement) is one of a coach's primary responsibilities. The purpose of this section isn't to point out these motor behaviors but to offer some simple suggestions for teaching motor behaviors based on operant conditioning theory. They are discussed next.

Remember that old habits die hard. In other words, once an athlete learns a motor skill, no matter how incorrect it might be, it can sometimes live forever—in part because the athlete receives reinforcing intrinsic feedback. Examples of these athletes abound: the basketball player with poor shooting technique, the quarterback with the awkward throwing motion, the swimmer with bad stroke mechanics, the golfer with the incorrect backswing, the wrestler with sloppy technique when shooting in on an opponent, and so on.

The point is that initial learning needs to be as error free as possible: Get it right the first time. If not, the athlete may be incapable of or highly resistant to altering the movement in the future. Therefore, the first coach an athlete works with is the most important coach. If you are the athlete's first coach, practice drills and skills until the motor movement is correct. For example, don't let the golfer in scenario 2 develop an incorrect backswing and practice it that way for years until she gets to college. Old habits die hard.

Catch athletes being good to reinforce correct behavior. I don't mean *good* in the disciplinary sense, but rather, in the motor movement sense. Coaches tend to focus on the bad; I know I did. I guess I reasoned that I don't need to dwell on what they do well. They already do it well, so why bother—right? However, for athletes, particularly young ones, it is important to point out the good—such as that perfect form for the overhead smash, the follow-through on the golf swing, the correct delivery for the fastball, the efficient flip turn in swimming, or the correct decision and execution of the pick and roll in basketball. Remember, reinforcement increases the likelihood that a behavior will reoccur. So, if you like that overhead smash, the follow-through, delivery, flip turn, and pick and roll, then reinforce the behavior.

Use both primary and generalized reinforcers. Some types of primary reinforcers at your disposal include a compliment, hand clap, pat on the back, and public praise—and, as you learned in chapter 3—even jelly beans. Brief one-on-one meetings between coach and player go a long way in reinforcing good motor movement. For example, your athlete finally performs correctly and you take the time to call him aside and tell him what an amazing job he just did, then you pat him on the back. This whole process only takes a few minutes at most.

Types of generalized reinforcers include player-of-the-week status, special T-shirts, selecting music for practice, a quote of the week, posting an athlete's good scores or newspaper article, a sticker for the football helmet, and so on.

For younger athletes it could be moving up from the bronze to the silver team or receiving a gold star for a new personal best.

Don't underestimate the power of the human touch. The human touch can be a powerful reinforcer. It can go a long way in communicating to your athletes that you genuinely care about them as people and are excited to see them learn and perform well as athletes. The scientific coach understands the principles of operant conditioning. The artful coach senses what, how, and when to provide appropriate consequences for behavior. Sometimes a handshake, pat on the back, high five, or hug can go a long way toward reinforcing behavior.

Remember that one of the most potent reinforcers is success. Consequently, you should arrange the practice environment in such a way that your athletes, no matter what their ages or ability levels might be, are challenged but through personal effort are ultimately able to achieve success. When working with young athletes, recognize their current developmental level. If you are a former athlete of your sport, it is easy to forget that a skill that might seem easily attainable to you is actually a complex skill comprised of many sub skills and, therefore, difficult for the young athlete to master.

Champion Behavior

To this point the discussion has included social behavior, learning behavior, and motor behavior. Another class of behavior worth noting and very much worth reinforcing is champion behavior. **Champion behavior** includes traits such as high effort, intensity, positive attitude, leadership, persistence, dedication, and resilience. All these traits and more are necessary for athletes to reach their greatest athletic potential.

Achieving a high level of athletic proficiency involves more than the three types of behavior (social, learning, and motor movement) discussed thus far. For example, in *Reflections on Success* (Gibbons et al., 2003), U.S. Olympians listed six individual characteristics they believe contributed to their success: dedication, persistence, natural talent, competitiveness, focus, and work ethic. While reinforcement cannot influence natural talent, it can certainly influence the other five characteristics, which are important not only for athletic success but success later in life after athletics. When your athletes try harder after a setback, when they are tired and still train hard, when they remain upbeat and positive after a loss, when they lead the team by example—when they exhibit any of these champion behaviors, it is important that you take time to administer reinforcement.

Let's take one final look at operant conditioning for the behavior of trying harder after a loss (figure 4.3). Trying harder after a loss demonstrates champion behaviors of dedication, persistence, competitiveness, and work ethic.

Many behaviors are worth reinforcing so that they reoccur and eventually become habitual. Perhaps of no greater importance among these behaviors are the champion behaviors. Before athletes become champions, they must first learn to behave like champions and exhibit the characteristics of champions

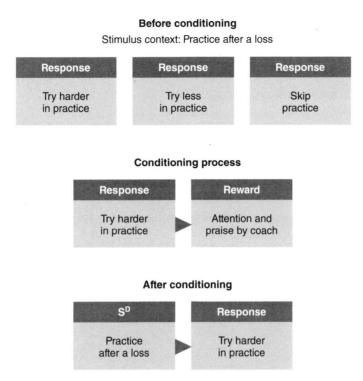

Figure 4.3   Operant conditioning for the response of trying harder after a loss.

(Huber, 2007). So, reward your athletes when they exhibit these characteristics. Sport, as is life, is not just about winning. As the Olympic creed reminds us, it is not about the triumph, but the struggle.

APPLYING OPERANT CONDITIONING THEORY IN COACHING ATHLETES

Get to know your athletes and what they find rewarding. For example, some athletes may find the use of constant praise a weak source of reward. In contrast, highly self-critical athletes may need to be constantly praised for the good aspects of their motor performances. For example, one former Indiana University diver, Kristen Kane, was a high achiever and perfectionist who was always highly critical of her diving. She was a national champion, an NCAA All-American, a Big Ten champion, and a remarkable student. But because of her extremely self-critical nature, she often needed to hear how well she was performing.

Another example of getting to know an athlete would be the athlete whose biggest reinforcer is being part of the team. I once had a diver who was reluctant to learn new dives but I discovered that being part of a team was his greatest reinforcement. Even though he was highly fearful of learning new dives, he was motivated to learn them to stay on the team. When I found this out early in his career, I used it often. I just had to say, "Either do this or you are off the team!" and Alex always did what was asked of him. After he graduated, his grandparents endowed a scholarship at IU in his name. What a fitting honor for a great young man.

Be aware of the consequences you hand out as a coach. You may be doing things that have the opposite effect of what you intended. For example, some athletes like being singled out and publicly praised and they find this experience highly rewarding. In contrast, some athletes find this experience embarrassing and uncomfortable. For Alex, being a part of the team was highly rewarding. For another athlete, however, being part of the team might not be as rewarding. When given the choice of doing something or being dismissed, this athlete might likely choose dismissal. Better to give this athlete other alternative consequences for his behavior. I am generally opposed to the ultimatum consequence: *Do this or you are off the team.* From personal experience it backs athletes into a corner and often forces them to make a poor decision they later regret. A wrestler, for example, who is fatigued from grueling practices and cutting weight, might in the heat of the moment decide to quit the team rather than follow the coach's directive.

Do not use external rewards too often or make these rewards too large or too obvious. The excessive use of reinforcement can have harmful effects on subsequent motivation (Lepper, 1981). In one experiment (Lepper & Greene, 1975), two groups of children were asked to solve a number of geometric puzzles. One group was told they would be allowed to play with toys as a reward. The other group was not led to believe that there would be any reward. Later, both groups were secretly observed to see if any of them spontaneously played with the puzzles. A significantly greater number of children who expected no reward played with the puzzles than the children who expected a reward.

The point of the study is that when external rewards are large and obvious, motivation and focus becomes more external. And, when the external rewards, or the prospect of rewards, are withdrawn, motivation is also withdrawn. Athletes should be internally motivated to practice. Why? Because the inner desire to practice and succeed will remain with them and sustain them during tough times when external rewards, such as attention, awards, and success, may be withdrawn. Also, humanistic coaches believe that based on theories and concepts, such as competence motivation, mastery learning, and self-actualization, athletes are prewired with an inner motivation; coaches, therefore, should encourage and nurture this internal motivation.

Structure the learning environment so that athletes are given challenging but attainable tasks. Asking athletes to master skills that are too difficult for them at their current level of ability and experience will lead to failure and discouragement rather than success and internal satisfaction. However, giving athletes tasks that are too easy offers them little challenge and, therefore, little intrinsic reinforcement. Choosing appropriate task difficulty helps your athletes receive intrinsic reinforcement.

Avoid comparing athletes to other athletes. Social comparison encourages athletes to look outside themselves and focus on external sources of reinforcement. Although competition between team members is a natural and healthy aspect of practice, the ultimate goal for each athlete is to reach his or her greatest personal potential irrespective of other players. At the end of the day, athletes need to be able to say that they gave their personal best effort.

Invite your athletes to participate in the decision-making process. For example, ask your athletes to design some of their practices. Also, ask your athletes to review their performances on videotape and give their impressions about what they need to change. Research reviewed by Ames (1992) suggests that teachers who provide students with opportunities for autonomy are more apt to encourage mastery orientations. According to Ames and goal theory, mastery orientation engenders intrinsic motivation and the development of goals that focus on the intrinsic value of learning.

Understand the uses and misuses of praise. Praise used too often can become almost meaningless to athletes. For more information on appropriate uses of praise, see chapter 10.

Remember that a reinforcer increases the likelihood of a behavior reoccurring. So, if you want a particular behavior such as good effort, a correct backswing, or attentiveness to the coach to reoccur, reinforce that behavior when your athlete demonstrates it. In other words, catch them being good.

THE ATHLETE IN THE SKINNER BOX

From a Pavlovian respondent conditioning perspective, it was helpful to view the athlete as the salivating athlete. Now, from a Skinnerian operant conditioning perspective it is useful to perceive the individual as the **athlete in the Skinner box**. With this perspective the practice environment is seen as a gigantic Skinner box in which you control your athletes' behaviors through the use of your operant conditioning tools. Like B.F. Skinner, you drop the *food pellet* of reinforcement when your athletes *depress the lever* of emitting the correct behavior. In other words, you reinforce and shape appropriate behaviors that include social, learning, motor, and champion behaviors.

THE COACH IN THE SKINNER BOX

Although you are the dispenser of consequences (i.e., reinforcement and punishment), you also are the recipient of consequences. You are the **coach in the Skinner box**. Like your athletes' behaviors, your behaviors are equally influenced by the principles of operant conditioning theory. Your actions are influenced by a variety of sources, such as athletes, parents, community members, colleagues, and a number of consequences, such as winning and losing. Be cognizant of the people and things that shape your behavior. Jon, my former athlete in the story at the beginning of this chapter, reinforced some of my positive coaching behaviors. In contrast, some athlete behaviors might cause coaches to emit negative coaching behaviors. For example, there might be a successful but annoying athlete on your team who's unpleasant and aversive behavior conditions you to avoid coaching the athlete or to relinquish decision-making power.

Using your understanding of operant conditioning principles, monitor the consequences that are controlling your behavior so that you emit the positive coaching behaviors you hope to see in yourself and your athletes. Winning and the expectation of future wins, for example, can cause some coaches to emit inappropriate behaviors. Recently, the head coach for the New Orleans Saints NFL football team was suspended for an entire season for condoning a bounty program (paying Saints players for injuring opposing players) and then lying about the program during an investigation. Don't allow the consequence of winning to reinforce unethical and inappropriate behaviors. Unpleasant and aversive athlete behaviors need to cease, even if the athlete is a successful athlete. And unethical and inappropriate behaviors need to be avoided, even if these behaviors bring about winning.

YOUR COACHING TOOLBOX

Now you have operant conditioning theory and the tools of positive and negative reinforcement, presentation and removal punishment, extinction, shaping, generalization, discrimination, and schedules of reinforcement. Like B.F. Skinner, you can shape the behavior of your *rat* in the *Skinner box* of practice. It may seem indelicate or crude to draw an analogy between a Skinner box and practice environment and to compare an athlete to a rat. However, the analogy is in many ways apt and it is useful. The practice environment is a perfect stimulus context in which to control athlete behavior. As coach you have great latitude in determining what consequences follow the responses your athletes make. Like Dr. Skinner shaping an animal's responses, you are capable of shaping your athletes' behaviors using the principles of operant conditioning

THE SCIENTIFIC AND ARTFUL COACH

The scientific coach understands the operant conditioning paradigm and utilizes this knowledge to extinguish poor behavior, reinforce good behavior (social, learning, motor, and champion behavior), and shape new behavior. The scientific coach administers punishment and reinforcement according to parameters established by research and operant conditioning theory.

The artful coach gets to know athletes on a personal level and discovers what they find rewarding. The artful coach also is sensitive to when and how often to use reinforcement and punishment. For example, overuse of praise renders positive comments meaningless and ineffective. The longer I coached, the less I praised, but when I did take time to praise a behavior I especially liked, it had a more potent impact on the repetition of that behavior in the future. In other words, the behavior was more likely to reoccur in the future.

A great deal of human behavior is shaped through reinforcement, both consciously and unconsciously. Sometimes, people shape behavior without really knowing it. As in scenario 7, you might unconsciously pay attention to the disruptive athlete and perhaps ignore the athlete who comes in every day and gives a good effort and sets a good example. Or, you might unconsciously ridicule an athlete's practice performance. All of these unconscious consequences you mete out have an impact on the future responses of your athletes.

Scenario 7

One of your athletes comes in every day on time, gives a good effort, never causes any problems and is easy to coach. You spend most of your time dealing with the disruptive athletes on the team, thinking that the well-behaved athlete is self-sufficient and doesn't need any attention.

The athlete in scenario 7 comes in every day and gives a good effort but never receives any attention from the coach. This athlete might eventually seek and respond to reinforcement from peers. This situation has the potential for good, but it also has the potential for bad because it could lead to undesirable responses from the athlete, such as disrespect and inattentiveness, depending on which behaviors the athlete's peers choose to reinforce.

The artful coach, therefore, works at being aware of the consequences he or she hands out so that no unconscious operant conditioning of behavior occurs and no hidden curriculum lies within the program.

IF YOU REMEMBER ONLY THREE THINGS

1. *Remember that the most powerful dispenser of childhood reinforcement is you.* Your comments, the look on your face, your body language, your emotional reaction, the privileges or punishments you give or withhold, and the rewards you dispense or delay are all powerful sources for shaping behavior, particularly in young athletes. Use this power scientifically, artfully, and wisely.

   Also, choose reinforcement over punishment. The most effective coaches spend little time yelling and admonishing their athletes. Instead, they spend most of their time, well, coaching—and reinforcing their athletes. They are quick to acknowledge good work and offer compliments to their athletes when due. They are masters at establishing a positive practice environment through operant conditioning techniques and adept at creating a practice plan that challenges but engenders success in their athletes. If you find yourself continually yelling at your athletes for not doing the right thing, perhaps the problem is with the coach and not the athletes.

2. *Remember to shape all four types of behaviors: social, learning, motor, and champion.* Early in my coaching career a number of kids came from a program coached by a man named Bruce Dart. I noticed after having two or three of his kids on my team that his athletes always seemed to understand behaviors such as hard work, being coachable, being good team members, and never giving up. In fact, it got to the point where I would take any of his athletes sight unseen because I knew that he taught all four types of behaviors to his athletes and, therefore, they would immediately be positive contributors to my program to one degree or another.

As a coach, particularly a beginning coach, it is easy to focus strictly on motor behavior and neglect other important behaviors associated with motor learning, motor performance, and becoming a champion. While it may involve more effort on your part, your hard work will not be in vain. Your athletes will grow as human beings, become better learners, improve their motor performances, and acquire champion characteristics that will serve them well during and after their athletic careers.

3. *Remember to create athlete experiences that are challenging, but lead to success.* This may be the single greatest coaching challenge and the most important coaching accomplishment for any coach of excellence: finding that balance between task difficulty and success. Success is highly reinforcing for many athletes, whether success means reaching a practice goal or achieving a competition goal. However, if the task is too easy, success doesn't mean much to the athlete because anyone could have done it. And if the task is too difficult, failure rather than success is sure to follow. So, this is your challenge, and one you must confront daily. You may lose some of these confrontations, but as you grow and become a scientific, artful, and, someday a wise coach, you will win more and more of these battles.

SUGGESTED READINGS

Huber, J.J. (2007). *Becoming a champion diver: Striving to reach your greatest potential.* DVD. Ames, IA: Championship Productions.

[In this DVD, I list the characteristics I believe to be important for becoming a champion athlete in any sport. After more than 37 years of coaching, I still believe becoming a champion begins with character.]

Schembechler, B. & Bacon, J.U. (2007). *Bo's lasting lessons: The legendary coach teaches the timeless fundamentals of leadership*. New York: Business Plus.

[I read this book when I was at the 2008 Beijing Olympic Games. It had a profound impact on my coaching and my program. I came home and made some major changes in my program that shaped the success of our season. Bo is old school but he still talks about lasting truths.]

Skinner, B.F. (1971). *Beyond freedom and dignity*. New York: Knopf.

[Although controversial, it has much truth. If you're too busy becoming a coach of excellence, read the annotated version.]

Walker, J.E. & Shea, T.M. (1999). *Behavior management: A practical approach for educators* (7th ed.). Upper Saddle River, NJ: Merrill.

[This book offers some practical suggestions for shaping behavior. It is where the rubber meets the road. Even if you only read part of it, it is worth a look.]

PART

III

Athletes and Theories of Cognitivism

Part III begins with social cognitive theory (chapter 5) because the theory is part behavioral and part cognitive, so it makes for a perfect transition between parts II and III. Human beings are indeed influenced by and learn from the consequences (rewards and punishments) of behaviors but, as Bandura rightly noted, they also are influenced by and learn from cognitive processes, such as observing the behaviors of others and anticipating rewards and punishments as a consequence of imitating these observed behaviors. The chapter introduces the *imitating athlete* and discusses the application of social cognitive theory for shaping various types of athlete behaviors.

Chapter 6 fully recognizes and explores the cognitive abilities of athletes and the critical cognitive component connected to motor learning and athlete performance. The chapter outlines not only what the *supercomputing athlete* looks like but also how coaches can construct supercomputing athletes by understanding cognitive theory and its numerous applications for developing cognition-enhancing practices and influencing athletes' thinking to accelerate motor learning and performance.

Part III concludes with chapter 7, which delves into the mind of the *expert athlete*, as well as the *expert coach*. The chapter outlines specific characteristics that differentiate the elite athlete and coach from the non-elite athlete and coach. The chapter then looks at a unique type of practice called *deliberate practice*, which experts engage in to achieve high-level performance, and how you and your athletes can create deliberate practice.

CHAPTER 5

The Imitating Athlete
Applying Social Cognitive Theory

Key Terms

affective valence
arousal level
champion behavior
complexity
direct reinforcement
disinhibitory effect
distinctiveness
eliciting effect
functional value
imitating athlete

imitating coach
inhibitory effect
learning behavior
model
modeling effect
motor behavior
observational learning
operant
past reinforcement

perceptual set
prevalence
sensory capacity
set
social behavior
social cognitive theory
social learning
symbolic model
vicarious reinforcement

When my son was about 5 years old, I took him to a national championship in Florida. One evening we were watching an action movie in our hotel room. After a particularly action-packed scene he blurted out, "Damn!" I was dumbstruck because I had never heard him utter anything like that. Suddenly, I realized what had happened. During the movie, I was unconsciously muttering the word *damn* whenever something happened and my son had simply observed me and decided to imitate my behavior.

The lesson was immediately clear: They are always watching. Children are always watching their caregivers, who serve as role models. In many cases, the same can be said for athletes. They are always watching, whether it be their coach, another teammate, a competitor, or an athlete they admire—and they are ready to imitate some of these observed behaviors. This concept can be somewhat daunting if you think that your athletes might scrutinize everything you do. On the other hand, it can be exciting and challenging to think that as a coach you have the ability to inspire, influence, and teach your athletes simply by having them observe your behavior.

As a young coach, I had an opportunity to have breakfast with the top diving coach in the United States. During the course of our meal he mentioned that the hardest working person on a team must be the coach. I never forgot his words because I intuitively knew they were true. I also knew that at that moment in my career I could not say I was the hardest working or even the most dedicated person on my team. There were athletes more inspired and more determined than I was and I realized that even though I had good intentions I was unconsciously acting as an impediment for them reaching their greatest potential. I vowed that when I returned home I would be a better role model and set a higher standard of excellence for my athletes through my behavior.

Athletes take their cues from their coaches. If you are hard working, they will be hard working. If you are passionate about your sport, they will be passionate. If you set high goals, they will set high goals. If you persevere in the face of adversity, they will learn to persevere. If you demonstrate good sporting behavior, they will demonstrate it, too. If you model optimism and a positive attitude, so will they. Athletes also have other models besides coaches to imitate. As we will see in this chapter, how these models are reinforced or punished affects athlete behaviors.

This process of learning through observation and imitation is known as social cognitive theory. This chapter is the story of the imitating athlete and how coaches can use social cognitive theory to shape social, learning, champion, and motor behaviors to help their players reach their greatest potential as athletes and human beings.

CHAPTER OVERVIEW

The chapter begins with a brief definition of Bandura's social cognitive theory. The chapter then looks at four types of behaviors worth modeling and imitating, the importance of models, and the four processes of observational learning. The chapter then examines sources of reinforcement and the effects of imitation and concludes with specific coaching applications of social cognitive theory for influencing athlete behaviors.

SOCIAL COGNITIVE THEORY

In researching respondent and operant conditioning, Pavlov studied dogs and Skinner studied rats and pigeons. However, one characteristic separating human beings from animals is that humans understand something about the consequences of their behaviors and they can anticipate, reason, and decide whether or not to initiate these behaviors. Behaviorists did not deny the existence of mental processes. They simply thought that it was improper for such a true field of science as behaviorism to study something that could not be directly observed and experimentally manipulated. However, some psychologists attempted to incorporate the concept of mental processes into human learning and behavior while still remaining true to the behaviorist's scientific perspective. One of these psychologists was Albert Bandura.

Bandura uses operant conditioning principles to examine cognitive aspects of social learning and human behavior. This theory, which can be viewed as a transition between behaviorism and cognitivism, is referred to as social cognitive theory. **Social learning** is the acquisition of patterns of behavior that conform to social expectations. In other words, social learning is the process of learning what is considered socially acceptable behavior and what is considered socially unacceptable behavior. According to Bandura's (1977) **social cognitive theory**, much of social learning results from imitation—a process also called observational learning—and the best way to understand how learning through imitation occurs is through considering operant conditioning principles.

According to Bandura, one can summarize **observational learning** with two statements:

1. *Much of human learning is a function of observing and imitating the behaviors of others or of symbolic models such as fictional characters in television programs and books.* From a Skinnerian point of view, imitative behavior can be considered an **operant**, which is a response not elicited by any known or obvious stimulus. In other words, the person simply chooses to make the response.

2. *When imitative behaviors result in positive contingencies or in the removal or prevention of aversive contingencies, they become more probable* (Masia & Chase, 1997). Remember that a reinforcer increases the probability that a response (i.e., behavior) will occur.

Besides being based on operant conditioning principles, Bandura's theory recognizes the importance of cognition: the ability of human beings to symbolize, imagine, decipher cause and effect, and anticipate the outcome of observable behaviors. In other words, from observing models, we learn cognitively how to do certain things and also what the consequences of our actions are likely to entail. For example, take the case in scenario 1 in which a freshman high school basketball player watches the star senior varsity basketball player shoot a jump shot and learns to imitate the same style of shooting. Unfortunately, the young basketball player also observes and learns to imitate the older player's boorish and poor sporting behavior in practices and games.

In this scenario the young athlete observes the star basketball player and this observation includes not only the shooting style of the senior basketball

Scenario 1

A freshman high school basketball player watches the star senior varsity basketball player shoot a jump shot and learns to imitate the same style of shooting. The young basketball player also observes and learns to imitate the older player's bad behaviors during practices and games, such as failing to acknowledge a teammate's assist, showboating, taunting an opposing player, and sloughing off on defense.

player but also the player's mannerisms and on-court behavior. After seeing the star player reinforced for making his shots and being lauded by other team members, the freshman imitates the senior's shooting style. Unfortunately, after seeing the star athlete receive the two reinforcers of attention and popular acceptance from teammates, the young player also learns to ignore the efforts of his teammates, gloat when he makes a good play, taunt an opposing player, and play weak defense.

In a sense, observational learning has everything to do with motor learning. For example, I once coached a diver named Lawrence, who crossed over his left leg on his last step into his hurdle. In other words, he would place his left foot near the right edge of the springboard and then jump into his hurdle. It is an odd way to jump. One day I asked him why he did this and he said he did it because when he was a young age group diver, he saw a really good older diver named Dave do it. It turned out I had coached Dave in college, and Dave had become a coach. One day I happened to run into him at a competition. The conversation came around to his hurdle and he mentioned that he learned to cross over on his last step by watching an older diver whom he admired; that diver also happened to be named Dave. Well, I had also coached this other Dave, who told me years later that he had learned to cross over in his last step by watching an older diver he admired.

As you can see from this story, models and imitative behavior are powerful influences on behavior; in fact, they are so powerful that they affect generations of athletes as well as entire teams. For example, I have observed programs in which teams from generation to generation resembled one another. Depending on the program and the behavior being modeled, this similarity can be a good thing or a bad thing. Some programs are steeped in tradition and pride and each generation of athletes seems to embody the same core values. On the other hand, some programs have a hard partying reputation or some other negative reputation that is passed on to each successive generation. For example, I know of one team whose behavior caused them to be banned from a particular hotel for 2 years.

Four Types of Behaviors Worthy of Imitation

Social cognitive theory is critical because it can positively and negatively affect so many aspects of your program. Besides socially acceptable behaviors, it also can affect acceptable learning behaviors, motor behaviors, and champion behaviors. A significant factor contributing to successful programs is that coaches of excellence consciously control the team environment by understanding observational learning and using this knowledge to influence different types of acceptable athlete behaviors. Whether it is having their athletes imitate good sporting behavior (social behavior), attentiveness to the coach (learning behavior), accurate motor skill (motor behavior), or high effort (champion behavior), coaches of excellence facilitate observational learning so that their younger athletes learn all types of acceptable behaviors from observing individuals who model good behavior.

Acceptable **social behavior** includes behaviors such as respecting teammates and coaches, respecting opponents, being a gracious winner, accepting defeat with class, supporting teammates, and setting a good example for younger athletes. People who model these behaviors include athletes—particularly your older athletes because they have a measurable influence on the younger athletes—parents, team administrators, and, most importantly, coaches.

Acceptable **learning behavior** includes behaviors such as attending to coaching instructions, remembering and following coaching instructions, asking questions when instructions are unclear, and making eye contact with the coach. Effective learning behavior is critical for beginning the learning process. The closer and more effectively an athlete works with the coach, the more successful and accelerated the learning curve becomes.

Acceptable **champion behavior** includes behaviors such as high effort, persistence, dedication, work ethic, positive attitude, focus, and competitiveness. These behaviors are the intangibles, the difference makers—the behaviors that separate the perennially great teams and the not-so-great teams. In highly successful programs these behaviors are modeled by the older athletes, and, of course, by the coach.

Acceptable **motor behavior** is obviously a critical component of motor performance success. Athletes need to learn to accurately reproduce motor movements modeled by highly successful athletes or symbolic models.

All of the aforementioned behaviors (social, learning, champion, and motor behaviors) can be modeled. What, or rather, *who,* are the models?

Models

A **model** refers to an actual person whose behavior serves as a stimulus for an observer's responses. As is apparent in the following section, the more power or value a model possesses, the more likely it is that other athletes will imitate that model's behavior. The concept and importance of a model for your athletes is discussed on page 157 of this chapter.

A model is not just limited to an actual person. Often the model can be a **symbolic model**, which is any model that is not a real-life person. Symbolic models for athletes include many different sources, such as book or magazine characters, written instructions, pictures, diagrams, televised athletes, and video replay of other athletes.

Symbolic models, like human models, can influence all four types of behaviors. For example, consider scenario 2. The injured athlete reads a story in *Sports Illustrated* about Tedy Bruschi, the New England Patriot's star linebacker who suffered a stroke but fought through adversity and injury to eventually resume his professional career. After reading the story, the young injured athlete is inspired to imitate Tedy's *champion behavior,* rededicate himself to rehabilitation, and set a goal to eventually return to the starting lineup just like Tedy did. Although Tedy is a real life person, to the athlete Tedy is simply someone in a magazine story but an inspirational model nonetheless.

Scenario 2

An athlete on your team who has given up hope of recovery after suffering a debilitating injury reads an inspirational story in *Sports Illustrated* about New England Patriots star linebacker Tedy Bruschi, who suffered a stroke after a football game. Tedy considered retirement, but then decided to continue his career, worked hard to rehabilitate his body, and eventually resumed his professional career. After reading the article, your athlete decides to work harder at rehabilitation and sets a goal to persevere and recapture the starting position on your team just like Tedy did.

As another example, consider an athlete who reads in the newspaper about a local athlete who volunteers at the local Boys & Girls Club. This athlete decides to imitate the *social behavior* and also volunteer for the local Boys & Girls Club. Another example of a symbolic model is when an athlete reads a book on a subject such as the fundamentals of pitching and attempts to imitate the *motor behavior* described in the book. Finally, consider this example of a symbolic model affecting behavior: A beginning gymnast watches an Olympic gymnast on television who stares intently into the eyes of her coach and listens carefully to every word her coach says before her performance. The next day in practice, the young gymnast imitates the *learning behavior* she observed the day before on television. She stares intently at her coach and pays close attention to everything her coach says.

In all four preceding examples, a symbolic model depicts a different type of behavior. Both symbolic and real models act as powerful learning sources for athletes through observational learning.

FOUR PROCESSES OF OBSERVATIONAL LEARNING

Four processes occur during observational learning. These processes are the attentional process, the retention process, the motor reproduction process, and the motivational process. The following text explains them.

Attentional Process

Attention is obviously important because if an athlete doesn't notice the modeled behavior, he or she won't be able to imitate that behavior. People constantly ignore all kinds of behaviors. They are likely and able to imitate only those behaviors that they attend to.

Several factors influence the attentional process. These factors have to do with both the characteristics of the modeled behavior and characteristics of the observer. Because these factors greatly determine whether or not an athlete will attend to and imitate a particular behavior, it is worth discussing them.

Characteristics of the Modeled Behavior

Many factors affect the way the modeled behavior captures the observer's attention. This section focuses on five of them: distinctiveness, affective valence, complexity, prevalence, and functional value. To effectively capture attention, the modeled behavior must have enough **distinctiveness** to be singled out from other behaviors that have similarities. The modeled behavior also must have **affective valence**. For example, like one atom attracting and combining with another atom, the modeled behavior must have some type of emotional appeal that attracts the observer's attention to the model.

Complexity is an important factor, too. If the behavior it is too complex to be fully observed, the athlete may not attend to it; if it is too simple, it might not be interesting enough to capture attention. **Prevalence** means the frequency with which the modeled behavior occurs. If the athlete only sees the behavior once or twice, the athlete may not have enough opportunity to adequately attend to the behavior. When it comes to sport, good behavior can't be modeled too frequently. Success in sport is derived to a great extent from doing the right things at the right time and doing them right all the time. Athletes who consistently observe good behaviors—whether it is social, learning, champion, or motor behavior—are likely to consistently imitate these behaviors.

Finally, the modeled behavior must have the right balance of **functional value**. If the behavior is of no ascertainable use or significance to the athlete, the athlete is not likely to attend to it; if functional value is high, the athlete is likely to pay close attention. Functional value has to do with the value the modeled behavior possesses. For example, if I am preparing to jump out of an airplane for the first time with a parachute, I am likely to attend very closely to the instructor's demonstration of how and when to open the chute. Modeled behavior also has to do with what Brewer and Wann (1998) consider the power of the model. Models that possess expertise, experience, success, and other similar defining attributes are considered to have *power* and, therefore, they attract the attention of the observer.

Characteristics of the Observer

At least four factors affect the observer's effectiveness in the attentional process: sensory capacities, arousal level, perceptual set, and past reinforcement. **Sensory capacity** has to do with the ability of the observer to functionally observe the modeled behavior. For example, the observer has to be in position to adequately observe the entire behavior from start to finish. **Arousal level** has to do with the level of alertness and motivation the observer brings to the observational learning situation. Athletes who are asleep or uninterested are likely to miss or ignore the modeled behavior. **Perceptual set** has to do with the mental readiness or mindset for observing a stimulus. **Set** is considered a predisposition to react to stimulation in a given manner. Finally, **past reinforcement** is an important factor for the observer. If the athlete has received reinforcement in the past for observing a modeled behavior, he is likely to do so in the future.

Retention Process

Paying attention to a modeled behavior isn't much good if the athlete doesn't do something to remember what has been observed. Usually a delay exists between the observation of a modeled behavior and the opportunity to practice imitating that behavior. Consequently, it is necessary to somehow retain the observed stimuli. According to Bandura, two types of mental representations exist: visual (imaginal) and verbal. So, once an athlete observes a modeled behavior, she can store a *visual* sequence of the action, perhaps remind herself *verbally* of key elements of the action, and then *mentally rehearse* (visualize) the action.

For example, as a young athlete I had the opportunity to observe Olympic gold medalist Bernie Wrightson compete in a local competition. I was impressed by his style of diving and couldn't wait to get home and imitate what I saw. Unfortunately, I had to wait two days before I could get on a diving board and practice what I observed. So, during those two days I visualized myself performing his hurdle, I reminded myself of key points in his hurdle that were different from mine, and I physically rehearsed the hurdle as well. When I came home from school, the sun perfectly hit our big sliding glass door and I would practice my hurdle as I watched my reflection in the glass.

As mentioned earlier in this chapter, besides motor behaviors, imitated behaviors also include social, learning, and champion behaviors. For some of these types of behaviors it is especially important to use the retention process. For example, when I was coaching at the Pan American Games in Santo

Domingo, Dominican Republic, I got to know Jack Huczek, who at the time was the number one ranked racquetball player in the world. I was able to watch his gold medal match, which he won (and he gave me the racquet he used to win the game!). I was amazed at his determination, aggressiveness, style of play, and overall fitness level.

When I returned home 2 weeks later I couldn't wait to begin imitating his style of play (motor behavior), his determination (champion behavior), and his aggressiveness (social behavior). During the 2 weeks I had to wait, I mentally rehearsed his motor movements, but I also felt the emotion he played with and re-created his mentality for approaching the game. My first game when I returned home was one of the best games I ever played in my life.

Having your athletes observe great performances is very valuable. It is difficult for athletes, particularly young athletes, to perform well if they have never had the opportunity to observe great performances. What does a great performance look like? Feel like? Sound like? What are the specific social behaviors, learning behaviors, motor behaviors, and champion behaviors associated with a great performance? For example, what does the exceptional athlete act like before, during, and after competition? When I observed Bernie Wrightson, I noticed everything about him: the clothes he wore coming in to the pool, his warm-up routine, how he interacted with his competitors, the look on his face during competition, and, much more.

It is also important to let your athletes observe great athletes not only in great performances, but also in great practices, too. Athletes can directly observe the types of day-to-day practice behaviors that ultimately lead to great competition performances. Some talented young athletes who were better than their competitors earlier in their careers erroneously believe that practice (i.e., effort) has little to do with competition; they think that they can take it easy in practice and then *turn it on* during competition. This naive approach only lasts so long and then a day of reckoning arrives. That is the day when all their competitors who had been doing the job in practice every day start putting things together and finding competitive success.

Motor Reproduction Process

All the arousal, observation, and mental rehearsal in the world don't take the place of the actual physical practice of the behavior. Once your athletes have observed the behaviors, you and your athletes must work hard to refine and shape behavior until it resembles the desired observed behavior. According to Bandura (1977), to achieve the desired observed behavior, the individual must possess the physical capability to imitate the behavior, receive accurate feedback during the learning process, and monitor attempts at reproduction. These steps are discussed next.

Determine physical readiness or capability. You can't expect your athletes to imitate a certain behavior if they aren't physically fit enough to imitate the behavior in the first place. For example, at my summer camp I often have campers who want to learn a backward 1 1/2 somersault in the pike position, yet they can't do one hanging pike up. Consider another example of a young and inexperienced football player who wants to imitate a linebacker he admires. This young football player should not be encouraged to imitate the more experienced football player until he has acquired sufficient shoulder and neck strength and has learned proper tackling technique.

Provide accurate feedback. While at my summer camp, I have seen athletes who observed one of my senior divers perform a particular motor movement and then went home and asked their coaches to help them learn the movement. The only problem was that their coaches didn't know how to teach the movement, provided inaccurate feedback, and the kids learned to imitate a distorted version of the movement. When they returned to my camp the following summer all I could say was this: "What is that?" It was so transformed that I couldn't recognize the original motor movement they were trying to imitate. Likewise, I have observed coaches trying to teach their athletes a movement that the coaches did not fully understand; consequently, their feedback to their athletes was inaccurate. Coaches must fully understand what they are teaching in order to provide accurate feedback.

Monitor reproductive attempts. This idea is somewhat different from providing accurate feedback. In this case, the athlete may correctly learn the observed behavior but lose the movement during practice unless the coach continues to monitor the reproduction process. The reproduction process takes hard work, spurred on by the motivated coach and athlete, to reach a high level of proficiency. This process may be considered the becoming process. It is as though coach and athlete are saying, "Okay, we have the idea and we know in which direction we are headed. We have achieved the movement to some degree, but need to further refine it. We have to stay on top of it, get it right, and work towards perfection."

From a safety perspective, the coach should monitor reproduction attempts to protect the athlete's well-being. Particularly for highly skilled movements where the potential for bodily harm exists, monitoring reproductive attempts is critical. When learning new and difficult movements such as a release move on high bar in gymnastics, reverse dive on springboard, pole vault, high jump, or headlock hip toss in wrestling, the coach should carefully monitor each reproductive attempt.

Motivational Process

Throughout daily life people observe many behaviors that they choose to never imitate. In fact, they may actually acquire these behaviors but choose to never perform them. For example, you might hear and remember an off-color joke but because of its inappropriateness and your subsequent dislike of the joke, you choose not to repeat it. What makes people choose to perform an observed behavior? According to social cognitive learning theory, the answer is motivation.

Motivation may be the most important of the four processes of observational learning outlined in figure 5.1. Without motivation, the observer is unlikely to be swayed to imitate the behavior. While Bandura identifies the motivation process as the final process before imitation occurs, motivation is the key component in all four stages or processes of observational learning. For example, during the *attentional process,* the model must possess enough emotional appeal (affective valence) and power (functional value) to motivate the athlete to pay attention. And the observer must be motivated (arousal level) enough to spend valuable attentional capacity watching the model. Next, the observer must be further motivated to organize and cognitively retain the information in the *retention process* and further motivated in the *motor reproduction process* to practice the observed behavior.

At the 2008 Olympic Trials in Indianapolis, Indiana, a few of my divers drove up from Bloomington to watch the men's 10-meter platform warm-up and competition. A few days later an assistant coach reported that after observing the competition our divers came home and had some amazing practices. They modeled some of the techniques they had observed as well as the level of intensity and motivation they had observed.

From an observational learning perspective, it is easy to understand my athletes' reactions and subsequent actions the next day. The gala of the trials captured their attention and motivated them to engage in the flow of processes for observational learning (see figure 5.1). The Olympic Trial divers were elite-level athletes being applauded and ogled by thousands of spectators (affective valence) and they demonstrated a level of diving competence that my divers aspired to reach (functional value and power). My divers also were able to watch both warm-ups and competition (prevalence). As for the observers, my divers were mentally ready (perceptual set) to understand and appreciate (sensory capacity) the complexity of the diving. All of this combined with reinforcement from the roar of the crowd, the NBC television cameras, and the honor of making the Olympic team and representing the United States induced a high level of arousal that captured my divers' attention and motivated them to closely observe and return home to imitate what they observed.

So, how do you motivate an athlete to imitate an observed behavior? From an operant learning theory perspective, the answer is reinforcement or the

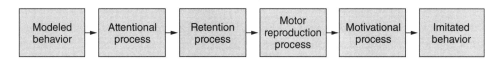

Figure 5.1 Flow of processes for observational learning based on social cognitive learning theory.

anticipation of reinforcement. Later this chapter will also answer the question of how you motivate an athlete to refrain from imitating an observed behavior.

SOURCES OF REINFORCEMENT

The two sources of reinforcement for imitative behavior are called *direct* and *vicarious*. **Direct reinforcement** is received when the consequence of the behavior results in reinforcement to the observer. In other words, the athlete is directly reinforced after imitating a certain behavior. For example, in scenario 3 one of your athletes observes another athlete thanking you after practice and you smile at that athlete. The next day, the athlete observing the modeled behavior comes up to you and also thanks you after practice and you smile and say, "Thanks for saying that. It means a lot to me." Your comments to the athlete act as reinforcement for the behavior.

Scenario 3

Darian, the best performer on your team, walks by you at the conclusion of practice and says, "Thanks for coaching me today!" You respond by smiling and saying, "Thanks, Darian. I appreciate your saying that. I enjoyed working with you." Phil, a young athlete on the team who isn't always very appreciative of things, especially your effort to coach him and make him better, happens to observe your conversation with Darian. The next day Phil imitates Darian's behavior and also thanks you upon leaving practice. You respond with a smile and tell Phil that you really appreciate his taking the time to thank you and you are looking forward to coaching him tomorrow.

Scenario 3 hopefully does or will happen on your team. It is important for athletes to recognize and express their appreciation for what you do for them and how much you care for them as athletes and people. Otherwise, they can take for granted what you do and how much of your heart and soul you give to them. Generally coaches are not highly paid for what they do. Your greatest reward (reinforcement) for coaching is often internal: knowing that you have helped your players become not only better athletes but also better human beings. Their expressed gratitude is also your reward.

When I graduated from college, I could have gone to work for my dad's company and made a fairly generous salary. After 3 or 4 years, the person who took the job I turned down bought a house on a golf course, joined a country club, and had a comfortable life. In contrast, my first 2 years of coaching were at Cypress College, a community college in southern California. I coached for free. My third year I accepted the coaching position at the University of

Nebraska in Lincoln and made $9,000. The following year my annual salary increased to $10,000. The next year there was a freeze on wages.

Despite the financial drawbacks, in my mind I made a decision that was in the right direction for me. I was fortunate to work with Cal Bentz, an experienced and exceptional swimming coach at Nebraska. He loved the sport of swimming and working with young people. Through observation I was able to imitate some of his outstanding qualities, coaching techniques, and interactions with his athletes. I adopted his passion, enthusiasm, and joy for working with athletes; that alone may have been the greatest behaviors I learned to imitate. And in imitating these behaviors, I received the direct reinforcement of athlete gratitude and appreciation, something money can never buy.

Another type of reinforcement for imitative behavior is **vicarious reinforcement**, which is derived from observing someone else reinforced for the same behavior. This type of reinforcement is called vicarious because it is received secondhand. Vicarious reinforcement is why Bandura's theory is called social *cognitive*. The observer makes the *cognitive* assumption that the model does something to receive reinforcement and, therefore, the observer will receive similar reinforcement for imitating the observed behavior.

Vicarious reinforcement can lead individuals to engage in behaviors—even inappropriate or ineffective behaviors—for quite some time despite a lack of any direct reinforcement. Research indicates that administering reward or punishment to a model has an effect on the behavior of the observer. It is as though the observer were directly rewarded or punished, even though it is not the case.

Bandura (1962) conducted a study in which three groups of children observed three different models. All three models behaved aggressively toward an inflated doll. The first model was rewarded for aggressive behavior. The second model was punished, and the third received no consequence for behavior. Next, the three groups of children were allowed to play with the doll. The group that observed aggressive behavior being rewarded was significantly more aggressive in play with the doll than the other two groups.

This result is significant because it suggests that athletes can be indirectly rewarded and the coach may or may not know who the model is or where the reinforcement is coming from. It also suggests that your athletes can be reinforced for inappropriate or ineffective behaviors and these behaviors can persist over time if they are vicariously reinforced. These notions have implications and applications for the coach of excellence, which are discussed later in the chapter.

EFFECTS OF IMITATION

According to Bandura and Walters (1963), imitation has three effects: the modeling effect, the inhibitory or disinhibitory effect, and the eliciting effect.

The **modeling effect** occurs when an observer acquires a new behavior as a result of viewing a model demonstrating that behavior. The term *model* can refer to an actual person whose behavior serves as a stimulus for an observer's response, or, as is often the case, it can refer to a symbolic model such as a character in a book or movie.

The **inhibitory effect** is defined as the suppression of inappropriate or incorrect behavior in an observer as a result of seeing a model punished for engaging in that behavior. The **disinhibitory effect** is the opposite effect. This effect occurs when an observer engages in a previously learned deviant behavior as a result of seeing a model rewarded, or at least not punished, for the same behavior. For example, consider scenario 4 in which the athlete talks back to the coach in front of team members. If the athlete is perceived as a role model by the team and the coach fails to reprimand the athlete in front of the other team members, then at some point the coach most likely can expect to see a similar behavior from other athletes because the model's initial inappropriate behavior was not punished and therefore not inhibited. In fact, if the other athletes laughed at the inappropriate behavior, the laughter can act as a reinforcer.

Scenario 4

You have gathered your team for an important team meeting. While you are talking to the team, you have an athlete talk disrespectfully to you in front of your team. It isn't the first time you have encountered this behavior from the athlete and you now realize that you must stop this kind of behavior before other athletes imitate it and you lose the respect and control of your team. What do you do?

The **eliciting effect** occurs when an observer engages in a similar but not identical behavior as a result of observing a model. For example, in scenario 5 an athlete on your team observes your team captain voluntarily mentoring a less experienced athlete on your team. Due to the eliciting effect, the athlete decides to imitate a somewhat similar behavior and volunteers to read

Scenario 5

One of your athletes observes another athlete on the team acting as a mentor to one of the younger and inexperienced athletes on the team. The observing athlete decides to imitate a similar behavior, so the next day he volunteers to read to children in the local elementary school.

to children in the local elementary school. The athlete also could choose to visit children in the hospital or become a better friend and spend more time outside of practice with the younger members of the team.

As mentioned at the beginning of the book, theories don't mean much, especially to coaches, if they can't be directly applied to the coaching and motor learning process.

APPLYING OBSERVATIONAL LEARNING THEORY IN COACHING ATHLETES

Following are specific ways that you can apply observational learning to improve coaching effectiveness, athlete performance, and program excellence.

Be aware of who your athletes are observing as role models and their sources of reinforcement for imitative behavior. One characteristic of a successful program is that athletes have good role models and a plentiful source of reinforcement. The opposite is also true: Unsuccessful programs have poor role models and, unfortunately, reinforcement is in place in these programs for athletes to imitate poor behavior. How does a coach of excellence turn this situation around? According to social cognitive theory, the answer is to use operant conditioning.

Use operant conditioning principles to control who becomes a model and what types of reinforcement are available to your athletes for imitating appropriate behavior. In other words, use operant conditioning principles to reward good models and athletes' imitation of good behavior; punish poor models and athletes' imitation of inappropriate behavior.

For example, early in my career I was afraid of losing my job unless I produced champions, but I was more afraid of the direction my program was taking and the inappropriate behaviors many of my athletes were learning. Our team captain was very talented and narrowly missed winning a conference title the year before (he was also NCAA All-American the year before), but he was not a model for dedication, effort, and commitment. After many meetings with him I realized that nothing was going to change on his part, so I decided to change things on my part.

The next day I went over to him and, knowing it might eventually cost me my job, I told him to clear out his locker. I then went over to my walk-on freshman diver who was the worst diver on the team, but the hardest worker and most dedicated, and told him he was my new team captain. It was a jaw-dropping moment for all three of us. The former captain was shocked that he no longer was a member of the team, the freshman was shocked to suddenly become the team leader, and I was shocked at my actions and secretly wondered if I would still have a job at the end of the season. Well, fortunately, I did keep my job and by substituting a new team captain (i.e., model) and providing reinforcement for team members imitating the new model, our team eventually found success through hard work, dedication, determination, and commitment. Four years later we were crowned national team champions.

Be aware of unseen sources of modeling and reinforcement and control these sources so that no hidden curriculum exists in your program. Sometimes the source of reinforcement can be hidden. Recall the concept of vicarious reinforcement. In this situation, the observer (athlete) doesn't directly receive reinforcement. Rather, the observer cognitively assumes that he will receive reinforcement for imitating the behavior. Therefore, administering of reinforcement is not overt. As a coach you must be vigilant and responsive to the models and types of reinforcement that affect your athletes' behaviors.

Remember that observational learning has far-reaching effects. If you don't think it is worth monitoring and controlling your athletes' observational learning, please reconsider. As mentioned earlier, observational learning can affect not only the behavior of your current athletes but also the behavior of future generations of athletes. Therefore, it is worth your time and effort to reinforce appropriate models and imitative behavior now so that each successive generation of your athletes acquires these same behaviors. It is amazing how much easier it becomes for new athletes to adopt the right behaviors once appropriate role models and reinforcements are in place. Incoming athletes join in lockstep with older athletes in imitating appropriate behavior. This is one sign of a healthy, thriving, and successful program.

Observational learning and reinforcement should include the four areas of behavior. In coaching, an obvious point of emphasis is motor learning. You want your athletes to learn sound techniques and perform well. Movements such as a good runner's stride, proper stance for a take-down in wrestling, good form in the backstroke, powerful tennis forehand, accurate basketball jump shot, and proper golf swing are important for athletes to observe. However, don't limit observational learning and reinforcement to merely motor movements. As previously mentioned, much goes into developing a competent athlete. Therefore, encourage your athletes to imitate good social, learning, and champion behaviors as well.

Model good behaviors that you hope to see in your own athletes. Your athletes look up to you, respect you, and follow your lead. So, your own behaviors should reflect the behaviors you hope to see in your athletes. As their coach, you serve as an important model and a powerful source for direct reinforcement. Even if you can't always model good motor behavior, you can model good social, learning, and champion behaviors. Good behaviors include behaviors already mentioned such as dedication, persistence, competitiveness, focus, and work ethic. Good behaviors also include acting calm under pressure, exuding confidence, reflecting optimism, accepting responsibility, showing compassion toward others, and learning more about your sport.

Develop yourself as a coach of excellence. A study by the USOC (Gibbons et al., 2002) suggests that athletes highly regard coaches who are knowledgeable about their sport, possess a high degree of strategic knowledge, and are effective teachers. Therefore, when you learn more about your sport and become a more effective coach, you command greater respect from your athletes and increase your affective valence (emotional appeal) and functional value (power) as a model.

Select team captains who can model good behaviors and not just good motor skills and performances. Team captains need to be athletes whom other team members admire and perceive as worthy of imitation; otherwise, the team may be unwilling to imitate their captains' behaviors. Your team captains don't necessarily need to be the best athletes on the team. Your team captains need to be individuals who are hard working, dedicated to the team and team goals, willing to put the needs of the team before their own needs, value the role of captain, willing to be outspoken when necessary, accept responsibility, and model the behaviors that reflect the persona of your team. Good role models are critical to the overall success of your team.

Pair a promising young athlete with a proven and successful athlete who models good technique, competitive skills, leadership, and social skills. This model may be another athlete on your team or it might be someone else such as a professional athlete or former athlete. For example, in his freshman year I asked Mike, one of my athletes, to study and imitate Dmitri Sautin, the famous Russian Olympic gold medalist. He would study Dmitri's diving for hours and then try to imitate his diving mechanics. Before most practices, he would view Dmitri's diving in my office and immediately go out to the pool and imitate what he saw. He not only imitated Dmitri's diving but also Dmitri's mental toughness, competitiveness, and single-minded focus. Mike went on to a very successful athletic career. Observational learning accelerated Mike's motor skill development as well as his emotional and mental toughness.

Many young athletes instinctively pair themselves with certain athletes: The young basketball player who dreams of becoming the next famous NBA player he idolizes imitates his idol's every move; the young baseball pitcher who watches every game and analyzes every pitch of his favorite MLB pitcher; the aspiring hockey player who has every instructional video produced by his star NHL player. If your athletes don't have a model, help them select one. If they have an inappropriate model (the model isn't right for them because of body type; poor, unusual, or difficult-to-imitate technique; or inappropriate social and champion behaviors), help them select a more appropriate model.

THE IMITATING ATHLETE

The **imitating athlete** is someone already on your team. In fact, the imitating athlete is everyone on your team. Much learning occurs through observational learning. Every athlete selects certain observable behaviors and chooses to imitate them. In fact, the best imitators on your team are likely to be some of your best athletes. They are your best athletes in part because they are adept at observing the behaviors of others and mimicking them. The imitating athlete is someone who imitates or attempts to imitate not just any behaviors, but appropriate social, learning, motor, and champion behaviors. This athlete not only imitates observed behaviors but eventually displays good behaviors and thereby ultimately serves as a model for other team members, especially your young and beginning athletes.

THE IMITATING COACH

The **imitating coach** is a compilation of her experiences of observing others, especially other coaches. We are not immune to the process of observational learning. We are the product of those whom we have observed, both good and bad. We strive to imitate the appropriate behaviors we have seen modeled and reinforced and to disregard the inappropriate behaviors we have observed modeled and punished—or at the very least unrewarded. Moreover, we are cognizant of the fact that we are one of the most important role models for our athletes and we endeavor to model the behaviors we hope to see in our athletes.

YOUR COACHING TOOLBOX

Now you have another tool for your coaching toolbox. Because observational learning occurs so frequently, as a coach of excellence you will take the time to understand the concept of social cognitive theory and use it to shape the learning environment and your athletes' behaviors. You will use this tool to help your athletes learn through the processes of observation, imitation, and reinforcement acceptable social behaviors, learning behaviors, motor behaviors, and champion behaviors. You also will use this learning theory tool to encourage your athletes to inhibit unacceptable social, learning, motor, and champion behaviors.

THE SCIENTIFIC AND ARTFUL COACH

As a scientific coach you understand the importance of social cognitive theory for shaping athlete behaviors. You use observational learning and operant conditioning principles to shape the imitating athlete's behaviors. And you don't limit these behaviors being learned to strictly motor learning behaviors. You also use this tool to shape social, learning, and champion behaviors.

As an artful coach, you are sensitive to the direction your athletes are taking. In other words, you are attuned to the models your athletes observe and attempt to imitate. You also monitor sources of reinforcement, both direct and vicarious, for imitative behavior. If you notice that things are headed in the wrong direction, you intervene and attempt to provide new role models, reinforce appropriate imitative behavior, and inhibit inappropriate behavior.

IF YOU REMEMBER ONLY THREE THINGS

1. *Remember that observational learning occurs naturally whether you want it to occur or not.* Consequently, pay attention to the models, observers, and reinforcement that is occurring on your team and learn to control these variables to positively influence athlete behavior. It is interesting to note that even birds such as black-capped chickadees (Hughes, Nowicki, & Lohr, 1998) and pigeons (Kaiser, Zentall, & Galef, 1997) learn by imitating observed behavior. Don't ignore this naturally occurring phenomenon; it affects your athletes daily.

2. *Remember to not limit your scope of behaviors.* Don't be satisfied that your players are imitating motor skills such as a correct jump shot, proper backhand, efficient swim stroke, or good bench press. Reinforce your athletes for imitating all four areas of athlete behavior: social, learning, champion, and motor behavior.

3. *Remember that you are the most important role model on your team.* Like my son who observed me say, "Damn," they are always watching. What you hope to see in your athletes you should model through your own behaviors. Thus, your behavior should set the standard for your team. Your behavior should reflect core values such as self-discipline, high effort, motivation, intensity, dedication, determination, fair play, ethicalness, good sporting behavior, calmness under pressure, and resilience. No one ever said being a coach of excellence would be easy.

SUGGESTED READINGS

Bandura, A. (1963). *Social learning and personality development.* New York: Holt, Rinehart & Winston.

Bandura, A. (1977). *Social learning theory.* Morristown, NJ: General Learning.

[Bandura can be slow reading, mainly because he is so brilliant. In this book I have tried to provide a faithful rendition of his theory in a more readable and applicable fashion for coaches.]

Howard, G.A. (2000). *Remember the titans.*

[Based on a true story, this movie recounts the integration of a high school in Alexandria, Virginia. I love this movie in part because it shows how one person can shape the behaviors of young athletes under his direction by modeling the behaviors and beliefs he hopes to see in others. It makes me want to be not only a better coach, but a better human being.]

CHAPTER 6

The Supercomputing Athlete

Applying Cognitive Learning Theory

Key Terms

action clause
action discrimination
action-plan-reconstruction hypothesis
anxiety
arousal
attributes
basic information processing model
chunking
closed skill
cognitive units
composition
concept
condition clause
condition discrimination
constant practice
contextual interference effect
cue-utilization hypothesis.
declarative knowledge
defining attributes

degrees of freedom
discrimination
dual coding theory
echoic
effector level
elaboration
elaboration hypothesis
encoding
episodic memory
executive level
expected sensory consequences
focus unit
forgetting or spacing hypothesis
generalization
generalized motor program
general motor program theory
gist
Hick's law
iconic
imaginal coding system

input
invariant features
knowledge base
knowledge compilation
links
long-term memory
macroproduction rule
mapping
memory
mind-to-muscle skills
modal model of memory
movement-output chunks
muscle-to-mind skills
network model of memory
nodes
open skill
organization
output
parameters
parameter values
perceptual narrowing
proceduralization

procedural knowledge
production
production rules
production systems
proposition
reaction time
recall memory
recall schema
recognition memory
recognition schema
rehearsal
relative timing
response programming

response selection
retrieval practice
ruminate
schema
schema activation
semantic memory
short-term memory
short-term sensory
   storage
speed of processing
spreading activation
stimulus

stimulus identification
stimulus–response
   alternatives
stimulus–response
   compatibility
strengthening
supercomputing athlete
supercomputing coach
surface features
tuning
varied practice
verbal coding system

❝ *It is possible that what has traditionally been considered memory research and what has been considered motor control research may be seen as related rather than distinct areas of motor behavior research.* **❞**

R.A. Magill, *Motor Learning: Concepts and Applications*

One day two young boys decide to simultaneously join a club team. They are approximately the same height and weight and both appear to have comparable athletic ability. They come from similar backgrounds, are the same age, and attend the same school. They train the same number of hours with the same coach on the same days, and they are similarly motivated to becoming great athletes. Two boys could not be more alike. But there is a glaring difference: One boy improves more rapidly than the other. How is this difference possible? The boys have the same physical component, same motivational component, same coach component, and same training component. What, then, is the difference? Is it due to a cognitive component? Does the rapidly improving boy process information differently than the other boy?

The observation that differences in motor learning and performance can be due to differences in cognition motivated me (Huber, 1997) to study two groups of subjects: four athletes who were U.S. national finalists and four athletes who were not finalists. All athletes were collegiate competitors with approximately the same number of years experience, similar ages, and similar physical ability. They were asked to perform, immediately view a video replay of their performance, and then verbally report the thoughts they had before, during, and after performance. Their verbal reports were then analyzed for differences and similarities in structure and content.

Results from this study were quite interesting. Discernable cognitive differences existed between groups. The elite group (national finalists) clearly did something different with the structure and content of information related to motor performance than the nonelite group. Perhaps of even greater interest in this study is that several years later two of the elite performers went on to earn Olympic medals—one a gold medal and the other a silver medal.

Does cognition play a major role in the development of elite performance? Consider the following story.

Kristin hailed from the Pacific Northwest, growing up not far from Puget Sound. She was a two-time high school state champion and an honor student. Her mother was a musician and her father was an electrical engineer. She competed at the junior level in the summers but never performed well enough to even qualify for the junior national championship. As for the senior national championship, to her way of thinking that level of competition was way beyond her physical reach and, quite honestly, completely off her mental radar. It was clear that she had talent and perhaps the potential to become a better athlete. What wasn't so clear was how well and how rapidly she could develop her talent and reach her greatest potential. To find out, she decided to continue her athletic career in college.

Kristin was an interesting character study: a driven individual both inside and outside the classroom. She studied so hard and practiced so hard, she was like a superwoman. Actually, she was more like super*computer* woman—a rapid processor of information. Certainly it is an understatement to say she was a fast learner. Her coach would give her data (coaching feedback) and, like a supercomputer, she would rapidly process the data, translating it into improved motor performance. After her sophomore year in college she was crowned U.S. national champion. Amazingly, in two years Kristin went from not being able to qualify for the junior national championship to being the best athlete in her sport at any level in the United States.

Like the other athletes we considered in earlier stories, Kristin wasn't necessarily more physically talented than her fellow athletes. Her rapid improvement and notable achievements could be traced to the *cognitive component*, her exceptional ability to process information and use that information to accelerate improved motor learning and performance. From a cognitive perspective, the difference between the athletes in each story is due to a difference in software rather than hardware. In other words, the difference between groups can be attributed to cognitive ability rather than physical ability.

This chapter is the story about the supercomputing athlete and how you can use cognitive learning theory in your coaching to transform your athletes into human processing machines—super learners capable of rapidly translating your coaching feedback into improved motor learning and performance to reach their greatest potential.

CHAPTER OVERVIEW

The chapter is divided into four sections, each with three subsections. The first section examines the three components of a simple but useful model of human cognition called the basic information processing model. The model's structure, the characteristics and limitations of each component, and their applications for affecting motor learning and performance are covered. The second section discusses the three stages of motor learning, a simple but useful paradigm for understanding and influencing athlete learning. The third section considers three cognitive theories—motor program theory, schema theory, and ACT-R—and their applications for helping you develop supercomputing athletes. The fourth section examines the three stages of information processing that occur during motor performance—stimulus identification, response selection, and response programming—and outlines applications for how you can help your athletes cognitively resemble elite athletes during each of the three stages. The chapter concludes with a composite picture of the supercomputing athlete.

THE COMPUTER AS METAPHOR

Cognitive learning theory is a much different approach to studying athlete behavior than behavior theory. While behavioral theories are effective tools for your coaching toolbox (recall, for example, that respondent conditioning is possibly the most important tool in the box), they overlook a critical factor of human behavior—human thought. Unlike Pavlov's dogs and Skinner's rats and pigeons, human beings are equipped with a brain capable of higher mental functioning. Unlike canines, rodents, and avian animals, human beings can analyze, sort, organize, code, store, and retrieve fairly large amounts of information. It is interesting to note that even the lowly rat demonstrates a minimal amount of cognition. For example, when rats are introduced to a maze, these little fellows are capable of **mapping**, a cognitive process of remembering the route of the maze.

Motor learning is closely connected to cognition because cognitive processes mediate motor learning much like they do for other types of human learning. As Magill (1985) has suggested, memory research and motor control research are related topics of study. In other words, motor learning relies on the same cognitive mechanisms as other types of mental tasks such as understanding a written paragraph, performing multiplications, and remembering new information. Although it is impossible to observe mental operations firsthand (it would be nice if we could lift the hood and take a peek at the engine), it is possible nevertheless to study human cognitive processes and how they relate to motor learning. Help guiding this study is the *computer as metaphor.*

Several factors influenced the cognitive revolution, including the frustration with the methods and limitations of behavioral theory and contradictory linguistic evidence for the behavioral explanation for language development

(Bruning, Schraw, & Ronning, 1995), but perhaps no factor was more influential than the emergence of computers (Baars, 1986). Cognitive theory uses the computer as metaphor and asks, "What if the human mind works like a computer?" What a fascinating question, and one that leads to other questions, such as "How does the mind receive new information? How does the mind organize, store, and retrieve, new information? What types of software programs does the mind generate?"

Cognitive theory research has expanded its scope of inquiry to include athletes and motor learning and performance. It asks, "What if the athlete's mind thinks like a computer? What does the supercomputing athlete look like and how can coaches use cognitive theory to help athletes learn?" This chapter begins with an examination of a simple but extremely useful model of human cognition called the basic information processing model.

THREE MEMORY COMPONENTS: THE BASIC INFORMATION PROCESSING MODEL

The **basic information processing model** most often referred to in literature is based primarily on the work of Atkinson and Shiffrin (1968) and is sometimes referred to as the **modal model of memory** (Baddeley, 1997). The basic information processing model of memory distinguishes among three types of memory: short-term sensory storage (STSS), short-term memory (STM), and long-term memory (LTM). These memory units and the flow of information are outlined in figure 6.1.

The differences among these three types of memory storage have to do with the different characteristics and the amount of processing of information required at each stage. *Processing* refers to mental activities such as attending, organizing, rehearsing, and storing information. Keep in mind that the basic information processing model is just that—a model. It is not a literal representation of the actual structure and workings of the mind. It is simply a metaphor for how the mind might function. The model of cognitive learning theory does not describe memory in specific neurological terms, but it does provide a simple and useful model of human thinking that helps researchers, educators, and coaches answer questions regarding teaching and learning. Characteristics of the memory storage units that make up the information processing model are examined next.

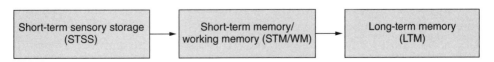

Figure 6.1 Basic information processing model and the flow of information.

Short-Term Sensory Storage

People are constantly bombarded with external stimuli. For example, consider a basketball practice for 9- and 10-year-olds. At any one time there might be kids talking to each other, basketballs flying in the air, players chasing one another, people calling the coach's name, people asking questions, or kids diving for balls. **Short-term sensory storage** (STSS) takes in most of this but it is fleeting. Two types of short-term sensory storage exist: echoic and iconic storage (Neisser, 1976). **Echoic** is the brief echo you hear when someone stops talking. For example, suppose you haven't been listening to someone's story and he suddenly asks, "What did I just say?" At this moment you might perhaps hear the echo of that last bit of information still in STSS. **Iconic** memory is the image you retain when you see something, close your eyes, and still see that image if only fleetingly. Information can be retained in STSS for less than 1 second.

From a cognitive perspective, attention may be defined as what athletes select from the bombardment of information into STSS and allow into short-term memory (STM), also known as working memory (WM).

Short-Term Memory (Working Memory)

Short-term memory (STM) holds information selected from STSS. When people attend to stimuli, it enters the system and is loaded into STM. STM holds the things people consciously attend to and work on, something akin to a chalkboard or writing tablet. Calfee (1981) likens it to a scratch pad for thinking. Somewhat more recently, most models of memory emphasize the processing component rather than the storage aspect of this part of the processing system (e.g., Anderson, 1976, 1983). For this reason it is referred to as working memory (WM). In this view, WM and LTM work together and are considered closely related rather than separate components. Throughout this chapter, this short-term portion of memory is referred to as working memory (WM).

Information can be sustained in WM for approximately 20 seconds or less. However, the information can be maintained through rehearsal. People rehearse information by consciously repeating (thinking about) items in WM. The capacity for WM is about seven separate items (plus or minus two), which is why phone numbers are seven digits, not including the area code. You might wonder how we remember 10-digit phone numbers that include the area code. Besides the fact that some people can maintain more information in working memory than others, a process called chunking helps to increase WM capacity.

Chunking is the process whereby related items are grouped together into more easily remembered items. For example, consider the phone number 812-856-1212 for a dorm room at IU. To remember this number, I need to remember only four items: [university area code] + [dorm prefix] + [12] + [12]. I might even chunk the last two items into one item: [12 repeated]. Miller

(1956) uses an apt analogy for understanding the concept of capacity and chunking in working memory. He likens working memory to a change purse that can only hold seven coins. It might hold just seven pennies, but it could also hold seven nickels, seven dimes, or seven quarters; each coin represents an increasingly higher number of pennies.

In summary, WM is the workplace for maintaining a relatively small amount of information people consciously attend to long enough to do things such as make sense of new information, solve math problems, and make decisions such as which motor program or strategy to employ. People also use WM to help anchor new information into long-term memory.

Long-Term Memory

Long-term memory (LTM) is the permanent storehouse of information for everything people know. Whereas information held in WM is in an active and ongoing conscious process, information held in LTM, which will be referred to as **memory** throughout the remainder of the chapter, is not in the immediate consciousness. For this reason information in working memory is more easily disrupted by external interferences. For example, consider an athlete who is attempting to listen to his coach's comments but is distracted by his teammate's banter. His coach's comments, temporarily stored in WM, are more than likely quickly forgotten. In contrast, information in memory is quite stable and retrievable over time. For example, if a dancer knows that the ballroom rumba is the slowest of the five competition Latin and American dances, she is likely to remember that forever.

From a cognitive perspective, information is selected from STSS, maintained in WM, and eventually anchored into memory. The process of anchoring new information into memory is called encoding. **Encoding** is a process whereby new information is given meaning and transformed or abstracted into representations and transferred to memory. Memory represents what Chi and Glaser (1980) call the knowledge base. The **knowledge base** is the accumulation of all the different types of information stored during a lifetime. Table 6.1 summarizes the characteristics of the three levels of memory just discussed.

Types of Knowledge in Memory

Various types of information make up your knowledge base: declarative (made up of semantic and episodic information), imaginal, and procedural memory information. **Declarative knowledge** is explicit, conscious long-term memory of all the facts, information, and experiences that are part of what you know. Declarative knowledge includes both semantic and episodic memory. **Semantic memory** refers to memory of general concepts and principles associated with these concepts. For example, the rules that athletes associate with their sports, such as the infield fly rule, allowable fouls to commit, and number of minutes in a game, constitute semantic memory.

Table 6.1 The Three Levels of Memory

	Short-term sensory storage (STSS)	Short-term memory (STM/WM)	Long-term memory (LTM)
Alternate names	Echoic or iconic	Working or primary	Secondary or memory
Duration	Less than 1 second	Less than 20 seconds	Indefinite
Stability	Fleeting	Easily disturbed	Fairly stable
Capacity	Extremely limited	Limited (7 ± 2 items)	Unlimited
General characteristics	Momentary, unconscious impression	Working memory; immediate; consciousness; active; maintained with rehearsal	Knowledge base; associationistic; encoded information; different levels of processing

Episodic memory refers to the storage and retrieval of personal experiences associated with specific times and places (Tulving, 1983, 1985). An example of episodic memory is when an athlete recounts a memorable trip to the state championship: "Well, we drove up the night before and got to stay in a really fancy hotel. In the morning we walked to the arena for warm-ups. That night the stands were packed and the crowd was crazy. We started out nervous but settled down and we won in the last seconds of the game."

One contribution of cognitive psychology has been the reintroduction of mental imagery into the realm of study. Alan Paivo (1971, 1986a) has proposed that information is represented in two separate memory systems. One system stores verbal information and the other system stores images. According to Paivo, words, sentences, stories, and the content of conversations are held in the **verbal coding system** while nonverbal information such as pictures, sensations, and sounds are stored in the **imaginal coding system**. Paivo's (1986b) theory is called a **dual coding theory** because incoming information can be held within one or both of the systems. Retention of information is enhanced when it is held in both systems rather than one system. Paivo has hypothesized that nonverbal memory traces are more resilient than verbal memories.

The final and most important type of knowledge for this chapter and book is **procedural knowledge**, which refers to things we know how *to do*, such as tie a shoe lace, solve a physics problem, drive a car, or perform a cartwheel. Procedural knowledge includes knowledge about procedures (e.g., how to perform long division), motor skills (e.g., how to serve in tennis), as well as conditioned responses (e.g., press the car brake when the traffic light turns red).

Types of Memory Units

Given the different types of knowledge in memory, one challenge for the field of cognition is finding what meaningful units make up cognitive operations (Bruning, Schraw, & Ronning, 1995). The four different types of cognitive units are concepts, propositions, schemata, and productions. A **concept** is the mental structure in memory that represents a meaningful category. Objects and events are grouped together within that concept based on perceived similarities. The similar features between objects are called **attributes** and features necessary for describing the concept are called **defining attributes**. For example, a game must have rules of conduct, competition, and other defining attributes to be classified within the concept of *sport*.

A **proposition** is the smallest unit of knowledge that can stand as a separate assertion. Propositions can be thought of as statements or assertions and they can be judged as true or false. Propositions are considered to be organized into propositional networks. An example of a proposition is the statement "A basketball hoop is 10 feet from the floor."

A **schema** is a hypothesized data structure that stores memory and controls the encoding, storage, and retrieval of information. A schema contains slots, which hold the content of memory as a range of slot values. A schema is a somewhat nebulous but useful concept for helping coaches understand how athletes learn. It is considered in greater detail later in this chapter.

A **production** is an IF-THEN rule that specifies a specific action and the condition in which the action should be activated. Like propositions, production rules are considered to be organized within a network called production systems. An example of a production rule for bunting in baseball would be the following:

IF the goal is to bunt

THEN pinch the middle of the bat with your top hand.

Like a schema, a production also is a useful concept for helping coaches understand how athletes learn. This concept is discussed in greater detail later in the chapter.

Types of Encoding

Encoding is transferring new information from WM to memory (LTM). The three processes for encoding are rehearsal, elaboration, and organization. **Rehearsal** is the recycling (repetition) of new information, such as when you want to remember a phone number long enough to get to a phone and dial it. Rehearsal is somewhat effective for maintaining new information in WM but not as effective for anchoring it into memory, perhaps because it doesn't make new information distinctive enough.

A more effective process for encoding is **elaboration**, which involves making new information more meaningful and distinctive by relating it to something athletes already know or making it somehow unique (Craik & Lockhart, 1986). For example, athletes are more likely to remember the starting date and time of the opening ceremonies for the Beijing Olympic Games if told that in China the number eight is considered to bring good luck. The starting date and time? 08-08-08 at 8:00 p.m.

The third process for encoding is **organization**, which involves athletes giving structure to new information. When one group of subjects is asked to remember new information and a second group is asked to organize new information but not try to remember it, both groups test the same on recall. In other words, remembering and organizing are essentially one and the same. You can help your players organize new information by giving them the underlying structure (organization) of things. For example, in the sport of track, it helps to remember the events by organizing the sport into three activities: running, jumping, and throwing.

Structure of Memory

A **network model of memory** represents knowledge as a web or network, which is hypothesized to contain **nodes** made up of **cognitive units** (usually concepts or schemata) and **links**, which represent the relations between cognitive units (Anderson, 1983). Nodes are networked (interrelated) to other nodes. Collins and Quillian (1969) proposed a network model in which nodes are concepts arranged in a hierarchy. These nodes are linked to other nodes as well as relational links, which are properties of each node. Figure 6.2 depicts an example of a crude network model of memory modeled after those developed by Collins and Quillian.

According to a network model, when memory is searched, activation moves across the links from the stimulated node to other nodes and relational links. This expanding movement is referred to as **spreading activation**.

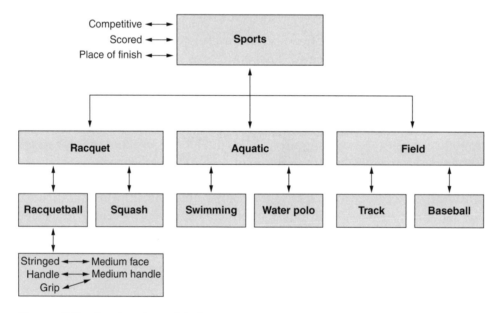

Figure 6.2 A network model of memory.

Perhaps the most important implication of a network model for effective coaching is to remember that information in memory is connected. As you will see, this notion of connectedness has huge implications for athletes understanding and remembering new information.

Applying the Basic Information Processing Model in Coaching Athletes

Now that you have learned all this information, it is time to learn how to apply it to make you a more effective coach and help turn your players into supercomputing athletes.

Short-Term Sensory Storage

When coaching athletes, follow these guidelines for applying short-term sensory storage (STSS).

Limit the amount of stimuli surrounding athletes when providing information. Human sensory systems (vision, hearing, taste, touch, and smell) are constantly inundated with external stimuli, but people are able to respond to only a fraction of all available stimuli at any given time. One way to limit stimuli is to find teachable moments. Pulling an athlete aside for a brief head-to-head conversation or gathering a few of your athletes together for a minilecture are both effective ways to remove your athletes from the ongoing distractions of practice and capture their attention.

Teach your athletes to focus on themselves and you during practice and competition. Suppose for a moment that one of your athletes is standing with two of her friends. One friend is on her right and the other on her left and each friend is simultaneously trying to tell her a different story. You can guess what is likely to happen: Your athlete is going to ask one friend to be quiet for a minute so she can listen to the other friend's story. Why? Because she can't attend to two different stories at once. Similarly, your athletes can't attend intently to you and simultaneously to their teammates or competitors. This point may seem obvious, especially in practice, but it is not quite so obvious in a competitive setting. More than a few athletes, particularly inexperienced athletes (but even experienced athletes too) develop sensory overload at competitions because they haven't learned to ignore or filter distracting sensory stimuli. They get caught up in the sights and sounds of the environment and, most distracting, watching their competitors.

I remember watching one of my divers stand in line on the 1-meter board at the U.S. national championship and his head was moving like a bobblehead doll on a dashboard. He would watch a diver on the 1-meter board, then one on the 3-meter board, and then on platform, and then back to another diver on 1-meter board, and so on. I called him over and instead of facing me and turning his back to the pool, he tried to stand to my left so that he could continue watching all the competitors. I kept backing up so that he couldn't stand to my side. After backing up about 10 feet he finally said, "What are you doing, coach?" I responded, "What are *you* doing?" At that point he realized what he was doing and apologized.

Most interesting is that he knew he should be focusing on my comments and his own performance and not on his competitors, but it was almost as though he couldn't help himself; it was like he was in a hypnotic trance. That wasn't a particularly good meet for him, but in subsequent nationals when he focused on my comments and his performance, he performed well, finishing as high as second! Every sport has athletes who have evidenced similar behavior: players entranced watching their competitors and oblivious to their coach's comments, warm-up routine, game strategy, and preperformance ritual.

Teach your athletes to maintain appropriate arousal level. Too little or too much arousal can cause your athletes to attend to irrelevant cues or too many cues, or cause them to entirely miss relevant cues associated with their performance. The effect of arousal level on stimulus identification is discussed later in this chapter.

Working Memory

When coaching athletes, follow these guidelines for applying working memory:

Avoid presenting too much information at one time. From a cognitive perspective, consciousness is considered attending to stimuli in short-term sensory storage. In other words, once you pay attention to stimuli (become conscious of them), that information passes from short-term sensory storage into working memory. As already mentioned, working memory is limited in its capacity to hold items. For example, in your eagerness to help your athletes, you might be tempted to provide far more information than they can cognitively process. Although it may not seem like a lot of information to you because you have been around your sport a long time, it may be too much data for your athletes, particularly your beginners, and you could overload them.

Provide athletes with ample time to process newly presented information. Even if you provide an appropriate amount of information, it may not get processed if you don't give them enough time to work on the information. Remember, one characteristic of working memory is that information has to be worked on to be maintained. That is why it is referred to as working memory. If you do not give them enough time to work on the information, that information will most likely be lost or maintained in an incomplete form. You can determine if athletes have processed the information when the information is evident in the motor movement. Asking them to recall the information on the next attempt is a good way to determine if they have processed the information. An even better test is to ask them to recall the information at the next practice. If they have processed it well enough in working memory it will have anchored in long term memory.

Consider the age of the athlete. One common way to test working memory capacity is to administer what is called a *digit span test*. In this test, random and unrelated single digits are read aloud and subjects are asked at the conclusion to immediately recall the span of numbers. Results indicate that adults and adolescents typically remember six or seven items or more (7 + 2). However, 6-year-olds, in contrast, are likely to remember only two or three items. Consequently, when working with young children, it is advisable to present small amounts of information at one time.

Teach athletes to chunk information. Because working memory capacity is limited, chunking is a cognitive process that allows individuals to maintain more information in working memory at one time. Sometimes athletes experience data overload. You might hear them say, "Ah! This is just too much to think about!" Chunking helps solve this problem. Teach your athletes to take a number of different cues and group them together so instead of thinking about, say, six things they are only thinking about one or two. You can encourage chunking by giving your athletes ample time to practice a series of actions until they can be performed as a single unit, such as the series of action necessary to hit a tennis serve: stance, toss, swing, and follow through.

Long-Term Memory

As mentioned earlier in this book, one way to define learning is *change*. However, real learning—real change—can't be said to have occurred unless it persists over time. And from a cognitive perspective this means that the change has to be retained in memory. Consequently, a major goal for coaches is the retention of information in memory. Based on the preceding discussion on information processing there are three processes that transfer information into memory (encoding): rehearsal, organization, and elaboration.

Teach your athletes to routinely use rehearsal. Since rehearsal is one method for retaining information in memory, have your athletes get in the habit of rehearsing new movements. For example, you can use *guidance* to manipulate your athletes' bodies through the correct movement and then have them rehearse the new movement several times before attempting to perform the movement. Rehearsal should be part of their preperformance routine. They should also repeat your coaching comments to themselves. In summary, to encode new information in memory, your athletes should routinely repeat your coaching comments to themselves and rehearse the corrections (physical movements).

Teach your athletes to cognitively organize new information. You can encourage cognitive organization by presenting information in an organized format so that your athletes see the big picture when it comes to comprehending the subtleties and nuances of your sport. For example, it is helpful for athletes to understand the different concepts besides fundamental mechanics that are associated (organized) with motor performance, such as relaxation, patience, rhythm, focus, and laws of physics. When you help your athletes create a cognitive organization, they are more likely to remember the information and translate that information into improved motor skill and performance.

Use elaboration when presenting new information. Coaches of excellence are masters at using the method of elaboration when presenting new information to their athletes. In other words, they are adept at finding ways to relate new information to something athletes already know and making new information distinctive and highly memorable. They achieve elaboration in many ways. For example, they may begin by saying, "Now, this new skill is a lot like . . . " or they might say, "The neat thing about this skill is that if you remember to . . . " or "The key point to remember about this new skill is . . . ." Often, athletes come to your sport with backgrounds in other sports and you can sometimes relate a new skill to something they did in another sport. For example, the takeoff for a backward armstand somersaulting dive with a twist on platform is similar to a swivel hips movement on trampoline. To remember to pivot the back foot when swinging a bat, young players are told to *squish the bug.*

Encourage your athletes to use dual coding. Retention of new information is enhanced when it is held in both verbal and imaginal coding systems. Therefore, when you present new information, present pictures along with the information and talk about the feelings and sounds associated with the information. For example, when talking about swinging a softball bat, a coach can have her players watch a video of a great hitter and then have them stand up and practice shifting their body weight from the back foot to the front foot, paying attention to the feel of the shifting body weight. In gymnastics, a coach might have her athlete pause after a particularly great routine, close her eyes, and visualize the performance and feel the performance so she is able to remember and replicate the routine on future attempts. Mental imagery should be part of an athlete's preperformance routine.

Use random practice to enhance motor skill retention. Most research indicates that when people practice a variety of skills randomly, they perform less effectively than people who practice the skills in blocked sequence. When tested at a later time, people who practiced under random conditions demonstrated superior retention compared to individuals who originally practiced under blocked conditions. This finding has been replicated in a number of different experiments (Lee & Magill, 1983; Shea, Kohl, & Indermill, 1990; Ste-Marie, Clark, Findlay, & Latimer, 2004). This phenomenon is known as the **contextual interference effect**, which occurs when random learning conditions initially decrease performance during practice but produce increased learning as measured on a retention test given at a later time.

Two interesting explanations exist for the contextual interference effect. They are both cognitive in nature and have to do with the unique characteristics of memory. In the first explanation, known as the **elaboration hypothesis**, Shea and Zimmy (1983) suggest that through random practice, movements become more distinctive or meaningful and therefore are more embedded in memory. They suggest that when athletes shift from one skill to another during random practice, they must become aware of the differences, similarities, and distinctiveness of each skill. Recall that elaboration is an important process for anchoring information in memory. The more distinctive (i.e., elaborative) something is, the more likely that it will be connected in memory with other information.

Another explanation for the positive retention effects of random practice is what is known as the **forgetting or spacing hypothesis**, which suggests that random practice prevents the repetition of a skill on successive attempts, thereby creating forgetting, which requires the athlete to regenerate (reconstruct) the action plan for that skill all over again. For this reason, the forgetting or spacing hypothesis is sometimes called the **action-plan-reconstruction hypothesis** (Lee & Magill, 1985). Perhaps the best way to understand this hypothesis is to use an example from mathematics.

Suppose you are a 10-year-old and you have to solve three different types of equations: $12 \div 4$, 12×4, and $12 - 4$. With blocked practice you begin with the first problem—$12 \div 4$—and cognitively work on finding the right solution. On the next attempt at solving $12 \div 4$, however, you are likely to simply remember the previous answer rather than repeat the mental processing you did to initially solve the problem. With random practice, you might be asked to solve each problem before trying to again solve $12 \div 4$. By this time, you have forgotten the answer to $12 \div 4$ and therefore you will have to retrieve and apply the appropriate rule for solving long division.

Random practice challenges athletes to generate a solution to a motor skill problem. This process is sometimes referred to as **retrieval practice** because through random practice athletes are required to retrieve the appropriate performance memory units from long-term memory (Bjork, 1975, 1979). This retrieval process helps explain how random practice enhances retention of new information. In one sense, it makes skill learning more distinctive. The athlete associates the skill with the appropriate motor information in memory, thus increasing elaboration. Random practice also encourages the process of organization, another tool for anchoring new information into memory. Going back to the mathematics problem, through random practice the young student begins to organize and distinguish between three types of problems: division, multiplication, and subtraction. The student learns to identify the type of problem and then apply the appropriate solution. The same organizational and retrieval process occurs in motor learning and performance. Through random practice, the athlete learns to organize and distinguish between different types of situational demands and then select the appropriate movement and movement parameters. For example, during catching practice a baseball coach might randomly give a young baseball player different types of throws so that the player learns to recognize and respond to different throws such as grounders, throws to the right, throws to the left, and throws over the player's head.

Teach your athletes learning strategies. Help your athletes better remember new information by helping them become better learners. You can help them become better learners by teaching them simple learning strategies. For example, for young divers (and sometimes collegiate freshmen divers) I like to teach them the following learning strategy called RIPS. In diving, a rip entry means the diver enters the water without a splash. In this case, however, RIPS is an acronym for a simple learning strategy:

R: *Review* quickly before hurdle or back press your coach's prior comments on your last dive and make the corrections on this dive.

I: *Immediately* look at and listen to coach after you perform your dive.

P: *Pose* questions if unsure of coach's comments.

S: *Strategize*—rehearse, elaborate, organize the comments and return to first step.

Be creative in your coaching and come up with your own acronym that is associated with something unique in your sport and conveys the same learning strategy. For example, RUNS in the sport of baseball: Review, Understand, Note changes, Strategize. I also like MURDER. Dansereau (1985) developed this more complex learning strategy for a classroom setting but you can easily modify it for athletes in your sport:

M: Set your *mood* before practice.

U: *Understand* what you want to accomplish during practice.

R: *Recall* what you learned from your last performance or last practice.

D: *Digest* your coach's comments.

E: *Expand* information.

R: *Review* mistakes.

THREE STAGES OF MOTOR LEARNING

At this point in the chapter, you might ask, "What does all this discussion about thinking and memory have to do with motor learning and performance?" You want your athletes to respond, not think. You want them to *grip it and rip it*. You want them to look and automatically react. Well, motor learning, particularly early learning, involves attempts by learners to acquire an idea of the movement (Gentile, 1972) or understand the basic pattern of coordination (Newell, 1985). To achieve these goals, learners must use cognitive (Fitts & Posner, 1967) and verbal processes (Adams, 1971) to solve problems. To this end, Fitts (1964; Fitts & Posner, 1967) suggests that motor skill acquisition follows three stages: the cognitive stage, the associative stage, and the autonomous stage.

As a coach I found this simple paradigm to be extremely helpful for understanding, guiding, and accelerating the motor learning process. Because of its importance, it is worth examining the three stages and their implications for effective coaching.

Cognitive Stage

For the new learner, the problem to be solved in the cognitive stage is understanding what to do (Schmidt & Lee, 2005). It would be extremely difficult for someone to learn a skill without receiving any prior knowledge about the skill, whether that knowledge is visual or verbal. For example, consider the butterfly stroke in swimming. It is a fairly complicated and somewhat unnatural stroke in which to syncopate the movement of the arms with the kick of the legs. It would be difficult indeed for a novice swimmer to learn such a stroke without ever seeing the stroke performed or ever receiving any declarative knowledge about how the stroke is performed. In other words, motor learning begins with the cognitive stage and the processing of information.

Surely the swimmer could discover how to roughly perform the stroke, but it probably would take many long hours of trial and error, experimentation, and some creative problem solving. It is much simpler to learn a skill by first acquiring information about the skill.

The cognitive stage is of great interest to cognitivists because this stage involves information processing. Also called the verbal–motor stage (Adams, 1971), this stage is verbal–cognitive in nature (Schmidt & Lee, 2005) because it involves the conveyance (verbal) and acquisition (cognition) of new information. In this stage, the person is trying to process information in an attempt to cognitively understand the requirements and parameters of motor movement.

Consider several young children taking beginning golf lessons. They might arrive early for their first golf lesson. Having never seen any golfers in action, they are excited and eager to see what golf is all about; each child is a mini tabula rasa ready to learn. They watch the preceding class of golfers and immediately begin collecting visual information. Next, the instructor explains the golf swing, beginning with the grip of the club and stance. Now they are gathering verbal information about the sport. In other words, they don't simply show up and begin golfing. Everything begins with the acquisition and cognitive processing of newly presented information. During this cognitive stage, the beginning athlete ingests information and organizes it into some meaningful form that will ultimately lead to the creation of a motor program.

The cognitive stage is characterized as having large gains in performance and inconsistent performance. During this stage instruction, guidance, slow-motion drills, video analysis, augmented feedback, and other coaching techniques are highly effective (Schmidt & Lee, 2005). Recall the discussion in chapter 4 regarding Adams' closed-loop theory and the importance of error-free learning in the initial learning stage (p. 133). During the cognitive stage it is important that the learner is provided with the necessary information, guidance, and time to establish sound fundamentals of movement. Sometimes making errors and taking a constructivist approach to coaching and learning can be useful (see the discussion on schema theory, p. 196).

Associative Stage

The associative stage is characterized as much less verbal information, smaller gains in performance, conscious performance, adjustment making, awkward and disjointed movement, and taking a long time to complete. During this stage the athlete works at making movement adjustments and stringing together small movement skills. This stage is also called the motor stage (Adams, 1971) because the problem to be solved in the associative stage is learning how to perform the skill (Schmidt & Lee, 2005). From the cognitive perspective, the athlete is attempting to translate declarative knowledge into procedural knowledge. In other words, the athlete is transforming *what* to do into *how* to do.

No diver in the history of the sport of diving has ever performed every single dive for perfect 10s in a single competition. There is always room for improvement. This is true for all sports. For example, a baseball or softball pitcher can improve delivery and learn new pitches, a pole-vaulter can learn to use a new pole and a new technique, a gymnast can refine a routine, a basketball player can improve shooting technique, and a swimmer can improve stroke or flip turn technique. Highly successful athletes and highly effective coaches are always looking for ways to get better. Consequently, they frequently revisit the cognitive stage and then the associative stage of motor learning. Revisiting these stages is the relearning process.

Some years ago, I had an opportunity to work with Professor Yu Fen at Tsinghua University in Beijing, China. Professor Yu Fen is one of the top diving coaches in the world and has produced numerous world and Olympic champions. One of the things I took away from working with her is the importance of continually revisiting the first and second stages of motor acquisition, no matter how accomplished an athlete might be. If a diver was not performing, say, a forward 3 1/2 somersault in the pike position, she would take the diver to the trampoline and begin working a basic jump or single somersault. During one of her practices, I observed Olympic gold medalist Tian Liang practicing on 1-meter springboard virtually the same drill as a beginning athlete on an adjacent springboard.

Let's say you have a new athlete who recently transferred from another program to your program. The reason for the transfer is that he has hit a plateau. In fact, his level of performance has begun to decrease. After observing him, you realize that the reason for his lack of progress is that some of his fundamentals are badly in need of remedial work. Where do you begin with this adopted athlete with a host of bad habits? Given what you now know about motor acquisition, the best approach is to first explain that if he wants to improve his performance he will have to make changes, and to make changes means letting go of old habits and learning new fundamentals by revisiting the three stages (cognitive, associative, autonomous) of motor learning. This relearning process means acquiring new information (cognitive stage) and then going through the frustrating associative stage.

Getting athletes to buy into relearning can be challenging. Some athletes, especially successful ones, might say, "Hey, I was high school state champion doing it this way! Why should I change? Besides, the new movement feels awkward." A coach might reply, "Well, you could have won by even more had you done it the new way!" When these athletes try something new it feels uncomfortable and awkward and they sometimes are reluctant to continue with the change. The verbal information you provide about the three stages of motor learning as well as the information about the new technique helps them establish or activate a learning schema (p. 179) and provides a rationale or perspective for persevering with the change. Next, you work with them on the skill in its simplest form until the skill is mastered, automatic, and integrated into the movement program.

Autonomous Stage

According to Fitts' and Posner's paradigm, this is the final stage of motor acquisition. It often requires years of training to arrive at the autonomous stage. But this stage is where it's at for elite athletes, where motor performance becomes largely automatic, where cognitive processing demands are minimal, and athletes are capable of attending to and processing other information, such as the position of defensive players, game strategy, or the form or style of movement (Schmidt & Lee, 2005) in sports such as ice-skating, dance, and synchronized swimming. It is the stage where they can now respond and not think (or think minimally), where they can *grip it and rip it*, look and automatically react, and enter a state of flow.

Both good outcomes and bad outcomes are associated with the autonomous stage. The good is that performance requires much less attentional and cognitive demand, which thereby frees the performer to engage in secondary tasks, such as the concert pianist who is able to follow random digits or perform arithmetic while simultaneously playing the piano (Shaffer, 1980), or the quarterback who is capable of surveying the defense and detecting an eminent blitz while simultaneously calling the signals and changing the play at the line of scrimmage.

The bad is that since less cognitive demand exists during performance, it leaves ample room for irrelevant and distracting thoughts to sneak into the workshop (working memory) of the mind. Examples of this occurrence are the elite athletes at the Olympic trials who get caught thinking about making the Olympic team instead of focusing exclusively on performance during the last moments of a gymnastics routine, swimming race, or wrestling match. Think of the gymnast who puts together a stellar routine only to make a silly mistake at the end; or the swimmer who swims magnificently but doesn't finish the race and gets touched out at the wall; or the wrestler who dominates the match but loses concentration and allows his opponent to gain an easy reversal in the waning seconds. Some mountain climbing accidents occur as climbers near the top of the mountain. This may be so because those experienced climbers

Table 6.2 Summary of Fitts and Posner's (1967) Three Stages of Motor Learning

Stage	Process	Characteristics	Other name
Cognitive	Gathering information	Large gains, inconsistent performance	Verbal-motor stage
Associative	Putting actions together	Small gains, disjointed performance, conscious effort	Motor stage
Autonomous	Much time and practice	Performance seems unconscious, automatic, and smooth	Automatic stage

used some of their available attentional capacity to suddenly begin thinking about reaching the peak—the outcome—rather than focusing on what got them to that part of the mountain in the first place—the process.

The other bad outcome about automatic performance is that it reinforces athletes to maintain incorrect movements because a certain amount of comfort and reinforcement is associated with automatic performance, even if it is incorrect. But just because a motor movement can be performed automatically doesn't mean the movement is correct or worthy of being maintained. Moreover, as soon as athletes stop thinking about the new movement during the cognitive and associative stages, they are likely to respond automatically, thereby reverting to the old and incorrect movement in their performance repertoire. The three stages of motor learning are summarized in table 6.2.

Applying Motor Learning Stages in Coaching Athletes

Provide your athletes with detailed information in the early stage of learning. If you want your athletes to perform correctly, give them the correct information. This means that you need to know what you are talking about and you need to be clear and concise with your instruction. If your athletes don't understand what they are supposed to do, they won't do it correctly. And if they don't understand, perhaps the problem is you, not them. In other words, you may need to do a better job of clearly communicating exactly what you want them to do and communicate it in laymen's terms—in language they can understand and at a conceptual level they are prepared to cognitively grasp. For example, you may understand the physics behind what you are teaching, but if your athletes don't comprehend concepts such as angular momentum, shear force, and action–reaction you will have lost them at "Hello."

Explain the three stages of motor learning and the relearning process. Relearning something is often more difficult than learning it correctly the first time. This difficulty can lead to frustration and frustration acts like a brick wall between the athlete and the desired goal movement being learned. Make sure your athletes understand the motor learning stages and which stage they are at during the relearning process. Continually remind them that if they trust you and stay committed to the new movement, eventually it will become automatic and integrated into their performance. The new movement seems awkward now compared to the old movement because they are in the associative stage, but after enough repetitions the new movement will become smooth, automatic, and, most important, more effective than the old movement. Some coaches are ineffective at fixing movements. They understand how to teach it correctly in the beginning, but not how to change (fix) a bad habit. Understanding cognitive theory and taking a cognitive teaching approach will help you effectively do both: Teach it correctly the first time and change a bad habit.

Be patient with your athletes during the associative stage. Based on the stages of learning, we now know that awkward and disjointed movements characterize the associative stage. Things aren't going to look or feel very smooth at first; it is part of the learning process. If you expect performance to be immediately smooth and flowing, you are going to be disappointed, disillusioned, and perhaps even somewhat distraught—and so too are your athletes. Fear not. It is all part of the learning process. Remain patient and facilitate learning. Your impatience is likely to make your athletes anxious and impede their learning, whereas your patience and confidence will motivate them to persevere during the associative stage.

Stress the importance of positive information in working memory. A goal for you is to get your athletes to be able to perform automatically. As already mentioned, however, automaticity creates empty space in working memory, which makes it easier for athletes to unintentionally entertain negative thoughts and **ruminate**, which means to repeatedly dwell on negative and unproductive thoughts. For example, some athletes focus on the outcome of competition and the thought *What if I lose?* Ruminative thoughts are often unconscious thoughts that through sheer volume of constant repetition become overwhelming and overtake working memory. For example, at a major competition some athletes get this blank look on their faces when their coaches talk to them. It's as though their entire focus is on some internal thought and they are lost to the external world of the here and now. Help your athletes keep working memory space filled with the right stuff; teach them to monitor their thoughts, use thought-stopping statements, redirect their thoughts, engage in positive self-talk, and answer negative thoughts and images with positive thoughts and images.

THREE COGNITIVE MOTOR LEARNING THEORIES

As highlighted at the beginning of this chapter with the examples of the different athletes, cognition plays a major role in both motor learning and motor

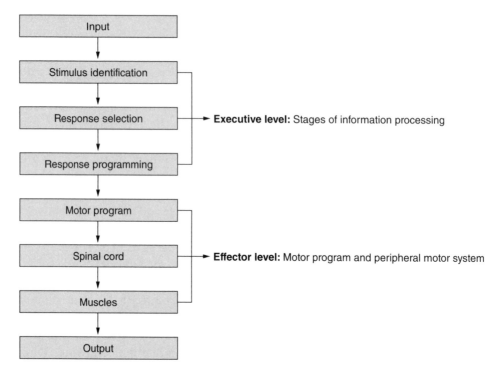

Figure 6.3 A conceptual model of cognition and motor performance.

performance. Consider the baseball pitcher in scenario 1 who is pitching in his high school regional championship. What is going through his mind? First and foremost, he considers the information of the situation—the men on base, the inning, the score, and, of course, the batter he is facing. He next selects a response—the pitch he thinks this batter will have the greatest difficulty hitting. In this case he selects a fastball down and in. The pitcher then programs the response—fastball down and in. Figure 6.3 provides a useful conceptual model of the role of cognition during motor performance.

Scenario 1

A baseball pitcher is pitching in his high school regional championship. Whichever team wins the game advances to the state championship. It is the bottom of the ninth inning and the there is a man on first base and a man on second base. There are two outs and the next batter comes to the plate. What types of information and cognitive processing are going on in the pitcher's mind?

The **executive level** involves information processing. As highlighted in scenario 1, at this level, working memory is selecting and processing incoming stimuli (e.g., What is the game situation? What is the count? Which batter am I facing?), selecting the best response (e.g., Which pitch to throw?), and activating the program from memory (e.g., Run the *fastball* program). The **effector level** is responsible for carrying out the program. At this level the selected motor program is activated in memory and delivered to the spinal cord and then to the muscles where contraction occurs.

To this point in the chapter the discussion has focused on the act of processing information into memory. But once that information is anchored into memory, what form or organization does it take? What eventually gets stored in memory appears to be sets of prestructured motor responses or programs. No one really knows for sure or has seen firsthand the structure of these motor responses, but several cognitive theories can help you speculate on their structure and how they might positively influence how athletes learn and how coaches teach. Let's look at three of these theories: general motor program theory, schema theory, and ACT-R theory.

General Motor Program Theory

For many skills, especially those that are brief in duration but rapidly executed in a relatively constant environment (e.g., platform diving, vaulting in gymnastics, free throw shooting in basketball, the start in swimming, shooting for a takedown in wrestling), it seems that performers select the movements in advance and then run the program without much modification. There is little conscious control over the movements once the program has been initiated because there is very little time for information processing to occur. Rapid actions are common occurrences but really quite astonishing if you stop to consider all of the muscle and joint activities required for even the simplest of skills (e.g., reaching for a glass of water, taking a drink, and placing it back on the table). All of the independent components of a movement and the number of ways each component can move are called **degrees of freedom**. For motor performance, the challenge is to learn how to manage the degrees of freedom so that the movement is produced in the most effective way (Schmidt & Wrisberg, 2008). How are all these degrees of freedom managed, especially for rapid movements?

General motor program theory suggests that generalized motor programs control these degrees of freedom (motor movements). According to the theory, a **generalized motor program** defines a pattern of movement rather than a specific movement. This lack of specificity provides for flexibility and allows the athlete to adapt the generalized program to generate variations of the pattern movement to meet the demands of the athletic situation recognized during the executive level of cognitive processing. At least two aspects of this theory are helpful for coaches: relative timing and speed of processing.

Relative timing is the temporal structure (timing) of a movement. A generalized motor program has variant (changing) and invariant (unchanging) features. Research has found that relative timing is a part of the generalized motor program but, interestingly, it is an invariant feature of the program. An athlete may change the speed, amplitude, force, or trajectory (i.e., variant features) of a movement but the relative timing of the movement will remain the same. In other words, the ratio of the time of each part to the total time of a movement remains essentially unchanged (Armstrong, 1970). All parts of a movement either slow down or speed up as a unit.

To better understand relative timing, Schmidt and Wrisberg (2008) use the analogy of a phonograph record. They liken the record to the generalized motor program and the speakers to the muscles and limbs. Their analogy is cited in The Phonograph Record Analogy for Generalized Motor Programs.

The Phonograph Record Analogy for Generalized Motor Programs

Our favorite analogy for generalized motor programs is that of the old standard phonograph record. In the "old days," large vinyl records used to be played on a device that contains a turntable and a needle, which sends signals from the record into an amplifier. The resulting output is then delivered to speakers. In this analogy the phonograph record is likened to the generalized motor program, and the speakers correspond to the muscles and limbs. The record has all of the features of the generalized motor program for a movement, such as information about the order of events (e.g., the trumpet comes before the drum, the right hand precedes the left), the fundamental timing structure of the events (i.e., the rhythm, or relative timing, of the sounds or of the movements), and the relative amplitudes of the output (e.g., the first drumbeat is twice as loud as the second; the hamstrings are contracted less forcefully early in the movement than they are later). This information is rigidly structured on the record and the generalized motor program in much the same way. And just as different records produce different types of music (rock, blues, classical, country, jazz, rap), so too do different generalized motor programs (throwing, jumping, shifting gears) produce different classes of movements. In both cases, though, each record or program contains a different pattern of stored information.

Notice again that the output of the record or the generalized motor program is not fixed: The speed of the music or the movement can be increased (by increasing the speed of the turntable or the rate of the commands sent to the muscles), yet the relative timing (rhythm) remains the same. Similarly, the amplitude of the output can be changed (by raising the volume or by increasing the force of muscle contraction). Even the effectors used can be changed (by switching the output from a set of speakers in the den to a second set located in the living room, or by producing a handball shot with either the left hand or the right; Schmidt & Wrisberg, 2008, p.139).

Speed of processing refers to the time it takes an athlete at the executive level to identify incoming stimuli, select a response, and program a response. Speed of processing is influenced by the number of stimulus–response alternatives and stimulus–response compatibility. According to **Hick's law** there exists a stable linear relationship between number of stimulus–response alternatives and choice reaction time. In other words, as the number of alternatives goes up, so does the amount of time it takes for an athlete to select a response. Hick's law explains the advantage of such movements as the head fake and the mixing up of the defense in sports such as basketball and football—each of these movements increases the number of stimuli an opponent must identify and respond to (**stimulus–response alternatives**). **Stimulus–response compatibility** has to do with the degree to which the relationship between a stimulus and a response is natural (compatible). The less compatibility between the stimulus and response, the greater the choice reaction time will be. For example, when forced to the left side of the hoop a young right-handed basketball player will take longer to select the response of a layup with the left hand than when forced to the right side of the hoop and select the natural right hand.

Applying General Motor Program Theory in Coaching Athletes

Recognize different generalized motor programs. There are different generalized motor programs for different classes of movements. For example, there is a generalized program for kicking, for hitting, and for running. Keep this in mind when coaching your sport. You may be teaching an athlete to develop a generalized program for one part of your sport but not another. For example, a softball coach might work with a player on her swing but not her run. It is great to be able to hit the ball but so too is it to run well to first base.

Recognize the importance of relative timing. Relative timing is the fundamental, temporal, deep structure of a movement. Asking an athlete, for example, to speed up an entire movement is a relatively simple request because it involves speeding up all parts of the movement, but asking an athlete to speed up just a part of the movement changes the relative timing for the entire movement. This request is essentially asking the athlete to relearn the movement. When making this type of request, be patient, take the athlete back through the three stages of motor learning, and give the athlete time to adopt a new rhythm (timing pattern) to the movement.

Improve speed of processing. You can help your athletes become quicker information processors in a number of ways. Practice is the most influential; you can't substitute for it. For example, the more a right-handed basketball player practices a left-handed layup, the more apt she is to not think twice about going left to the hoop because it feels natural. The more times a player confronts a fake in practice, the less likely he is going to be to take the fake.

Other applications of general motor program theory include cue utilization, anticipation, automaticity, and arousal management. Successful athletes use cues, such as the eyes of an offensive lineman, the angle of the blade of a hockey player's stick, and the position of the hips of a basketball player, to anticipate their opponents' movements and quickly select their motor program movement. Automaticity is helpful because it involves little if any information processing. As mentioned earlier in the chapter, a stimulus can bypass working memory and elicit a motor program directly (automatically) from long-term memory. And arousal management is important because athletes can't be quick and proficient processors of information if they are running around like their pants are on fire.

Schema Theory

Head (1926) was the first to introduce the concept of schema and Bartlett (1932) emphasized it. Schema is the label Piaget used to describe a unit in cognitive structure. Schema is the term used for the abstract memorial representations for events, stories, or skilled actions, where the representation can be thought of as a concept, generalization, or rule about the event but lacking in many of the actual details. According to Rumelhart (1981), schemas (also called *schemata*) are hypothesized data structures containing slots that hold the contents of memory as a range of slot values. The term has been extended to the area of motor learning. Rumelhart postulated that schemas can be applied to sequences of actions. Schmidt (1975), dissatisfied with Adams' theory, developed a schema theory arguing that a motor response schema controls movement.

Central to Schmidt's view of schema learning is the idea of the generalizable motor program (GMP) with **invariant features** (features of the GMP such as impulse timing, relative timing, and relative force that remain unchanged) that is modified by parameters that determine how the program is to be executed. According to Schmidt, after a GMP has been selected and a movement has been made, four types of information are held briefly in working memory:

1. Initial conditions (IC) information (e.g., weight of ball, distance to be thrown)
2. Parameters (P) assigned to the GMP (e.g., duration, forces)
3. Movement outcome (MO) feedback (e.g., distance ball was thrown, speed at which it was thrown)
4. Sensory consequences (SC) of the movement (e.g., how the movement felt, sounded, looked)

According to schema theory two types of memory exist: recall memory and recognition memory. **Recall memory** is responsible for movement production and **recognition memory** is responsible for movement evaluation. Recall memory is called into play for rapid, ballistic movements where the motor program and parameters are structured in advance since peripheral feedback has little involvement after the movement has been made. In contrast, recognition memory is used to evaluate the movement-produced feedback after the movement is complete. For slower movements, such as drawing a line, recognition memory can be used to evaluate movement-produced feedback during the movement.

According to schema theory (Schmidt, 1975), when individuals practice a class of movements they acquire a set of rules they use to establish the parameters and parameter values (similar to the slot values postulated by Rumelhart) necessary to produce different versions of the action. A schema, then, is a set of rules relating the various outcomes of an action to the parameter values of an action to attain the desired outcomes. **Parameters**, also referred to as **surface features**, are the modifiable features such as speed, amplitude, and muscle and limb usage of a generalized motor program. **Parameter values** are the values assigned by performers to the parameters of a generalized motor program that adjust a movement pattern to meet specific environmental demands. For example, divers performing a forward 3 1/2 somersault will adjust the parameter value of the arm throw to throw stronger and perhaps further into the somersault than, say, a forward 1 1/2 somersault.

In developing a schema, the performer sets parameters and parameter values for dimensions, such as force, movement time, movement distance, and movement height, based on past drills with the motor program. The performer is then able to effectively produce skilled movement as well as novel movements never before practiced.

According to schema theory, two types of schemas influence motor movement: the recall schema and the recognition schema. The **recall schema** is responsible for movement production and is developed by establishing a relationship between the sizes of the parameter (P), the nature of the movement outcome (MO) along with the initial conditions (IC).

Similarly, a **recognition schema** is responsible for movement evaluation and is developed by establishing a relationship between the initial conditions (IC), movement outcomes (MO), and sensory consequences (SC). Before the athlete performs the movement, the movement outcomes and initial conditions are selected and then the recognition schema is used to estimate the sensory consequences if that movement outcome is produced. These consequences, called **expected sensory consequences** (ESC), are used to evaluate the movement in much the same way that Adams used the perceptual trace.

Applying Schema Theory in Coaching Athletes

Use varied practice to help your athletes generate schemas with appropriate parameters and parameter values. In many learning situations, particularly during early learning, it is a good idea to avoid generating error and avoid variability in practice because it is less effective and perhaps harmful to motor learning. However, significant research suggests that in certain situations, varied practice is indeed helpful to motor learning (Shea & Kohl, 1990, 1991), presumably because it helps learners construct schemas by establishing relationships and parameter values.

Any particular skill has a number of variations based on certain dimensions, such as speed, force, direction, and distance. For example, when throwing a baseball, the ball can be thrown a short distance, a long distance, very high or very low, and in many different directions. **Constant practice** involves repeatedly performing a single variation of a skill, such as throwing the ball 20 feet 20 times, before moving on to a different skill. In contrast, **varied practice** (also known as variable practice) involves performing a number of variations of the same skill, such as throwing the ball 10 feet 10 times, then 15 feet 10 times, and finally, 20 feet 10 times.

Varied practice is useful for establishing schemas also for tennis players, quarterbacks, and basketball players who must learn how to swing a racquet, throw a football, or shoot a basketball, respectively, from a variety of positions, angles, and speeds. Consider a basketball player who practices that last-minute buzzer beater from every spot on the court, or the quarterback who scrambles and has to throw off-balanced and across the field, or the tennis player who hits a return shot from every conceivable angle (sometimes from between the legs). All these athletes practice shots, passes, and strokes from a variety of initial conditions. This variability of practice allows them to develop a relationship between the size of the parameters, the nature of the movement outcome, and the expected sensory consequences.

Help your athletes learn to activate the appropriate schema. **Schema activation** is the process of activating relevant schemas prior to a learning activity. Schema activation is important for helping people relate new information to prior knowledge and thereby encode it into memory (Pearson, 1984). When appropriate schemas are not activated during learning, the assimilation of new information is difficult. The appropriate schemas affect what athletes pay attention to, what meaning they give to new information, what they select for encoding, and what they ultimately remember—in other words, how well they learn. If the appropriate context is not activated, assimilating new information during learning is dubious.

When using varied practice, consider the learner's age. Although varied practice is useful in developing schemas, it is important to consider the age of the learner. Some research (Wrisberg & Mead, 1983) suggests that young children may benefit from repetitive, nonvaried, practice during practice of an open skill. An **open skill** is defined as a skill performed in an environment that is unpredictable or in motion and requires the performer to adapt movement in response to these changes. Some examples of open skills are football, basketball, and hockey, where the environment is constantly changing. In contrast, a **closed skill** is defined as a skill in which the environment is predictable or stationary, such as discus throwing, throwing a baseball, and swinging a golf club.

Consider the boundaries of the schema. It is important to consider the boundaries of the schema and carefully select drills that do not encourage individuals to exceed the parameter values of the desired movement. A program's boundaries are exceeded if the individual's movement changes dramatically and is outside the desired parameter values. In other words, you want to give your athletes enough variation and latitude in practice to discover the parameters of a movement but not go beyond the boundaries. All coaches have seen athletes who when they were young exceeded the parameter values during the learning process and developed bad habits: the pitcher with the goofy windup and delivery, the basketball player with the idiosyncratic jump shot, the diver with the funky springboard hurdle, or the tennis player with the awkward backhand.

Schema Theory Resolves Problems With Adams' Closed-Loop Theory

Schema theory resolves problems that exist with Adams' closed-loop theory. The storage limitation problem is resolved because according to schema theory, rather than store separate and specific references of correctness for each specific movement, people gist (to **gist** means to extract the general meaning or essence of something) information from past experiences and create rules or relationships. In the case of motor learning, the recall schema establishes a relationship between movement parameters and movement outcome. The recognition schema establishes a relationship between the initial conditions, the environmental outcomes, and the sensory consequences. As Schmidt and Lee (2011) put it, "This evidence suggests that motor learning may be primarily rule learning and not the learning of specific movements" (p. 443).

Schema theory also resolves the novelty problem. According to schema theory, applying general rules to adapt or modify a motor program, which results in a brand new movement, can generate never-before-seen motor movements. In other words, schema theory suggests that a particular movement outcome need not be previously produced to be produced in the future. Research has shown that after varied practice similar but not identical responses can be produced almost as accurately as the same response repeatedly practiced (Catalano & Kleiner, 1984).

Schema theory also resolves the problem behaviorism had with ignoring the human mind as part of the motor learning and control process. Schema theory recognizes cognition as part of motor learning and control. According to schema theory, the human mind is actively involved in processing information by selecting, abstracting, organizing, and storing information in the form of schemas in memory.

Problems and Limitations With Schema Theory

Like most theories, some problems or shortcomings exist with schema theory and, although it is one useful tool in the coaching toolbox, it does not satisfy the demands of every coaching and learning situation. One problem with schema theory is a structure problem. As you can probably tell, the schema concept is nebulous and ill-defined. What exactly is a schema? Schema is defined as a set of rules or data structures, but what form do these rules or structures take? The concept of a schema has been criticized for being too general and too vague (Alba & Hasher, 1983).

Another problem with schema theory is a definition problem. Different researchers define schema differently. It has been referred to as a script, rule, representation, data structure, and generalization. Perhaps because of its vagueness researchers cannot agree on its structure.

Another problem with schema theory is an application problem. Because of its vagueness, schema is in some ways unusable because it is difficult to apply both in computer simulation models and coaching situations. If schemas act as generalized motor programs, it is difficult to see how they can be applied to motor performance.

A fourth problem with schema theory is an action problem. As Anderson (1983) states, "One serious question about schema theories is how one gets any action from them" (p. 37). From an information processing perspective it is unclear how schemas can be used to generate action. Part of this problem involves the fact that schemas are better suited for declarative knowledge rather than procedural knowledge. Recall that procedural knowledge encompasses things *to do,* such as tie a shoe, solve a math problem, or swing a racket, whereas declarative knowledge refers to facts and information. Another part of the action problem is that the units of knowledge in schemas tend to be too large and force the processing system into self-limiting modes of behavior (Anderson, 1976). The scientific principle of parsimony suggests that an effective schema theory and schema system should be more simple and frugal.

For all of the preceding reasons, it is useful to look at a theory that provides a more concrete form for the structure of motor programs. Anderson (1983) has suggested that schemas can be better understood as production rules.

ACT-R Theory

Anderson (1976, 1983, 1990, 1993, & 2007) has proposed a theoretical framework for the architecture (structure) of memory and cognition that attempts to describe the encoding, storage, and retrieval processes for declarative and procedural knowledge. His theory overcomes the problems and limitations of schema theory. This section briefly outlines Anderson's ACT-R theory and discusses implications and applications for effective coaching and learning.

According to ACT-R theory the basic building blocks of memory are propositions. A proposition is the smallest unit of knowledge that can stand as a separate assertion and be judged as true or false. According to Anderson, a basic cognitive unit consists of a unit node (a proposition) and a set of elements (the relation and arguments of the proposition), which are all encoded as one unit in memory.

Like other cognitive theories, ACT-R is a network model of memory with spreading activation. Spreading activation in network models means that input units cause other units to be activated through their connections until the activation eventually spreads to response units. Activation begins with a **focus unit**, which is the point where activation begins. For example, if I think back to a championship I attended last summer, this recollection (focus unit) will help me recall (spreading activation) the athletes, events, and results (spreading activation). Because working memory overlaps, activation can spread from working memory to associated units in long-term memory.

In the ACT-R model of cognition, well-learned concepts produce more activation and are therefore more easily retrieved from memory than less-learned concepts. Concepts with strong activation have many associations and a broad range of activation with multiple access routes and more activation occurs on paths leading to stronger nodes. In other words, well-learned nodes are more easily accessed and it follows that new information should be related to existing information to encourage recall.

Production Rules

Anderson proposes that it is more useful to think of procedural knowledge as taking the form of production rules rather than schemas. As mentioned earlier in the chapter, **production rules** have an IF-THEN construction, where IF is the **condition clause** and THEN is the **action clause**. The condition clause indicates when the action clause should be activated. For example, a production rule for driving a car might look like this:

IF the light turns red

THEN press on the brake

Anderson (1983) postulates five learning mechanisms that influence the development and structure of production rules: composition, proceduralization, discrimination, generalization, and strengthening. These five concepts are subsumed under two learning processes that Anderson calls knowledge compilation and tuning.

Knowledge Compilation

Together composition and proceduralization make up what Anderson calls knowledge compilation. **Knowledge compilation** is the process whereby new production rules enter the system. Anderson suggests that through the two processes of composition and proceduralization, production rules enter memory and begin directly controlling behavior through memory, thereby bypassing working memory. The following text examines each of these two processes.

Composition

Composition is the process whereby a series of production rules is collapsed into what Anderson calls a **macroproduction rule**, which does the work of two or more production rules that occur in a sequence. For example, consider the process of shifting gears while driving a car with a manual transmission. In the beginning, the series of production rules might look like this:

IF goal is to shift gear

THEN take foot off gas pedal

IF foot is off gas pedal

THEN depress clutch pedal

IF clutch pedal is depressed

THEN shift gear

IF gear is shifted

THEN depress gas pedal

This is a process novice drivers take during the associative stage of motor learning. The process is fairly conscious, generated from working memory, and literally performed step by step. Anyone who has ever learned to drive a manual transmission car can likely remember their initial learning of shifting gears. However, once the production rules have been composed (the process of composition), the series of separate production rules collapse into the following macroproduction rule:

IF the goal is to shift the gear

THEN take foot off gas pedal

    depress clutch pedal

    shift gear

    depress gas pedal

Proceduralization

According to Anderson, **proceduralization** is the process whereby production rules become automatic. Once proceduralized, production rules no longer require loading into working memory. Instead they are automatically activated and executed directly from long-term memory. This automatic process therefore frees up space in working memory and allows performers to store additional information in that work space. Thus, going back to the previous example, the macroproduction rule for shifting gears is now activated and executed directly from memory.

Tuning

Learning continues even after a skill has been compiled. Anderson (1983) calls this continued learning **tuning**. This term closely resembles the way Rumelhart and Norman (1978) use the term. Anderson, Kline, and Beasley (1977, 1980) have proposed three learning mechanisms to account for the tuning process: discrimination, generalization, and strengthening.

Discrimination is the process by which rules become narrower in their range of application. In other words, the discrimination process restricts the application of production rules to a stricter set of circumstances.

Two subprocesses accomplish discrimination: action discrimination and condition discrimination. **Action discrimination** involves learning a new or altered action with an old condition. Through action discrimination, action clauses become more specific, relevant, and appropriate to the conditions under which they are activated. **Condition discrimination** involves restricting the condition for an old action. Going back to the example of shifting gears, say the driver is experienced and decides to race the car. So, through discrimination the production rule might look like this (italics indicate the discriminative changes):

IF the goal is to shift the gear in *a racing mode*

THEN take foot off gas pedal

    depress clutch pedal *rapidly*

    shift gear *forcefully*

    depress gas pedal *immediately*

The rule has now become more discriminating because the condition clause is more restrictive and the action clause more specific.

Generalization is the process by which rules become broader in their range of application. In other words, the condition clause becomes broader in its ability to apply actions to more numerous situations. Generalization may occur by expanding the condition clause or replacing constraints with variables within the condition clause. In other words, the condition becomes less restrictive and thereby more often applied. Looking again at the macroproduction rule for shifting gears, you can easily tune it to become more general so that it applies to all fast starts (not just a racing mode) while at the same time maintaining its discriminative properties (italics indicate the generalized changes):

IF the goal is to shift the gear *for all fast starts*

THEN take foot off gas pedal

    depress clutch pedal *rapidly*

    shift gear *forcefully*

    depress gas pedal *immediately*

Notice that the rule is now more general and applies to all fast starts but is still somewhat restrictive because it does not apply to shifting other gears (second, third, fourth, fifth, and sixth gears).

Strengthening is a mechanism for using feedback to select the most appropriate or workable production rule and to eliminate the inappropriate rule. The strength of a production rule determines the amount of activation it receives in competition with other production rules during pattern matching.

The strongest production rule will be matched and the weaker rule will be automatically repressed (Anderson, 1983).

An example of strengthening is when elite athletes are confronted with a sudden change in movement outcome and quickly make corrections to adapt. Look again at the production rule for shifting gears. Say that the driver releases the clutch too soon or doesn't push the gas pedal down enough and the engine begins to stall. A beginner driver is likely to simply stall the car. A more experienced driver, however, reacts immediately by pushing the clutch back down while simultaneously pressing down on the gas pedal to prevent the engine from stalling. Production rules are organized in networks called **production systems**. When the engine begins to stall, the experienced driver immediately represses the action clause of the production rule and activates a new rule within the production system:

IF the engine begins to stall

THEN depress clutch pedal immediately

   depress gas pedal rapidly

Strengthening helps explain the retention effect seen with random practice. During random practice athletes must continually go through retrieval practice to activate the appropriate production rule. This repeated activation strengthens the node and makes it easier and more likely to be activated in a performance situation. In other words, through a great deal of practice, elite athletes are much quicker at accessing appropriate productions during motor performance.

Applying ACT-R Theory in Coaching Athletes

Teach your athletes appropriate production rules. Highly effective coaches are masters at teaching their athletes correct production rules. In other words, their athletes know exactly *what to do* (the action) and *when to do* (the condition). Their athletes have no uncertainty. In contrast, less effective coaches seem to emphasize *what to do* but not *when to do.* Or, they might emphasize *when to do* but not *what to do.* Their athletes often have great performance uncertainty. *If* this is the case with your athletes, *then* consciously teach both the actions you want your players to take and the conditions under which the actions should be taken. (Notice the production rule in the last sentence.)

Teach your athletes to tune their production rules. So, you have taught your athletes the appropriate condition associated with the appropriate action. But how finely tuned are these production rule responses? Tuning involves the cognitive processes of discrimination, generalization, and strengthening. In observing coaches of excellence, their players not only seem to know *what to do* and *when to do,* but also *what not to do, when not to do,* and *when to do something different.* In other words, their players know when to discriminate, when to generalize, and when to invoke a different and more appropriate response (strengthening). It is a thing of beauty to observe a defensive football unit working as one finely tuned machine, each player automatically making the correct action under the correct condition, 11 players responding as of one mind.

You can teach discrimination and generalization by taking the time to point out the subtle nuances of the conditions and actions associated with your sport's movements and going over step-by-step exactly what they should do under specific conditions. In my experience, athletes think they know exactly what they should do, but often times really don't. Ask your athletes to tell you and to slowly model what they should do. In most instances they will probably have a *close, but not quite* idea of what they should be doing . With very young or inexperienced athletes, less discrimination and generalization is probably best until they become more advanced.

You also can teach discrimination and generalization by teaching these two concepts to your athletes and encouraging them to use the concepts. Explain to them that if something works for them in one context it probably can be applied and work equally as well in a similar but not identical context. For example, the action that a diver uses on a reverse somersaulting dive is the same for a backward somersaulting dive.

You can help your athletes strengthen appropriate production rules with the use of random and varied practice. Challenge them with practice situations that upset the apple cart, that give them unexpected *oops* situations that they must respond to. In this way, they learn to discard a suddenly inappropriate production rule and invoke a now more appropriate one. For example, it is not uncommon, to hear an athlete say, "Shoot. I knew what to do, I just couldn't think enough to do it at the time." There is nothing worse for a coach to hear after an athlete's performance than the words "I should have. . . ." With enough practice, your athlete will become adept at discarding one rule and activating another rule without even having to consciously think about the process.

Teach your athletes to compose their production rules. Since composition is the process of collapsing or reducing a series of production rules into one production rule, encourage composition by teaching your athletes to focus on a narrow set of performance cues. Some athletes overthink their sport and focus on too many cues. Help your athletes select those cues that help them perform automatically. For example, when I played racquetball, it helped my backhand if I simply thought about turning my shoulders and bringing my right hand up to my left ear. When I focused on those two cues, everything else seemed to fall into place for my shot.

Teach your athletes to proceduralize their production rules. Proceduralization is a function of practice. After enough repetitions, production rules become automatic; they are activated directly from memory. In other words, your athlete doesn't have to think much about the movement. For example, after enough practice I rarely thought about even the two cues for my backhand. I simply responded with a backhand when my opponent drove the ball to my left. Give your athletes the practice time and situations necessary to proce-duralize performance.

Help your athletes strengthen backup production rules. Backup production rules are rules that must be activated when something goes wrong with the previous production rule. For example, the beginning driver lets the clutch out too quickly or doesn't give the engine enough gas. The backup production rule has to be immediately activated or the engine stalls. Beginners stall the engine; experienced drivers don't. The other day I was watching two differ-ent but similar football games. Both games were tied with about 3 minutes left in the game. One quarterback was a veteran NFL player and the other was a true freshman collegiate quarterback. Both players were faced with the exact same situation—drop back to pass, no one open, game tied. The NFL quarterback used his backup production rule—IF no receiver open, THEN hold the ball. The collegiate quarterback stayed with his activated production rule—IF dropping back to pass, THEN find a receiver and throw the ball. The NFL quarterback's game went into overtime and his team won. The collegiate quarterback's pass was intercepted and his team lost in the closing seconds.

Teach your players backup production rules (contests rarely go the way we plan; there is always some road block) and purposely give them practice situations where they have to learn to rapidly invoke these backup rules. With practice, these backup rules become automatic and your players learn to do the athletic equivalent of keep the engine from stalling.

THREE STAGES OF INFORMATION PROCESSING FOR MOTOR PERFORMANCE

Based on the three motor learning theories just examined, it is interesting to consider the information processing stages that athletes, particularly elite athletes, engage in during performance and how they are able to quite rapidly cognitively identify a game situation (*stimulus identification*), decide what to do (*response selection*) as well as what not to do in terms of movement during that situation, and then activate (*response programming*) that correct move-ment—often within the blink of an eye. Speed and accuracy of information processing is important because without it, success is unlikely. For example, a tennis player who is slow to detect that his opponent's booming serve is going to his backhand is probably not going to be able to return serve very well.

Stimulus identification is the first stage of processing and involves the detection and identification of input as outlined earlier in the chapter in figure 6.3. During this stage, an athlete's task is to identify incoming information referred to as the **input**, also known as the **stimulus**. In other words, the athlete analyzes environmental information using sensory systems of vision, audition, touch, kinesthesis, and smell and assembles a representation of the situation. For example, a soccer player is a covering defender and suddenly the ball is deflected and she is confronted with an attacking offensive player.

She must analyze the situation and determine factors such as the number of offensive players and defensive players, speed and distance of the offensive players to each other and the goal, hip position of her opponent with the ball, and field placement of the players. Once the representation has been formed, it then passes to the response selection stage for further processing.

During **response selection**, the athlete must decide what, if any, response needs to be generated based on the incoming information from the stimulus identification stage. In the preceding soccer example, the covering defender must make a response, otherwise there certainly will be a shot on goal. She can decide to intercept her opponent's pass, switch to another player, drop back and defend her goal, among many other choices. She has a host of responses to choose from, but whatever she decides, she must decide quickly.

Once the response has been selected, the athlete must prepare (organize) the motor system to produce the selected movement. This stage is called **response programming** and the action that is produced as a result of information processing is referred to as the **output**. During this third stage, it is thought that a number of processes occur, such as activating the motor program, preparing the musculature for the commands of the motor program, orienting the sensory system, and readying the postural system for the action (Schmidt & Wrisberg, 2008).

In the case of the soccer player, let's say she decides to cover the opponent with the ball and intercept a pass. Given this selected response, she will activate some sort of defensive *pass interception* motor command, prepare her leg muscles to steal the ball, perhaps focus her eyes on her opponent's hips to anticipate the direction of the pass, and position her body to face up with the opposing player.

Applying Information Processing Stages in Coaching Athletes

Understanding the characteristics and limitations of the mind as computer makes it easier to understand the demands, obstacles, and processes that occur between input and output during athlete performance and how to help athletes become supercomputing athletes. Some suggestions follow.

Teach your athletes to accurately identify appropriate cues. During the stimulus identification stage, you know that short-term sensory storage and working memory are limited in both duration and capacity. In other words, your athletes can only attend to so many incoming stimuli at one time. Consequently, it is important to teach your athletes to identify the most salient cues and disregard the other distracting *noise*. For example, in studying ice hockey goaltenders, Bard and Fleury (1981) found that expert goaltenders were faster in initiating a blocking movement than novice goaltenders because they tended to fixate more on the stick rather than the puck. In other words, the expert goaltenders were able to use stick cues rather than puck cues to predict the flight of the shot.

Williams and Davids (1998) found a similar result between experienced and inexperienced soccer players. Experienced soccer defenders in a one-on-one situation tended to fixate longer on an opponent's hips while less experienced players tended to watch the opponent's feet and ball. A similar result has been found in field hockey players (Starkes & Deakin, 1984) as well as athletes in other sports.

Teach your athletes pattern recognition. You want your athletes to look and immediately react, but brief reaction time is predicated on quickly identifying a pattern or structure of the game situation. Allard, Graham, and Paarsalu (1980) found that basketball players could more accurately recall game structured situations than nonplayers. In other words, these basketball players seemed to possess what Allard and Burnett (1985) call *meaningful units,* which they define as a group of elements that form a unit of activity on the court. It is interesting that basketball players fared no better than nonplayers at recalling nonstructured (nonmeaningful units) situations. Consequently, teach your athletes to recognize meaningful game situations, patterns, and structures and the corresponding response programs. The solution to a problem often involves simply recognizing the structure of the problem, which then leads to the selection and activation of a workable solution. For example, recognizing that a geometric structure is a right triangle with two of the three perimeter lengths known, one would apply the Pythagorean theorem to solve for the third variable.

Teach your athletes speed of retrieval. When responses become automatic they are rapidly retrieved and activated directly from memory. When these responses are not automatic, they are retrieved from memory, loaded into working memory, and then activated. This extra cognitive step is a time-consuming process that slows response time. Consequently, give your athletes sufficient practice time rehearsing these responses so that they become embedded in memory and automatically activated. Also, teach your athletes to associate the correct cues and patterns (conditions) with the correct response programs (actions) so that they develop strong production rules.

Finally, teach your athletes to chunk response programs. As mentioned earlier, Anderson (1983) refers to these chunked programs as macroproduction rules. Schmidt and Wrisberg (2008) call them **movement-output chunks**. Through chunking, your athletes retrieve and produce several movements as a single unit rather than produce several units in slow, serial fashion. To promote chunking, have your athletes repeatedly practice associated actions until the actions are consolidated into a single program unit. Some athletes find it helpful to remember multiple movement units by using short two- or three-word phrases. I once listened to a U.S. Olympic coach say to his athlete, "Load-pop-spot-spot." Besides having a nice ring to it, this little ditty helped his athlete remember and perform well.

Teach your athletes to make quick and accurate decisions. **Reaction time** (RT) is generally a good indicator of an athlete's speed and effectiveness at decision making. Several factors influence RT and decision making. Two of these factors are number of stimulus–response alternatives and stimulus–response compatibility. With regard to stimulus–response alternatives, you know from Hick's law that a linear relationship exists between the number of stimulus–response alternatives and RT. As the number of alternatives increases, so does RT. Therefore, decreasing the number of alternatives will decrease RT. To decrease the number of response alternatives, teach your athletes to focus on cues and patterns that help eliminate irrelevant responses and anticipate (predict) certain movements so that they can initiate sooner response selection and response programming. For example, the softball batter might use the angle of a pitcher's elbow during delivery to eliminate all pitches except a fastball. Also, teach your athletes how to increase the number of stimulus–response alternatives for their opponents. For example, if you are working with a softball pitcher, you might teach her to disguise her delivery for throwing a fastball, making her delivery look similar to other pitches she throws.

Stimulus–response compatibility has to do with how natural a motor response is in relation to a particular stimulus. For example, if someone suddenly throws something at you, you are likely to automatically respond by catching it with your dominant hand. For a number of sports, some responses seem more compatible that others. For example, in racket sports such as squash, racquetball, and tennis, a forehand swing is more natural than a backhand swing. In the sport of diving, forward somersaults are more natural (compatible) than reverse somersaults in which the athlete takes a forward approach and then somersaults backward in the direction of the springboard. Find the movements in your sport that are incompatible for your athletes and have them practice these movements as frequently as or more frequently than the compatible movements so that the incompatible movements become compatible and automatic.

Teach your athletes to maintain individualized optimal arousal and anxiety levels. **Arousal** is the level of activation or excitement of an athlete's central nervous system. **Anxiety** is an athlete's level of uneasiness and distress about perceived capability to meet the demands of an impending situation. As anxiety increases, so does arousal. Both arousal and anxiety levels affect information processing by impacting perceptual narrowing and cue utilization. **Perceptual narrowing** is the reduction or narrowing of attentional focus as arousal level increases. This narrowing can be beneficial to athletes because it helps them ignore peripheral or meaningless information such as cues or stimuli and identify information important for response selection and programming. But sometimes perceptual narrowing can be detrimental to athletes, as suggested by the cue-utilization hypothesis.

Cue-utilization hypothesis (Easterbrook, 1959) suggests that athletes use cues to guide performance and these cues are influenced by arousal level. When arousal is too low, the perceptual field is relatively wide and cues are too numerous. Consequently, athletes identify too many cues resulting in extended information processing or athletes attend to irrelevant cues and miss relevant cues, thereby decreasing performance. On the other hand, when arousal is too high, the perceptual field becomes excessively narrow and restrictive. Consequently, athletes begin missing important relevant cues and performance decreases. Teach your athletes to use relaxation and energizing techniques to maintain an optimal arousal level. Williams and Harris (2006) identified two categories of such techniques: muscle-to-mind skills and mind-to-muscle skills. **Muscle-to-mind skills** are techniques for regulating arousal using somatic (body) techniques, such as breathing exercises and progressive relaxation, to relax or energize the mind. **Mind-to-muscle skills** involve techniques for regulating arousal using cognitive activities, such as meditation, visualization, self-talk, and cognitive restructuring, to relax or energize the muscles.

THE SUPERCOMPUTING ATHLETE

The beginning of this chapter considered two very similar boys and decided that all things being equal, the difference in motor learning and performance was the result of a difference in *software* rather than *hardware*. In other words, the defining difference was the cognitive component, not the physical component. Both boys tested the same in factors such as height, weight, vertical jump, strength, flexibility, and reaction time. However, the boys were different in processing information. Distinct cognitive differences exist between the supercomputing (elite) athlete and the nonelite athlete. These differences give coaches a clearer picture of the supercomputing athlete. What does the **supercomputing athlete** look like?

Research (e.g., Huber, 1997) suggests some strikingly noticeable cognitive differences between elite and nonelite athletes. These differences also are evident in experts and nonexperts in such diverse domains as physics problem solving, mathematics, chess, field hockey, basketball, ice hockey, and volleyball. In general, supercomputing athletes possess a broader and deeper knowledge base in memory related to their sport and motor performance. In other words, they know a lot more than nonelite athletes about their sport and about what they need to do to perform at a high level. Moreover, their knowledge base isn't limited to simply the movements of their sport. Supercomputing athletes represent the problem of performance on a scientific level, connecting concepts such as relaxation, rehearsal, visualization, self-talk, practice versus performance, arousal level, attentional focus, automaticity, and laws of physics, with high-level motor performance (Huber, 1997).

Using a production rule analysis, supercomputing athletes operate with much more sophisticated knowledge structures (Huber, 1997). Their production rules display greater knowledge compilation (composition and proceduralization) and tuning (discrimination, generalization, and strengthening). Composition simply means that production rules for the supercomputing athlete are more condensed and activated automatically directly from memory.

The supercomputing athlete doesn't have to try very hard cognitively to perform. This is in contrast to the nonelite athlete for whom motor performance is often a conscious cognitive labor.

From a production rule analysis, the supercomputing athlete also operates with rules that are more finely tuned for elite-level performance. In other words, they seem to understand what it takes to perform at a high level. Their rules are highly discriminating. They associate specific features and subtle nuances with conditions and actions and distinguish when and when not to invoke the production rules. They also understand when to generalize—use certain production rules under similar but not identical conditions. They also have the advantageous ability to repress certain production rules when during the course of performance the rules become inappropriate and activate other more appropriate rules (the process of strengthening). Supercomputing athletes rarely utter, "I knew what to do; I just couldn't think of it at the time." They simply cognitively respond to a changing situation automatically.

Supercomputing athletes also incorporate higher order concepts directly into their production rules. Concepts already mentioned, such as relaxation, visualization, attentional focus, and laws of physics, are considered higher order concepts because they are associated with the underlying principles of the problem rather than the superficial surface features of the problem. Chi et al. (1981) suggest that novices tend to operate with a naive representation while experts operate with a scientific or higher order problem representation. The nonelite athlete sees performance as simply a matter of performing basic movements—good jump, good reach, fast run, hard throw, and so on. In contrast, the supercomputing athlete understands the underlying problem. For example, in the high jump, getting a good jump involves good mechanics, relaxation, patience, attentional focus, and physics. Getting a good rotation in a backward 3 1/2 in platform diving involves in part Newton's third law of motion using action–reaction to initiate somersaulting action.

Supercomputing athletes also are skilled from input to output at the three stages of information processing. They quickly identify and process meaningful cues, structures, and patterns, judiciously decide what responses to make (and not make), and rapidly retrieve and produce these responses. They also are cool under fire. They understand their cognitive characteristics and limitations and the effects of anxiety and arousal on information processing and performance. They associate anxiety and arousal with the problem of performance and use techniques for managing relaxation and energy levels.

THE SUPERCOMPUTING COACH

The **supercomputing coach** deeply processes cognitive learning theory to the point of comprehending the mind of the supercomputing athlete and even thinking like the supercomputing athlete. In cognitive terms, the supercomputing coach downloads software to the athlete to radically alter cognition and program the supercomputing athlete. The supercomputing coach possesses a broad, deep, and richly interconnected sport-specific knowledge base more extensive than the knowledge base of his athletes. The structure of the supercomputing coach's knowledge base is finely tuned and includes higher order concepts. Moreover, the supercomputing coach represents the problem of high-level performance in scientific terms and higher-order concepts and understands the cognitive processing demands from input to motor movement output. This coach frequently asks athletes, "What were you thinking about?" and understands the importance of cognition in motor learning and performance.

YOUR COACHING TOOLBOX

Cognitive learning theory provides a number of useful new tools for your coaching toolbox. The basic information processing model helps you understand athletes' cognitive characteristics, limitations, and processes for understanding, remembering, and putting new information into action. The three stages of motor learning help you understand the importance of cognition as athletes learn new skills. The three cognitive theories each in their own way help you understand and impact athlete motor learning and performance. Generalized motor program theory helps you better understand what form new information takes as *software* for motor performance. Schema theory helps you further understand the importance of a motor program and the usefulness of varied practice, parameters and parameter values, and activation of relevant and related information in memory with new information. ACT-R theory (specifically, production rules) provides a concrete conceptual form that motor programs might take, that you can use to influence athletes' motor learning and performance. Finally, the three stages of information processing that occur during motor performance help you understand the cognitive demands of performance and how you can transform your players into supercomputing athletes.

THE SCIENTIFIC AND ARTFUL COACH

Cognitive learning theory redefines the notion of getting into an athlete's head. While such a statement may have once connoted something to the effect of controlling an athlete mentally or understanding what an athlete is thinking, cognitive theory and the computer as metaphor give coaches a conceptual model for understanding specifically how athletes learn. As a scientific coach, you take the paradigms, models, and theories discussed in this chapter to not only understand how your athletes learn and perform but, more importantly, better understand how coaches teach. You use cognitive theory to become an even more effective coach. For example, because you understand the importance of your athletes having a broad base of knowledge, you provide them with lots of information but you present it in pieces so that they have time to attend to and process the new information. You also don't limit your coaching to the simple Xs and Os of your sport. Besides providing information on the basics of your sport, you also include higher order concepts, such as relaxation, perceptual narrowing, and laws of physics.

Even though cognitive learning theory might easily fall under the category of the science of coaching, much about it also involves the art of coaching. Take, for example, the following statement by Bruning, Schraw, and Ronning (1995): "The idea underlying schema activation is that students at any age will have some relevant knowledge to which new information can be related" (p. 94). This statement is worth examining. Notice the words "any age," "relevant," and "related." Successful coaches are masters at connecting with their athletes by getting in touch with where their athletes are at cognitively and relating new information to something relevant to their athletes. This is part of the art of coaching: tuning into your athletes (no matter what their ages might be); understanding (as best you can) their past experiences, personal interests, and previous learning; and creating through schema activation a conceptual bridge between what they already know and what they need to learn. As a scientific coach, you use schema theory to guide the structure of practice. As an artful coach, you find a way to bridge the gap between old and new information.

IF YOU REMEMBER ONLY THREE THINGS

1. *Remember that athletes are like computers—processors of information.* Sure, this reminder may sound rather obvious after reading this chapter, but I have observed coaches who choose to ignore athletes' cognitive ability. These coaches prefer to teach their athletes much like an animal trainer would train a dog. But athletes aren't cognitively like dogs, rats, or pigeons. They are human beings with a unique capacity for processing loads of information. So use cognitive learning theory to help your players become supercomputing athletes. All you need are the tools from the theory and a desire to coach the cognitive component.

2. *Remember the concept of production rules.* It is such a simple but useful and easily comprehended concept. Drop in and observe a practice of any sport and listen to what the coach has to say. You are likely to hear the words *if* and *then* or derivatives of those words such as *when* and *now*. Listen to yourself next time you coach. You will be surprised at how often you verbalize production rule-like statements to your athletes. When you become conscious of this hypothetical construct of procedural knowledge you are able to be more effective in teaching your athletes the appropriate conditions and actions associated with the motor performances of your sport.

3. *Remember the three stages of motor learning.* Like the basic information processing model and the concept of production rules, the three-stage motor learning construct is a simple but useful paradigm for understanding, facilitating, evaluating, and accelerating your athletes' motor learning development. The paradigm also helps you and your athletes remain patient and recognize where you are at along the sometimes frustrating road of motor learning.

SUGGESTED READINGS

Anderson, J.R. (1983). *The architecture of cognition.* Cambridge, MA: Harvard University Press.

[This is not an easy read and is recommended only for those looking for a perusal challenge. Still, the whole notion of production rules is so appealing and so useful for coaches wanting to become great teachers of their sport that it is worth reading even if only sections of the book.]

Schmidt, R.A. & Wrisberg, C.A. (2008). *Motor learning and performance: A situation-based learning approach* (4th ed.). Champaign, IL: Human Kinetics.

[This book is the bible for motor learning and performance. It should be on every coach's book shelf. It has sections on cognition and motor learning that are more readable and more comprehensible than Anderson's book.]

The Expert Athlete
Applying Expertise Theory and Deliberate Practice

Key Terms

deliberate play

deliberate practice

ego orientation

expert athlete

expert coach

expertise theory

involvement
  opportunities

metacognition

perceived competence

sport enjoyment

TARGET

task orientation

teaching games

Andy was a tennis player who decided he wanted to become a state champion. He was only 14 but he had been playing with the sport of tennis for a number of years. As a little kid, he hit a tennis ball against his garage door; he also played impromptu games of soccer, basketball, baseball, and even wrestling with his dad and friends in their backyard. He enjoyed these games so much that as he got a little older, he participated in more organized versions of soccer, basketball, and baseball. But now he was heading into his freshman year of high school and wanted to focus his efforts on a sport in which he could really excel and become high school state champion. Fortunately, he belonged to a local tennis club with some outstanding players who either formally competed in college or were currently competing in college.

One day Andy came home from school and said to his mother, "Mom, from now on I am going to devote myself exclusively to tennis and I want to see how far I can go with the sport. I would really appreciate any help you and Dad can give me to help me reach my goals." His parents were only too happy to support their son. The next day Andy met with the club pro, who was a masterful teacher, and told the pro of his plan. The pro was excited about Andy's commitment because he had watched Andy's development over the past year and believed that with the right coaching Andy could not only be good but possibly the best high school player in the state.

Andy's background in soccer, basketball, and baseball helped him develop great foot speed and coordination, a rocket arm, and mental toughness, and this background would be to his advantage. Sure, he hadn't been playing tennis exclusively for many years, but his years in the other sports had taught him many things he could apply to tennis. Also, because he had played *with* tennis for many years, he had developed a real love and passion for the game, which now motivated him to train with great effort, intensity, emotion, and persistence.

The first thing Andy did when he began practicing at the club was to pair up as often as possible with Paul, the best player in the club. Paul was a former high school state champion and currently ranked in the top five of college players. It wasn't a lot of fun for Andy in the beginning; he got his butt kicked most days. But he persevered. He observed how the older player stretched: how he warmed up, his conditioning routine, his intensity, his practice habits, and how he warmed down; in short, he watched everything he did. Andy picked his brain as well, asking what his goals were for each practice. Andy also worked closely with the club pro, carefully listening to everything he said and doing everything he asked. A year and a half went by and suddenly Andy was holding his own with the older player. By the end of his sophomore year, Andy actually won a tournament match against him. After the match Paul congratulated him and said "Well, you little snot, you finally beat me. Congratulations."

After the match, his parents asked him how he managed to improve so quickly in little over a year's time. His response was "Well, I figured if I wanted to become a champion I had to train like a champion. So, every day I tried to do everything Paul did! I also tried to do everything the coach told me to do!"

This chapter is the story of an *expert athlete* and how you can use the theory of expertise and the concept of deliberate practice to help your athletes train like elite athletes to reach their greatest athletic potential and perform like champions.

CHAPTER OVERVIEW

The chapter first defines the study of expertise and the characteristics of experts. Then it covers the characteristics of a type of expert training called deliberate practice and the athlete developmental phases for engaging in this type of practice. Next, it examines how you can develop the characteristics of deliberate practice within your athletes and your training regimes. It concludes with a discussion about how the expert athlete needs the expert coach and the characteristics of the expert coach.

EXPERTISE THEORY

Sometimes the best way to achieve elite or expert performance is simply to imitate what the great ones do, much like Andy the tennis player did. But what exactly do the great ones do that makes them great? It isn't often easy to ascertain the factors that separate good from great. **Expertise theory** is the study of expert performance across a wide range of performance fields that examines differences between experts and nonexperts in an attempt to identify those factors that differentiate the two groups of performers and account for superior performance.

In 1973 Herbert Simon and William Chase studied perceptual-cognitive differences between grandmaster and lower-level chess players. They found that differences between skill levels were not due to superior memory capacity but rather the ability to organize information. Simon and Chase postulated that this ability to organize could be attributed to time spent training. They famously suggested that it takes roughly a decade or 10,000 hours of intense preoccupation with the game of chess to reach the level of grandmaster.

This 10 year or 10,000 hour rule encouraged some researchers in cognitive science to adopt a nurture-over-nature perspective to explain expert performance. One of these researchers was Anders Ericsson, who postulated that the difference between expert and nonexpert performances could be explained by differences in the amount and type of practice rather than differences in genetic superiority. According to Ericsson and his colleagues, not just any type of practice will help an individual achieve expert status; they must engage in what he calls *deliberate practice*.

Over the years I have had the good fortune to work with a number of elite athletes. These athletes were physically talented but they shared another trait that differentiated them from their teammates and other highly talented athletes: the way they trained. They trained with the same intensity, effort, motivation, concentration, and other characteristics typified by experts in other domains such as chess, physics problem solving, ice skating, and wrestling. In other words, they engaged in deliberate practice. The point to this chapter is that if you can teach your athletes to train like expert (elite) athletes, you can help them reach new levels of performance they never dreamed of attaining.

So, what are the characteristics of expertise, what are the characteristics of deliberate practice, what are the developmental phases for an athlete engaging in deliberate practice and how can you help your athletes learn to train and eventually become elite level athletes? The discussion begins with the characteristics of expertise.

CHARACTERISTICS OF EXPERTISE

What exactly is an expert performer? Identifying expertise is not always easy, because it tends to be a relative, not absolute measure. Most often when people call someone an expert, they mean they are superior in relation to other performers. Experts tend to be outstanding people who rank in the very upper level, perhaps the top 1% to 5% of all performers in their fields. Researchers believe that studying expertise and expert performance in many different domains can lead to discovering the underlying general mechanisms that account for superior performance (de Groot, 1978; Chase & Simon, 1973). Chase and Simon (1973) suggested that expertise for any skilled task such as football, music, and chess is not a result of superior and inheritable intelligence and physical giftedness, it is the result of vast amounts of knowledge and pattern-based retrieval acquired over many years of experience in the particular domain.

Certain physical characteristics, such as height and body–limb proportionalities, are unchangeable. However, research on expertise has found other characteristics related to high-level performance that are malleable and therefore worthy of consideration for coaches and athletes. The nonphysical characteristics of experts across domains are listed and discussed next.

Characteristics of Expert Performers

Knowledge base

Problem representation

Accuracy of recall

Speed of performance

Problem-solving strategies

Preparation time

Deliberate practice

Knowledge Base

Research indicates that elite performers in sport (e.g., wrestling, ice skating, and springboard diving) and nonsport domains (e.g., chess and physics problem solving) possess a large body of knowledge related to their particular domains. This knowledge base may be characterized as conceptually complete, highly specific, densely interrelated, well organized, and readily activated. Specifically, the elite knowledge base contains a large number of central concepts with very specific defining features (details and values associated with each concept). These concepts are intricately interrelated, meaning each concept is connected to a greater number of other concepts and features. In contrast, nonelite performers appear to possess a less complete and limited knowledge base.

For example, experienced nonelite collegiate divers were compared to experienced elite collegiate divers who had competed internationally (Huber, 1997). Although both groups of divers had approximately the same amount of experience, the elite divers demonstrated a much richer and more detailed knowledge base. Similar results have been found in examining baseball players (French, Spurgeon, Graham, Rink, & McPherson, 1996; French, Spurgeon, & Nevett, 1995), basketball players (French & Thomas, 1987), and tennis players (McPherson, 1999), as well other nonsport domains such as chess (Pfau & Murphy, 1988) and mathematics (Webb, 1975). It is presumed that simply having experience is not enough. For elite-level performance, it is necessary to make cognitive sense of that experience, learn along the way, and organize information into an applicable form that results in improved performance.

Problem Representation

Another characteristic that differentiates the elite from the nonelite is problem representation. Chi, Feltovich, and Glaser (1981) have proposed that novice problem solvers, particularly in the domain of physics, operate with a naïve mental representation while expert problem solvers operate with a scientific, higher order representation. In other words, elite and nonelite performers represent the problem (high-level performance) differently. For instance, physics problem solvers operate with scientific representations, in terms of idealized objects and physical concepts such as force, momentum, and energy (Chi et al., 1981; McDermott & Larkin, 1978).

Similarly, elite divers represent the problem of dive execution in terms of scientific or higher order concepts. Some of the concepts elite divers mention are relaxation, self-talk, attentional focus, visualization, level of arousal, automaticity, principle of motion (i.e., Newton's third law), rehearsal, and performance (competition) versus practice (Huber, 1997). In studying tennis players (McPherson, 1999), it appears that higher-level players represent the problem of playing tennis as matching current and sophisticated game conditions (e.g., score, position of opponent, information about the opponent's strengths and weaknesses) with situation prototypes that guide decision making, action plans, and movement parameters.

Accuracy of Recall

Research indicates, as does experience and commonsense, that experts have better recall than nonexperts. For example, when briefly shown a chessboard expert chess players can recall more accurately the positions of pieces on a chessboard than nonexpert chess players. This accuracy of recall appears to be specifically related to learned performance because when a chessboard with randomly placed pieces (in other words, a nonsensical positioning of the pieces) is shown, accuracy of recall for both expert and nonexpert is similar.

This same accuracy of recall also can be seen in elite athletes and elite coaches who can recall every practice scenario, game situation, good play, miscue, hit, shot, and skill movement. Elite athletes and coaches have an uncanny ability to accurately store and recall an amazing amount of information. Great baseball hitters can remember every pitch that was thrown at them in a current game and past games.

Speed of Performance

Another characteristic of expertise is the speed at which experts can perform. This characteristic is evident in a chess grandmaster who glances at a chessboard, quickly selects a strategy, and makes a move. It is evident in a basketball player who recognizes an offensive play and immediately makes the correct defensive adjustment. It is evident in a gymnast who quickly transitions from one movement to the next in a floor routine. A similar speed of performance is also evident in elite springboard divers. Elite divers transition easily and quickly from the hurdle to the takeoff to the flight and then to the entry. Perhaps of greater interest, it appears that elite springboard divers are able to rapidly respond to perceived errors in dive performance (Huber, 1997). They quickly and automatically initiate backup (i.e., corrective) movements that adjust for errors and right the dive just as a pilot might right a plane, a gymnast adjust for a bobble on the balance beam, a baseball hitter adjust the swing for a curveball, a sailor adjust the sheets in response to wind change, and a quarterback adjust the angle of the throw in response to a cornerback's position.

Speed of performance is about decision making and decision making has a great deal to do with pattern recognition, object recognition, advance cues, and visual search. For example, expert basketball players are quicker at recognizing sport-specific patterns of on-court player formations (Allard, Graham, & Paarsalu, 1980) and expert volleyball players are faster at detecting and recognizing objects, such as the position and direction of the ball within the visual field (Allard & Starkes, 1980). These types of differences allow expert athletes to anticipate and more quickly select and program an appropriate motor response.

Problem-Solving Strategies

Because elite performers represent problems differently from nonelite performers, they also employ different problem-solving strategies. Chi, Feltovich, and Glaser (1981) found that expert physics problem solvers worked differently than novice physics problem solvers. The novices solved problems by working backward from the unknown solution to the given quantities, while expert physics problem solvers worked forward from the givens to the desired solution.

Likewise, elite divers appear to employ different problem solving strategies from nonelite divers (Huber, 1997). Because elite divers represent the problem of dive performance in terms of fundamental diving mechanics and higher order concepts, such as automaticity and attentional focus, two differences in problem solving can be identified between elite and non-elite divers. The first difference is that elite divers appear to focus on causes rather than effects in solving the problem of how to dive well. In other words, elite divers tend to focus on specific mechanics (e.g., body position and arm timing) that create good results (e.g., good height off the board and fast rotation). Just like expert physics problem solvers, then, elite divers appear to work forward by working on the causes. And just like novice physics problem solvers, nonelite divers work backward by focusing on the effects. Even novice coaches operate similarly. It is not uncommon to hear a novice coach say, "Get a stronger jump. Swing the arms faster."

A similar nondiving example would be a novice baseball or softball hitter who concentrates on swinging the bat faster and hitting the ball harder. In contrast, the expert hitter is more likely to think about the things that will achieve a fast bat swing and better contact with the ball, such as engaging the lower abdominals, relaxing the upper body, and rotating the hips to transfer energy from the legs and arms to the ball.

The second difference is that elite divers appear to translate higher order concepts, such as automaticity and attentional focus, into higher order problem-solving strategies that employ metacognition. **Metacognition** is our knowledge about our thinking process (i.e., simply our knowing about our knowing). Metacognitive strategies include approaches such as monitoring thoughts, redirecting attention, talking to oneself, and mentally controlling muscle tension. Returning to the question "What do I need to do in order to achieve a good jump and reach?" the elite diver might solve this problem by focusing on several specific causal actions, such as timing and arm swing in the approach, and several metacognitive strategies, such as redirecting thoughts through self-talk, redirecting concentration by changing attentional focus, and employing a thought-stopping technique to encourage automatic performance as opposed to self-conscious performance (Huber, 1997).

That same thing can be said about experts in most sports. Expert baseball and softball hitters see the solution for hitting a baseball as not so much the quality of the swing (of course that too is important) as a novice might but, rather, the concentration and mental attitude that precede the swing, particularly in a game situation. In a game situation, the batter needs to have as much or more concentration than the pitcher and a mindset stronger and more determined than the pitcher.

Preparation Time

Many people believe that innate natural talent causes people to rapidly and easily attain expertise in their particular fields. However, biographical information disproves this misconception (Ericsson et al., 1993). Simon and Chase (1973) observed that no chess player attained the level of grandmaster in less than a decade of intense preparation with the game. Likewise, in the domain of music, Hayes (1981) confirmed that it takes 10 years to reach a level of expertise. Research in other domains, such as mathematics (Gustin, 1985), tennis (Monsaas, 1985), swimming (Kalinowski, 1985), and long-distance running (Wallingford, 1975), corroborate Simon and Chase's 10-year or 10,000-hour rule. Preparation time is undoubtedly necessary for reaching a high level of performance. However, preparation time must be of a specific quality to achieve expert performance. This type of expert preparation time is referred to as deliberate practice.

Deliberate Practice

Inherited physical talent is to a large degree necessary for becoming a great athlete. Few coaches would disagree with this statement. However, physical talent is relatively fixed and, consequently, unchangeable. In other words, a coach can't give a kid more natural talent than he was born with. However, through the right type of training, people can improve and continue improving almost forever. For instance, early studies observing highly experienced performers, such as typists (Dvorak, Merrick, Dealey, & Ford, 1936), Morse Code operators (Bryan & Harter, 1897), and typesetters (as described in Book & Norvell, 1922) found performance could continually be enhanced through restructured, improved training.

What exactly is *improved training*? It has long been believed that merely engaging in practice regardless of the structure, intensity, and purpose of the practice was enough to lead to superior performance. However, as Ericsson et al. (1993) write, "In sum, the belief that a sufficient amount of experience or practice leads to maximal performance appears incorrect" (p. 366). In other words, merely showing up and practicing is not enough to become an elite athlete. To become an elite performer, one must participate in what Ericsson calls deliberate practice. Research examining experts in different domains suggests that experts engage in a specific type of practice that is quantifiably different from nonexperts and this **deliberate practice** leads to increased high-level performance.

CHARACTERISTICS OF DELIBERATE PRACTICE

Deliberate practice may be distinguished from another important type of practice referred to as deliberate play. **Deliberate play** is a type of sport involvement young athletes engage in during their sampling (i.e., early) years in which activities, such as recreational games of hockey and soccer, involve direct competition between individuals or teams and are constrained by rules (Côté & Hayes, 2002; Ericsson, 2003). Deliberate play is an important antecedent for eventually engaging in deliberate practice. During the early years young athletes engage in a high frequency of deliberate play and a low frequency of deliberate practice (Côté & Hayes, 2002), much like Andy the tennis player.

As athletes continue in the sport they engage in increasingly more deliberate practice. There appear to be at least 13 characteristics of deliberate practice. These characteristics are listed here and discussed next.

Characteristics of Deliberate Practice

Motivation and desire

Preexisting knowledge

Explicit goals

Highly relevant

High level of effort

High level of concentration

Not inherently enjoyable

Highly structured

Careful monitoring

Working closely with an authority

Immediate information feedback

Using different methods and refining methods in response to feedback

Time and energy

Motivation and Desire

In approaching deliberate practice, the first characteristic elite athletes bring with them is an extremely high level of motivation and desire. They come to each practice motivated to give a high level of effort and concentration. Their desire motivates them to do whatever is necessary to reach their practice goals and thereby improve performance. In many cases, their desire enables them to overcome their fears, fatigue, doubts, disappointments, and in some cases even their physical limitations. In looking at factors important in the development for success in skating, for example, elite skaters and elite skating coaches both agreed that desire was the most important factor (Starkes et al., 1996). Without a high level of desire, deliberate practice cannot occur. As mentioned earlier in this book, motivation might be the single most important factor for achieving athletic success.

Preexisting Knowledge

Another factor important for approaching deliberate practice is preexisting knowledge. One distinguishing characteristic of the expert athlete is knowledge base, the breadth and depth of information that athletes possess about their sport, themselves as athletes, and other information related to performance. Simply put, elite athletes know more about their motor performance than nonelite athletes. Moreover, their knowledge base contains a wider range of concept domains such as fundamentals of the sport, highly specific motor movements for each phase of performance, physiology of conditioning, stretching, laws of motion, sport psychology, and metacognition.

Although it might be suggested that elite athletes have a broader and denser knowledge base simply because they are indeed elites, research suggests that athletes become elite-level performers because they first become students of the sport and develop a richly connected and dense knowledge base. As their knowledge base expands, their performances improve. As Richman et al. (1996) put it, "The important overall point is that the expert's ability to perform in his or her domain of expertise rests solidly on a large accumulation in long-term memory of knowledge that is (often) evoked when it is relevant for solving the problem at hand" (p. 172).

Explicit Goals

Expert performers appear to have very specific goals for each practice. Their overriding goal for every practice is to improve performance. They are never content to rest upon their laurels or previous practice accomplishments. This may seem obvious, but for many nonelite athletes, their goal often seems to be to simply show up for practice. Perhaps they mistakenly think that attending practice is enough, that being physically present for practice will automatically produce improvement in performance. Experts know better.

Beyond the goal of improvement, however, experts have specific goals for every phase of practice and these goals directly contribute to improved performance. No warm-up exercise, no drill, no movement, and no activity is done without first setting an explicit goal. Even the simplest and most mundane exercise has purpose and meaning to the elite athlete. Before each practice task these athletes ask themselves this question: "What can I do right now on this practice set to get better?"

Highly Relevant

For the elite athlete, everything done in practice has to be relevant. In this case, *relevant* is defined as contributing to improved performance. If the activity does not result in improved performance, then the activity is dropped from the training program and a more beneficial activity is added.

Expert athletes appear to value practice activities that are most closely related to what they do in competition (Starkes, Deakin, Allard, Hodges, & Hayes, 1996). In other words, relevance is associated not only with improvement in performance but also with the specific performance to be executed in competition. Expert athletes associate mental work rather than physical work as most relevant practice activities. In this case, mental work is focused, intense, mental concentration on practice activities. From the study of Starkes et al. (1996), mental study appears to be equivalent to what Ericsson et al. (1993) identifies as concentration.

High Level of Effort

Expert athletes perceive a high level of effort as a necessary factor for improving. While mental effort is important, elite athletes see physical effort as most important. For example, research examining elite wrestlers and figure skaters (Starkes et al., 1996) indicates that these elite athletes perceived effort as pertaining to physical effort. Some of the practice activities that wrestlers rated as high effort were mat work, weights, and running; mat work received the highest rating. Some of the practice activities that skaters rated as high effort were on-ice training, weight training, and lessons with coach; on-ice training received the highest rating.

For athletes aspiring to reach the elite level, it is important to remember that a high level of effort is necessary on a daily basis. It is easy to come in well rested on Monday and train like an animal, but what about the rest of the week? Elite athletes sustain a high level of effort for all practices and all practice activities. Sustaining high effort may be the greatest challenge for becoming an elite athlete.

High Level of Concentration

For deliberate practice, a strong positive relationship (correlation) exists between relevance, effort, and concentration. In other words, all three factors—relevance, effort, and concentration—are characteristics of expert practice. Concentration is deemed necessary not only for physical performance but also ancillary practice aspects such as video review, mental training, and instruction. For example, in a study examining wrestlers and skaters (Starkes et al., 1996), practice activities rated as requiring high concentration for wrestlers included mat work, work with coach, video, and mental rehearsal; mat work received the highest rating. For skaters the practice activities receiving a high concentration rating included on-ice training, lessons with coach, and mental training.

In short, expert athletes have their heads in the game in everything they do. They are dialed in mentally whether it is performing in practice, reviewing performance, visualizing, or simply listening to their coach's instructions. Their daily high level of concentration becomes a habit for them, a habit that automatically transfers to their elite-level competition performances.

Not Inherently Enjoyable

Research suggests that expert performers do not find deliberate practice to be inherently enjoyable (e.g., Ericsson, Krampe, & Tesch-Römer, 1993; Starkes et al., 1996). In other words, they do not practice in order to find enjoyment. For nonexpert performers, it is just the opposite; they practice because they love the sport and enjoy the practice activities associated with the sport. However, expert performers are motivated to practice because they believe practice will lead to enhanced performance and success. They derive their enjoyment from the mastery of a new motor skill, the consistency of a routine, and the perfection of a performance: the arc and swish of the basketball through the net for the tenth consecutive shot, the rhythmic flow and follow-through of the baseball pitch that catches the outside corner of the plate, the improved dismount from the uneven bars, and the well-timed backhand and follow-through on a tennis swing.

Perhaps elite performers are wired differently genetically than nonelite performers. Like geese genetically predisposed to fly south for the winter, elite performers seem almost preternaturally compelled to seek improvement. Some kids just have to keep doing something over and over until they get it right. However, as a coach you must remember that enjoyment (defined here as having fun) is an important part of an elite athlete's early development; it is one of the reasons the athlete persists in the sport, eventually commits, and decides to engage in deliberate practice. Even at the elite level a small amount of deliberate play is good for maintaining a positive practice environment and keeping a healthy perspective.

Some research suggests that elite athletes do actually find enjoyment of deliberate practice or at least parts of deliberate practice. Starkes et al. (1996) found that deliberate practice activities that were rated as highly relevant and involved social interaction were reported as highly enjoyable by elite performers. Csikszentmihalyi, Rathunde, and Whalen (1993) had a similar finding for talented teenagers. In my coaching experience, those driven and passionate elite athletes who find enjoyment while working hard are more successful than those elite athletes who just work hard. The same may be said for coaches as well: Those driven and passionate coaches who find enjoyment while working hard are more effective and successful as coaches than those who just work hard.

Highly Structured

For elite athletes, the overriding practice goal is improved performance. To achieve this goal, practice activities need to be highly structured. *Highly structured* means that each phase of practice is well defined and efficient and transitions between phases are clear and rapid. Very little, if any, time is spent idly waiting to do something. Elite athletes may sometimes even finish practice before other athletes, not because they practiced less but because they were efficient and their practice was well structured with no time wasted. In fact, elite athletes are so efficient that they can often do much more than nonelite athletes and still finish early.

Careful Monitoring

Within the structure of practice is the continual process of carefully monitoring performance to ascertain any errors in performance. As errors are detected, additional drills are employed to correct the errors. The expert's performance is monitored to see if the new drills are successful in correcting performance. If they are not, then other drills are added and performance is once again monitored. If these drills are not successful, then new drills might be invented to continue the process of improving performance.

Careful monitoring is important throughout the daily and weekly course of deliberate practice. Monitoring of performance includes diagnostic tools such as videotape review, biomechanical analysis, performance charting, mood state questionnaires, and blood analysis. As research indicates (Ericsson et al., 1993), perhaps the most important source for monitoring the expert athlete's performance is the coach. However, as athletes progress to the elite level they become more self-regulatory and take increasingly greater responsibility for monitoring all aspects of their training.

Working Closely With an Authority

In studying skaters and wrestlers, Starkes et al. (1996) found that these elite athletes rated working with the coach as the second most relevant activity. The most relevant activity was rated as on-ice training for skaters and mat work for wrestlers. In other words, the two most relevant activities for elite athletes appear to be working on the actual performances for competition and working closely with their coaches or other authorities highly knowledgeable about their particular sports.

Researchers and educators generally recognize that individualized teacher supervision is superior to group instruction. Bloom (1984) examined research in education and found that students randomly assigned to instruction from a tutor outperformed by two standard deviations students randomly assigned to conventional teaching. In the case of elite athletes, they understand the significant impact that a close working relationship with an authority can have on improving performance.

Whereas nonelite athletes might want to learn by themselves and sometimes ignore instructional or critical comments regarding their performances, elite athletes seek out these comments. For the elite performer the only thing that matters is getting better. Practice doesn't have to be fun; it doesn't have to be friendly (not that it can't be so); but practice, without a doubt, does have be productive and culminate in improved performance. Establishing a close working relationship with the coach helps accomplish this objective.

Immediate Information Feedback

Experts in all fields are interested in immediate and informative feedback (Ericsson et al., 1993). This should come as no surprise given some of the characteristics of deliberate practice already discussed. Since the overriding practice goal is improved performance, experts want to know immediately whether or not they are doing a skill correctly, making a specific correction, or reaching an intended practice goal. If immediate feedback informs them that progress is being made, then they continue with the current course of action. If feedback information tells them progress is not being made, then a new direction is taken.

Elite athletes don't want to wait until tomorrow to find improvement. They want it now and know that they need to find it now or relatively soon because their competitors are getting better day by day; those athletes who wait until tomorrow to get better make great doormats for those athletes entering the elite level of their sport. Elite athletes train with a sense of urgency and welcome immediate informative feedback.

Using Different Methods and Refining Methods in Response to Feedback

Experts are more apt than nonexperts to actively seek different methods and refine old methods in response to repeated errors and performance levels that fall below expectations. In other words, when experts realize that repeated attempts to correct performance are ineffective, they quickly make changes in their training by trying new methods, refining old methods, and in some cases inventing new methods that will lead to improved performance. For example, a golfer having trouble with her swing might confer with her coach and together invent a new drill using an elastic band for reshaping her swing. Professional golfer Tiger Woods revamped his already successful swing to find even greater performance success.

This image of the elite athlete as experimental, refining, and inventive is in stark contrast to the nonelite athlete. The image of the nonelite athlete is characterized as unimaginative, conservative, rote, and status quo. Nonelite athletes are like diners who always order the same dish off the menu. They reach a certain level of performance and then become stuck, performing the same way every time, and they rarely evaluate what they do, make changes in their performances, or try anything new and adventurous.

Time and Energy

Although it seems obvious, deliberate practice requires available time and energy. It is impossible for a hockey player to improve without available ice time. And once on the ice, the player must exert a high level of energy and maximize ice time. The same can be said for any athlete in any sport; the athlete needs high energy and a maximization of practice time. An athlete can't attain the expert level without putting in the time.

This time and energy requirement extends to the support people surrounding the athlete. Because experts engage in sport at an early age, time and energy is required of the parents to get the child up in the morning, have uniforms cleaned, feed the child at irregular hours, and transport the child to and from practices. It also takes a great deal of time and energy to attend special training sessions, regional training camps, and competitions. Without a willingness on everyone's part to give their time and energy, expertise will be more difficult for the athlete to attain.

ENGAGING IN DELIBERATE PRACTICE: THREE PHASES OF DEVELOPMENT

So, becoming an expert in any field involves, in part, engaging in deliberate practice. But how do athletes develop to a point where they are motivated to engage in such practice? Bloom (1985) interviewed many international-level performers from several different domains and he was able to distinguish three phases of development toward deliberate practice and expertise.

During *phase 1* the subjects started out in childhood being introduced to the domain and engaging in playful and enjoyable activities. After a period of time, they revealed a talent for the domain and showed promise of possibly excelling. Phase 1 appears to end with the introduction of instruction and deliberate practice.

Phase 2 consists of an extended period of preparation and ends with the person's commitment to pursue the activity on a full-time schedule.

Phase 3 is the period of time people are actively involved on a full-time basis and ends when they have reached a performance level that allows them to make a living as a professional. If this is not possible, they usually end their full-time commitment.

Ericsson et al. (1993) suggested a fourth phase of development that should be included. During *phase 4*, people progress beyond the scope and expertise of their coaches to make unique and innovative contributions to their domains.

More recently Côté and colleagues (2008) have derived the developmental model of sport participation (DMSP) that more accurately depicts the stages of athlete development toward elite performance and sport expertise. The DMSP model outlines three distinct phases: the sampling years (childhood; age 6-12), the specializing years (early adolescence; age 13-15), and the investment years (late adolescence; ages 16+).

During the *sampling years*, athletes engage in a variety of sports with the emphasis primarily on deliberate play. As mentioned earlier in the chapter, deliberate play involves activities such as backyard football and street basketball where rules and monitoring are established by the children or participating adults. According to Côté and Fraser-Thomas (2008) deliberate play is intrinsically motivating, provides immediate gratification, and is specifically designed to maximize enjoyment. Recall from the opening scenario of this chapter that Andy the tennis player first participated in sports by engaging in deliberate play with his friends and dad in their backyard. Deliberate play is highly important for athlete retention, motivation, and progression to the specializing years and investment years when athletes increasingly engage in deliberate practice.

During the *specializing years* athletes engage in fewer sporting activities and deliberate play is combined with deliberate practice. During this phase, Andy participated in organized sports and played soccer, basketball, and baseball but dropped out of wrestling. The specializing years are a transitional phase between the sampling years and the investment years.

During the *investment years*, athletes generally focus on one sport and engage primarily in deliberate practice. So, at the age of 15 and heading into his sophomore year of high school, Andy elects to focus solely on tennis and engage full-time in deliberate practice.

Applying the DMSP Model to Coaching Athletes

Sometimes coaches make the mistake of forcing athletes to invest too early—or too late—in a particular sport. Investing too early can reduce deliberate play, dampen enthusiasm and motivation for the sport, and eliminate learning opportunities (i.e., aspects and information that only certain sports can teach an athlete). Investing too late can result in missing a critical window of opportunity (i.e., too late to learn certain skills and become competitive in the sport). The DMSP model helps coaches conceptualize the developmental progression athletes make with regard to practice commitment, identify what stage their athletes are in, and determine appropriate amounts of deliberate play and deliberate practice for athletes.

The following sections offer some specific applications of the developmental model of sport participation for coaching your athletes. These applications promote enjoyment, increase motivation, and encourage increasingly greater engagement in deliberate practice.

Identifying Your Athlete's Developmental Stage

Andy's club coach was smart to let him have fun and sample other sports. He recognized Andy's talents early on but rather than force him to choose tennis over another sport and demand 100% deliberate practice, he let Andy have fun, participate in other sports, and decide for himself when to focus solely on tennis and engage in deliberate practice. Identify which stage your athlete is in—the sampling years, the specializing years, or the investment years—so you can determine how much deliberate play versus deliberate practice to offer, how much coaching to provide, how much encouragement to give to participate in other sports, and how much emphasis you place on performance and organized competition.

Notice in Andy's case that it was Andy who made the decision to progress to the investment stage. This is often the case—but not always. Sometimes athletes are unaware of their full ability; the opportunities, advantages, and rewards of investing; or the often short window of sport opportunity available to them. Following is an overview of the three phases of the DMSP and how your coaching and your practice plans might vary for individual athletes depending on their stage of sport participation.

Working With Athletes in the Sampling Years

Children's desire to remain in sport and continue on to the elite level is primarily influenced by their experiences during the sampling years. Consequently, during this developmental stage coaches should nurture children's intrinsic motivation to engage in sport. To accomplish this, support and encourage your young athletes to engage in deliberate play rather than deliberate practice, and to participate in a variety of sports. During this stage you should deemphasize performance through deliberate practice as well as organized competition. You should avoid overcoaching; however, children should be allowed to engage in a small amount of deliberate practice across different sports so that they learn fundamental movement skills that are transferable across sports. Côté et al. (2008) suggest deliberate play 80% of the time and deliberate practice 20% of the time.

To keep practice fun, engage your athletes in **teaching games**, which are loosely structured experiences that promote entertainment, enjoyment, and sport understanding. For example, consider scenario 1, in which you have a talented young athlete who could someday be quite good in your sport. Because she is in the sampling years, you know she isn't ready to specialize, but you want to keep her loving your sport so that when it comes time to get more serious she remembers how much fun your sport is. Consequently, you encourage her to play at your sport and you create teaching games that surreptitiously educate her about important fundamental skills. You also encourage her to participate in other sports, even though that participation sometimes means missing some of your practices.

Scenario 1

You have a talented athlete who likes playing your sport and could go a long way in the sport. But she is young and has interests in other sports. You don't want to turn her off to your sport. In fact, the opposite is true: You want to keep her loving the sport until she gets to a point where she wants to invest 100% of her time in it. Your concern is how to accomplish this feat. What should you do to not chase her off but rather keep her interested and connected to the sport?

When you have your athletes engage in teaching games, deliberate play, and different sports, you not only create a fun environment in organized sport but you also promote the development of self-regulation, decision-making skills, competence, and connectedness, all of which are important for progressing to the expert level.

Working With Athletes in the Specializing Years

During this stage, your athletes have decided to increase their involvement in one sport at the expense of other sports and commit to a more serious approach to training. At this stage, deliberate practice becomes a greater proportion of the workout, although deliberate play is still available to the athlete. Côté et al. (2008) suggest that an equal balance should exist between deliberate play and deliberate practice; however, as the athlete progresses through the stage deliberate practice should increasingly become a larger proportion of the workout.

During this stage you encourage your athletes to engage in practice activities that may seem less inherently enjoyable but necessary for advancement toward the elite level of performance. You accomplish this by explaining the relevance of the practice activity both now and for the future development of the athlete. Consider scenario 2 in which you have a young basketball player in the specializing stage of his athletic career. He has successfully used a two-handed set shot for a number of years but now is the time to make the change in his shooting mechanics if he is to continue his successful progression in the game of basketball. So, you sit down with him and explain that he needs to change his shot mechanics and routinely practice his shooting every day. You tell him that while the change and practice routine might not be as enjoyable as playing pickup basketball with his buddies, the deliberate practice is necessary for his continued improvement. You remind him that he will still have time to play with his friends during portions of his practices.

Scenario 2

You have a 13-year-old basketball player who has used a two-handed set shot since he was very young. You believe he could develop into a great basketball player, but he needs to change his shooting fundamentals if he wants to become a better offensive player in the future. Now, during the specializing year, is the best time for him to make that change. How do you approach this athlete and what should you do?

Working With Athletes in the Investment Years

During the investment years, athletes tend to focus on one sport and commit to training and performance. Most of their training time should be spent on deliberate practice. Côté et al. (2008) suggest that a small number of deliberate play activities should be incorporated into practice to remind your athletes of the intrinsic enjoyment they gain from participating in your sport. Athletes in this stage also need to engage in competition and competitive practice scenarios. Competition helps develop perceptual and decision-making skills as well as handling nervousness, anxiety, and stress.

Now that these athletes are continually engaged in deliberate practice, they will need your knowledge as a coach more than ever. They will look to you for guidance about things such as tactical knowledge, periodization of training, skill learning, effective drills, training and competition stress management, conditioning, mental training, and preperformance routines. Moreover, you will need good communication skills to impart this knowledge and the ability to incorporate this knowledge within your practice structure.

Let's say you are faced with the situation in scenario 3. One of your athletes wants to immerse herself in your sport. She is ready to enter the investment stage and devote all her efforts toward deliberate practice, much like Andy the tennis player did in the chapter-opening scenario. You are excited because you have been secretly hoping since she was a young athlete that she would take this step. But you are simultaneously apprehensive because you understand that her commitment will require a comparable level of commitment on your part as well as a depth of knowledge necessary for her to reach the elite level. That night at home you begin spending more time structuring your daily practices, paying greater attention to the finer details and goals of practice. You also decide to attend some coaching clinics, analyze more performance replays, and read articles from your sport's monthly periodical. You know that for her to improve as an athlete, you need to improve as a coach.

Scenario 3

You have a 16-year-old sophomore girl on your high school volleyball team who has come to you and asked for more practice time and more coaching because she has decided that this is the sport for her. She thinks about volleyball day and night. She wants to devote all of her time and energy to see how good she can become. She is putting her trust, her future, and her development in your hands. What does her commitment mean to you? How will it affect your development as a coach?

CREATING DELIBERATE PRACTICE

Deliberate practice doesn't happen on its own. Deliberate practice is the result of a collaborative effort between coach and athlete. Recall the 13 characteristics of deliberate practice from page 222. How can you help create these characteristics within your athletes and your training program?

Increasing Motivation and Desire

Not every athlete readily embraces the notion of deliberate practice. It's not that they object to it; it's just that they are accustomed to less formal training—they have engaged more in deliberate play than deliberate practice—and they simply have not yet grasped the concept. I once coached a very talented freshman who came from a junior program that emphasized fun (which is probably a major reason why she loved the sport and wanted to continue in it) but did not emphasize goals, effort, concentration, structure, making changes, and other characteristics of deliberate practice. She basically transitioned from the sampling years directly into the investment years, skipping over the specializing years. In other words, she went from 90% deliberate play and 10% deliberate practice to 90% deliberate practice and 10% deliberate play. Needless to say, the transition was challenging for her.

How can you motivate your athletes to transition into deliberate practice and also help them maintain the high level of motivation and desire necessary for engaging in deliberate practice? The next section addresses this question.

Elevate Perceived Competence

Perceived competence is an athlete's judgment about his ability in a sport. Athletes who feel competent tend to have positive expectations for success, persist in their sport, choose challenging tasks, and expend high effort, all of which are desirable traits for engaging in deliberate practice. Consequently, you can increase athlete motivation to engage in deliberate practice by increasing his level of perceived competence. Three sources contribute to increased athlete perceived competence: successful past experiences, positive information derived from observing models, and verbal persuasion.

To ensure *successful past experiences*, particularly during the early learning years, give your athletes difficult but attainable practice challenges. Tailor practice tasks so they are attainable by simplifying complex skills, modifying drills and equipment, or assigning attainable practice sets, among other things. Stress mastery, enjoyment, and effort. You can stress mastery and effort by encouraging your athletes to focus on the learning and performing processes rather than on winning and losing.

An increase occurs in perceived competence and motivation to engage in deliberate practice when athletes receive *positive information* by observing a successful performance by either a model or their own performance. Consider scenario 4 in which a young gymnast doesn't feel competent enough to perform a new vault maneuver. In this case you find a way to break down the vault into several simple skills and then have her watch a gymnast her own age successfully perform the vault. You also have her watch some of her past vaults as well as some of the skills she has been rehearsing in preparation for the new vault. This self-observation can instill greater perceived competency and motivation to attempt the new vault.

Scenario 4

A young gymnast is unsure of her ability (competency) to successfully and safely perform a new vault movement and has balked numerous times. You know she is ready to do the vault but she isn't so sure. She doesn't believe she is competent enough to perform it and, therefore, is unmotivated to learn it. Lately she has begun shying away from important practice drills and spending more time playing around with younger team members.

Another way to help your athletes achieve a heightened sense of competency is *verbal persuasion*. If your athletes regard you as trustworthy, credible, authoritative, and knowledgeable, they are likely to believe you when you tell them that they have the competence to perform. For example, in scenario 4, besides having the gymnast successfully perform lead-up skills and watching other gymnasts, you sit down with her and tell her that based on your observations and experience she is ready to competently perform her new vault and all she has to do is trust you, herself, and her preparatory training.

Promote a Task Orientation

Task orientation is a perspective in which success is based on mastery and effort. This is in contrast to an **ego orientation**, in which success is based on outperforming or beating others and achieving more with less effort. A task orientation positively affects perceived competency which in turn positively increases motivation. How exactly do you establish a practice environment that promotes task orientation? The answer lies in emphasizing factors such as the learning process rather than outcomes, skill mastery, goal attainment, personal improvement, cooperation, individual challenges, effort, and self-referenced evaluation. A helpful practice scheme designed to accentuate these factors and develop a task orientation is called **TARGET**.

T: Task design involves using a variety of tasks and assignments that allow your athletes to develop a sense of their own competency without comparing themselves too much to other athletes.

A: Autonomy involves allowing athletes when possible to take part in the learning process by distributing responsibility and authority and giving them choices. Let your athletes occasionally select some of the drills and tasks for the practice and ask them to evaluate their progress on them.

R: Recognition occurs when you notice and reward things you want to see from your athletes. Rewards should be used as a form of positive information and feedback regarding skill acquisition, champion behavior, and effort.

G: Grouping is something to avoid when possible. Because of differences in maturation, experience, and age between young athletes, some athletes would have trouble finding success and would draw erroneous comparisons about their level of competence. When possible, provide individual drills; if this is not possible, offer small cooperative group tasks.

E: Evaluation refers to allowing athletes to self-evaluate. Encourage your athletes to evaluate improvement, effort, mastery, persistence, and other factors associated with a task orientation.

T: Timing refers to the time you allocate for your athletes to complete practice tasks. You should be flexible, taking into account differences between athletes in the time it takes for them to complete tasks.

Beginning around the age of 12, young athletes tend to judge their capabilities relative to others. Practice schemes such as TARGET promote task orientation, which is good for the development of athlete perceived self-competence during late childhood and early adolescence.

Use Reinforcement

You also can increase athlete motivation through the use of reinforcement. A number of sources of reinforcement exist to maintain athlete motivation and persistence in engaging in their sport. These sources include parents, the first coach, and the community. Research indicates that of these sources, parents are the most important influence on socializing children into sport. Parents introduce their children to the sport, locate an instructor, set practice routines, instill value for the sport, and encourage high expectations. Reinforcers available to parents include praise and material rewards.

Even though parents are important, don't forget the importance of the first coach or a coach in the early period of an athlete's career. Elite athletes report that reinforcement they received from these coaches motivated them to return to play the next season and persist in their sport. Reviewing interview research by Bloom (1985) and Young and Medic (2008) identifies four sources coaches use to reinforce an athlete's early motivation to practice: showing special interest in the child, praise and approval, tangible rewards and prizes, and, close observation and tracking.

Encourage Self-Regulation

Bloom's research indicates that a coach's positive reinforcement is an important source of motivation in the first 2 or 3 years of training for athletes whose starting ages range from 7 to 11. However, for athletes to reach the elite level they need to ultimately transition to *self-regulation*, at which point they take on much greater responsibility for their motivation for practicing, planning, monitoring, and evaluating. Consequently, as athletes develop, reinforcement is gradually reduced and they are encouraged to self-regulate. In the later stage of development, elite athletes take on increasingly more responsibility for self-regulation. At the expert level, practice motivation and self-regulation become the primary responsibility of the athlete.

Cleary and Zimmerman (1998) have proposed a four-step cyclical model for self-regulated learning for athletes. Step 1 is goal setting and strategic planning. Step 2 is monitoring of strategy implementation. Step 3 is monitoring of strategic outcomes in training. Step 4 is self-evaluation of outcomes. As noted earlier in the chapter, all four of these steps are part of the deliberate practice process.

Enhance Sport Enjoyment

Another way to motivate your athletes to engage in deliberate practice is to enhance sport enjoyment. **Sport enjoyment** refers to the positive experiences, pleasure, and fun that athletes derive from their sport experiences. In studies of youth athletes from a variety of sports, enjoyment is perhaps one of the strongest predictors of continued sport commitment for youth. For example, in a study by Scanlan, Russell, Beals, and Scanlan (2003), adult international-level rugby players identified enjoyment as a significant influence on their persistent commitment to their sport. Athletes experience joy and satisfaction through activities such as deliberate play, free play, discovery learning, performance success, and mastery accomplishments.

Athletes also can find enjoyment through competition. Enjoyment might be found in the outcomes (e.g., winning), level of performance (e.g., setting a personal best), awards, social recognition, making new friends, new experiences, and travel. As mentioned in chapter 3, pairing positive emotions such as joy and success with your sport conditions your athletes to love their sport. Consequently, look for ways to make your athletes' sporting experience enjoyable.

Increase Involvement Opportunities

Involvement opportunities are the enjoyable conditions that athletes anticipate will be part of their sport experience at some point in their careers. If they perceive greater opportunities within their sport in the future, they become increasingly more committed to their sport. These opportunities include things such as friendships, travel, awards, outfitting, selection to international teams, and recognition. You can increase these involvement opportunities and thereby increase athlete motivation to engage in deliberate practice by helping your athletes take advantage of as many of these opportunities as possible. For example, athletes don't often become eligible for certain awards and special recognitions unless their coaches nominate them. They can't qualify for selected teams, trips, clinics, or programs unless their coaches enter them and prepare them for the qualifying competitions.

Encourage Appropriate Developmental Path

Athletes are more motivated to specialize in one sport and ultimately engage in deliberate practice if they are allowed to sample other sports in the early years and be exposed to the benefits and activities that each sport offers. Sampling protects the young athlete from an overemphasis on one sport, which research suggests is associated with later negative outcomes such as loss of enjoyment, injury, burnout, and early retirement. You can increase your athletes' motivation to engage in deliberate practice later in their careers by respecting their wishes to participate in other sports and by avoiding ultimatums that make them choose one sport over another. You also can tweak your practice schedule and seasonal schedule so your athletes have time to participate in other sports, particularly in the off-season. Along the way, making your sport as enjoyable as possible increases the likelihood of them eventually choosing your sport in which to specialize. You also can encourage them to select optional sports that provide for cross-training and enhance their preparation for engaging in your sport.

Building a Knowledge Base

The second characteristic elite athletes bring to deliberate practice is a broad knowledge base. The more athletes know about their sport, their training, and themselves, the more power and control they exert in creating and sustaining deliberate practice. Research indicates that this knowledge base contains declarative knowledge about response selections and executions as well as the procedural knowledge for carrying out these movements. French and McPherson (2004) have suggested that this sport expert knowledge base also includes sport-specific memory adaptations and structures, such as action plan profiles, current event profiles, game situation prototypes, scripts for competition, and domain-related strategies.

You can help your athletes develop a rich and varied knowledge base in many ways. For example, reserve 10 minutes at the end of each practice for a brief minilecture. Once a week give your athletes a handout about some aspect of your sport. Invite a guest coach to work with your team or talk with your players. Play an audiotape before or after practice. Play a digital recording. Make copies of an article you like and hand them out to your athletes or post the article in your team locker room. Arrange a panel discussion with current and former players. Share new information that you recently acquired from reading a book, attending a clinic, studying game film, talking with a colleague, and so on. The possibilities are endless.

The great thing about a knowledge base is that it has unlimited growth potential. It can continue growing indefinitely, which explains why many elite athletes even into their thirties and forties continue improving. But this growth only continues as long as athlete and coach seek new knowledge. Just as a tree cannot grow without sunlight and water, athletes and coaches cannot grow without the acquisition of new information. The onus for building a knowledge base, then, rests not only on athletes but also on coaches. Elite athletes need elite coaches who can help them bring an ever-expanding knowledge base to the game of deliberate practice and elite performance. Therefore, as an elite coach you will be a lifelong learner, continually looking for ways to improve practice and performance, and a voracious reader with a wide variety of interests because you know that elite performance and elite coaching involve knowledge from a wide variety of domains.

Setting Explicit Goals

Every aspect of training for elite athletes has explicit goals. Everything they do inside and outside the practice venue is goal directed. As coach, you want to help your athletes do two things: be goal directed and set their own goals. When working with your athletes, give them daily, weekly, and monthly goals. You can write them down and give them to your athletes or communicate them verbally. For example, when I observed a practice in China, I noticed the coach would give each diver a piece of paper with that day's individual practice and goals. Remember, don't limit goals to just the physical practice. They should also have goals for other parts of training such as their warm-up routine, mental training, and conditioning. Also, have your athletes take their sport home with them. Encourage them to keep a journal in which they reflect on their practices and competition performances, set new practice goals, evaluate their short-term and long-term goals, and so on.

If you want your players to become elite athletes, they ultimately need to become responsible for setting their own goals and regulating progress toward achieving these goals. You begin this process by having your athletes be a collaborative part of the goal-setting process. Besides the goals you set for them, ask them what goals they would like to include. Eventually, you retreat from the goal-setting process and the athlete assumes responsibility for setting goals and monitoring goal attainment.

Making Practice Relevant

As experts in other domains have defined them, aspects of practice are relevant if they specifically relate to improving the actual competition performance. So, everything done in practice must be directly related to improving the performance athletes will ultimately execute in competition. At no point during practice is time wasted on anything that doesn't positively impact competition performance.

You can make practice more relevant in several ways. Analyze your practice routines, drills, and tasks to see if they are relevant to the end product: improving competition performance. Practice is a means to an end. Is everything you are doing in practice helping your athletes become better performers? After careful analysis, you might want to modify some aspects of practice routines and some aspects you might want to delete all together. Next, continually look for improved drills, techniques, and training methods. Pick the brains of elite coaches. See what elite athletes do in training to make their practices relevant. Also, don't be afraid to experiment. Try new approaches and methods. Be creative. Concoct new drills and invent new training methods. Solicit ideas and suggestions from your athletes. Since they are the ones in the trenches fighting the good fight every day in practice, they will have some provocative suggestions. Finally, be vigilant, forever looking for ways to make your practices more relevant.

Increasing Effort

For individuals aspiring to become elite athletes, they may not completely comprehend the effort level necessary to train like an elite athlete. It is easy for nonelite athletes to misgauge the high effort level elites give for every practice, especially if they have never trained side by side with elite athletes. In descriptive terms, explain to your players the effort necessary to become an elite athlete. If you were an elite athlete, talk about your experiences. If you weren't, like most of us coaches, have an elite athlete talk to your team.

Consider the athlete in scenario 5 who has the tools to become an outstanding performer but only if she increases her effort. In this real life story, I asked Amelia what she thought it meant to be a champion. She said, "To perform better than everyone else in competition." I responded, "It means to give a level of effort in practice on a daily basis that no one else in the country is willing to give. To do the things no one else is willing to do." Our conversation had an immediate impact: She began to sustain a high level of effort from one practice to another. By her sophomore year, Amelia, the walk-on athlete, set a Big Ten conference record and was U.S. national champion.

Scenario 5

You have a talented walk-on freshman athlete who from all indications can become a breakout phenomenal player. After several weeks, however, you notice that she likes to train hard for one or two practices and then sloughs off for three or four practices. You believe she can become a champion but not at her current level of effort in practice.

Talk sometimes isn't enough though. Athletes have to see it to fully understand it. Therefore, take your team to watch elite athletes train. For example, visit a national training center and watch practice and talk with some of the athletes and coaches there. When I took my team to the national training center to watch their dryland and water practices, it was definitely an eye-opener for my athletes, especially the freshmen and sophomores. Also have an elite athlete train with your team for a brief time or have an elite coach work with your team alongside you.

High effort, or more precisely, *sustained* high effort is perhaps the one characteristic that truly separates the elite from the nonelite athlete. Many athletes dream of being champions, but only those athletes who sustain high effort for every practice become champions.

Increasing Concentration

Performing well involves concentrating on the right things at the right time. Concentration is a skill like any other skill, therefore it needs to be practiced so that athletes learn to control it and sustain it for extended periods of time. When individuals begin deliberate practice, the initial duration of weekly practice is typically limited (Bloom, 1985). Limited duration has to do with physical readiness, but also mental readiness. Because of the high mental demands required of deliberate practice, beginning athletes and young children are not fully prepared mentally to sustain this level of concentration.

As athletes become more knowledgeable about their sport, they learn to concentrate on the right things at the right time and sustain their concentration for longer durations. Athletes can't focus on everything because attentional capacity is limited; human beings can only attend to so much incoming stimuli at one time. Therefore, athletes must learn to select the most appropriate cues related to task performance. To assist your athletes with their concentration, identify appropriate cues on which to focus and inappropriate cues to ignore. Of course, this means that as an elite coach you need to be knowledgeable about these cues if you want to teach them to your athletes.

Finally, remember that according to research a high level of concentration is associated with and influenced by the deliberate practice characteristics of relevance and effort. Athletes will bring a high level of concentration to practice activities if they are motivated and see relevance in what they are doing. Consequently, when you motivate your athletes and make practice activities relevant, you simultaneously increase concentration.

Making Practice Enjoyable

Despite the earlier discussion about how practice for experts isn't inherently enjoyable, elite athletes really do enjoy practice. If they didn't, they wouldn't have remained in the sport and become elite athletes. They just enjoy practice differently from nonelite athletes. Elite athletes generate a natural high from making improvements and knowing they are moving toward greater performance and goal attainment. In contrast, nonelite athletes find enjoyment simply through participation in their sport. While they would like to get better, their enjoyment of the sport isn't predicated on improvement. They love their sport and simply like being associated with it.

Perhaps the most effective way to make practice enjoyable for elite athletes, then, is to structure practice so that they are constantly finding improvement in their performances. In some cases elite athletes change coaches because practices have become stale, monotonous, and unproductive, and therefore are not very enjoyable. For this reason, elite coaches should constantly seek new training methods, make changes to their practices, and tune the system. Think about this: If everything is exactly the same for each of your practices within each segment of your annual training plan, how much improvement are your athletes likely to make from one season to the next?

Remember, too, that even at the elite level deliberate play should be part of the practice experience. Elite athletes should never forget the fun and enjoyment they experienced earlier in their careers during the sampling and specializing years, the fun and enjoyment that transformed them into salivating athletes. For very young athletes, sport enjoyment is important for keeping them in the sport and motivating them to eventually engage in deliberate practice. But just because these young athletes are now no longer young and have advanced to the investment years doesn't mean they shouldn't experience deliberate play occasionally.

It is safe to suggest that driven, focused, and dedicated elite athletes can sometimes get a little too serious, as can coaches. Therefore, humor, deliberate play, proper perspective, and enjoyment should be important parts of the deliberate practice process. Sometimes we may have to tell an athlete (or ourselves), "Listen. Let's lighten up. You know, it's just a game and, yeah, we want to do our best and reach our greatest potential—and we will—but no one is dying of cancer today and we aren't going to get any better by acting after each workout set as if a family member just keeled over and died."

Structuring Practice

Structuring practice means that every practice activity is outlined and every transition between activities is smooth and rapid. To create practice structure and efficient transitions, take time to thoughtfully design each practice. Moreover, the practice design must take into account individual needs and differences, time of season, individual goals, and other considerations. Given these considerations, structuring practice is no easy task. For example, developing a three-month daily practice structure leading up to the Olympic Trials required approximately 10 hours of planning on my part.

In structuring practices, take the time and effort to map out an annual training plan that reflects training periodization and peaking for championship competition. Also, analyze each practice and structure the next practice in response to not only the yearly training schedule and long-term outcome goals such as winning a championship, but also in response to short-term training goals and the preceding practice (e.g., sickness, injury, overtraining). In general, the process of structuring practice is an ongoing daily activity that involves both athlete and coach, takes into consideration many factors, and is sensitive to the results of the preceding practice.

Monitoring Practice

Since improvement is most important for elite athletes, your responsibility as coach is to determine if improvement is indeed occurring. Improvement isn't always easy to gauge. For example, you are in the middle of your season training the heck out of your team. They are dead tired and performing badly, which is understandable given the time of season and work load. But are you doing the right things? Are you overtraining them or is the workload appropriate? Are all your athletes responding physiologically the same, or do some need more training and some need less?

Elite athletes are so driven and so determined that they will do any amount of work to improve and succeed. Unfortunately, they can sometimes be the cause of their own undoing. Through overtraining they may put themselves in a position where they are susceptible to injury or illness. As an elite coach, you need to monitor their physiological responses to training. Sometimes you have to pull in the reins and be the one who says, "Okay, that's enough for today." In my experience I have seen overtraining cause serious and even career-ending shoulder and back injuries.

Your other responsibility as coach is to monitor practice to ensure that it resembles the characteristics of deliberate practice. You can't develop elite athletes without creating an elite training environment and sustaining that environment. Ask yourself these questions: Do your practices reflect the characteristics of deliberate practice necessary for your athletes to reach the elite level? Are you providing them with knowledge about their sport? Are you helping them set explicit goals? Are you making practice activities relevant? Are you demanding a high level of effort and concentration? Are you making practice enjoyable by making sure that your athletes are not simply present at practice but improving? Is your practice structured? Are you monitoring every aspect of it? Are you working closely with your athletes and providing immediate feedback? Are you continually refining your practice methods and looking for new ways to help your athletes improve? And most important, are you putting in the time and energy to help your athletes reach their greatest potential?

A deliberate practice is impossible without a deliberate coach. The same is true for the athlete: There is no expert athlete without the expert coach. Your program will only reach greater heights when you reach for the stars just as you demand your athletes reach for their greatest potential.

Working Closely Together—Athlete and Coach

The athlete–coach relationship is one of the most important factors for athlete success. Elite skaters and wrestlers indicated that the second most important aspect of deliberate practice is working closely with their coaches (Starkes et al., 1996). How can you develop a close working relationship between you and your athletes?

From a humanistic perspective, developing a close relationship is possible when emphasizing genuineness, open communication, honesty, and trust. These humanistic qualities create an atmosphere that invites your athletes to connect with you and work more closely with you on a deeper and more meaningful level. You also foster a close working relationship when you have shared goals. After your athletes have selected short-term and long-term goals, these goals become your goals.

Sean McCann (2002), head of the United States Olympic Committee (USOC) sport psychology department, provides suggestions for developing a strong coach–athlete relationship, particularly with elite-level athletes. His first suggestion is *don't overlook emotions*. Coaches need to be aware of and sensitive to the emotional states of their athletes. As indicated in chapter 9, emotions have a significant impact on performance. Consequently, be aware of your athlete's emotional state.

Another suggestion McCann offers is to *develop good questions*. Getting in the habit of asking rather than telling athletes helps elicit more information from them. Asking questions can assist you in quickly ascertaining your athlete's thought process, emotional state, and physical condition. In addition, asking questions also allows your athletes to find their own solutions rather than simply agreeing with your solutions. Some good questions include the following:

How are you feeling physically right now?

How are you feeling emotionally right now?

How are you feeling mentally right now?

What is it you need to do now?

What are you thinking about right now?

What is your goal for this next set or practice?

What would you like to do differently?

Do you have any suggestions?

What do you think?

McCann also suggests *developing trust* so athletes can express weaknesses. Some elite athletes mistakenly believe that mental toughness means ignoring or hiding distracting and debilitating thoughts, anxieties, fears, and self-doubts. They believe that talking about these types of things makes them appear to be mentally weak athletes in your eyes, that talking about these things makes them real, and that mental toughness means pushing these things away. In reality, distracting and debilitating thoughts and feelings need to be acknowledged and treated (Grand & Goldberg, 2011). If athletes don't find resolution or develop coping strategies then these thoughts and feelings can and will rear their ugly heads during practice and competition, particularly during times of high stress, such as heavy training periods and critically important competitions. Feeling free to express their weaknesses allows your athletes to put the problem out in the open. Then the two of you can work closely together to solve it.

Finally, McCann also suggests that coaches should know the difference between *good quiet* and *bad quiet*. In other words, know when your athletes are ready to perform and when they are not ready to perform. They could be quiet because they are nervous, tense, and unready to perform, or they could be quiet because they are focused and ready to perform. On the first day of a major competition, I missed recognizing that one of my athletes was simply not mentally ready to perform. He arrived late for warm-ups, wore a frown the whole time, and never said a word. It was definitely a *bad quiet*. The next day I had him come in early for warm-ups. We sat down and joked and then formulated a warm-up plan that more closely resembled his normal routine, reviewed performance goals, and outlined a competition strategy that involved the two of us working closely together. By the end of the morning warm-up session he was back to his old self and I was convinced he was going to perform better than he did the preceding day. And he did: He won a national championship.

Providing Immediate Informative Feedback

Expert performers seem to crave immediate and specific feedback, particularly knowledge of performance. Perhaps the most accurate and immediate feedback athletes can receive is from an automatic digital replay system. In the past few years, many programs in a variety of sports have installed this type of system. As immediate and accurate as this system is, however, it loses something in translation. These systems cannot provide feedback regarding aesthetics, necessary movement corrections, and quality of performance. For all of these reasons and more, a coach is necessary.

One challenge for coaches is the ability to be succinct, specific, relevant, and immediate, often in a matter of seconds. In practice you have to say the right thing at the right time; say it fairly immediately; and say it succinctly. When I first came to IU as a young coach I had the opportunity to work with future Olympic gold medalist Mark Lenzi. It didn't take long working with Mark to realize that I had to up my coaching game in practice. If I forgot to look at a particular aspect of a dive or forgot what correction I had told him to make, he let me know the error of my ways. I also realized that I needed to learn a lot more about my sport and coaching. Research indicates that elite athletes want their coaches to possess knowledge of their sport and knowledge of competition tactics and strategies. Therefore, you should be a lifelong student, continually acquiring new ideas about all aspects related to your sport.

Finally, remember that you provide two types of feedback: knowledge of performance (KP) and knowledge of results (KR). Elite athletes want to know about the correctness of their movements (KP), but they also want to know about the quality of their movement and how well it would be evaluated in competition (KR). As noted earlier, elite athletes are most interested in improving the actual competition performance. Consequently, provide both KP and KR.

Using Different Methods and Refining Methods in Response to Feedback

In studying an expert hockey coach, researchers (Horton & Deakin, 2008) noted that there was a minimum of practice stoppage and if drills weren't accomplishing the coach's objective, the drills were rapidly altered or replaced by other drills. They noted that facilitating a smooth transition from one drill to another required considerable planning, preparation, and evaluation by the coach. In other words, using different methods or refining methods doesn't happen by accident; they are the result of the coach's hard work. They also are the result of hard work on the athlete's part. Two heads are better than one, so engage your athletes, particularly your more experienced athletes, in the processes of planning, preparation, and evaluation.

With regard to evaluation, collect objective feedback that helps you accurately determine the success of your methods, refine some methods, and invent new ones. Objective feedback includes things such as biomechanical analysis, slow-motion replay analysis, blood analysis, performance charting, competition rehearsal, and challenge sets. Without objective feedback it is impossible to accurately assess the effectiveness of your methods. For example, I believed that one of my athletes was performing inconsistently in practice and that I needed to alter her training. However, examination of her weekly performance chart indicated otherwise; she was indeed consistently meeting her performance goals and no refinement of our training methods was necessary.

Devoting Time and Energy

An athlete who has decided to enter the investment stage of sport participation has decided to put time and energy into focusing exclusively on one sport and one type of practice—deliberate practice. The problem at this point is helping this athlete find the time and energy. Researchers in the area of expertise (Sloane, 1985) have noted the importance of a support group for helping aspiring elite athletes find the time and energy to train deliberately. It takes a village to raise an elite athlete. Of primary importance are the caregivers. Parents and significant others must find the time and energy to support the athlete in many ways, including making meals, driving to and from practice, making arrangements for competitions, rearranging their schedules to accommodate their son or daughter's practice schedule, and providing words of encouragement and rewards for training.

Other support members include coaches, athletic trainers, tutors, teachers, mentors, and peers. All of these people are important for helping athletes engage in deliberate practice. For example, an athlete may have an unavoidable conflict with practice and the coach offers practice at a different time. My senior year in high school my coach, Morry, came in on his day off so that I could train. For athletes to put in the time and energy, the support group must do the same. More and more young athletes are choosing to home school or attend an online school so they can train 8 hours a day and become elite athletes. This type of commitment requires an equal commitment by the support group.

THE EXPERT ATHLETE

The **expert athlete** represents the problem of high-level performance in a uniquely different way from nonexpert athletes that aids in recall, anticipation, speed of performance, and decision making. The expert athlete also willingly engages in deliberate practice, which means this athlete is highly motivated and desirous of attaining excellence; possesses a large body of domain specific knowledge and continually seeks to learn more each day; sets daily practice goals and practices with intensity, a sense of urgency, and a high level of effort and concentration; practices not so much for enjoyment but for goal attainment; thrives with structure and self-monitoring; works well with a coach and embraces immediate feedback; highly values practicing the actual performance and is willing to make changes to improve; and is willing to invest a great deal of time and energy to reach his or her greatest potential. In short, the expert athlete is a coach's dream athlete.

THE EXPERT COACH

As Arnove (2009) makes clear in *Talent Abounds: Profiles of Master Teachers and Peak Performers*, youthful talent needs master teachers to become world-class talent, whether it be in classical music and conducting, jazz, opera, modern dance, chess, mathematics, or sport. So, in one sense this chapter has been as much about the expert coach as it has been about the expert athlete. Throughout this chapter a picture of the expert (elite) coach has gradually emerged. Let's now take a look at the complete picture.

The Deliberate Coach

The **expert coach** in many ways resembles the expert athlete who trains deliberately. Like the deliberate athlete, the deliberate coach is highly motivated and desirous of attaining excellence. The deliberate coach is knowledgeable about all aspects pertaining to the sport and sets explicit practice goals. Moreover, this coach makes sure that everything done in practice is relevant to improving competition performance. The deliberate coach brings a high level of effort and concentration, finds enjoyment in seeing athletes improve, structures and carefully monitors practice, and enjoys working closely with athletes. The deliberate coach is adept at providing immediate informative feedback, and not afraid to use different training methods or refine these methods or discard them and create entirely different methods. Finally, this coach is fully vested in the program and athletes and willing to spend the time and energy necessary to attain excellence.

In support of this picture of the expert coach, research by Horton and Deakin (2008) indicates that expert coaches design practices to re-create game conditions by emphasizing pressure, intensity, and relevance to performance situations. These researchers found that expert coaches maximize practice time, precisely plan practices, and thoroughly evaluate previous practices.

The Skilled Coach

Beyond these characteristics, an expert coach should possess other skills, too. In a survey (Pankhurst, 2009) by the United States Olympic Committee (USOC), Olympic coaches were asked to rank the five most important coaching skills. They cited the following skills:

1. Communication skills
2. Knowledge of sport

3. Skill development

4. Team development

5. Passion

These same coaches also were asked to write their own job description and list the top five job requirements. It is interesting that this list varied from the coaching skills list:

1. Technical knowledge

2. Planning and organizational skills

3. Teaching skills

4. Interpersonal skills

5. Experience and leadership

The Lifelong Learner

Irrespective of their sport, Pankhurst identifies several characteristics of expert coaches worth noting. The first characteristic is that expert coaches tend to be *lifelong learners*. These coaches are always looking for ways to improve their practices and coaching effectiveness. They tend to be voracious readers interested in a wide range of topics pertaining to their sport.

The USOC survey asked four elite coaches to cite their top five books that should be in a coach's library. Following are their selections.

- Bob Bowman, U.S. Olympic swimming coach and coach of Michael Phelps

  Theory and Methodology of Training, Tudor Bompa

  Mindset: The New Psychology of Success, Carol Dweck

  The Science of Winning, Jan Olbrecht

  My Personal Best, John Wooden

  The Tao of Leadership: Lau Tzu's Tao Te Ching Adapted for a New Age, John Heider

- Guy Baker, U.S. Olympic head coach for two silver medals (2000 & 2008) and one bronze (2004) medal in women's water polo

  Peak Performance, Clive Gilson, Mike Pratt, Kevin Roberts, & Ed Weymes

  Built to Last, James C. Collins & Jerry I. Porras

  Sacred Hoops, Phil Jackson

  Vision of a Champion, Anson Dorrance

  Who Will Do What by When?, Tom Hanson

- Adam Bleakney, U.S. Paralympic coach for gold, silver, and bronze medalists

  Theory and Methodology of Training, Tudor Bompa

  Flow: The Psychology of Optimal Experience, Mihaly Czikszentmihaly

Athletic Development: The Art and Science of Functional Sports Training, Vern Gambetta

Emergence: The Connected Lives of Ants, Brains, Cities, and Software, Steven Johnson

Sport Specific Speed: The 3S System, Gary Winckler & Vern Gambetta

- Vern Gambetta, conditioning coach for a variety of sports and teams including the Chicago White Sox and New York Mets and a consultant for the U.S. Men's World Cup Soccer team

  Running: Biomechanics and Exercise Physiology Applied in Practice, Frans Bosch & Ronald Klomp

  You've Got to Be Believed to Be Heard: The Complete Book of Speaking in Business and In Life, Bert Decker

  Mindset: The New Psychology of Success, Carol Dweck

  Mastery: The Keys to Success and Long-Term Fulfillment, George Leonard

  A Whole New Mind: Moving from the Information Age to the Conceptual Age, Daniel Pink

  Presentation Zen: Simple Ideas on Presentation and Delivery (Voices That Matter), Gar Reynolds

- Following are several books that influenced my coaching.

  The Physiological Basis of Physical Education and Athletics, Edward L. Fox & Donald K. Mathews

  New Voices in Counseling The Gifted, Nicholas Colangelo & Ronald T. Zaffrann

  Emotions in Sport, Yuri Hanin

  Motor Control and Learning, Richard A. Schmidt & Timothy D. Lee

  Psychology for Teaching, Guy Lefrançois

  The Force of Character—And the Lasting Life, James Hillman

Janelle and Hillman (2003) suggest that to obtain elite status, athletes must excel in four domains: physiological, technical, cognitive (tactical skills and decision-making ability), and emotional (emotion regulation and psychological skills). When you consider the depth and breadth of knowledge that expert coaches must possess, it is easy to see why they are lifelong learners.

Other Characteristics of the Expert Coach

Expert coaches are problem solvers. If something isn't right, they search for answers to make it right. They have no problem refining, changing, deleting, or inventing methods. They also tend to have a network of advisors or confidantes who provide advice and confirm or disconfirm some of their solutions.

Expert coaches are leaders. They are able to capture the allegiance of their athletes and coaching staff while simultaneously managing a host of responsibilities such as budget, logistics, and other issues unrelated to coaching athletes.

Expert coaches are relationship builders. Expert coaches are good at developing and sustaining relationships. The relationship between the expert athlete and expert coach is a long-term working partnership typically lasting 8 years or more. It is a relationship of trust and respect and mentally the two are on the same page working toward shared goals. According to Pankhurst, the best relationships are those in which the coach acts as guide: The athlete is self-regulatory and self-reliant but willingly accepts the coach's advice and suggestions on how to improve performance.

Expert coaches are passionate about coaching and their involvement at the elite level. If time and energy are important characteristics of deliberate practice for expert athletes, they are equally important for expert coaches. After athletes go home, the expert coach is still there planning the next day's practice, answering voice messages and emails, perhaps talking with an athlete about a problem, or planning next week's travel itinerary. I am reminded of former IU and Hall of Fame soccer coach Jerry Yeagley, who in the early years would coach the team all day and then wash the practice and competition jerseys, line the soccer field, and make travel arrangements for the next away game. Expert coaches are passionate about what they do and willing to devote as much time and energy as is necessary for success.

YOUR COACHING TOOLBOX

Here is another valuable tool for your coaching toolbox. Understanding expertise theory and how to develop deliberate play and deliberate practice makes you a wiser, more knowledgeable, and more effective coach—the expert coach. In one sense it is a simple plan. See what the great ones do and then imitate them just like Andy the tennis player did. But Andy only observed the best player at his club. The study of expertise examines hundreds of experts across a variety of domains and captures the unique characteristics and essence of expertise. These characteristics are capable of being reproduced in your program.

THE SCIENTIFIC AND ARTFUL COACH

The lists of skills and job requirements for an expert coach as indicated by Pankhurst (p. 247) are an interesting mix of science and art. According to the Olympic coaches, the scientific coach should possess knowledge about the sport as well as technical knowledge, and knowledge about skill and team development, planning, organizing, and teaching. On the other hand, according to these same Olympic coaches, the artful coach should possess communication and interpersonal skills (humanistic attributes), leadership, and passion. Successful U.S. Olympic coaches recognize that effective coaching at the elite level involves both science and art.

With regard to deliberate practice, the scientific coach possesses a large knowledge base. For this reason, expert coaches tend to be voracious readers of scientific literature. Knowledge is power and the more you know about your sport and related fields of study, the more powerfully you affect athlete development. The scientific coach understands technical aspects of the sport, the 13 characteristics associated with deliberate practice, and how to integrate these characteristics into practices and coaching.

The scientific coach also determines an appropriate amount of deliberate practice and deliberate play. As skill level increases, so should the amount of deliberate practice. No precise formula exists for how much weekly deliberate practice should be done at any particular age. The determining factor is number of years of experience in the domain rather than age of the individual. Thus, the number of hours of deliberate practice depends on the individual's career stage.

Ericsson et al. (1993) examined pianists and violinists and Starkes et al. (1996) looked at figure skaters and wrestlers. Despite different starting ages and despite comparing different domains, increase in hours spent each week on deliberate practice was approximately the same for all individuals in all domains. Some performers reported higher number of hours, but these hours included activities, such as jogging, stretching, and weight training, not considered part of deliberate practice. When these extracurricular activities were separated out, all performers were similar in number of hours dedicated to deliberate practice as a function of number of years involved in the domain.

Following are several general guidelines for increasing the amount of deliberate practice. First, if children start at an early age, 10 to 20 minutes per session for deliberate practice is appropriate. The children should be encouraged to adopt a regular weekly schedule with practice periods of fixed duration (Bloom, 1985). Practice time may be longer, but the amount of actual deliberate practice should be approximately 10-20 minutes.

Then, after a period of time when individuals have attained an acceptable level of proficiency, adapted physically to the demands of practice, and arranged their lives to incorporate practice time, you can increase the amount of deliberate practice gradually and slowly (Ericsson et al., 1993). Too rapidly increasing deliberate practice can result in overtraining (Silva, 1990), staleness (Raglin & Wilson, 2000), burnout (Bailey & Martin, 1988), failure, and injury (Ericsson et al., 1993). Table 7.1 outlines the approximate hours per week for deliberate practice based on the number of years of involvement.

The numbers in table 7.1 are simply guidelines for determining the appropriate amount of hours per week for deliberate training. Since they are based on results from studying a wide range of performers (pianists, violinists, skaters, and wrestlers), some variation exists. For example, for 6 years of involvement,

Table 7.1 Time Spent in Deliberate Practice

Years of involvement in the sport	Approximate hours of deliberate practice per week
2	5-7
4	6-11
6	8-16
8	12-17
10	17-21
12	22-26

the amount of weekly hours ranges from 8 to 16 hours. However, the numbers are useful for establishing an approximate range of hours. Remember, these are hours of deliberate practice and therefore do not include additional activities such as stretching, weight training, video analysis, deliberate play, or structured practice. These hours also do not reflect individual differences among athletes. Some young athletes are more motivated and in some cases prewired to engage in more deliberate practice than other athletes of similar age.

It is interesting to note that besides scientific literature, expert coaches tend to read a lot about the art of leadership and business success. This combination makes perfect sense. Coaches may be highly knowledgeable about their sport but if they can't gain the respect, admiration, and loyalty of their athletes and they lack interpersonal skills, they will have a difficult time establishing the close working relationship necessary for deliberate practice and the development of athlete expertise.

Finally, the artful coach is also the passionate coach. One characteristic of elite athletes is their passion, which translates into high motivation, effort, concentration, and relevance in everything they do. The artful coach's passion equals that of the elite athlete and translates into the same high level of motivation, effort, concentration, and relevance. Although passion is difficult to measure, its importance to deliberate practice and the development of expert performance can't be understated.

IF YOU REMEMBER ONLY THREE THINGS

1. *Remember that for very young athletes deliberate play precedes deliberate practice.* In your zeal to create a dynasty and develop expert athletes, you might forget that your first priority is to hook your athletes on your sport. When you allow your athletes to participate in deliberate play, probably much like you did when you were a young athlete, they get turned on to your sport and eventually engage in an increasingly greater amount of deliberate practice just like Andy the tennis player eventually did. And just like Andy, let your athletes participate in other sports during the sampling years and even the specializing years. Don't

give your athletes an ultimatum and make them choose between sports when they don't have to.

2. *Remember the 13 characteristics of deliberate practice.* Let these characteristics be your guide for shaping athlete behaviors, practice activities, training atmosphere, and coaching traits. You have the blueprint; you simply need to follow the plan. Like Andy, imitate the best to become the best. Train your athletes like expert athletes to become expert athletes. And don't forget about your own development as an expert coach, which leads to the next reminder.

3. *Remember that the expert athlete needs the expert coach.* Athletes can't reach the elite level on their own. Like Andy the tennis player did with his club coach, they need that authority figure with whom they can work closely. They need the expert coach to facilitate their transition from nonelite to elite athletes. What level coach are you? What are you doing to up your coaching game? What are you doing to be the expert coach you want to become? Do your actions reflect the intensity level and characteristics you hope to see in your athlete? Before you can develop the expert athlete, you must first develop yourself into the expert coach.

SUGGESTED READINGS

Arnove, R.F. (2009). *Talent abounds: Profiles of master teachers and peak performers.* Boulder, CO: Paradigm.

[This is an entertaining book with background information on many great teachers and performers. Also reminds us that great performers need great teachers.]

Bloom, B.S. (1985). *Developing talent in young people.* New York: Ballantine.

[This is an interesting and lengthy but not difficult read that opened my eyes to the study of expertise and developing elite athletes.]

Colwin, G. (2008). *Talent is overrated.* New York: Penguin.

[The author makes the case that great performance is not reserved for the genetically gifted but, rather, available to anyone who wants it bad enough and believes that through the heavy burden of deliberate practice they can attain it. A very enjoyable read.]

Ericsson, K.A. (1996). *The road to excellence: The acquisition of expert performance in the arts and sciences, sports and games.* Mahwah, NJ: Lawrence Erlbaum Associates.

[Ericsson's book helped me realize what I could do with my athletes. No excuses; if we train the right way we can succeed. I don't need the genetically superior athlete; I need the superior (expert) practice structure and the athlete willing to train deliberately. This book inspired me and convinced me my athletes could make the U.S. Olympic team. And they did.]

Fried, R.L. (1995). *The passionate teacher.* Boston: Beacon Press.

[Coaches at heart are teachers and if we want to facilitate the development of passionate athletes engaged in deliberate practice then we need to be equally passionate. Reading this book gave me a shot of adrenaline and reminded me why I entered the coaching profession in the first place.]

Athletes and Theories of Humanism

Part IV is a sharp detour from the previous seven chapters. Humanistic learning theory embraces a vastly different perspective because human beings are not like the dogs, rats, pigeons, or computers used as analogies in previous chapters. Also, while humanism is interested in individuals reaching their greatest potential, it is more about human potential than athlete potential. Still, humanism is not at odds with athletes reaching their greatest athletic potential; in fact, the next two chapters show that it is a helpmate for them doing so.

Chapter 8 introduces one of the most noteworthy theorists of humanistic approaches to learning—Carl Rogers—and some concepts germane to the humanistic perspective. The chapter then outlines five major characteristics of the theory along with some common emphases and their application to your coaching. The chapter introduces the *fully human athlete* and offers a specific coaching approach—the nondirective model of coaching—for interacting with your athletes to facilitate change. The chapter concludes by examining another humanistic-based theory called constructivism.

Chapter 9 inspects another very human aspect of athletes—emotions—and the fascinating interplay between emotions and motor learning and performance. The chapter discusses athlete differences with regard to range and types of emotions and introduces the *emotional athlete*. Perhaps most interesting are the lists of emotions that, according to research, enhance and impair performance. Many coaches and athletes will find these lists somewhat surprising and contrary to their previously held notions about emotions and athlete performance. The chapter concludes with some effective preventive and coping strategies for helping athletes stay in the game by playing the emotion game.

CHAPTER 8

The Fully Human Athlete

Applying Humanistic Learning Theory

Key Terms

authenticity

catharsis

congruence

constructivism

direct instruction

discovery learning

emphasizing affect

existentialism

fully human athlete

fully human coach

genuine

humanism

humanistic psychology

mastery learning

nondirective

nondirective model of
  coaching

person-centered therapy

phenomenology

positive self

Pyramid of Teaching
  Success in Sport

self-actualization

self-determination

task analysis

One day I happened to run into a friend whom I have known for many years. I first met him when he was either 13 or 14 and an up-and-coming athlete. He wasn't very good back then, but he made remarkable improvements in a hurry. It wasn't too long before he was making the finals at the national championships. About that time his parents divorced and shortly thereafter he was involved in a car crash. People speculated that alcohol or drugs might have been involved in the incident. He recovered after major surgery and a year of rehabilitation. Eventually he was off to college and a new beginning for his athletic career.

His athletic ability flourished in college even though other issues of his life worsened. Throughout college he was able to maintain a quasi-separation between his athletic life and his social life. He eventually made an Olympic team and even medaled at the Olympic Games. On paper, his life looked like a total success. He even made a second Olympic team and medaled again. Young athletes idolized him and strove to imitate him. But his life wasn't nearly as successful or as happy as it appeared. He had moments when he could barely keep the troubles of his private life from bleeding into his athletic life and ruining everything. At one point, he was involved in another accident that he was lucky to survive.

When I talked with him that day he was very open and forthcoming about his life during athletics and after athletics. After the thrill of two Olympic Games and the fame of being an elite-level athlete and living on the national and international stage, he was, by his own admission, a mess. He went through several years of therapy and counseling. After much effort at improving himself as a human being, he finally arrived at a point in his life where he could find peace, happiness, and self-worth. I will never forget his parting words: "I wonder what I could have accomplished as an athlete if I had had my life together as a human being." He believes he could have won two gold medals and thoroughly enjoyed the experience along the way. Knowing him, I too believe he could have accomplished both goals.

What good does it do for coaches to develop individuals as athletes and not as human beings? Fame is fleeting and medals tarnish. So, what is of lasting meaning and value? What is most important for the development and long-term well-being of the athlete? It is easy to see that a well-adjusted and more actualized individual ultimately makes for a more effective, successful, and happier athlete.

This chapter is the story of the *fully human athlete*—the athlete developing as a person. This chapter covers how you can understand and apply humanistic learning theory to help your players reach their greatest potential as athletes by concomitantly helping them grow as human beings.

CHAPTER OVERVIEW

Much of the book up to this chapter has examined scientific approaches to how athletes learn and how coaches teach. While a scientific approach is worthwhile and often necessary, it somehow neglects a part of what makes athletes human. Scientific approaches tend to dehumanize athletes and overlook issues such as feelings, personal values, personal growth, and other factors important to athletes as human beings. As this chapter shows, these issues also are important for how athletes learn and how coaches teach.

This chapter briefly defines humanistic psychology and some fundamental concepts associated with humanistic theory as identified by psychotherapist Carl Rogers. The chapter then outlines five major characteristics of humanistic learning theory. Next, it examines some common emphases of humanistic teaching and how they can be applied in your coaching. Then it explains in detail a unique humanistic model of teaching adapted for coaches and how you can apply this model when interacting with your athletes. Following is a look at a humanistic learning theory called constructivism and its implications for effective coaching. It also considers a humanistic-based paradigm for effective coaching known as the pyramid of teaching success in sport. The chapter concludes with a look at seven humanistic principles that you can apply to your coaching.

HUMANISTIC PSYCHOLOGY

Humanistic psychology originated from the musings of philosophers, particularly existentialist philosophers such as Jean-Paul Sartre, Martin Buber, and Karl Jaspers. These philosophers pondered the nature and purpose of humanity and of human existence; thus, the term **existentialism**. These writers considered what it means to be human and how humanity matures and is expressed through each individual.

Humanistic psychology is concerned with the dignity and self-worth of all people. It focuses on the individuality, the humanity, and the uniqueness of each person. This uniqueness of self is most central to humanistic psychology. Humanists object to the technological orientation of approaches such as behaviorism that coldly analyze and dissect the educational experience into two factors: the teaching process and the learning product. The humanistic orientation emphasizes the uniqueness of each individual learner and the teacher's attitudes toward learners.

Rogerian Humanistic Theory

Carl Rogers is among the most influential theorists in the area of humanistic approaches to learning. Carl Rogers was a psychotherapist interested in finding alternative approaches to understanding and changing human personality and to bringing happiness to lives filled with sadness. He rejected currently popular approaches to therapy such as Freudian theory and behaviorism and looked for a more humane approach that respected the individual dignity and self-worth of clients. His writings emanated from his effort to place the individual client at the center of therapy. Like those of existential philosophers, Rogers' writings are based on his answer to questions about humanity and human existence: How do people perceive the world? How do they feel? How do they perceive their relationships with others? What are the necessary conditions needed for them to learn (change)?

Rogers' theory had, and continues to have, a significant influence on psychotherapy and counseling. More important for teachers and coaches, his theory also has significance for effective teaching and learning. Rogers' theory is much different from scientific-based theories and provides teachers with a different way of dealing with students. Similarly, a humanistic approach to learning can provide coaches with a different way of dealing with athletes. To best understand Rogerian theory, it is useful to first understand several concepts associated with his theory.

The first concept is **person-centered therapy**. Rogers' approach is therapeutic in nature and deals with counseling clients. According to Rogers, counseling (and teaching and coaching) revolves around the person, not the counselor (or teacher or coach). Also, the client–counselor relationship is **nondirective**. In other words, the counselor sets the stage so the client defines the problem and works toward a solution, rather than the counselor attempting to solve the problem.

The second concept associated with Rogerian theory is **phenomenology**. This concept suggests that reality is what each individual perceives it to be. The counselor should be concerned with the client's own personal view of the world, not as it appears to others.

The third concept is **humanism**. Historically, humanism has been concerned with human worth, human development, and self-determination. Consequently, Rogerian theory is influenced by these ideas. Based on the notion of human worth, Rogerian theory deemphasizes material goals and emphasizes personal self-worth and development. Based on the idea of human development, Rogerian theory stresses the importance of self-actualization. According to Rogers, **self-actualization** is the process of striving to become a complete person. Rogers suggests that all human beings have an innate desire to strive toward this self-actualization.

Finally, Rogerian theory is concerned with the notion of **self-determination**. Rogers wants the individual to acquire autonomy and the ability to self-regulate, which is why he emphasizes person-centered therapy. Person-centered therapy means individuals solve problems for themselves and take greater personal responsibility for making decisions that affect their lives.

Later, this chapter looks at ways for coaches and athletes to integrate these concepts into their coaching and training. First, it is worthwhile to look at some defining characteristics of Rogerian theory.

Five Major Characteristics of Rogerian Theory

In the eleventh chapter of *Client-Centered Therapy* (1951), Rogers summarizes his therapeutic approach in 19 propositions. The five most important propositions germane to teaching and coaching are highlighted in this section. These characteristics of Rogers' theory are important for helping you better understand and work with your athletes. To achieve a better understanding of humanism and Rogerian theory, it is useful to listen to "On Becoming Fully Human," an audiotape by Leo Buscaglia (1984), which is cited at the end of this chapter in the Suggested Readings. Although he says he is not a humanist, many of the things Buscaglia says clearly and succinctly state the humanist's position.

Reality Is Phenomenological

"No two of us have the same world" (Buscaglia, 1984a).

This first characteristic of Rogerian theory suggests that reality for each person consists of private experiences that are different from another person's experiences. Therefore, what is real for one person is not necessarily real for another. One athlete might have an entirely different perspective of your sport than you have for your sport. I remember an athlete of mine who never approached competition as competition, at least in the same way that other team members did. Yet, that reality worked for him, and worked quite well. To this day I am not sure what exactly that reality was for him, even though I tried to understand.

As an outsider to this private experience, you can never completely know someone else's phenomenological world. This means that when trying to relate to what someone is going through or when trying to understand someone's perspective, you can say, "I had an experience that might be somewhat similar" but you can never say, "I know exactly what you mean" or "I had the very same experience." This doesn't mean that you shouldn't try to understand an athlete's viewpoint. When you try to understand, you provide empathy, an important characteristic of effective humanistic coaching.

It may seem discouraging to consider the possibility that no two people see the world in the same way. However, this difference is part of what makes coaching interesting, challenging, and often rewarding. As Buscaglia (1984a) says, "It's our sameness that brings us together, but it's our differences that keep us together and that keep life going and exciting."

Behavior Occurs Within the Context of Personal Reality

"Never have a short argument. Always argue long enough so you know what you're arguing about" (Buscaglia, 1984a).

This second characteristic suggests that people react from the reality they perceive. Consequently, the best way to understand another person's behavior is to try and adopt that person's point of view, which is why humanism emphasizes open and nonjudgmental communication. To understand others' viewpoints, it is necessary that they openly and freely talk about their feelings and perceptions. Sometimes coaches are quick to make judgments and suggest solutions rather than try to simply understand an athlete's perceived reality.

If a disagreement, misunderstanding, or argument occurs, it is important that both sides openly and honestly communicate until each person has an understanding of the other person's personal reality. Buscaglia suggests that if you do have a disagreement, you should communicate long enough until you really understand each other's points of view.

The Individual Constructs the Self

"I need you to reflect me. I need you to show me who I am" (Buscaglia, 1984a).

According to Rogers, everyone constructs a notion of self from direct experiences with the environment. You can control the experiences your athletes encounter. You can offer your athletes direct experiences such as acceptance, love, belongingness, and success. These types of experiences lead to the development of a **positive self**, which is a consistent pattern of beliefs about who you are.

You also can offer your athletes indirect experiences that usually come in the form of evaluational interactions with others. Coaches are powerful *others*. You are an important source of evaluational interaction for athletes, particularly young athletes struggling to develop a notion of self. The information and the way you deliver it to your athletes helps them construct a belief about who they are. Therefore, it is important to provide them with positive feedback that contributes to the development of a positive notion of self. This feedback can take the form of praise, positively stated and constructive criticism, positive reinforcers, and especially positive expectations.

People's Behaviors Conform With Their Notion of Self

"If I'm fearful, I teach my fear. But if I am together and secure, I can help you to become together and secure" (Buscaglia, 1984b).

People act in accordance with their self-concept. In other words, people select behaviors that are compatible with their notion of self. If athletes perceive themselves to be capable, then they act capable. If they perceive themselves to be powerless, then they act powerless. If they perceive themselves as good competitors, they are likely to perform well in competition. For this reason it is especially important for you to provide both direct and indirect positive experiences that help your athletes, particularly your young athletes, develop strong notions of self.

It also is important for coaches to develop a strong notion of self because you will coach in accordance with your self-concept. If you perceive yourself to be insecure, then you will coach insecurely. But if you perceive yourself to be competent and confident, then you will coach competently and confidently. How do you perceive yourself? How do you wish your athletes to perceive you? You don't have to be perfect, but enhancing your self-concept helps you become a more effective coach and leader.

Behavior Is Motivated by a Need to Self-Actualize

"You are more potential than you are actuality" (Buscaglia, 1984a).

According to Rogers, each person has an inner need or tendency to strive toward becoming a complete, healthy, and competent person. This becoming process is directional; it is growing and moving toward one's fullest potential. This process also involves self-government, self-regulation, and autonomy. Self-actualization is a notion basic to the humanist viewpoint, which sees people as essentially good and forever striving toward a better state of being. What a healthy and positive perspective for athletes and coaches to possess when approaching training and coaching. Keep in mind that this striving toward a better state of being applies to coaches and not just athletes.

Over the years, Buscaglia's statement has come to mean more and more to me: "You are more potential than you are actuality." This concept brings me back to coaching every year. When I met a new group of summer campers or greeted each year's incoming freshmen, I was overwhelmed by the amount of potential in the room and overjoyed by the expectation of what these young athletes would become and accomplish both in athletics and in life. I have had the privilege of witnessing many athletes actualize their potential over the years and I am grateful to have had the opportunity as a coach to facilitate this becoming process.

APPLYING FOUR COMMON EMPHASES OF HUMANISTIC COACHING

Humanism can manifest itself through the coaching process in four ways. These common emphases are affect, self-concept, communication, and personal values.

Affect

Emphasizing affect means paying greater attention to thinking and feeling and less attention to acquiring specific information and skills. Following are some suggestions for emphasizing affect.

Set affective objectives. Setting specific affective objectives means you commit to making a conscious effort to integrate humanism into your program. Examples of affective objectives include encouraging and leading athletes to demonstrate a love for their sport and themselves and to demonstrate a concern and respect for teammates. Another affective objective is to demonstrate a concern and respect for your athletes and acceptance of them as unique individuals, not just as a group of athletes. Another goal is to act as a role model and model a love for the sport and belief in the importance of becoming a more complete person.

Pay greater attention to athletes' feelings. Simply asking athletes how they are feeling and what is going on in their lives, showing a genuine concern for them as human beings, listening to their problems, and being sensitive to their emotional responses are all ways of paying greater attention to athlete's feelings.

Have athletes become more aware of their teammates' feelings. Awareness of others' feelings emphasizes affect and helps athletes move outside their egocentrism. One way to facilitate this greater awareness is to hold a team meeting and ask your athletes to express their feelings, understand their teammates' needs, and find ways to support each other at practices, competitions, and outside the practice venue. Also, when disagreements occur between athletes, ask each athlete to try understanding the other's viewpoint.

Stress the importance of learning and thinking strategies. According to Rogers emphasizing affect also means emphasizing thinking. When you emphasize thinking, the information and skills being taught are not as important as the process and strategies for learning. Consequently, a humanistic coach emphasizes learning how to learn and teaches athletes specific strategies to help them become good learners. For example, having athletes mentally review information about drills before, during, and after each practice helps them learn how to learn drills. Many athletes tend to leave a practice and never think about that practice ever again. When taking time to review information discussed in practice, athletes are more apt to organize the information, give it meaning, remember it at the next practice, and, consequently, improve at a faster rate.

Self-Concept

Helping your athletes develop a positive self-concept is another way to emphasize humanism. Remember that your athletes develop their self-concept in part through interaction with you and how you communicate to them about who they are as human beings. How can you facilitate this process? Following are some suggestions.

Maintain positive perceptions and expectations of your athletes. It is easy to form limiting notions of your athletes and unconsciously communicate these limitations to them. These notions then become part of a hidden curriculum: the things you unconsciously teach as the unintended outcome or by-product of your coaching. Statements such as the following ones can become part of a hidden curriculum: "This athlete is mentally weak." "This athlete will never make it." "This athlete can do skills A and B great but will never learn skill C." "This athlete will always be a B-level player." Rid yourself of preconceived limiting notions of your athletes and avoid any hidden curriculum. Expect the best. When you expect the best, you generally get the best. Don't count out any of your athletes. Like Jimmy, the young lanky boy I coached many years ago, just when you think someone can't do something, you may be surprised.

Communicate these positive perceptions and expectations through word and deed. It is good to have positive perceptions and expectations of your athletes, but make sure you communicate them to your athletes both by what you say and what you do. Take the time to tell your athletes what you think of them and what they are capable of achieving and communicate these expectations through your coaching. Saying, "Well, you didn't make it this time but I know you will at the next competition" is an effective example. Also, demonstrate your confidence in them through your actions. For example, you tell one of your athletes that she can become a champion if she puts in more work and then you stay after practice or volunteer to come in on your day off to work with her.

Maintain positive perceptions and expectations publicly and privately. Coaches sometimes disparage their athletes behind their backs. Getting frustrated and needing to vent some frustration is part of coaching, but you have to support your athletes and believe in them, even when they aren't looking. Being a humanistic coach means, in part, being genuine as a person. Being **genuine** means acting as you really are as a person and having your words match your internal feelings. In other words, you openly let others know how you feel. Venting is part of human nature and part of dealing with stress. But you have to be true to your athletes. You can't say one thing publicly and then turn around and say something contrary privately. Besides making you a hypocrite and disingenuous, your words ultimately get back to the athlete and ruin the coach–athlete relationship.

Invite rather than disinvite athletes. According to Purkey and Novak (1996), teachers *invite* students by communicating to them that they are capable, self-directed, and valued, and by expecting behaviors and achievements commensurate with their worth and emerging self-concept. In contrast, teachers who *disinvite* students send a message that students are irresponsible, incapable, worthless, and undirected. As a coach, do you invite or disinvite your athletes?

Build a positive self-concept by promoting success rather than failure. To promote success, break down learning tasks into small and attainable increments. Coaches sometimes ask athletes to do too much too soon. Perhaps this is because they forget how many smaller tasks comprise a particular movement. They ask athletes to do a skill that actually involves many skills, none of which the athletes have yet mastered. When you ask athletes to do too much too soon, you set them up for guaranteed failure. The result of repeated failure can be a poor self-concept, a feeling of external control, and a sense of helplessness.

Promoting success and a positive self-concept also includes implementing mastery learning (Bloom, 1976). The concept of **mastery learning** suggests that all learners can learn; the only difference between learners is the amount of time each person requires to learn the material. While Bloom's concept of mastery learning deals mainly with concept learning, mastery learning can be applied to motor learning as well. Not all athletes will learn to perform at the elite level. However, most athletes can learn much of what you teach to some level of proficiency. The humanistic coach focuses on helping each athlete master as many skills as possible for their particular sport and level of experience and ability.

Mastery learning means learning a particular skill to a certain level of proficiency before moving on to the next skill. For example, when you break down a skill into smaller increments, make sure your athlete masters each smaller skill before moving on to the next skill. It may take time and patience on the part of both athlete and coach, but it will be well worth the effort later in the athlete's career.

Communication

A third major emphasis of a humanistic approach to coaching is communication. Communication includes attention to the principles and skills of effective human relations, honest interpersonal communication, and constructive conflict resolution. Following are some suggestions for emphasizing communication in your coaching.

Establish effective human relations through honest and open interpersonal communication. Honest and open communication means being real with your athletes, rather than aloof and unapproachable. Honest communication also means really listening to what your athletes have to say. A shortcoming for many coaches is that they don't take the time or give enough effort to really listen to what their athletes are trying to say. Being a good listener is not easy but sometimes it is all an athlete really wants or needs.

One season I had trouble establishing a relationship with one of my athletes. I was angry with her because I thought she never listened to me. Over the course of the season, our relationship became increasingly distant. Finally, another athlete said to me, "Coach, you need to talk to her." At first I dismissed her comment, but the more I thought about it, the more I knew she was right. So, one afternoon I took some time to talk with her. I said a few things about how I felt, but then I just listened to what she had to say. The more I listened to her, the more she listened to me. I am positive that our meeting was a turning point in her season and career. And it literally happened overnight. We met on a Wednesday and on Thursday she competed in the NCAA championship. She finished third with a lifetime best performance, a performance that far exceeded anything she had done to that point in her season.

Take time from your daily routine to communicate with your athletes. Maybe it is just a few minutes as they are coming into practice or while they are stretching. Or maybe you connect with a few of your athletes before they leave practice. The more you communicate with them, particularly on a personal level, the more of a relationship you establish with them. Take the time to occasionally meet one-on-one in your office. Have an open-door policy so that your athletes feel comfortable stopping by even if it is only to say hello. Schedule individual goal-setting sessions. Besides nourishing the athlete–coach relationship, these meetings provide athletes with the opportunity to express their feelings and talk about things important to their athletic careers and their personal lives.

Arrange team meetings and team goal-setting sessions. These sessions give your athletes the opportunity to communicate among themselves. It is worthwhile to attend some of these meetings to lay the ground rules for athlete interaction and discussion topics. For other meetings, it is more important that the athletes take responsibility for the meeting and you need not be present. Some of the topics your athletes can consider are how to support one another inside and outside of practice, how to communicate effectively with each other, and how to openly talk about problems and their resolutions.

Use the principles and ideas of humanism and Rogerian theory to constructively resolve conflict. No matter how effective you are as a coach or how great your athletes are as people, you will have conflict at some point within your team and within your program. And the quicker it is resolved, the sooner you right the ship and continue moving forward. It might be a conflict between you and a player, between two players, between an assistant coach and a player, between two assistant coaches, between coach and parent, or between the offense and the defense. The number of potential conflicts lurking on the horizon is great and you and your athletes need to be trained and ready to confront these battles. Humanism and Rogerian theory provide a perfect battle plan.

According to humanism and Rogerian theory, the best way to resolve conflict is for both sides to sit down and communicate. Since people act in accordance with their phenomenological reality, this communication involves having each person really listen and attempt to understand the other person's private world of experiences. Because humanism emphasizes self-direction, self-determination, autonomy, and self-evaluation, it is expected that each person, with the coach acting as facilitator, will assume responsibility for resolving the conflict.

Personal Values

Personal values should be a part of your coaching philosophy and your coaching curriculum. You teach values whether you know it or not. If you are unaware of the values you teach, then they have become part of your hidden curriculum. As mentioned a number of times in this book, effective coaches are aware of everything they teach. Consequently, be conscious of the values you teach—or want to teach—and incorporate them into your coaching curriculum so that you teach positive values and eliminate negative values you might be inadvertently teaching your athletes.

Encourage your athletes to discover their own personal values. Simon, Howe, and Kirschenbaum (1972) suggest 79 strategies for helping students elaborate and clarify values. Personal values you might teach include acceptance of self and others, acceptance of personal faults and mistakes but still maintaining self-worth, and valuing effort and performance more than winning. One personal value worth teaching is personal responsibility. Historically, humanism has valued autonomy: the individual taking responsibility and control for his or her life.

Stress personal responsibility as a value. You can nurture personal responsibility in many ways. Having athletes set their own goals and select appropriate ways of reaching their goals gives them a sense of control and autonomy. Also, setting up athletes for success helps establish an internal locus of control. According to attribution theory, athletes with an internal locus of control see success as a result of personal effort and not an external factor such as luck. In other words, an athlete with an internal locus of control believes that he is in control of the outcome of events.

Stress personal problem solving as a value. Rather than solve a problem for an athlete, you can facilitate the athlete's effort to solve the problem. This concept is at the center of Roger's client-centered therapy, in which the client, not the counselor, solves the problem. Based on Rogerian theory, a nondirective model of teaching has been developed for fostering a sense of personal responsibility in athletes. The following section outlines the nondirective model.

NONDIRECTIVE MODEL OF COACHING

The **nondirective model of coaching** described in this section is based on the nondirective teaching model as outlined by Joyce, Weil, and Calhoun (2009). Their model is influenced by the work of Carl Rogers and reflects several humanistic concerns. The model places the learner at the center of the learning process and assumes that people are willing to be responsible for their own learning. Also, the model is more concerned with long-term learning styles and the development of the individual self than with short-term instructional or content objectives or the particular short-term problem the individual might be confronting.

The primary goal of the model is to assist people in attaining greater personal integration, effectiveness, and realistic self-appraisal. In other words, the goal is to help individuals become more self-actualized. A secondary goal of the model is to create a learning environment conducive to examining perceptions and forming new perceptions. While it might not be necessary to change perceptions, the model assumes that it is worthwhile to reexamine perceptions, such as needs and values, so that individuals can effectively direct their own decision making.

The nondirective model of coaching is not meant to be used as your sole coaching strategy, but it should be blended in with your daily coaching. The model is particularly useful when dealing with individual athletes who are experiencing personal problems or athletic problems and failures; rather than being spoon fed solutions to their problems the model encourages them to actively seek solutions for themselves. However, having said this, the model can be used as well when dealing with happy, problem-free, and successful athletes. For example, the nondirective model can be used during goal setting when athletes evaluate progress and development and establish expectations and future goals.

In addition, this model of coaching is particularly useful when dealing with gifted athletes. Gifted athletes tend to have a positive self-concept and need to feel part of the learning process and part of the decision-making process. When you engage them in these processes, they feel at the center of the learning process and assume greater responsibility and autonomy for their learning.

Setting the Atmosphere

According to Rogers, the best interview atmosphere has four defining qualities. These qualities can be applied to the athlete–coach interaction scenario. First, the coach demonstrates warmth and responsiveness toward the athlete and expresses a genuine interest in and acceptance of the athlete. Second, the coach demonstrates permissiveness with regard to the expression of feelings and thoughts. In other words, the coach does not judge or moralize on feelings expressed and comments made by the athlete. Third, the athlete is allowed to freely express feelings symbolically but is not allowed to control the coach or to carry impulses into action. During the interview, limitations exist in terms of responsibility, time, affection, and aggressive actions. Fourth, the counseling relationship is free from pressure and coercion. In other words, the coach avoids demonstrating personal bias or reacting in a personally critical manner toward the athlete during the interview.

During the interaction between athlete and coach, the coach acts as a facilitator and reflector, helping the athlete when possible and necessary to define problems and feelings, take responsibility for her actions, and plan objectives and how to achieve the objectives. Typical reinforcement and punishment in the form of approval or disapproval are not part of the interaction between athlete and coach. Instead, reinforcement in the nondirective interview is more subtle and intrinsic—acceptance, understanding, and empathy from the coach.

Phases of Personal Growth in the Nondirective Interview Process

During the nondirective interview, it is hoped that the athlete will experience four phases of personal growth that ultimately lead to a fifth phase: a new orientation. The following list outlines these five phases.

Phases of Personal Growth in the Nondirective Interview Process

> *Phase 1:* Release of feeling—Catharsis
>
> *Phase 2:* Insight—New perception of the self
>
> *Phase 3:* Action—Decisions: New choice of goals and self-initiated action
>
> *Phase 4:* Integration—Independence and confidence
>
> *Phase 5:* New orientation—New perceptions and growth

JOYCE, BRUCE R.; WEIL, MARSHA, MODELS OF TEACHING, 8th Edition, ©2009. Reprinted by permission of Pearson Education, Inc., Upper Saddle River, NJ.

Teams can go through these phases, too. For example, a little later in this chapter, scenario 3 looks at how a team deals with a problem and eventually moves from anger to insight to action and eventually integration and a new orientation.

The Model

Despite the fact that the interview process can be unpredictable, Rogers indicates that there is a sequence to the process that involves five phases. The next section outlines these five phases of the athlete-coach interview.

Phase 1: Defining the Helping Situation

Before starting this phase, make sure to greet the athlete in a way that will set the tone for the interview process. Opening remarks to the athlete are important because they let the athlete know several things. Remarks such as "What brings you here today?" or "Something seems to be bothering you; tell me about it" let athletes know you are glad to see them, interested in them and their problem, and willing to listen to what they have to say.

At the beginning of the meeting, define the athlete's freedom to express feelings and provide him with a nonjudgmental and caring environment. Agree with the athlete about the general focus of the interview and establish the procedures for the interview.

At the beginning of phase 1, it is not unusual for people to release a great deal of emotion. They might be angry, upset, worried, or tearful. This release of feeling, called **catharsis**, helps people release emotions that can prevent them from clearly and rationally beginning to explore their problems. Once these emotions have subsided, people should be encouraged to explore exactly what is bothering them, which is the goal of phase 2.

Phase 2: Exploring the Problem

During this phase, the athlete is encouraged to explore and define the problem. The coach accepts and clarifies feelings using nondirective responses that encourage the athlete to continue talking and exploring the problem. Nondirective responses include simple acceptance, reflection of feelings, and paraphrasing of content.

After some time, the athlete may have trouble narrowing the topic or defining the problem. At this point the coach can use nondirective lead-taking responses. These types of responses include structuring, directive questioning, and forcing the athlete to choose and develop a topic. Structuring involves helping the individual organize what has been said (e.g., "Okay, you have mentioned three specific concerns, which are . . . "). Directive questioning means using questions that point the individual in a specific direction (e.g., "You mentioned three concerns; talk more about the second one."). Sometimes, the athlete has trouble getting to a specific topic and the coach might have to force the issue (e.g., "Which of the three concerns is most urgent for you to solve and how might you solve it?").

When asking directive questions, avoid using questions that start with the words *can, should,* or *would.* The problem with these words is that they elicit simple *yes* and *no* responses that don't encourage the athlete to continue exploring the problem. Instead, use nondirective leads and open questions. Open questions that start with *how* and *what* ask for information. For example, you can answer the question *Can you think of an alternative?* with the word *no.* In contrast, the question *What are some alternatives?* elicits more information.

Table 8.1 summarizes the different types of nondirective responses to feelings and nondirective lead-taking responses available to coaches when meeting with their athletes.

Table 8.1 Nondirective Responses

Responses to feelings	Lead-taking responses
Simple acceptance	Structuring
Reflection of feelings	Directive questioning
Paraphrasing of content	Forcing athlete to choose and develop topic
	Nondirective leads and open questions
	Minimal encouragements to talk

Phase 3: Developing Insight

Once the problem has been identified, the athlete is encouraged to further discuss it. During this phase, the coach supports the individual's efforts to examine the problem and gain insight into all aspects of the problem.

This model works well for minor problems. However, you should be aware that major problems, such as thoughts of suicide, are problems best left for trained professionals. Should a problem of this nature arise, immediately inform the parents and refer the athlete to a professional.

Phase 4: Planning and Decision Making

This is the action phase. During this phase, the athlete makes decisions about the best approach for solving the problem. Then the athlete develops a plan for implementing the approach. During this phase, the coach clarifies possible decisions by repeating what the athlete may have said, paraphrasing, and pointing out potential alternatives that may have been overlooked.

Phase 4 concludes with the athlete prepared to implement the plan. Before adjourning, it is important to set a specific date and time to meet again. This second meeting is important because it gives the coach and athlete an opportunity to meet and see if the original plan was successful. If it was not, then the athlete can formulate a new plan at this second meeting.

Once the meeting is adjourned, the athlete initiates the plan of action outside the interview scenario.

Phase 5: Integration

After the plan of action has been implemented, the athlete meets again with the coach at the prearranged time and place. The athlete reports the actions taken, develops further insight, and plans increasingly more integrated and positive actions. During this second interview, the coach is supportive of the athlete's efforts to gain insight and develop and integrate new perceptions and actions.

If further work is deemed necessary, once the athlete has made plans of action the athlete and coach agree to meet again at a predetermined time and place to once again evaluate the effectiveness of the newly formulated plan.

New Orientation

Recall that the fifth and final phase of personal growth for the athlete is a new orientation. In other words, through the coach's facilitation, the end result of the nondirective model of coaching should be a new perspective adopted by the athlete, a new perspective that from a humanistic viewpoint reflects the growth of the athlete as a human being.

Phases of the Nondirective Model of Coaching

Phase 1: Defining the helping situation—Coach encourages free expression of feelings.

Phase 2: Exploring the problem—Athlete is encouraged to define the problem. Coach accepts and clarifies feelings.

Phase 3: Developing insight—Athlete discusses the problem. Coach supports athlete.

Phase 4: Planning and decision making—Athlete plans initial decision making. Coach clarifies possible decisions. Action outside of interview: Athlete initiates positive action.

Phase 5: Integration—Athlete gains further insight and develops more positive actions. Coach is supportive.

Positive Effects of Using the Model

Why use the nondirective model of coaching? Why not just tell the athlete what the problem is and how to solve it? From a humanistic perspective, the answer to this question is that acting as facilitator and having the individual solve the problem produces several positive, long-lasting effects for the athlete.

The athlete learns how to solve problems for himself. While it may be important to solve a particular problem an athlete might be experiencing at that moment, it is more important in the long run for the athlete to learn general problem-solving skills for later in life. As Rogers (1995) writes, "It is my hypothesis that in such a relationship the individual will reorganize himself . . . to cope with life more constructively, more intelligently, and in a more socialized as well as a more satisfying way" (p. 36).

Through the nondirective process the athlete becomes personally aware of his ability to control external factors through personal effort. This awareness helps establish an internal locus of control and a heightened sense of self-efficacy. Again, Rogers (1995) writes, "He changes his perception of himself, becoming more realistic in his views of self. He becomes more like the person he wishes to be. He values himself more highly. He is more self-confident and self-directing" (p. 36).

With newly acquired problem-solving skills and heightened self-efficacy the athlete is likely to take greater responsibility for personal actions and become more autonomous. As Rogers (1995) pens, "He is less frustrated by stress, and recovers from stress more quickly. He becomes more mature in his everyday behavior . . .

He is less defensive, more adaptive, more able to meet situations creatively" (p. 36). Creating autonomous athletes is a major goal for the humanistic coach.

Finally, the athletes become more effective in setting and attaining social and athletic goals. As the athlete grows as a person and learns new perceptions, problem-solving skills, orientations, and personal actions, he becomes more effective socially in resolving problems with teammates, taking on more responsibility, and providing leadership. As Rogers (1995) says, "He becomes more accepting in his attitudes towards others, seeing others as more similar to himself" (p. 36). The athlete also becomes more effective athletically in setting challenging goals and conquering particularly difficult athletic challenges and obstacles.

Applying the Nondirective Model in Coaching Athletes

Coaches can apply the nondirective model to four types of problems: personal problems, social problems, motor performance problems, and team problems. The following four scenarios provide real-life situations and specific dialogue that demonstrate the model in action.

Scenario 1

Your athlete is having a *personal problem*. She is beginning to achieve some remarkable success in her sport and is qualifying for both national and international competitions, but her mother is becoming more and more of a distraction at these competitions. While at these competitions, when your athlete does find some down time between events, her mother demands she spend time with her. Moreover, when she and her mother do get together, her mother tells her the mistakes she is making and how she could do better if she only made certain changes in her performance and in the things she does leading up to and during competition. All of this has reached a breaking point and your athlete is miserable and has finally decided to come see you.

Coach: Hi, Sally. Thanks for stopping by. What brings you into my office today? You don't look so happy?

Sally: Hi, Coach. Sorry to bother you but I haven't been feeling so good lately. [Sally begins to cry.]

Coach: What do you mean you don't feel so good lately?

Sally: I don't know. I just don't want to compete anymore. [More crying.]

Coach: Not compete anymore?

Sally: Yeah. It just isn't any fun when I go to a competition.

(continued)

Scenario 1 *(continued)*

Coach: Why is that?

Sally: I don't know. It just doesn't seem fun.

Coach: Well, Sally, there must be a reason for this. Can you think of a reason?

Sally: Well, my mom has really been bugging me lately. [Sally quits crying]

Coach: What do you mean? How has your mom been bugging you lately?

Sally: Well, every time I go to a competition she wants to go out for a *long* lunch or dinner. But at the end of the day I am tired and want to get some rest and get ready for the next day's competition.

Coach: How does this make you feel?

Sally: Angry. My mom doesn't get it. I need to rest and get ready for the next day. And she is always telling me what to do.

Coach: Telling you what to do?

Sally: We sit down to eat and she starts telling me all the things I did wrong and how I could have done better.

Coach: How does this make you feel?

Sally: It really upsets me. She is my mom and should be supporting me. Her job isn't to coach. That's your job. Besides, I don't want to talk about the day. I want to talk about something else.

Coach: What do you want to talk about?

Sally: Nothing really. Just something that takes my mind off the competition.

Coach: That is a very good comment, Sally. How can we accomplish this and solve the situation?

Sally: Well, I would like my mom to know how to support me at meets.

Coach: How can we make this happen?

Sally: Well, for one, I don't want to go out to a sit-down meal that lasts hours.

Coach: What else?

Sally: I don't want her coaching me. That's your job.

Coach: That is a good point, Sally. Anything else?

Sally: Yes. She needs to know all this. But I'm not sure how to tell her. But she needs to know. How can I tell her? Can you talk with her? Or better yet, can you make up some rules for her?

Coach: Well, we could develop a set of parental rules that outlines how parents can support their kids at competitions. I could send it to all the parents so that your mom doesn't think she is being singled out.

Sally: Coach, that is a great idea. Thanks so much. How about if I write up a list of rules and give it to you tomorrow?

Coach: That's a great idea. Then I will look it over, make any changes I think appropriate, have you look it over again, and then send it to all the parents on the team. How does that sound to you?

Sally: That sounds perfect.

Coach: Great. Let's do that and then meet back tomorrow at this same time to agree on the wording of the rules.

Sally: Coach, you are amazing. Thanks for using the nondirective model of coaching. [Of course, she wouldn't really say this, but you might think it!]

Scenario 1 is something I went through with one of my athletes. Notice how the athlete moves through the five phases of the model. She begins by releasing her feelings, then gaining insight and, finally, moving toward action and integration. Now consider a different problem in scenario 2, in which an athlete is experiencing a motor performance problem.

Scenario 2

Your athlete is having *motor performance problem*. The problem is that she is in a slump and can't break out of it. In desperation she has come to you for help.

Coach: Hi, Asha. Thanks for stopping by. What's going on?

Asha: Hi, Coach. I think I am going to quit the team. [She feels dejected and lost.]

Coach: Quit the team. Why, you are one of our starters. What's the matter?

Asha: Coach, I just can't do it anymore. You've seen my last four games. Basically, I suck. I can't do anything right. Everything I do is wrong.

Coach: What do you mean, everything you do is wrong?

Asha: I mean just that. I can't do anything right and instead of getting better I'm getting worse. It's not worth playing anymore. I'm letting you down, my parents down, and the team down.

Coach: What do you mean? Tell me more.

Asha: I'll tell you more. I suck! You shouldn't keep me on the team! [At this point she breaks down in tears.]

Coach: Listen, Asha, you wouldn't be a starter if you didn't earn it. And you wouldn't continue to be a starter if you didn't deserve it. It sounds like

(continued)

Scenario 2 *(continued)*

you are being way too hard on yourself. Besides, you don't play for your parents or for me. You play for yourself and for the love of the game and all I ask is that you give your best effort, which you do.

Asha: But I can't let everyone down.

Coach: You haven't let anyone down.

Asha: But I can't break out of this slump.

Coach: Well, from what I know of slumps, they are caused by either a technical problem with execution or a problem with mental thoughts. And from what I can see your technique seems fine.

Asha: Then maybe my problem is mental.

Coach: In what way do you think it might be a mental problem?

Asha: Well, maybe I'm putting too much pressure on myself to perform for you, my parents, and my team. When I was younger, I just played for the enjoyment.

Coach: That is an interesting thought. Do you enjoy it now?

Asha: Well, I use to until I was made team captain. Then I started feeling like I had to play for the team and for you. I don't want to let anyone down.

Coach: How could you let us down?

Asha: By not winning.

Coach: Remember the Olympic Creed: It's not the triumph but the struggle. As I have told you and the team many times, I only ask for your best effort physically, mentally, and emotionally.

Asha: I know. I guess I kind of forgot that. But I'm team captain.

Coach: What are the responsibilities of our team captain?

Asha: To work hard, set a good example—both in practice and in the classroom—support my teammates, and provide leadership.

Coach: I didn't hear anything about winning.

Asha: I'm sorry, Coach. I guess I got things mixed up.

Coach: It's easy to get mixed up in life. So what is it you want to do?

Asha: I want to lead. I want to do the things a captain is supposed to do.

Coach: And, as you mentioned earlier, have fun.

Asha: Yeah. I forgot how much I love the game. I want to get back to that phase of my career.

Coach: How do we do that?

Asha: I guess it's simple, by getting back to what I used to do: working hard and having fun.

Coach: How do you have fun?

Asha: By loving the sport like I used to and concentrating on performing the best I can.

Coach: That sounds like a simple but great plan. Let's try that this week and meet back on Friday at the same time to see how things go.

Asha: Thanks for listening, Coach. I feel much better.

Coach: Thanks for coming to see me and being open with me. I appreciate it very much. See you Friday, Asha.

Notice in scenario 2 that Asha gets stuck in the initial phase of the interview and the coach interjects to help move her along in the interview process. No interview is perfect and no interview is the same. Some athletes are better than others in this type of interview process. This was a situation I confronted as a coach and found that this athlete needed a little more assistance. It was also a critical time of the season and neither one of us had the time or opportunity to meet as long as we would have liked.

Although the problem is different, the athlete moves through the same phases of personal growth during the interview process. Rogers (1995) suggests that the nondirective interview process is effective for many types of problems and for different types of relationships: "The excitement comes from the fact that these findings justify an even broader hypothesis regarding all human relationships" (p. 37).

Scenario 3 provides a different problem. In this case, the coach is experiencing a problem with his team and decides to use the nondirective model to solve the problem.

Scenario 3

You—and your team—are having a *team problem*. Your team isn't sustaining their training intensity throughout the week. By Friday morning the team starts shutting down physically, mentally, and emotionally. It's as though they are resting up and getting ready for Monday morning practice. You decide to use a nondirective teaching approach by confronting the team with this problem and asking them to take responsibility for solving it.

Coach: Listen, guys. We have a problem and if we don't solve it we aren't going to reach the goals we set for ourselves at the beginning of the

(continued)

Scenario 3 *(continued)*

season. We simply aren't training hard enough throughout the entire week from Monday morning to Saturday morning. We aren't giving the type of sustained physical, mental, or emotional effort we need in order to perform at our highest level. This has to change if we want to reach our team goals.

Player: Coach, I haven't noticed anything wrong. [Athlete is somewhat angry and defensive.]

Player: I haven't noticed anything either! [Athlete is also somewhat angry.]

Coach: Has anyone noticed the problem?

Player: Absolutely. [Athlete is also angry] I feel like some Fridays I am the only one giving a good effort in practice and I am tired of it. We need to get our butts in gear every day, not just some days.

Coach: Anyone else feel like this?

Player: Well, I will admit that last week I didn't give the effort I should have.

Coach: Thanks for your honesty. Being honest is the only way we are going to play like a team and reach our goals. So how do we solve this problem?

Player: Well, I think we've already started by identifying the problem. We've got to try harder.

Player: But just saying that doesn't mean it will happen. We've got to do more and look for more solutions to the problem.

Coach: Great idea. How about if we brainstorm some ideas for solving this problem? Remember that in brainstorming there are no wrong or bad ideas. So don't judge anyone's ideas. Let's just throw the ideas out there and I will write them down.

Player: Let's put up inspirational signs in the locker room reminding us to give a 100% effort.

Coach: That's a good idea.

Player: Let's monitor each other during practice.

Player: Yeah, but you can't complain when someone tells you something.

Player: Let's give an award each week to the player who works the hardest.

Coach: These are all great ideas. Keep them coming!

Player: Let's write down the things it takes to practice like a champion and post them in the locker room.

Player: Let's post them in the practice area.

Player: And it isn't just in practice. Let's talk about giving 100% in the weight room and stretching and everything we do during the week, including the classroom.

Coach: Great idea.

Player: And if you don't give 100% during the week, you don't compete.

Coach: Now we are getting somewhere. What should we do next?

Player: Well, it doesn't do us any good to just talk about the solutions. We have to make sure we follow through on things like Coach always tells us.

Coach: How do we do that?

Player: Let's write them down, then have another meeting after practice tomorrow so we can decide on the rules. Then we can post them and start monitoring ourselves.

Player: And we shouldn't just monitor ourselves at practice. It should be outside of practice as well.

Coach: Good point.

Player: I will write all these things down. I have paper and pencil.

Coach: Okay. Now we are getting somewhere. Let's continue brainstorming for another 15 minutes and then we will meet again tomorrow to discuss them immediately after practice. I want to remind you that this is *your* team and what *you* decide will dictate the direction *you* take and the level of success *you* achieve.

Player: Thanks, Coach.

In scenario 3 the nondirective model of coaching works well for allowing the team to discuss the problem and, more important, to consider a number of different solutions. The coach facilitates the meeting by introducing the problem, encouraging brainstorming, providing simple acceptance, and directive questioning. The players provide inspiration, ideas, and solution paths.

Most coaches would like to say they spend 100% of their time simply coaching but the truth is, coaches wear many hats and one of these is the fireman's hat. There are times when coaches must douse brushfires before they become raging infernos. And sometimes coaches must even extinguish the occasional inferno. Whether you like it or not, athletes have problems and for the well-being and success of the athletes, betterment of the team, and advancement of the program it becomes necessary for you to become a facilitator of change by helping athletes find resolution. The nondirective model of coaching is one of the most useful tools available to you for helping your athletes find resolution. Helping athletes improve performance sometimes boils down to helping them resolve their problems so they can regroup, refocus, and ready themselves to learn, train, and perform.

CONSTRUCTIVISM

Constructivism is a general term for an instructional approach that places the learner at the center of the learning process. It posits that meaningful learning is constructed by, not given to, the learner. Another term for constructivism is **discovery learning** because the learner acquires knowledge through self-exploration and discovers solutions to problems.

Constructivism does not mean that coaches should completely remove themselves from the learning process and that athletes should assume complete responsibility for learning. With a constructivist approach the coach's responsibility includes determining athlete ability, readiness, skill level, and goals. To make this determination it is important that coaches do a **task analysis** to determine the hierarchy of skills that make up a particular motor movement. From there the coach can help provide learning situations that match the athlete's skill level. When using a constructivist approach, keep in mind the instructional principles discussed next.

• *Provide varied physical opportunities.* Giving athletes different situational demands, varied practice scenarios, and diverse practice drills provides them with a number of opportunities to explore, discover, and learn. From a motor learning perspective, these multiple opportunities help them construct motor programs (e.g., schemas and production rules), stimulus identification, and response selection.

• *Provide optimal difficulty.* A task that is too easy or a task that is too difficult both have the same net result: very little learning. An easy task means the athlete already knew what to do and, consequently, no learning occurs. An impossibly difficult task will culminate in failure and, consequently, no learning occurs. As mentioned throughout this book, finding an optimal level of task difficulty is important for a myriad of reasons. In this case it is important for promoting discovery learning.

• *Understand how children think.* Children don't always think rationally, logically, abstractly, or maturely (and neither do adults on occasions for that matter). Consequently, recognize situations when you will need to intercede and provide direction, advice, or concrete examples. Piaget (1972) found that young children have difficulty comprehending abstract concepts. An example of an abstract concept is Newton's third law, which states that for every action exists an equal and opposite reaction. This concept and how it applies to the movement may be conveyed better by a concrete physical demonstration. Also, young athletes may become frustrated because of their inability to comprehend or perform a movement, in which case coach intervention may be helpful.

• *Provide social interaction.* Encourage athletes to interact and work cooperatively with each other. The adage *two heads are better than one* is certainly true for discovery learning and athletic teams. Coaches who encourage their athletes to interact and learn together create a positive, motivating, and successful athlete-centered learning atmosphere. One example of social interaction would be to have two athletes on your team work together on learning a specific skill. As they work together, they give each other feedback, discuss nuances of the skill, and suggest changes. From my own experience, this scenario works well primarily because the athletes like it. It is a dramatic change of practice from their coach giving them feedback every 5 seconds of practice. Social interaction also helps young athletes become aware of the feelings and thoughts of others, develop moral and game rules, and construct and practice their own logical thought processes (Lefrançois, 2012).

• *Assess athlete readiness.* My team and I were at a training camp in California during winter break and a diver from another team mentioned that he was going to dive off the 10-meter platform. He had never done it before and wanted to give it a go. I told him it would be prudent to work his way to 10 meters by diving off the 5-meter platform first and then getting acclimated to the 7.5-meter platform so he could *discover* what an impact feels like and how to hold his lineup from the 10-meter platform. He declined my suggestion and headed immediately to the top platform. He dislocated his shoulder on his first dive. For obvious reasons, coaches need to assess athlete readiness before letting them gallivant off in pursuit of some goal. For example, you wouldn't put a beginning baseball player in the batting cage and tell him to discover how to hit a 90 mile per hour fastball or throw someone into the deep end of a pool and say, "OK, now discover how to swim!"

Although assessing athlete readiness is obvious, many coaches break this rule more often than they perhaps realize. Have you observed a coach in your sport give free rein to athletes by allowing them to try something they simply aren't physically, mentally, or emotionally prepared to tackle? No coach likes to discourage an athlete, but at times you need to say, "OK, but let's try this later. You aren't quite prepared to do it—yet. Learn X, Y, and Z skills and then we will give it a shot."

Much is to be said, then, for a constructivist approach to coaching. It recognizes an athlete's need to prove self-competency. Constructivism also encourages discovery learning, cooperative learning, and active athlete participation in the motor learning process. However, times do exist when a constructivist approach is inappropriate. Adams' closed-loop motor learning theory suggests that early learning should be error free. But a constructivist approach encourages errors and learning from these errors. And for some skills, it may be injurious to the athlete to use a constructivist approach. In addition, for young athletes dreaming of becoming future champions it is important to establish good fundamentals from the outset of their careers. For any motor skill—shooting a basketball, swinging a golf club or tennis racket, drawing a violin bow, throwing a football, or pitching a softball—it is important to lay a foundation of accuracy and proficiency in the simple, fundamental movements that underlie great performances.

How do we reconcile these two contradictory approaches to coaching athletes? How do we use both the tool of constructivism and the tool of error free learning? For successful coaching, the trick is to find an appropriate ratio between **direct instruction** (i.e., coach-directed approaches to coaching) and a constructivist approach to coaching. Finding this ratio is part of the art of coaching.

PYRAMID OF TEACHING SUCCESS IN SPORT (PofTSS)

Chapter 1 considered Maslow's hierarchy of needs and how basic and meta-needs are important for the development of the athlete. The hierarchy is humanistic because it recognizes some very important needs embraced by humanists, many of which have already been touched upon or alluded to in this chapter: safety, belongingness, love, self-esteem, cognitive and aesthetic needs, and self-actualization—the inner desire of all individuals to strive toward reaching their greatest potential. Like Maslow's hierarchy of needs, the **Pyramid of Teaching Success in Sport** (PofTSS) (Gilbert, Nater, Siwik, & Gallimore, 2010) is hierarchical and recognizes concepts near and dear to the hearts of humanists, concepts such as love, friendship, cooperation, and self-examination (an important concept for self-development of the coach). The Pyramid (figure 8.1) identifies the building blocks for becoming an effective coach.

The first tier is considered the foundation of teaching success and consists of five humanistic blocks. These concepts are love, friendship, loyalty, cooperation, and balance. The authors define the cornerstone of love as the selfless, altruistic, and unconditional dedication coaches should have to help athletes succeed at all times. The other cornerstone is balance—the ability to maintain moderation and perspective and congruence, "the alignment between what the coach thinks, says, and does" (p. 90). The blocks between the cornerstones—friendship, loyalty, and cooperation—create a humanistic teaching and learning atmosphere that engenders collaboration, trust, and relationship building.

The second tier is called the coach's learning community because it recognizes that coaches don't learn in a vacuum. They learn from others such as former coaches, mentors, coaching colleagues, and opposing coaches. The four blocks—industriousness, curiosity, resourcefulness, and self-examination—are essential concepts for learning because they contribute to increasing knowledge base, developing emotional durability, and building character. Industriousness means working hard physically and, just as important, intellectually. Curiosity motivates coaches to ask the question *Why?* and look for ways to improve coaching effectiveness. Great coaches are curious seekers of information and are resourceful at discovering answers to questions, finding solutions to problems, and creating novel responses to puzzling situations. The fourth block, self-examination, contributes to continued learning and personal growth because the successful teacher continually asks the question *How can I improve as a teacher and person?* As the authors write, "Self-examination spurs future

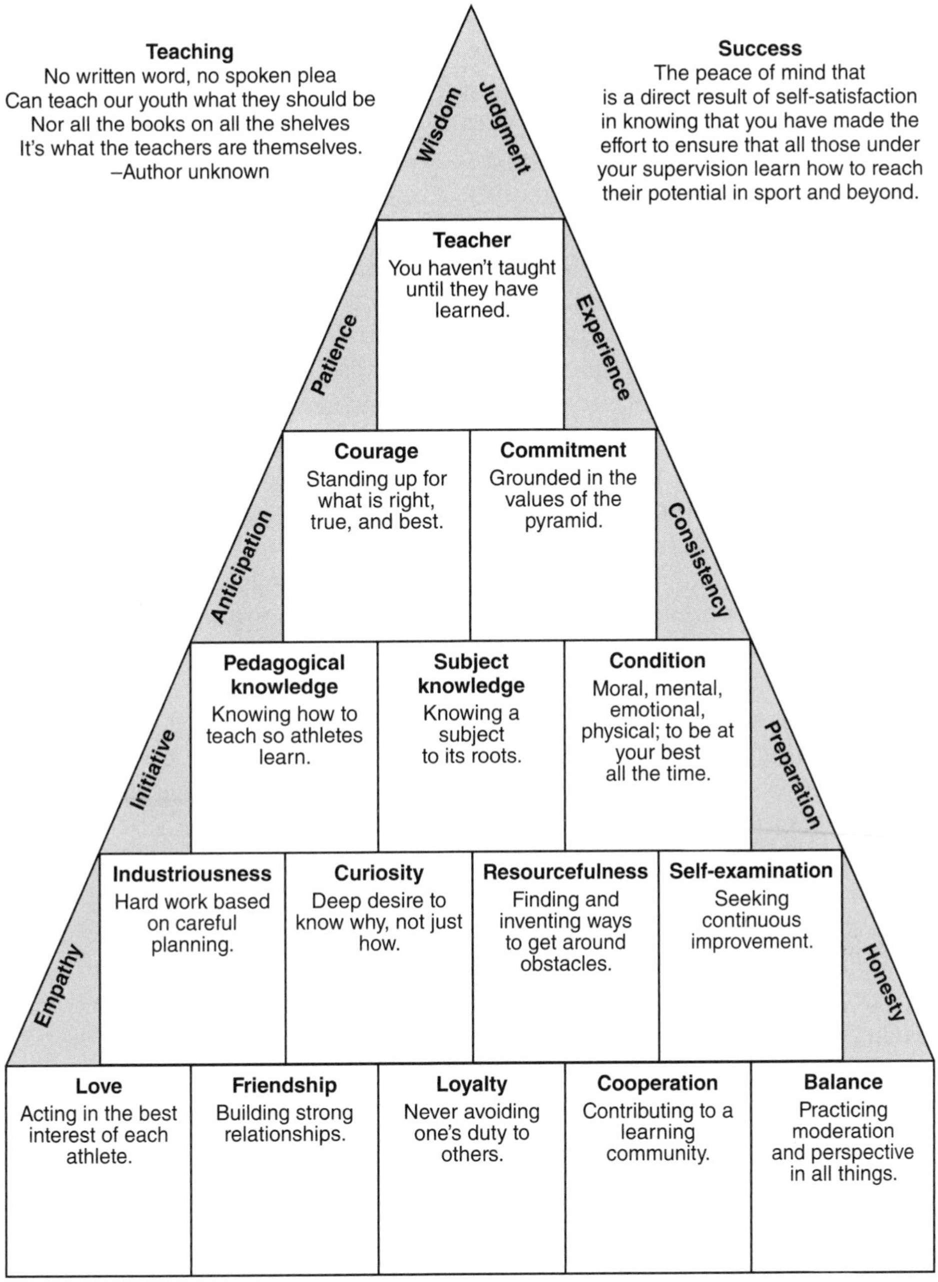

Teaching
No written word, no spoken plea
Can teach our youth what they should be
Nor all the books on all the shelves
It's what the teachers are themselves.
–Author unknown

Success
The peace of mind that
is a direct result of self-satisfaction
in knowing that you have made the
effort to ensure that all those under
your supervision learn how to reach
their potential in sport and beyond.

Wisdom Judgment

Teacher
You haven't taught
until they have
learned.

Patience Experience

Courage
Standing up for
what is right,
true, and best.

Commitment
Grounded in the
values of the
pyramid.

Anticipation Consistency

Pedagogical knowledge
Knowing how to
teach so athletes
learn.

Subject knowledge
Knowing a
subject
to its roots.

Condition
Moral, mental,
emotional,
physical; to be at
your best
all the time.

Initiative Preparation

Industriousness
Hard work based
on careful
planning.

Curiosity
Deep desire to
know why, not just
how.

Resourcefulness
Finding and
inventing ways
to get around
obstacles.

Self-examination
Seeking
continuous
improvement.

Empathy Honesty

Love
Acting in the best
interest of each
athlete.

Friendship
Building strong
relationships.

Loyalty
Never avoiding
one's duty to
others.

Cooperation
Contributing to a
learning
community.

Balance
Practicing
moderation
and perspective
in all things.

Figure 8.1 Pyramid of Teaching Success in Sport.

growth by eliminating weaker ideas and ineffective practices, setting new goals to pursue, and aligning everyday behavior with core values, especially love and balance" (p. 90).

The third tier is the heart of the pyramid because it identifies the core elements of effective teaching: pedagogical knowledge, subject knowledge, and conditioning. No matter how humanistic a coach might be, that attribute won't overcome or compensate for a lack of understanding of how to teach (pedagogical knowledge) or what to teach (subject knowledge). Effective coaches are essentially effective teachers. They understand how athletes learn and how coaches teach (thus, the purpose of this book). They understand different learning theories and how these theories guide teaching. These same coaches also know the technical aspects of their sports and continue to learn more with each passing season because they are curious lifelong learners. Conditioning refers to the necessity for coaches to maintain physical, mental, emotional, social, and moral endurance not just for one practice or game but for an entire season. Endurance is perhaps a coach's greatest challenge. It is easy to be the occasional leader, but it is an entirely different matter to lead on a daily basis.

The fourth tier contains the blocks courage and commitment. There are moments in every coach's career when coaching seems to be the most difficult profession in the world. Becoming a successful coach takes courage and commitment. You need courage to fight for what you believe in: your program, your goals, your standards, your philosophy, your actions, your decisions, your values. You need courage to confront those who prize such things as expediency, mediocrity, and winning-at-all-cost over the welfare and development of people as athletes and as human beings. This courage is bolstered by a commitment to deeply considered and clearly defined values and principles that are the bulwark of your coaching philosophy.

The apex of the pyramid is the teacher, the ultimate goal for every successful coach. In defining coaching success, the authors write, "If a coach can say that he or she has done everything possible to help an athlete learn, that coach will have reached the apex of the Pyramid which is Teacher. Like the Courage and Commitment blocks, Teacher is not something you work on but rather it is a perpetual state of becoming that flows from working on the 12 blocks in the first three tiers" (p. 91). Their perspective is indeed humanistic.

If you look closely at the pyramid in figure 8.1, you will notice that along the sides of the pyramid are 10 concepts that act as mortar for binding the blocks to produce like the Egyptian pyramids a resilient and enduring structure. These concepts are well worth remembering and including in your coaching philosophy:

Empathy	Anticipation	Experience
Honesty	Consistency	Judgment
Initiative	Patience	Wisdom
Preparation		

APPLYING SEVEN HUMANISTIC PRINCIPLES IN COACHING ATHLETES

In his influential book on the humanistic coach, Lombardo (1987) suggests seven humanistic principles that can be applied to coaching. These principles and their application are listed in table 8.2 and summarized next.

- *Success promotion.* Lombardo suggests that the best way to promote success is to have athletes set personal and meaningful goals and to self-evaluate progress toward attaining these goals. When giving athletes the freedom to set goals and evaluate goal attainment, coaches demonstrate their belief in their athletes' ability to self-determine and self-evaluate. As Lombardo (1987) writes, "In short, the process of preparing athletes to independently determine goals is, in effect, an inherently success-promoting technique" (p. 43).

- *Positive regard.* Application of positive regard involves valuing individuals as human beings and not just as athletes. It means looking beyond the jersey, uniform, and equipment and recognizing each athlete's uniqueness and humanness. Coaches can demonstrate positive regard by respecting the dignity of each athlete and providing acceptance, encouragement, support, and inspiration. In providing feedback and criticism, coaches should make a distinction between the athlete and the individual person. You may dislike an athlete's motor performance yet like and value the individual person and her potential for goodness and growth.

- *Involvement.* In programs influenced by a humanistic perspective, athletes are motivated, excited, enthusiastic, exuberant, and energized in part because of their personal involvement. They feel that the program is their program because they participate in making decisions. They feel accepted and can be themselves. They have personal and meaningful goals they set for themselves rather than goals set by their coach. In this type of program a pervasive sense of freedom, joy, and excitement is brought about by genuine acceptance and an athlete-centered approach to coaching.

Table 8.2 Applying Seven Principles of Humanism in Coaching Athletes

Principle	Application
Success promotion	Athletes set and attain goals.
Positive regard	Coaches value athletes as human beings.
Involvement	Athletes experience excitement and engagement.
Interaction	Athletes voice their thoughts and are heard.
Cognitive processes	Athletes use learning strategies and think.
Congruence	Coaches are authentic.
Empathy	Coaches consider athletes' feelings.

- *Interaction*. Interaction has to do with the manner in which athletes are permitted to speak and be heard. Humanistic programs not only provide continuous opportunities for athletes to speak and be heard, they also encourage athletes to speak out, question things, and provide input and suggestions. Research (Carron & Bennett, 1977) suggests that when more interaction exists and when both athletes and coaches are allowed to be in control, athlete motivation is maintained and the number of dropouts is reduced.

Interaction also has to do with coaches and their ability to interact with their athletes. As Lombardo (1987) puts it, "An important characteristic that distinguishes humanistic athletic leaders from their colleagues is their capacity to truly listen to and hear the athlete, to clearly perceive what the athlete is saying, to comprehend the hidden message conveyed, and to discern the covert agendas within the player's communication" (p. 45).

- *Cognitive processes*. The humanistic coach recognizes, values, and encourages the athlete's ability to think and finds opportunities to engage athlete cognition, opportunities such as decision-making, problem solving, goal setting, performance evaluation, introspective self-assessment, and training periodization. Athletes in a humanistic program have the freedom to disagree and are encouraged to think independently. In this environment, the humanistic coach is willing to consider oppositional ideas and deal with disagreements, divergent thinking, and conflict.

- *Congruence*. **Congruence** occurs when a person's behaviors (i.e., emotions, feelings, thoughts, and actions) honestly and accurately reflect his private inner being. Closely related to the concept of congruence is the concept of **authenticity**, which occurs when people don't play a stereotypical role (e.g., coach, teacher, or supervisor) but, rather, behave in accordance to who they are. Authentic coaches (and athletes) present their real selves to others rather than feel the need to "'play' the role of the coach or don a "coaching face" when confronted with athletes" (Lombardo, 1987, p. 28).

Congruent and authentic coaches are not afraid to show their weaknesses or admit their mistakes. These coaches are open and honest and their physical behavior matches their verbal behavior. Heitmann and Kneer (1976) quite astutely note, "Non-verbal messages often communicate feelings which reinforce or contradict what is said verbally . . . People tend to believe behavior—which is harder to hide" (p. 70). Athletes, like most human beings, are perceptive and quickly detect on their mental radar when coaches' actions don't match their verbal messages. Truly great coaches develop trust, devotion, and connection with their athletes in part because of their authenticity.

- *Empathy*. Empathetic coaches are sensitive to athlete feelings and never lose touch with what the athletes are experiencing both as athletes and human beings. Although coaches can never fully understand exactly what the athlete is going through, the empathetic coach endeavors to comprehend from the athlete's point of view the athlete's thoughts and feelings. Empathetic coaches are also sensitive to and respectful of the athlete's dignity and self-worth and reflect this respect in their interactions with their athletes both publicly and privately. In his book, Lombardo lists some specific and effective coaching behaviors for emphasizing the seven principles of humanistic psychology listed in this section.

THE FULLY HUMAN ATHLETE

The fully human athlete does not exist on your team, nor does the fully human coach. According to Rogers, self-actualization—striving to reach one's greatest potential—is a forever becoming process, a destination no person every quite reaches. The **fully human athlete**, then, is the person continually striving to become a better person in all aspects of life: a better athlete, student, friend, citizen, role model, son or daughter. To this end, the fully human athlete has the innate desire and ability to self-determine, self-direct, set personal goals, resolve problems, accept personal responsibility, and engage in discovery learning. This athlete maintains a positive self-concept and regard for self and teammates, an internal locus of control, and a personal set of values.

The fully human athlete is a one-of-a-kind person who brings something unique to your team that no other athlete can offer. This athlete's behavior is motivated by a desire to self-actualize and conforms to her notion of self—a self-concept formulated to an extent by interactions with the fully human coach.

THE FULLY HUMAN COACH

The **fully human coach** is also someone who continually strives to become better: a better coach, leader, role model, citizen, student of the sport, and so on. The fully human coach has a strong sense of self and, therefore, sees himself as competent and efficacious. This coach is caring, genuine, empathetic, congruent, authentic, and attentive to athletes' feelings, problems, verbalizations, and viewpoints. The fully human coach places the athlete at the center of the motor learning process, emphasizes humanistic values through personal behavior, and practices the nondirective model of coaching.

The fully human coach isn't afraid to admit making a mistake or embracing humanistic concepts such as love, friendship, loyalty, cooperation, and balance. This coach facilitates athlete success, maintains a positive regard toward athletes, engages and interacts with athletes, accepts criticism, and practices self-examination to continually seek improvement as a coach and as a human being.

YOUR COACHING TOOLBOX

So here is a very atypical tool for your toolbox. From the outset of the chapter, it has been clear that humanism is different from the other theories examined.

However, its differences make it most useful. Like respondent conditioning, you won't see this theory in many, if any, motor learning books, but it is a theory that will have a profound impact on your coaching and, therefore, your athletes.

From a longitudinal analysis, humanism is one of your most important learning theories in your coaching toolbox because of its long-term effect on your athletes. By taking a humanistic approach to coaching, you help your athletes develop as athletes while concomitantly helping them grow as human beings. This personal growth–promoting process results in greater personal insight, maturity, self-functioning, self-confidence, and coping skills, which in turn positively affects the quality and success of their athletic careers as well as their lives after sport.

To have in some small way facilitated the development of individuals as athletes and human beings is a wonderful coaching accomplishment. Some years ago, I was invited back to the University of Nebraska–Lincoln where I had the good fortune to coach for 11 years. Some of my former athletes organized a reunion in which almost every past athlete attended. I thought it was simply a chance to reunite, but it turned into a coach love fest. I was surprised and deeply touched by their stories, appreciation, and gratitude. Never have I received a greater honor than their praise nor felt more accomplished as a coach than after listening to how much their experiences meant to them and the positive impact it had on them later in their lives.

Coaches make a difference in the lives of their athletes. It is a great reward to be able to say, "I reached that athlete. I made a difference in that person's life." Make humanism an important tool in your coaching toolbox.

THE SCIENTIFIC AND ARTFUL COACH

Unlike several of the other theories discussed in this book, humanism is clearly on the side of art. Consequently, its outcomes are often difficult to observe and measure. For example, how do you observe and measure the athlete who has heightened self-esteem and an improved self-concept? How do you measure the athlete who seems to have matured and become a well-adjusted person who is better able to solve personal problems? These outcomes are difficult, if not impossible, to measure.

The discussion on humanism may indicate a clear division between art and science and that a coach must take either a behavioristic/cognitivistic approach or a humanistic approach. However, in reality, nothing is so clearly divided. Behaviorists and cognitivists are often not as technologically oriented as a humanist's description might suggest. And humanists often borrow useful techniques from the behaviorist and the cognitivist. Both scientific and humanistic orientations contribute something of value to the learning process. In many ways, humanism is compatible with cognitivism and behaviorism.

While humanism leans heavily on the side of art, humanists might agree that a scientific perspective is not altogether bad and in many cases necessary and useful for impacting and measuring learning. Because much of humanism is difficult to quantify (e.g., how do you measure concepts such as self-actualization? How do you identify when appropriate emotions, communication skills, openness, and genuineness have improved or been attained?), humanists might agree that much useful learning and measurement can be derived from a scientific approach to learning, as long as this approach simultaneously recognizes individuals' humanness and those things that differentiate us from dogs, rats, pigeons, and computers.

As a scientific and artful coach, you will want to be a blend; consider yourself a behaviorist, a cognitivist, and a humanist.

IF YOU REMEMBER ONLY THREE THINGS

1. *Remember to let the theory of humanism permeate your coaching and program.* While humanism doesn't necessarily lead to specific coaching methods, it does lead to some specific emphases for coaching. Let these emphases imbue your coaching and your program. Among these emphases are the following:

   - Emphasize the learning process rather than specific learning: Teach learning strategies and encourage your athletes to think for themselves.

   - Emphasize self-determination: Encourage your athletes to take responsibility for their athletic careers and become autonomous, self-directed, and self-evaluative.

   - Emphasize personal growth: Want to see your athletes develop as individual people and not just as athletes.

   - Emphasize communication: Help your athletes learn to listen and make an effort to understand each other. Model good communication skills as a coach.

   - Emphasize individualism: Team is important, but so is each athlete. Cultivate an attitude that appreciates and nurtures the uniqueness of each athlete.

   - Emphasize affect: Feelings and personal experiences of each athlete matter and are often more important than what is actually being taught. Maintain an attitude that is sensitive to and values athletes' feelings and experiences.

2. *Remember that the development of the person positively correlates with the development of the athlete.* Therefore, remember that when you facilitate the growth of your players as human beings, you simultaneously facilitate their development as athletes. Avoid thinking that everything you do is

about the Xs and Os. What you do to develop your athletes as human beings matters—to them as athletes and to them as human beings after they conclude their athletic careers. This development is facilitated by the use of the nondirective model of coaching.

3. *Remember that the development of the person is facilitated through a helping relationship.* The coach creates this relationship by being genuine and transparent about feelings, warmly accepting and prizing of the athlete as a separate person, and perceiving the athlete's world as the athlete sees it. Because of the coach's humanistic approach to the relationship, the athlete can experience personal insight and become more self-directed, more self-confident, more capable at problem solving, more acceptant of others, and more self-expressive. The Pyramid of Teaching Success in Sport is an invaluable resource for helping coaches understand the building blocks for establishing this helping relationship.

While Rogers (1995) was referring to the client–counselor relationship, he also was referring to any helping relationship. He defines a *helping relationship* as one ". . . in which at least one of the parties has the intent of promoting the growth, development, maturity, improved functioning, improved coping with life of the other" (pp. 39-40). From a humanistic perspective, the coach–athlete relationship is such a relationship. In fact, Rogers saw a helping relationship both as one-on-one and also as an individual–group interaction. So, the helping relationship extends to a coach-team relationship.

SUGGESTED READINGS

Benjamin, A. (1981). *The helping interview.* Boston: Houghton Mifflin.

[This book is about the counseling interview process and helped me develop a more effective way of interacting with my athletes.]

Bloom, B.S. (1976). *Human characteristics and school learning.* New York: McGraw-Hill.

[Not all athletes can become Olympic champions, but all athletes can attain a certain degree of mastery. I take this as a coaching challenge to see how far I can progress each athlete. This goal brought me back to coaching every year.]

Buscaglia, L. (Speaker). (1984a). "Love." Cassette recording titled *On being fully human.* Chicago: Nightingale-Conant.

[I first heard Dr. Buscaglia speak when my high school English teacher brought in a tape she had made of one of his speeches. It profoundly affected my consciousness and made me want to become a teacher. It perfectly captures the humanistic perspective.]

Buscaglia, L. (Speaker). (1984b). "Love." Cassette recording titled *Together with Leo.* Chicago: Nightingale-Conant Corporation.

[Another recording worth listening to.]

Joyce, B., Weil, M., and Calhoun, E. (2009). *Models of teaching.* Englewood Cliffs, NJ: Prentice Hall, 328.

[This book outlines some effective teaching models. The chapter on nondirective teaching captures the essence of Rogerian theory and puts Rogers' concepts into practice. I have used the model many times in interacting with my athletes.]

Rogers, C.R. (1995). *On becoming a person*. New York: Houghton Mifflin.

[Howard Gardner postulates that several types of intelligence exist. One is interpersonal intelligence: the capacity to understand the intentions, motivations, and desires of other people and to work effectively with others. Rogers was hugely gifted in this area of intelligence. Even if you only read one or two chapters of this book you will get a sense of the depth, breadth, and sensitivity of his feelings, thinking, and theory.]

Rosenthal, R. & Jacobson, L. (1968). *Pygmalion in the classroom: Teacher expectations and pupils' intellectual development*. New York: Holt.

[While substantiating research is unclear, is there any coach who doesn't believe that coach expectations affect athlete development?]

Simon, S.B., Howe, L.W., & Kirschenbaum, H. (1972). *Values clarification: A handbook of practical strategies for teachers and students*. New York: Ballinger.

[If you are unclear of your values and you want to teach values to your athletes, this book is helpful.]

CHAPTER 9

The Emotional Athlete
Applying Emotion Theory

Key Terms

action tendencies

anxiety

arousal

attribution theory of
    emotion

burnout

cognitive appraisal

cognitive interference

cognitive restructuring

control

cue utilization
    hypothesis

denial

determined coping

direction of attention

distress

dysfunctional effect

dysphoria

ego involved

emotion

emotion game

emotional athlete

emotional coach

hardwired emotional
    responses

individual zones of
    optimal functioning

inner game

interpersonal
    consequences

intrapersonal
    consequences

intuitive appraisal

locus

maladaptive fatigue
    syndrome

negative emotions

optimal

optimal effect

paralysis by analysis

physiological changes

positive emotions

reflective appraisal

seven Rs

stability

state anxiety

stop technique

subjective experience

task involved

trait anxiety

unacknowledged
    distress

A t a U.S. national championship, Mike, a promising young athlete, had a breakout performance that surprised everyone. Well, everyone except Mike and his coach. But it almost didn't turn out that way.

Before his first event Mike had a lousy morning warm-up. In the past, a poor warm-up would automatically flip his anger switch, which would trigger an even poorer performance, which in turn would transform his anger into rage. At this point he would typically do something stupid like go into the locker room and punch a locker (he broke his hand doing just that his freshman year). Once he reached this emotional furor his performance instantaneously deteriorated. Over the past few months, however, he had been reading about emotions and how they relate to cognition and motor performance. His coach encouraged him to read about emotional intelligence (Goleman, 1997) and how an emotion such as rage can negatively affect his thinking and actions. He and his coached talked about how certain antecedent events can trigger negative thoughts, which engender emotions that in turn negatively affect performance. Together they devised a mental game plan for controlling his emotions so that instead of falling into his habitual emotional trap, he activated a strategy he and his coach developed and used during practices, particularly frustrating ones.

Their strategy involved self-monitoring, self-talk, self-direction, and relaxation. Mike performed well when he was somewhat edgy or angry but he had to be careful to not let his anger escalate into rage. He knew that when he became enraged he could be his worst enemy and things would quickly unravel. Consequently, Mike monitored himself. The moment he noticed he was becoming too angry during his morning warm-up at nationals, he activated his plan. He immediately told himself to calm down and then redirected his thoughts to his performance goals, preperformance routines, and relaxation. It wasn't easy for him, but he stuck with his plan. His first preliminary event didn't set the world on fire, but then again, it wasn't terrible either. He performed well enough to barely make finals. In the finals he performed better than he did in preliminaries. The next day he performed even better and suddenly he was a man on a mission, an unstoppable force. By his third and final event Mike achieved a lifetime best performance, received the Athlete Performance Award as the outstanding male athlete of the championship, and was selected to represent the United States at several international competitions as well as the World University Games in Palma de Mallorca, Spain, where, ironically, Mike was elected team captain in part because of his emotional stability and maturity.

This amazing success story began with Mike as an inexperienced walk-on and unknown rookie and ended with him as one of the top athletes in the country in his sport. And to think that the happy conclusion to his story hinged on a brief moment in time when he controlled his emotional state during his first morning warm-up, thereby channeling his emotions to achieve peak-level performance.

This chapter is the story of the *emotional athlete* and the fascinating interplay between emotions and performance. It explains how you can teach your athletes to utilize enhancing emotions and avoid impairing emotions in order to maintain an optimal range of emotional functioning and attain high-level performance when it matters most.

CHAPTER OVERVIEW

The chapter first defines emotion and then considers a simple but useful paradigm for understanding the sequence of events that generates emotions within your athletes and the potential consequences of these emotions. The antecedents—the things that generate emotions—are examined first. Then two particular emotions—anxiety and arousal—and the interplay of these emotions on athlete performance are examined. The chapter also considers differences between athletes and optimal ranges of emotions for individual athletes and then looks at specific emotions that enhance athlete performance and emotions that impair performance, some of which may surprise you. Next is a look at some of the consequences of emotions on your athletes, their performances, and their well-being. Finally, it offers some effective preventive and coping strategies for helping your athletes find and maintain the emotions and range of emotions that will help them achieve high levels of performance.

EMOTIONS AND PERFORMANCE

Emotion and athlete performance are strange bedfellows. Consider again the emotion of anger cited at the opening of this chapter. A defensive lineman psyches up until he transforms himself into a raging animal and then bursts through the offensive line to make a spectacular quarterback sack. In contrast, a golfer becomes angry after double bogeying a hole and then misses a simple routine putt on the next hole. Anger is a performance-enhancing emotion for the lineman, but a performance-impairing emotion for the golfer—and for Mike, when his anger transformed into rage.

Consider some other emotions. A basketball player feels nervous and tense before a game and then goes onto the court and plays a great game. However, a different basketball player also feels nervous and tense before a game but goes out and plays absolutely awfully. Finally, a gymnast feels nervous, tense, and irritated before a competition and then performs phenomenally. But a different gymnast feels relaxed, satisfied, and pleasant before a competition and then performs poorly in the meet.

Curiously, you might think feeling nervous and tense is a bad thing just as you might think feeling relaxed and pleasant is a good thing for performance. And you might think that if certain emotions and range of emotions are good for one athlete, they should be good for all athletes. But are these assumptions true? Which emotions enhance performance? Which emotions impair performance? Which emotions are best suited for your particular sport? Which emotions are most appropriate for each individual athlete? What range of emotional response is appropriate for each athlete? How can you help your athletes stay in their emotional zone?

The first question to answer is *What exactly is emotion*? People often use the word *emotion* to describe athletic performances. For example: "The athlete played with a lot of emotion." "The team was on an emotional roller coaster." "Emotions ran high in the club house." "She played on emotion." "The team's emotional chemistry was good." What does *emotion* mean?

Deci (1980) offers this definition of emotion:

> An emotion is a reaction to a stimulus event (either actual or imagined). It involves change in the viscera and musculature of the person, is experienced subjectively in characteristic ways, is expressed through such means as facial changes and action tendencies, and may mediate and energize subsequent behaviors. (p. 85)

According to Deci's definition, an **emotion** is a reaction to some real or imagined antecedent stimulus that results in physiological, experiential, and behavioral changes in the athlete. To understand how emotions affect athletes, consider the simple emotion paradigm outlined in figure 9.1.

The Emotion Paradigm

The emotion paradigm is a simple but effective coaching tool for understanding the sequence for how emotions are generated and their consequences on human behavior. Antecedents are the psychological processes that precede the emotions. Affect refers to emotions, feelings and mood. This chapter focuses mainly on specific emotions. Consequences are the physiological and psychological effects the generated emotions produce. The following sections expand on these three aspects of the emotion paradigm.

Antecedents are the things that initiate specific emotions. Obviously, something has to happen to impact an athlete's emotions. It may be a sudden change in game situation, the prospect of losing, the exploits of a competitor, or the jeers from the crowd. However, all of these stimuli don't influence emotions; the athlete's psychological perception and appraisal of these stimuli

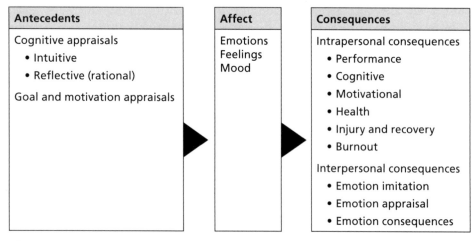

Figure 9.1 The emotion paradigm: the antecedents and consequences of emotions.

Adapted, by permission, from R.J. Vallerand and C.M. Blanchard, 2000, The study of emotion in sport and exercise: Historical, definitional, and conceptual perspectives. In *Emotions in sport*, edited by Y.L. Hanin (Champaign, IL: Human Kinetics), 9.

influence emotions. Athletes make three types of appraisal: cognitive, intuitive, and reflective.

Cognitive Appraisal

The brain plays a primary role in generating emotion. According to appraisal theorists people abstract information from events and from this antecedent information they make an assessment (**cognitive appraisal**) that determines their emotional response. These appraisals have a greater impact on emotion than the actual objective event. After all, what is an event other than the meaning you give to it?

According to Weiner's (1995) **attribution theory of emotion**, how an athlete appraises an event determines the specific emotion the athlete will experience. For example, if athletes attribute success to effort, they will experience joy. If they attribute success to luck, they are likely to experience complacency. In other words, a connection exists between an attribution and a specific emotion linked to that attribution.

According to Weiner, emotions are derived from three sources. One source is the impact of the event. For example, joy follows success and sadness trails failure. These outcome-dependent emotions are generally the first and also the most potent emotions the athlete experiences. The second source is the attributions the athlete assigns for the outcome of the event. These attributions lead to specific emotions, such as pride when an athlete attributes success to ability and effort. The final source is the causal dimension. These attributions influence emotions over time. The three causal dimensions are **locus** (the cause is internal or external to the athlete), **stability** (the cause is permanent or changing), and **control** (the cause is under the athlete's direct control or it is not).

To understand these three sources of emotions, consider a softball pitcher who throws a phenomenal game and her team wins the conference championship. She is immediately happy about winning the game and knows she threw well, but wonders if it was just one of those days when things went right or if she has the right stuff to be a consistently good pitcher. Because of the importance of the event she feels great happiness. Because she attributes her high level of performance to her ability and effort (internal locus of control), she also feels pride and competence. After further appraisal she believes her stunning performance is something she can control and replicate in the future. This appraisal causes her to feel an abiding sense of self-esteem and self-efficacy. The next game she plays in results in another masterful performance.

Intuitive Appraisal

Athletes make conscious cognitive appraisals all the time and these appraisals lead to the generation of specific emotions. However, sometimes appraisals aren't so conscious or deeply processed. Vallerand (1987) has proposed an intuitive-reflective appraisal model. **Intuitive appraisal** is a minimal and nearly automatic subjective cognitive assessment of performance. Consider a golfer who starts off badly after two holes of a tournament. Even though it is a 36-hole contest, after 2 holes he makes the intuitive appraisal that he isn't playing well, which leads to the emotion of depression, which in turn leads to increasingly poor performance with each subsequent hole. His intuitive appraisal has taken him out of the game almost before the game has started.

Reflective Appraisal

Unlike intuitive appraisal, **reflective appraisal** involves deliberate and rational cognitive processing of external and internal (e.g., memory) environmental information. Reflective appraisal occurs at some point in time after intuitive appraisal, which is often fairly immediate. Reflective appraisal modifies, minimizes, or augments intuitive appraisal and its effects on emotions.

For example, a swimmer wins three events in a dual meet against her arch rival high school. At the end of the competition she feels happiness at her success and satisfaction with the results of her training regimen. But the following day she reflects on her accomplishments and modifies her appraisal, creating a change of emotion. She realizes that her competition wasn't very good and, even though she won, her times weren't nearly as fast as she expected them to be for that time of the season. She now feels anger at her poor performance and dissatisfaction with her training. She vows to train harder for the remainder of the season.

Goal and Motivational Appraisal

A number of theorists have suggested that goals and motivation play a key role in producing emotions (Frijda, 1988; Lazarus, 1991a, 1991b; Mandler, 1984; Ortony, Clore, & Collins, 1988). Mandler (1984) suggests that emotion results from goal blockage. Ortony et al. (1988) suggest that emotions occur because of appraisals of events related to a personal goal. As Frijda (1988) puts it, "Emotions arise in response to events that are important to the individual's goals, motives, or concerns" (p. 351). This seems a rather obvious point when you witness an athlete who is emotionally devastated after losing a race in the final meters or an athlete who is overcome with happiness after scoring a personal best. However obvious this connection between goals, motivation, and emotion might be, it is important to understand this connection theoretically so you teach your athletes to establish appropriate goals, motives, and concerns, and make sound appraisals that engender psychologically healthy and performance-enhancing emotions.

Goal Orientation

Research (Ames, 1992; Duda, 1992) indicates that people tend to engage in sports because of ego or task involvement. Athletes are **ego involved** when they engage in sports to demonstrate their level of competence to others and they are **task involved** when they seek to master challenges for themselves. Nicholls (1984) suggests that these two types of antecedent goals or motivational orientations influence different emotions, which result in quite different consequences.

Athletes who are task oriented tend to experience more enjoyment and worry less about their performances than do ego-oriented athletes (Newton & Duda, 1993). Task-oriented athletes also tend to experience more satisfaction (Duda & Nicholls, 1992) while ego-oriented athletes tend to experience feelings of boredom. Finally, ego-oriented athletes experience more cognitive anxiety than task-oriented athletes (Duda, Chi, & Newton, 1990).

In general, research indicates that ego orientation is associated with negative emotion while task orientation is associated with positive emotion. Consequently, goal orientation theory suggests a rather important implication for athletes and for coaches, parents, and anyone else working with athletes: It is important for athletes to be task oriented. In other words, athletes should focus on performing and mastering specific drills, skills, and activities. They should not focus on demonstrating or proving their competence to others. Athletes should not put their ego on the line when performing. What matters is not whom they beat or what other people will think about them if they win or lose. What matters is simply giving their best effort emotionally, psychologically, and physically to the task at hand.

AROUSAL, ANXIETY, AND PERFORMANCE

Before a contest a former athlete of mine would march angrily around as though he was upset about some sort of insult or injustice. The first time I noticed his behavior I wanted to say something, but he performed well in the competition, so I decided that whatever upset set him probably wasn't that important and I didn't say anything to him. At the next competition, I noticed the same precompetitive behavior and, again, he performed well. His precompetitive behavior persisted and finally one day I asked him, "Lawrence, why do you always look so upset and angry before a meet?" His reply surprised me: "Coach, I've found that when I get angry it keeps me from getting nervous and I compete better that way!" As a young coach, I took note of his response. I began to consider the importance of emotion and how athletes can harness their emotions to positively affect their performances.

Some years later, I was searching for a way to help one of my athletes perform better in competition. Since it was early in the season and a relatively meaningless dual meet, I decided to experiment and see what emotions might work best for her. Before the competition I asked her to get angry, much like Lawrence did, and get after her dives. She performed horribly in the meet and afterward she said, "Coach, that just isn't my style. When I get angry I get too amped up and can't perform." Well, at least we found out what didn't work for her. So I asked her, "Well, when you think back to some of your good performances, what emotions did you feel?" After some thought, she replied, "I think when I perform well, I am excited and having fun and being myself." I replied, "Well, then, let's try that the next time you compete!"

Second semester of that same academic year, we went to the U.S. national championship, which was also the qualifying meet for the world championship in Changzhou, China. Before the women's 10-meter platform event I told her, "Amy, go out there and be Amy and get excited and have fun!" And she did! This once unknown and inexperienced walk-on from Naperville, Illinois shocked her competition by putting together two amazing lists of dives, beating the defending national champion, and qualifying for the world championship.

Emotion can be an athlete's strongest ally during the heat of competition if you and your athletes know which emotions and range of emotions are most effective for them. Anger worked well for Lawrence but a completely different emotion worked better for Amy. Perhaps the two most studied emotions are arousal and anxiety. Let's now turn our attention to these emotions.

In a great deal of research on motor performance and emotion, emotion has typically referred to anxiety and arousal. **Arousal** has to do with the physiological and psychological state of activation and readiness that may range from very low (e.g., sleep) to extremely high. Spielberger (1972) defines **anxiety** as an emotional reaction to a stimulus perceived as dangerous. This stimulus, or stressor results in dysphoric (**dysphoria** is an emotional state characterized by anxiety, depression, or unease) thoughts and feelings, unpleasant sensations, and physical changes in the athlete (Raglin & Hanin, 2000). These physical changes include physiological responses such as elevated heart rate and increased muscle tension. The key word in the definition of anxiety is *perceived*. If an athlete does not perceive a stimulus as threatening, then no change should occur in anxiety level. Depending upon the athlete's perception, the stimulus can be perceived as helpful, threatening, or neutral. What is the relationship between arousal and anxiety to performance?

The Inverted-U Hypothesis

In their study, Yerkes and Dodson (1908) examined the effects of stimulus intensity (electric shocks) on habit formation in mice using a maze discrimination task. An interaction between stimulus intensity and discrimination difficulty was observed. The highest-intensity shocks slowed learning under the most difficult trials, but some shocks increased learning, suggesting that moderate stimulation was best for learning under such conditions.

Yerkes and Dodson's results have been generalized to a variety of other constructs, such as drive, motivation, and learning; but the hypothesis is most often associated with arousal (Teigen, 1994; Winton, 1987). Arousal level has been correlated with physiological responses, such as heart rate, muscle tension, and galvanic skin response (GSR) (Gould & Krane, 1992). Arousal has

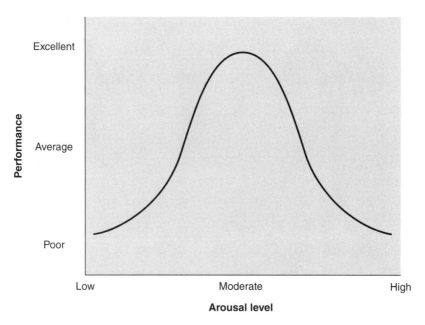

Figure 9.2 Inverted-U hypothesis: Correlation between anxiety-arousal and motor performance.

Reprinted, by permission, from R.A. Schmidt and C. Wrisberg, 2008, *Motor learning and performance*, 4th ed. (Champaign, IL: Human Kinetics), 40.

been associated also with dysphoric emotional states, particularly the emotion of anxiety (Duffy, 1957).

Basically, the inverted-U hypothesis states that as arousal or anxiety increases, so does performance, but only to a point. Beyond a certain point, performance begins to decrease as arousal or anxiety increases. Figure 9.2 describes the correlation between anxiety-arousal and performance.

Modifications of the Inverted-U Hypothesis

The inverted-U depicted in figure 9.2 has some glaring shortcomings. The inverted-U hypothesis does not account for differences in motor requirements between sports. For example, for sports such as golf and billiards (or say, playing the piano), which require precise motor control and minimal physical effort, performance is highest when anxiety or arousal is relatively low (Oxendine, 1970). For a high level of performance in a sport such as golf, the inverted-U would be skewed to the left. However, in sports requiring greater physical effort, such as football and weightlifting, performance is facilitated when anxiety or arousal is relatively high. In this case, the inverted-U would be skewed to the right. Figure 9.3 summarizes this modification.

The inverted-U hypothesis also needs to be modified when considering the skill level of the performer. It is generally assumed that a highly skilled athlete should be able to function using a higher anxiety or arousal level than

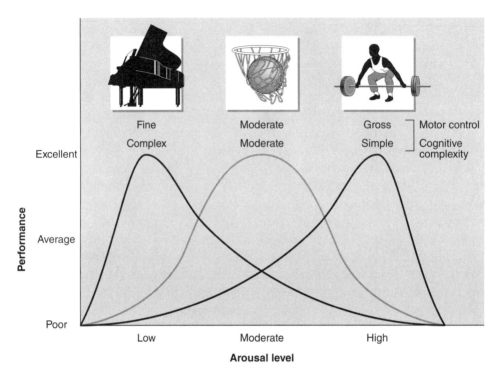

Figure 9.3. Skewed inverted-U for sports requiring high and low anxiety and arousal.

Reprinted, by permission, from R.A. Schmidt and C. Wrisberg, 2008, *Motor learning and performance*, 4th ed. (Champaign, IL: Human Kinetics), 41.

a less skilled athlete (LeUnes & Nation, 1996). In other words, in any sport optimal anxiety or arousal should be highest for the most skilled performers.

Problems With the Inverted-U Hypothesis

Although the preceding modifications answer a number of criticisms concerning the inverted-U hypothesis, a number of other criticisms still remain. First, research concerning the negative effects of anxiety and arousal on cognitive processing and attentional capacity does not consistently support the inverted-U hypothesis (Raglin & Hanin, 2000). Second, in some cases high physiological activation does not seem to be particularly harmful to athletes in fine motor skill sports, such as pistol shooting (Landers & Boutcher, 1998). Because of lacking empirical evidence with regard to elevated muscle tension and other physiological changes, some researchers conclude that physiological factors are of little importance to the anxiety–performance relationship (Eysenck & Calvo, 1992). Third, indicators of arousal, such as elevations in heart rate, have been found to be missing during episodes of intense anxiety (Aronson, Carasiti, McBane, & Whitaker-Axmitia, 1989). Fourth, sport research shows a lack of empirical evidence to support the inverted-U hypothesis (Fazey & Hardy, 1988; Krane,

1992; Raglin, 1992). In fact, Kleine (1990), in a meta-analysis of sport anxiety literature, concluded that evidence for the inverted-U hypothesis is scarce.

The final and perhaps most damning criticism of the inverted-U hypothesis is that the hypothesis does not account for the fact that athletes respond differently to different levels of anxiety (Fazey & Hardy, 1988; Kleine, 1990; Raglin, 1992). In other words, not all athletes perform well at the same intensity level of arousal and anxiety. Some highly skilled athletes appear to perform well at a higher arousal and anxiety level than other highly skilled athletes. For instance, I knew an athlete who seemed to thrive on a high level of arousal and anxiety. It seemed to me that he would sometimes do poorly in a class just so he would have to pull himself from the fire at the last minute by performing remarkably well on the final exam. In competition, he would perform poorly in preliminaries and then have to nail his last attempt just to make finals—and then he would win finals. It was as though he was an arousal-anxiety junkie. He went on to win numerous U.S. national championship titles.

To account for these criticisms of the inverted-U hypothesis and for the differences between individual athletes Hanin (1995) developed the Individual Zones of Optimal Functioning (IZOF) model. The following section discusses this model and its significance to your athletes and their ability to perform at a high level.

Individual Zones of Optimal Functioning (IZOF)

The development of the IZOF model was based on research assessing anxiety in several thousand athletes before competition. Examining a general level of anxiety, as measured by the Russian language version of the State-Trait Anxiety Inventory (STAI), Hanin (1978) found that his research identified anxiety as a significant factor in athletic performance, but only at the individual level, not the group level. Consequently, Hanin proposed the **individual zones of optimal functioning** model, which suggests that each athlete possesses an optimal zone or range of anxiety for peak motor performance. This zone may be different between athletes and may be anywhere on a continuum between low and high anxiety. The following text gives you a breakdown of the IZOF model, beginning with the individual.

Individual

The IZOF model places the individual athlete at the center of the model. According to the model, *individual* differences exist between athletes with regard to their emotional states and successful performances. For example, some athletes perform better at a higher level of anxiety, while other athletes perform better at a lower level of anxiety. The emphasis on individual differences in the IZOF model is a radical departure from the inverted U-hypothesis, which suggested that athletes in all sports have the same emotional responses. This emphasis on the individual is of increasing interest to sport psychologists

(Gould & Krane, 1992; Weinberg, 1990; Vanden Auweele, Cuyper, Mele, & Rzewnicki, 1993).

Zones

According to the IZOF model, athletes perform best when their emotional states are within their individual *zones*, or intensity levels that in the past have resulted in successful performances. The concept of zone variance was derived from research involving several hundred athletes in a variety of sports and examining precompetition anxiety levels prior to performance and levels of performance success (Hanin, 1978, 1983a). Results from this research suggest several things. It seems there is no specific optimal level of anxiety resulting in successful or unsuccessful performances for athletes in the same sport, which argues for individual zones for individual athletes. Second, this zone of optimal functioning appears to be relatively narrow (Hanin, 2000a). In other words, while variance does exist, this variance is relatively slight.

Optimal

In terms of the IZOF model, **optimal** means the most relevant and appropriate emotional state for a particular athlete under specific motor performance conditions (Hanin, 2000). Optimal performance includes emotions you would consider both positive and negative (positive and negative emotions are discussed later in this chapter). Also, this concept of optimal is multidimensional. In other words, emotional state is related not only to intensity level, but also to form, time, and context. For example, consider the emotion of anger. An angry outburst might be acceptable or tolerated in practice but a more modest expression of displeasure might be more tolerable in competition (form). Also, anger might be optimal before, but not during actual performance (time) and anger might be acceptable if directed toward an athlete's own performance, but not toward a competitor or referee (context).

Functioning

The term *functioning* refers to the optimal or dysfunctional effects that specific emotional states have on the quality of the performance. The model is based on the results of systematic observation of elite performers in real-life situations. The research has stressed how and why athletes experiencing different levels of emotion intensity, such as high, moderate, and low precompetition anxiety, are consistently successful or unsuccessful.

Successful performance requires the recruitment of energy and appropriate available resources. For athletes to perform well, they must be excited and eager (energy) but also calm enough to focus and concentrate (resources) on specifics of performance. For example, a runner who becomes too excited and eager at the start of the race is likely to get off pace. Consequently, the IZOF model considers two functions inherent within the emotion–motor performance relationship: energizing versus deenergizing and organizing versus disorganizing effects of emotion on performance. In other words, functional emotions have the behavioral consequences of energizing the athlete to action and keeping the athlete physically and mentally on track (organizing). Dysfunctional emotions have the opposite effect.

The IZOF model also examines interactional effects of how emotion influences performance and how performance influences emotion. For example, consider the athlete in scenario 1, a high jumper who is expected to win the state championship. Her initial anxiety affected her first jump and her first mistimed jump increased her anxiety. This caused her to perform even more poorly on her second jump at the next height.

Scenario 1

Just before competition, the favorite to win the state championship in the high jump starts feeling anxiety because of everyone's expectations that she should win. Consequently, she moves outside her zone of optimal functioning, causing her to badly mistime her first jump. She manages to barely clear her opening height but because of her disjointed first approach, she becomes even more anxious, moving further outside her optimal zone of functioning. She can't seem to get into the flow of her routine and approach; she misses her next jump and fails to win the championship.

From an applied perspective the IZOF model can be useful in helping elite-level athletes cope with the extreme stress that comes with high-level competition and intensive day-to-day training. Based on the model, you can compile an athlete's profile that indicates the emotions and zone of optimal functioning for these emotions for successful performance. Also, based on the model, several interventions are useful for elite performance. These interventions are discussed later in the chapter.

The IZOF Model Versus the Inverted-U Hypothesis

The IZOF model resolves several of the problems inherent within the inverted-U hypothesis. The IZOF model explains why research concerning the effects of anxiety and arousal on cognitive processing and attentional capacity does not consistently support the inverted-U hypothesis, why high physiological activation does not seem to harm some athletes in fine motor skill sports, why indicators of arousal have been found to be missing during episodes of intense anxiety, and why athletes respond differently to anxiety. According to the IZOF model, these research results are due to the fact that individual athletes are performing within their distinct, individual zones of optimal functioning.

If individual zones of optimal functioning are important for understanding differences between athletes and for helping athletes improve their performances by staying within their zones, how do athletes determine their optimal zones?

Establishing Optimal Anxiety Zones

Hanin has developed two methods for establishing athletes' optimal anxiety zones: the direct method and the indirect method. In the *direct method*, precompetition anxiety is assessed until an athlete has a personal best performance. The upper and lower limits of the optimal range are determined by adding and subtracting four anxiety units (1/2 standard deviation) from the anxiety score obtained prior to best performance. Several problems exist with the direct method. The first problem is that anxiety scores must be taken until the athlete achieves a best performance, which may take a great deal of time, from several weeks to many months. Another problem is that the direct method requires self-ratings immediately before competition, which are not always possible or desirable to obtain, since such intrusiveness can distract the athlete and disturb precompetition preparation. Also, repeated assessment, especially for a team of athletes, is time consuming and cost ineffective.

Because of the problems associated with the direct method, an *indirect method* based on retrospection was developed. With the indirect method, athletes complete the state-trait anxiety inventory (STAI), which is a general measure of anxiety (Spielberger, Gorsuch, & Lushene, 1970; Spielberger, Gorsuch, Lushene, Vagg, & Jacobs, 1983). The athletes are given instructions to respond by indicating how they recall feeling before their best past performances or, more generally, how they recall feeling when their performance was optimal or near optimal. The optimal anxiety zone is set by adding and subtracting 1/2 standard deviation from the recalled best score. Research indicates that the accuracy of the recall method at the group level yields results comparable to those obtained using the direct method for establishing optimal anxiety ranges (Jokela & Hanin, 1997; Randle & Weinberg, 1997). Some critics have argued that performers cannot make accurate attributions with regard to past performance. However, research consistently indicates that the indirect method for assessing optimal precompetition anxiety is sufficiently accurate for establishing optimal zones for most competitive and highly skilled athletes (Harger & Raglin, 1994; Turner & Raglin, 1996).

Variability in Optimal Anxiety

The IZOF model assumes a significant difference exists between athletes regarding the level of optimal anxiety associated with successful performance. In other words, as mentioned already, some athletes perform well within a zone of moderate anxiety while other athletes perform well within a zone of relatively high anxiety. However, research (Hanin, 1978, 1986) indicates that a significant number of athletes report that high levels of anxiety are optimal for performance. Using the recall method, research with North American athletes has replicated this finding (Morgan, O'Connor, Sparling, & Pate, 1987).

Prediction of Precompetition Anxiety

Research (Hanin 1978, 1986) suggests that athletes are capable of predicting how anxious they will feel immediately before upcoming competitions. In conducting these studies, athletes completed anxiety questionnaires several days before competition. In these questionnaires, athletes were asked to indicate how they anticipated feeling immediately before their events. Then, before the actual event athletes were again asked to complete the questionnaire. Correlations between predicted and actual precompetition anxiety scores ranged from 0.60 to 0.80, with higher coefficients for more competitive contests.

If you establish athletes' optimal zones of anxiety and look at their predicted zones, it is possible to identify athletes who may need some type of intervention before competition. For example, consider scenario 2, in which one of your athletes performs well at her sectional meet and qualifies for the state championship.

Scenario 2

One of your athletes performs well at her sectional meet and qualifies for the state championship. As you discuss plans for the state meet, the athlete senses within her a heightening level of anxiety that did not exist for the sectional meet. She intuitively predicts she will be outside her optimal range of anxiousness and so together the two of you discuss strategies for helping her stay within her optimal zone for successful performance.

Scenario 2 is not uncommon among athletes who continually improve and reach new levels of performance. A rise in the level of athlete performance is often accompanied by a comparable rise in the level of competition and, quite possibly, athlete anxiety. For example, if your athletes perform well at conference, they qualify for sectionals. If successful at sectionals, they qualify for state. If your athletes do well at a qualifying meet, they advance to nationals. If successful at nationals, they qualify for Olympic trials, and so on. With each success exists the potential for increased anxiety.

The IZOF model considers not only anxiety, but also a number of other emotions that the athletes themselves have reported. Research (Hanin, 1997a) has shown with athletes of different sports and age levels that both positive and negative emotion can predict positive performance. The next section discusses these emotions.

Other Emotions

Theorists have suggested that emotion consists of three main components: physiological changes, action tendencies, and subjective experience. **Physiological changes** include increased heart rate and blood pressure, increased muscle tension, and skin response. Some researchers (e.g., Arnold & Gasson, 1954; Frijda, 1986) argue that **action tendencies** represent the core elements of emotions. For example, fear may prompt an action to run away; sadness may result in lethargy. I have little doubt that some emotions are critical for athlete success. For example, an athlete who feels self-pity does not respond well to adversity. In contrast, an athlete who feels anger more than likely will respond in an attack mode. **Subjective experience** refers to what an individual consciously experiences during an emotional experience.

Research on emotions and their effects on motor behavior suggests that both positive and negative emotions have optimal and dysfunctional effects on performance. Simply put, **positive emotions** are emotions you might typically think of as emotions that are good for performance, such as easygoing, tranquil, relaxed, and satisfied. **Negative emotions** are emotions you might generally think of as bad for performance, such as tense, dissatisfied, irritated, and angry. Surprisingly, some positive emotions can actually be bad for athlete performance while some negative emotions can, in truth, be good for athlete performance, as you are about to see.

Optimal effect may be defined as having an enhancing effect on performance, while a **dysfunctional effect** may be defined as having an impairing effect on performance. Analysis of emotion patterns in the IZOF model is based on the idea that skilled athletes are aware of and able to report their subjective emotional experiences related to their performances. Consequently, assessments use a variety of self-report scales (Zevon & Tellegen, 1982).

Tables 9.1 and 9.2 present selection frequencies for positive and negative emotions that athletes perceived as optimal or dysfunctional. The results for these tables were derived from a study sample that included 138 skilled athletes representing 7 sports: badminton, ice hockey, orienteering, cross-country skiing, swimming, squash, and soccer (Hanin, 2000b).

Positive emotions can have either an optimal or a dysfunctional effect on motor performance. For example, the positive emotion energetic was the most often cited emotion for enhancing performance (39.9%). In contrast, the positive emotion easygoing was the most often cited emotion for impairing performance (30.4%). With regard to negative emotions, the most often cited negative emotion for optimal (enhancing) performance was tense (49.3%), while the negative emotion tired was selected as dysfunctional (impairing) by 44.2% of the sample.

Notice in table 9.1 that the top 15 optimal positive emotions, such as energetic, charged, motivated, and purposeful, are strong (Hanin, 2000b) action-oriented emotions that suggest a certain amount of momentum and high level

Table 9.1   Top 15 Positive Emotion Markers Selected as Optimal or Dysfunctional

Predominantly optimal (P+) emotions (%)			Predominantly dysfunctional (P–) emotions (%)		
	P+	P–		P–	P+
Energetic	39.9	5.8	Easygoing	30.4	6.5
Charged	39.9	3.6	Excited	22.5	18.8
Motivated	37.7	—	Tranquil	18.1	2.9
Certain	30.4	13.8	Relaxed	16.7	10.3
Confident	29.0	2.2	Animated	16.7	0.7
Purposeful	29.0	—	Overjoyed	15.2	0.7
Willing	22.5	2.2	Fearless	15.2	8.7
Resolute	21.7	—	Satisfied	14.5	3.6
Alert	21.0	1.4	Exalted	13.8	6.5
Excited	18.8	22.5	Certain	13.8	30.4
Rested	18.1	7.2	Pleasant	13.0	1.4
Brisk	18.1	2.2	Comfortable	13.0	1.4
Cheerful	14.5	5.1	Nice	10.9	—
Enthusiastic	14.5	3.6	Daring	10.1	3.6
Brave	13.8	0.7	Calm	9.4	9.4

Note: *n* = 138 athletes, 7 sports.

P+ = emotion descriptors selected as positive and optimal (enhancing) for performance. P– = emotion descriptors selected as positive but dysfunctional (impairing) for performance.

Reprinted, by permission, from Y.L. Hanin, 2000, Successful and poor performance and emotions. In *Emotion in sport*, edited by Y.L. Hanin (Champaign, IL: Human Kinetics), 157-187.

of performance. In contrast, the top 15 dysfunctional positive emotions in table 9.1, such as easygoing, satisfied, and pleasant, are weak emotions and suggest a certain amount of complacency, inactivity, and low level of performance. I cite the emotions easygoing, satisfied, and pleasant because I think some athletes and coaches erroneously believe these emotions are enhancing when in fact research suggests otherwise. I have never witnessed an athlete perform exceptionally well when he was easygoing, satisfied, or pleasant. When athletes are in that emotional state, I am worried and dubious.

Like the optimal positive emotions, Hanin (2000b) describes the top 15 optimal negative emotions in table 9.2 as strong emotions because they suggest a need to continue strong, forceful, and deliberate action despite the fact that the competitive performance level may be low. In other words, you might be performing poorly, but you are dissatisfied and attacking rather than uncertain, depressed, and unwilling, which are inactive, impairing, and negative, emotions. Her sophomore year, Amelia missed making the finals of both the

Table 9.2 Top 15 Negative Emotion Markers Selected as Optimal or Dysfunctional

Predominantly optimal (N+) emotions (%)			Predominantly dysfunctional (N−) emotions (%)		
	N+	N−		N−	N+
Tense	49.3	10.1	Tired	44.2	2.9
Dissatisfied	49.3	5.8	Unwilling	39.9	1.4
Attacking	34.5	—	Uncertain	37.0	5.1
Vehement	24.6	—	Sluggish	29.0	0.7
Intense	21.7	2.9	Depressed	26.8	—
Nervous	20.3	10.1	Lazy	23.2	0.7
Irritated	19.6	4.3	Distressed	20.3	5.8
Provoked	13.0	4.3	Sorrowful	17.4	—
Angry	12.3	4.3	Afraid	15.9	3.6
Furious	10.9	2.2	Exhausted	14.5	—
Uneasy	10.1	2.2	Dejected	11.6	—
Tight	8.7	8.7	Sad	11.6	—
Restless	8.0	5.1	Concerned	10.9	6.5
Concerned	6.5	10.9	Unhappy	10.9	—
Distressed	5.8	20.3	Nervous	10.1	20.3

Note: *n* = 138 athletes, 7 sports.

N+ = emotion descriptors selected as negative but optimal (enhancing) for performance. N− = emotion descriptors selected as negative but dysfunctional (impairing) for performance.

Reprinted, by permission, from Y.L. Hanin, 2000, Successful and poor performance and emotions. In *Emotion in sport*, edited by Y.L. Hanin (Champaign, IL: Human Kinetics), 157-187.

conference championship and the NCAA championship. After failing to make finals, her mood state could best be described as dissatisfied and irritated. In that mood state she set a conference record in the consolation finals. In the consolation finals at the NCAA championship she set a school record and would have contended for the NCAA title that evening had she made finals. For the upcoming USA national championship I encouraged her to maintain the dissatisfied and irritated emotions. Amelia didn't win her individual event in finals but she did win semi-finals, qualified for the Pan American Games in Guadalajara, Mexico, and she and her partner won the national 10-meter synchronized diving title. Emotions may be the key to unlocking athlete performance excellence.

In contrast to the optimal negative emotions, the top 15 dysfunctional negative emotions, such as tired, uncertain, and afraid, are considered weak and impairing because they reflect a lack of action, personal resources, or ability to actively cope with the competitive situation.

CONSEQUENCES OF EMOTIONS

Up to this point, the discussion has focused on the different emotions that can be engendered by antecedent appraisal. But what about the effects of these elicited emotions on your athletes? What consequences do these emotions have on your athletes' performances, psychological and physiological well-being, and interaction with teammates? The following section discusses these consequences.

Intrapersonal Consequences of Emotions on Performance

According to Izard (1993), emotions constitute the primary human motivational system and these emotions have intrapersonal and interpersonal consequences. Intra means within. Therefore, the term **intrapersonal consequences** refers to the effects emotions have within or on the individual athlete. This definition is in contrast to inter, which means between, among, or within a group. In this case **interpersonal consequences** refer to the effects emotions have between and among your athletes. The following section first focuses on the intrapersonal consequences of emotions on individual athletes.

Performance Consequences

Most obvious and most important of the consequences of emotion is the enhancing and impairing effects on performance. Many coaches focus so intently on the Xs and Os—the tangible factor—that they overlook the intangible factor—the emotion factor.

After a lecture at Tsinghua University in Beijing, China, on the interplay between thoughts, emotions, and motor performance I was asked a question the gist of which was this: *Since Chinese athletes are immune to the effects of emotions because of their training regimen, why bother with emotions?* A few years later at a world championship in Rome, Italy I watched an incredibly close men's platform event go down to the last dive. Two Chinese, one Australian, and one British diver all had a chance to win and all had spectacular dives left. Farthest back was young Thomas Daly from Great Britain. Performing fourth to last in the competition, Thomas drilled a reverse 3 1/2 for straight10's—a perfect dive. The two Chinese divers, one of whom had a nice lead, and the Australian diver (defending Olympic champion) all looked unnerved and all missed their last dives. At the age of 15 Thomas Daly surprised the diving community by becoming the youngest male 10-meter world champion in the history of the sport. Did emotion play a part in the demise of the Chinese divers? Most certainly so.

No matter what kind of training regimen you use, no human being is devoid of emotion or immune to the effects of emotion; to believe otherwise is to deny your athletes' humanness, their fallibility, their susceptibility—and perhaps their most noble attribute. The unstoppable athlete, the resilient athlete, and the salivating athlete are proof that athletes filled with powerful emotions such as determination and passion can accomplish almost anything. Emotions do indeed have consequences on motor performance. Coaches and athletes need to recognize both the enhancing and the impairing effects of emotions on performance and make the emotion factor part of training and competition preparation.

Cognitive Consequences

Researchers looking at sensory processing (LeDoux, 1993, 1994) have discovered that the brain's circuitry is wired differently than previously thought and that when people become highly emotional brain functioning changes dramatically. When people are excessively emotional, sensory stimuli from the eyes and ears travel as signals first to the thalamus and then across a single synapse to the amygdala; a second signal from the thalamus is routed to the neocortex, which is the thinking part of the brain. This architecture enables the amygdala to begin responding before the neocortex has a chance to respond. The amygdala is associated with the fight-or-flight response, which alerts the body's emotional centers and stimulates us to action.

According to this research, people think differently depending on their emotional state. When you are emotionally balanced, you think rationally with the neocortex, but when you are overly emotionally charged, you react (as opposed to think and respond) emotionally with the amygdala. Sometimes this emotionally charged state helps athletic performance (e.g., the defensive lineman who makes a spectacular quarterback sack). Other times, however, this emotional state impairs performance and causes athletes to perform errantly (e.g., the golfer who double bogeys and then misses a routine putt on the next hole), or do irrational things (e.g., the athlete who punches a locker with one's fist as Mike did). When the game is tied in the final seconds and a basketball player charges the referee and receives a technical foul, which causes his team to lose the game, he is most likely responding emotionally from the amygdala.

Other emotions besides anger also can have cognitive consequences. For example, a reigning national champion goes to the Olympic trials fully prepared both physically and mentally to win trials and compete for the United States at the Summer Olympic Games. After all, Russ is the defending national champion. However, he is not prepared to see his formerly healthy father, with whom he had become estranged, unexpectedly show up at the venue in a wheelchair and in extremely frail health. The sight of his disabled father has a powerful emotional effect on him from which he never recovers. He becomes emotionally upset and cognitively distracted and performs well below his ability level in the trials. He finishes fourth and does not make the team.

Emotions can have significant cognitive consequences for athletic performance. One of these consequences is **cognitive interference**. Smith (1996) states,

> Cognitions have both stimulus and response properties, and cognitive interference occurs when the stimulus properties of task-irrelevant cognitions interfere with the effective processing of task-relevant cues, or when they evoke responses (e.g., emotional arousal) that are incompatible with task-relevant responses. (p. 262)

In other words, cognitive interference occurs when athletes think about things unassociated with the task, such as the outcome of the contest, and these task-irrelevant thoughts in turn generate inappropriate emotions, such as worry and anxiety, that further disrupt thinking and cause athletes to make mistakes. For example, a highly trained athlete begins to worry about not performing well in the finals and not making the national team. As a result, the athlete becomes cognitively distracted, misses specific performance cues, and performs poorly.

Three factors contribute to cognitive interference (Carver, 1996). One factor is stepping outside the cognitive stream and assessing the likelihood of achieving the desired goal. For example, an athlete might be preoccupied with thinking about the outcome of the meet: "What happens if I don't win?" "What happens if I don't make finals?" These concerns about performance outcomes and goal achievement rather than performance processes generate negative emotions such as fear, anxiety, and worry. And these negative emotions in turn, help sustain or generate additional cognitive interfering thoughts.

Stepping outside the cognitive stream can also cause athletes to become self-aware, to attend to themselves while performing (Smith, 1996). In sports, this self-awareness is referred to as **paralysis by analysis**, which is the process of consciously focusing on the mechanics of a performance that is normally performed automatically and nearly unconsciously. When athletes perform at peak levels, they feel as though they are on automatic pilot and they react with very little cognitive effort (Williams, 1986). The expression *grip it and rip it* refers to the fact that successful performance is often automatic. To paraphrase hall of fame baseball player Yogi Berra, *You can't think and hit at the same time.*

A second factor that can cause cognitive interference is having an unfavorable expectation of success which can cause athletes to disengage from further effort. In this scenario, when athletes confront adversity they have negative ruminations that often focus on feelings of self-doubt and inadequacy (Carver, 1996). These emotions in turn lead them to disengage both physically (physical withdrawal) and mentally (daydream, fantasize, focus on task-irrelevant thoughts, sights, or sounds). This disengagement cannot be sustained, however, because they are, for a variety of reasons, brought back to the task at hand. Consequently, there is a recurrent cycle of sporadic effort, interruption, assessment (which often only exacerbates their feelings of self-doubt and inadequacy), and disengagement. As the cycle continues, negative emotions and cognitive interference only increase.

For example, a college freshman who had some moderate success with his sport in high school decides to continue in the sport at the collegiate level. He is attending his state school and convinces the coach to let him walk on to the collegiate team. He enters the program with a moderate to low expectation of success. At the first sign of adversity or failure (e.g., he doesn't do well in the first week of practices), he begins to ruminate on his feelings of self-doubt and inadequacy. Consequently, he comes to practice the next week mentally unprepared and gives less effort than he did the first week. He is required to practice but, because he has another bad week of practice, even more self-doubt and self-deprecating thoughts cause him to disengage even further. Before the end of his second month on the team, he decides to quit.

Finally, a third factor that can cause cognitive interference is connecting the success of the task to self-esteem. When performance declines, as it assuredly will for all athletes at some points in their careers, athletes who connect success with self-esteem will experience heightened negative emotions such as fear and anxiety because they perceive a poor performance as not just a lapse in execution but also as a failure of the self. When athletes put their egos on the line, they also put enormous pressure on themselves. When performance decreases, negative emotions increase and athletes experience cognitive interference because they think about task-irrelevant things, such as personal inadequacies, rather than particular inadequacies about the performance. Such is the case when an athlete puts his ego on the line every time he competes. If he wins, he feels good about himself and is happy and motivated. If he loses, he generalizes his poor performance to include that he is somehow inferior as a person and then he feels sad and unhappy. This generalization and ensuing emotions causes him to ruminate on his inadequacies and interfere with his concentration in preparing and performing for the next competition. Consequently, at the next competition he has to deal with the pressure of competing and also the pressure of protecting his self-esteem, which is a daunting task for any athlete.

Another negative consequence of emotion is that emotions can influence cognitive perception. Individuals tend to perceive stimuli (situations, cues, etc.) based on their emotions (Niedenthal & Setterlund, 1994). For example, an overly anxious athlete might focus on the judges' scores and think the judges are out to get her, rather than focus on performing. Unfortunately, focusing on cues consistent with the emotion only serves to reinforce the emotion and, consequently, increase the level of anxiety.

Another consequence of emotion can be a shift or narrowing of attentional focus. According to Easterbrook's (1959) **cue utilization hypothesis**, athletes utilize relevant cues during successful motor performance and disregard

Width of focus

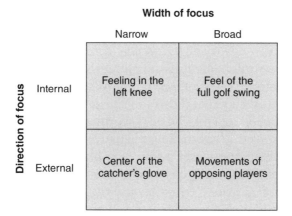

Figure 9.4.   Directions of attention.

Reprinted, by permission, from R. Schmidt and C. Wrisberg, 2008, *Motor learning and performance*, 4th ed. (Champaign, IL: Human Kinetics), 222.

irrelevant cues. Under conditions of high arousal or anxiety, attention may become too narrow and the athlete may not attend to relevant cues. Nideffer (1989) has hypothesized a dual **direction of attention**. According to his hypothesis, arousal affects two dimensions of attention: narrow or broad and external or internal. Figure 9.4 represents these dimensions.

Arousal affects attention in different ways because athletes can react differently under high levels of arousal. Some athletes might become too broad in their attentional focus while others might become too narrow. Some might become too internally focused while others might become too externally focused. The notion of internal focus suggests that athletes use internal cues such as feelings, thoughts, level of arousal, self-talk, or self-monitoring, for high-level performance.

Another dimension seems equally important for athlete performance, namely, time. This dimension includes past, present, and future. Figure 9.5 represents the dimension of time and its relationship to the other two dimensions.

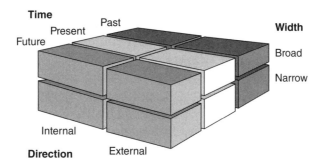

Figure 9.5.   Direction of attention with time as an additional dimension.

To understand the dimension of time, consider a basketball player who takes a jump shot. Before her feet touch the floor she is thinking to the future and preparing to run down court and play defense. This scenario could be different. The player might focus in the present and wait to see if the ball goes in the net. If she misses the shot, she might focus on the past, continuing to think about the missed shot, and then be late getting back on defense.

Another consequence of emotion on performance is that emotion can influence personal judgment. When making evaluative judgments about themselves, people often use their emotion as a source of information (Schwarz, Strack, Kommer, & Wagner, 1987). For example, when basketball players report their level of life satisfaction after a win, they use their current positive emotional state to determine that things are going well and will report higher levels of life satisfaction than athletes who have just lost (Clore, Schwarz, & Conway, 1994; Schwarz & Strack, 1991).

Motivational Consequences

A number of authors have suggested that emotions significantly influence motivation (e.g., Arnold, 1960; Deci, 1980; Frijda, 1986; Weiner, 1977). Arnold and Gasson (1954) and Frijda (1986) have suggested that action tendencies are inherent in emotions. In other words, certain emotions motivate people toward an object, as in the case of anger, and certain emotions motivate individuals away from an object, as in the case of fear. Izard (1993) goes even further in suggesting that emotions represent the main motivational system for dictating that people address immediate concerns and needs.

Weiner (1977) has proposed that emotions are major determinants of motives and that specific emotions are associated with specific motives. For example, anger leads to an aggressive motive and pity to a helping motive. Very little research to date, however, has been pursued to examine Weiner's proposal. Still, many coaches would agree that emotion acts as a strong motivating factor for athletes. For example, the young diver who is afraid of learning a new dive might be motivated to avoid practice.

Health Consequences

The relationship between emotions and health has been of longstanding interest to researchers in the area of health psychology (Vallerand & Blanchard, 2000). There are three principles related to emotions and health (Oatley & Jenkins, 1996). *The first principle is that inner conflict leads to illness.* From a psychoanalytical perspective (Alexander, 1950), this perspective suggests that unresolved emotional conflict can lead to physical health problems. A familiar example would be an athlete who participates in a sport to avoid disappointing his parents, even though he isn't very good in the sport or doesn't like the sport. Unfortunately, I have seen this scenario far too often. This continued struggle, often an unconscious struggle, may lead to chronic stress and resulting mental and physical health problems.

The second principle is that people who express their emotions are less inclined to develop illness. Some research suggests that people who are able to express their feelings about traumatic experiences are healthier than people who are not able to express their feelings. For example, a study by Pennebaker and Beall (1986) showed that subjects who were able to write about their traumatic experiences for 3 to 5 days experienced health benefits, such as fewer visits to the doctor's office, in comparison to subjects who simply wrote about other topics.

This research suggests that athletes can benefit from finding ways to express their feelings, particularly during a long season of heavy training and rigorous competition. Coaches can develop an open door policy to let athletes know they can come in and talk about anything and that it will be kept private. (See chapter 8 for a review on the nondirective model of coaching.) Before an NCAA championship, one of my athletes came into my office and exclaimed, "Everything is wrong with my diving!" After sniffling and crying for about 15 minutes and complaining about everything under the sun, she finally released enough emotion to begin talking about some of the things in her life, such as pressure from parents and choosing a college major, that were bothering her. In the end, she discovered there was nothing wrong with her diving, but there were things outside the pool that had been building for a long time that she needed to address. I am sure that had she continued to bottle up her emotions her physical and mental well-being would have worsened.

The third principle is that the immune system mediates between life stresses and illness. This means that when athletes become emotionally imbalanced (*stressed out*) the immune system intervenes to keep the athlete healthy. However, if this emotional imbalance persists over an extended period of time, the immune system eventually breaks down and health problems occur. Although sport research has not yet examined the impact of the immune system on emotion and health, it has examined the relationship between emotion (e.g., stress) and health in athletes. In particular, sport research has looked at the link between emotion and athlete injury, recovery, and burnout. Negative emotions such as anxiety, depression, and fear can contribute to a greater likelihood of injury, longer recovery time, and athlete burnout.

Injury and Recovery Consequences

Andersen and Williams (1988) have developed a model to try to explain the connection between emotion and injury. In their model, three factors— personality (e.g., trait anxiety), history of stressors (stressful life events), and coping resources (e.g., stress management strategies)—influence an athlete's appraisal of a situation as stressful. A negative appraisal can lead to negative physiological and attentional consequences, which increase the risk of athletic injury. Research supports parts of the model. For example, several studies have noted a relationship between life stressors and athletic injuries (Bramwell, Masuda, Wagner, & Holmes, 1975; Cryan & Alles, 1983; Hardy & Riehl, 1988). In addition, Hanson, McCullagh, and Tony-mon (1992) found that sport competitive anxiety predicted the severity of injuries for National Collegiate Athletic Association (NCAA) division I and II athletes. Research also indicates that the stress–injury relationship seems to be greater for athletes whose ineffective coping skills and low social support system keep them from effectively managing stress (Smith, Smoll, & Ptacek, 1990).

Besides affecting injury, emotion also can affect recovery from athletic injuries (Vallerand & Blanchard, 2000). Early efforts to understand the emotional responses to athletic injuries initially relied on the work of Dr. Elizabeth Kubler-Ross (1969), who suggested that patients move through stages in struggling to cope with terminal illnesses. These stages are denial, anger, bargaining, depression, and acceptance. Instead of a stage theory, Heil (2000) has suggested that the injured athlete moves through a cyclical process of emotional recovery and he has developed an affective cyclical model of injury recovery that includes three components: distress, denial, and determined coping. **Distress** reflects the effects of injury on the athlete's emotional balance. Distress includes emotions such as anxiety, depression, fear, anger, and guilt. Subtle forms of distress manifest themselves in the form of resistance-like behaviors (Heil, 2000) such as redirected anger, complaining, and self-doubt. For example, when athletes become injured, they sometimes redirect their anger at the trainer, training program, or coach.

Denial is what Heil calls **unacknowledged distress**. In other words, the injury creates psychological tension within the athlete that the athlete either unconsciously does not recognize or consciously refuses to acknowledge. Ranging from mild to profound, denial includes behaviors and emotions such as avoidance, minimizing, shock, disbelief, and failure to accept the severity of the injury. Denial may be either functional or dysfunctional in its application. Denial can be functional for an athlete who is trying to remain positive and optimistic because denial can prevent the athlete from ruminating on distressing thoughts and becoming overwhelmed by negative emotions. On the other hand, denial can be dysfunctional for an athlete when, for example, the athlete does not consciously or unconsciously acknowledge a serious injury and ignores rehabilitation or prescribed limitations on movement.

The third component of Heil's model is determined coping. **Determined coping** refers to an athlete's ability to move beyond passive acceptance toward proactively channeling her knowledge, skill, and energy into overcoming the injury. Coping skills include exploration (looking for possible solutions, clarifying goals, seeking available resources, considering alternative solutions, learning new skills) and commitment (new focus, vision, teamwork, cooperation).

According to Heil's affective cycle of injury recovery, the athlete moves through each of these components during each stage of the rehabilitation process. In other words, athletes can go through a distress-denial-determined coping minicycle at various stages of the recovery process. For example, an athlete has shoulder surgery after her junior year in college. She expects to begin light practice about 3 months after surgery. In fact, her recovery takes over 2 years. During this time, she experiences numerous minicycles. Her shoulder feels better and she begins to feel enthused and energetic about her prospect of competing in the near future. Soon, however, she begins to feel tenderness and rubbing when she moves her arm, which makes her anxious and the cycle begins anew. At times she despairs and becomes depressed. After having her shoulder scoped, the irritation in her shoulder disappears and she begins to channel her intelligence, enormous energy, positive outlook, and commitment into getting better. She immerses herself in her rehabilitation program, begins an extensive strength program, and changes her stretching program. Her shoulder improves dramatically. But her real improvement began when she overcame her emotions of distress and denial and became determined to cope with her injury. In this real-life scenario, Kimberly went on to eventually win several U.S. national championships and make the U.S. Olympic team.

Burnout Consequences

Burnout is most commonly defined as a multidimensional syndrome characterized by feelings of emotional exhaustion and depersonalization and a reduced sense of personal accomplishment (Maslach & Jackson, 1986). Research suggests that burnout affects a significant percentage of athletes, as high as 47% according to Silva (1990), and the syndrome is a reaction to long-term, chronic stress (Dale & Weinberg, 1990). Smith (1986) has developed a model of burnout that borrows from his anxiety model, which was outlined earlier in this chapter. Smith's burnout model stresses that the appraisal process of the situation determines perceived stress. Cognitive appraisals are influenced by personality (e.g., trait anxiety) and motivational factors (high need for achievement) and lead to cognitive (e.g., rumination), physiological (e.g., arousal), affective (e.g., anxiety, anger), and behavioral (e.g., staleness, withdrawal) consequences that characterize burnout. Preliminary research indicates that stress-related emotions can predict burnout (Kelley & Gill, 1993; Taylor, Daniel, Leith, & Burke, 1990; Vealey et al., 1992).

Additional research examining training programs and mental states has attempted to demonstrate that overtraining creates a negative affective state that may cause athletic burnout (Morgan, Brown, Raglin, O'Connor, & Ellickson, 1987). For example, a study of 41 German junior national rowing team members found that increased training led to mood disturbance and decreased training resulted in mood improvement (Kellmann, Kallus, Steinacker, & Lormes, 1997). While this result and results from other studies suggest that overtraining may eventually lead to burnout, at this time no empirical support exists for this hypothesis.

Interpersonal Consequences of Emotion on Performance

Up to this point, the discussion has focused on intrapersonal consequences, or how emotion affects the person who is experiencing the emotion. In this section, the focus is on **interpersonal consequences**, how emotion affects the interaction between one or more individual athletes.

Little research has been done on the importance of interpersonal consequences of emotion on sport performance (Vallerand & Blanchard, 2000). As suggested by Vallerand (1983), three areas of interest concerning interpersonal consequences might be of value when applied to the sport setting.

Emotion Imitation: Influencing Emotional Behavior

An emotional display by one athlete has consequences on the behavior of others, including emotional behavior. For example, seeing a teammate become excited and happy during practice might cause another athlete on the team to become excited and happy. Unfortunately, the same thing might be said for an athlete who becomes frustrated and angry. One or more athletes might also become frustrated and angry. For this reason, it is important to have a team role model—an athlete who sets the pace every day in practice, not only for the level of effort and determination, but also for the level of emotion other athletes will imitate. Coaches most often refer to this athlete as the emotional leader of the team.

Emotion Appraisal: The Emotional Message

The appraisal of the emotional message influences an individual athlete's emotions. In other words, how an athlete interprets another's emotional response can influence that athlete's emotions. For example, if you show pity towards an athlete after a poor performance, the emotional message is that you don't think your athlete has the ability to perform any better. The athlete interprets this message and experiences feelings of sadness and self-pity. However, if you show displeasure or anger toward your athlete (or your athlete's performance), the athlete interprets the emotional message to be that you think he has ability but needs to give more effort. In this case the athlete will also experience displeasure or anger and a desire to work harder in practice.

Another person's emotional display need not be displayed directly to an athlete in order to affect that athlete's emotions and behavior. For example, an athlete might view a video clip of another elite athlete modeling positive emotions during a winning performance and then imitate those emotions in his or her own performance. Hackfort (1996) has shown that simply viewing video clips that highlight emotional qualities in different sports enhances athletes' levels of arousal and aspirations, and their motor performance on an endurance task.

Emotion Consequences: Affecting Future Behaviors

Interpersonal emotions have consequences on interpersonal behavior. In other words, an emotional response to an interaction with a person will affect future interactional behavior with that person. For example, if you unduly criticize a referee, the referee will experience anger and in future competitions is likely to look unfavorably at your athletes. If you unfairly criticize an athlete publicly, the athlete is likely to experience feelings of shame and anger, which will negatively affect the athlete's future interactions with you.

In summary, if you want to build team unity and cohesion, facilitate good interpersonal emotional consequences. Make sure you and your athletes, particularly your team leaders, model good emotional behaviors by sending the right emotional message to your athletes, and by monitoring the emotional interactions among teammates so that positive emotional responses are being elicited by your athletes. Negative emotional responses can cause team tension, discord, and disunity.

APPLYING EMOTION THEORY IN COACHING ATHLETES

Nothing discussed to this point in the chapter is important—at least from a coaching perspective—unless it can be applied to the most important factor in the emotion–performance equation: the athlete. What are some strategies for helping your athletes maintain appropriate emotions and remain within their zone of optimal functioning? Table 9.3 summarizes these preventive and coping strategies and they are discussed in the following sections.

Preventive Strategies

The easiest and most effective way to maintain appropriate emotions and remain in the zone is to avoid inappropriate emotions and stay in the zone in the first place. Following are some preventive strategies you can apply to help your athletes maintain emotional balance and stay in the zone.

Play an Effective Affective Game

Help your athletes understand the interplay between emotions and motor performance; encourage them to play the emotion game. Like the **inner game** of sports such as golf and tennis, in which athletes focus on the influence of the mind on performance, the **emotion game** of sport focuses on the interplay between emotion and performance. The following strategies can help your athletes stay within their emotional zone, but the first step to applying these strategies is recognizing the importance of emotions in motor performance and playing an effective affective game.

Table 9.3 Preventive and Coping Strategies for Staying in the Emotional Zone

Preventive strategies	Coping strategies
Play an effective affective game.	Deal with burnout.
Embrace enhancing emotions.	Use coping strategies for MFS.
Avoid impairing emotions.	Use cognitive monitoring and restructuring.
Establish a zone.	Resolve inner conflict.
Stay in the zone.	Express emotions.
Predict anxiety level before competition.	Use self-talk.
Make appropriate appraisals.	Take care of body and injuries.
Develop psychological defensive coping strategies.	Practice determined coping.
Determine state-trait anxiety personality.	Filter emotional messages.
Expect success.	Change body language.
Prevent maladaptive fatigue syndrome and burnout.	Avoid distractions.
Avoid boredom.	
Practice dealing with the unexpected.	
Learn to ignore hardwired responses.	

Embrace Enhancing Emotions

Athletes can't be emotional clones of someone else; they have to be who they are. They need to embrace their own emotional personality and recruit the emotions that fit their approach to performance and competition. Anger works well for some athletes, but not at all for others. Review the list of positive and negative enhancing emotions in this chapter and, like buying a new pair of shoes, have your athletes *try on* different emotions to see which ones are the most comfortable fit for them. Once they have identified the enhancing emotions that work for them, they can next work on developing personal strategies and skills for recruiting and utilizing these emotions.

Avoid Impairing Emotions

This may seem obvious, but not always so for some athletes. Perhaps because they had some moderate success with these emotions when they were young athletes, they continue to utilize emotions that are no longer optimal for them. For example, I coached an athlete who would become giddy, chatty, and animated during major competitions. It was her standard emotional approach to competition when she was a junior competitor. After several national competitions in which she performed poorly, I sat down with her and strongly suggested she find other emotions and alter her preperformance routine. The following year, we attended the NCAA championship. In the first day's event she reverted back to her old emotions and routine and, consequently, performed horribly. After the contest I sat down with her and in quite force-ful terms told her to discard her old emotional approach to competition and adopt the emotions and routine we had worked on all year. The following day she earned the bronze medal in a very tough contest.

Establish a Zone

Have your athletes get in touch with their emotional limits for practice and competition performances. Some coaches may not have the time, manpower, or resources to administer something like the state-trait anxiety inventory (STAI) to help athletes determine their emotional boundaries. You can, however, assess their limits directly by asking them how they feel immediately before and after a competition. This informal assessment provides your athlete and you with a sense of the optimal range for their emotions. You can assess their limits indirectly by having them recall how they felt in past competi-tions, particularly when they performed at an optimal level and when they performed at a dysfunctional level. Often the best learning experience about emotions comes on the heels of a terrible performance.

Many athletes, however, are reluctant to honestly report their feelings when they perform poorly because they believe it is a sign of weakness or that their coach will think less of them if they reveal that they were nervous, scared, or afraid. Consequently, you may need to be persistent in coaxing them into being forthcoming about the emotions and range of emotions they experienced during competition. If they chocked, they chocked, plain and simple. The first step toward establishing emotional equilibrium is for athletes to admit that their emotions got the best of them. Openly and honestly assessing their emotional disequilibrium allows them to begin framing the emotional problem and finding a solution for keeping themselves in the zone of optimal functioning.

At the December winter U.S. national championship, which was also the last chance to qualify for the U.S. Olympic Trials, Darian had a disastrous event, an event that every athlete experiences, but only the great ones learn from. He was understandably disappointed but it took 20 minutes of talking with him on the pool deck before he admitted that he choked. After much denial he looked at me and said, "Coach, I froze. My mind went blank." My response was "Great. You just admitted to doing something that every athlete I have ever worked with has done. Now, we move forward, find a solution, and prepare for the conference and NCAA championships." After a second lengthy meeting (still on the pool deck) we formulated a plan of attack. As I started to walk away, I suddenly turned around and said, "Darian, you are going to have an amazing second semester." Two months later he was crowned Big Ten conference champion, Big Ten diver of the championship, and NCAA All-American.

Stay in the Zone

It's fantastic when athletes are in the zone but it doesn't do them much good if they can't stay in the zone. But staying in the zone doesn't happen by accident;

it takes effort and practice. Teach your athletes to continually monitor and self-regulate themselves to make sure they are staying within their zone. Sometimes a quick mental check and offering a short self-statement, such as "Hey, I am starting to get a little frustrated, so calm down and refocus" is all it takes to get back on track emotionally. It is much easier to stay in the zone than it is to get back in the zone. Once that invisible 2,000-pound gorilla gets on an athlete's back it is virtually impossible to get it off.

It is inevitable during competition that an athlete will make a mistake and, whether it is big or small, how that athlete responds to the error will influence emotions. One way of keeping the gorilla off an athlete's back and staying in the zone is to practice the **seven Rs**: responsibility, recognize, respond, release, regroup, refocus, ready. Responsibility means taking personal responsibility for the mistake and also responsibility for moving on rather than dwelling on the mistake. Recognize means being aware of the situation and the necessity of proactively dealing with it. Respond means taking positive actions after the mistake. Release involves letting go of negative emotions and putting the mistake in the past, which for many athletes is no easy task. Regroup means retracing the performance preparation steps and getting redialed in—again, no easy chore for some athletes unless they consistently practice the seven Rs. Refocus means zeroing in on the next movement and its performance cues. Ready involves initiating the preperformance routine and readying oneself physically, mentally, and emotionally for the next movement with no further thought of the previous movement or quality of the movement unless information about the movement (but not the emotional baggage tied to it) is beneficial for the following movement.

Predict Anxiety Level Before Competition

Research (Raglin & Hanin, 2000) indicates that athletes can be fairly accurate in predicting how they will feel immediately prior to competition. Through direct and indirect assessments (if they are honest like Darian was), you can get a true sense of which of your athletes are likely to be emotionally out of the zone for competitions, particularly major competitions. Knowing this, you can sit down with them and formulate a plan and implement preventive strategies (e.g., relaxation, visualization, and cognitive restructuring) well in advance of the competition. If you wait until competition time to cope with it rather than prevent it in advance, it will probably be too late to make any measurable difference, hence, the 2,000-pound gorilla.

Make Appropriate Appraisals

Because appraisal influences emotion, help your athletes make clear and accurate appraisals that engender enhancing emotions such as motivated, attacking, vehement, intense, and resolute. To accomplish this, show your athletes persuasive data (e.g., video clips, performance averages, statistical evidence) that confirms their performance is getting better, or close to their goal, or that with more effort they can reach their goal.

Avoid the quick and intuitive appraisal, especially immediately after a competition. Emotions can run high right after a competition, particularly after a poor performance. So, rather than make an appraisal influenced by the heat of the moment, you and your athletes should wait until some time has elapsed and then make a reflective (rational) appraisal. I have seen several instances soon after a contest where a coach and athlete, both emotionally charged, tried to talk about what went wrong and the discussion wasn't pretty. As mentioned earlier in the chapter, when people are emotionally charged, they don't always think logically or rationally.

When making reflective appraisals, seek objective and accurate performance feedback. Comments from competitors, teammates, parents, and others should be taken cautiously. It should be a simple thing to accomplish but sometimes it isn't so easy to evaluate an athlete's progress. For example, maybe she placed lower in the standings than the last competition but her score was a personal best and the field of competitors was really deep. If she looks solely at place of finish she may feel disappointment, but if she looks at her personal best score she should attribute the outcome to personal effort and therefore experience joy.

Develop Psychological Defensive Coping Strategies

Smith (1996) suggests that psychological defenses act as coping strategies by distorting the perception of the competitive situation. When lessening the seriousness and gravity of competition, athletes appraise the competitive situation as less threatening so they experience less anxiety. For example, before any major competition, an athlete of mine always had an excuse or reason why she probably wouldn't perform well in the upcoming competition: Her arm hurt. She wasn't feeling well. There were personal problems. Of course, she almost always performed well at the competition. Her excuses acted as a psychological defensive coping strategy because they provided her with an alibi, a reason for not performing well, which made the looming competition less formidable and allowed her to relax and experience less anxiety. It is as though she was telling herself and others, "Listen, this is probably not going to be my day to shine; I've got some issues going on, so don't expect much from me." In this real-life scenario, the athlete did indeed shine and went on to win several U.S. national championships and become a member of the U.S. Olympic team.

According to Smith, athletes can make four types of appraisals:

- *Appraisal of situational demands.* How demanding is the sport situation?
- *Appraisal of resources to deal with the sport situation.* Do I have what it takes to meet the sport challenge?
- *Appraisal of the nature and likelihood of potential consequences if the demands of the sport situation are not met.* What will happen if I fail?
- *The personal meanings attached to the consequences.* What will it mean to me or about me if I win or lose?

How well athletes make these four types of appraisals positively or negatively affects their perceptions of the significance of the sport situation, their level of anxiety, and the types of emotions they might experience. Successful athletes appraise a sport situation as moderately demanding, rather than highly demanding, because they have worked hard and they believe they are prepared and have the ability to meet the challenge to succeed. Successful athletes have adequate defensive coping strategies that help them perceive the situation and the consequences as less threatening. They have a response to the question *What will happen if I fail?* Their answer, of course, is *Nothing threatening; life will go on.* Also, these athletes understand that their self-esteem and self-worth are not linked with winning or losing.

Determine State-Trait Anxiety Personality

State anxiety refers to a person's response (level of anxiety) to a specific situation. **Trait anxiety** refers to a person's general response tendency (level of anxiety) when exposed to stressors. Athletes differ in their normal level of anxiety. Research suggests that athletes with high levels of trait anxiety typically tend to experience high levels of state anxiety in competitive sport situations (Martens, Vealey, & Burton, 1990). In other words, athletes who tend to become highly anxious outside a sport setting also tend to become highly anxious in a competitive situation. Consequently, encourage your athletes to get to know themselves and how they are likely to respond in competition and then help them prepare for the emotional demands of the situation. Pay close attention to athletes with high trait anxiety. If they perform well in competition with high state anxiety, that is all right; if they don't perform well then they will need to use strategies for reducing anxiety.

Expect Success

A favorable expectation for success is important for promoting enhancing emotions such as confidence, certainty, and motivation. In contrast, having an unfavorable expectation can cause athletes to disengage in further effort and experience feelings of self-doubt and inadequacy (Carver, 1996). Your athletes have trained hard, made the most of each practice, and prepared for the competition. Why not expect success? Frequent positive self-talk, posted signs (e.g., "Expect the Best!"), objective data (e.g., performance reviews, training times, past successes), the coach's affirmation of success, positive comments, explaining the importance of expecting success, and encouraging a positive outlook are all ways of encouraging an expectancy of success.

Prevent Maladaptive Fatigue Syndrome and Burnout

Maladaptive fatigue syndrome (MFS) is physical and mental fatigue caused by a combination of stressors from mental, physical, and social sources. Gould (1996) accurately describes it as a "psychological, physical, and emotional withdrawal from a formerly enjoyable and motivating activity" (p. 276). Since MFS is associated with a number of impairing emotions such as anxiety, depression, and sadness, it is important to prevent it. There are a number of ways to prevent MFS (Henschen, 2000). Some of these preventive strategies include proper training, periodic time-outs, avoiding monotony, positive reinforcement from coaches, management of pre- and postcompetitive anxiety, mental practice (relaxation, concentration, imagery, self-talk, and performance routines), and participating in the decision-making process concerning training.

Avoid Boredom

Boredom may be the single greatest cause of MFS (Henschen, 2000). If this is indeed the case, you and your athletes need to consider creative ways to avoid boredom in practice. One way to avoid boredom is to use a random rather than blocked practice schedule to increase cognitive attention and enhance learning (Shea & Morgan, 1979). Another way to avoid boredom is to make sure that practice demands are challenging but attainable. If practice is too easy, athletes become complacent; if it is so difficult that success is unattainable, they feel unmotivated to try. Find the right balance between challenge and attainability. Part of the beauty of the flexible practice environment is the ability of athlete and coach to constantly shape and reshape it. Each day practice can be something new, exciting, challenging, puzzling, instructive, and rewarding for the creative thinking coach and athlete. Remember, too, the importance of making deliberate play part of your practices.

Practice Dealing With the Unexpected

You can never completely prepare for the unexpected, but you can use several strategies to help your athletes learn to deal with it so they come to expect the unexpected and maintain emotional balance. One strategy is planning unexpected scenarios in practice. For example, right before an athlete performs, you have a fellow teammate perform well and have the rest of the team cheer. In this scenario the athlete rehearses having to follow a great performance with one of his own. These types of practice scenarios are probably as old as the games of sport. For example, many basketball players rehearse in practice hitting the game-winning shot at the buzzer. And many golfers imagine having to sink a practice putt to win the championship. The possibilities are as varied and numerous as your imagination can create.

Another way to deal with the unexpected is to teach athletes to visualize random, unusual, or challenging scenarios. I know a number of Olympic athletes who visualize themselves in as many different competition scenarios as possible so they are prepared if one or more of those situations arises. Some of these scenarios include falling behind and catching up, feeling fatigued and reenergizing, playing poorly and regrouping, feeling ill and performing well, dealing with inclement weather, adjusting to new surroundings, performing with audience noise, competing in poor facilities, using bad equipment, and dealing with distractions.

To facilitate athlete visualization start by reserving 10 to 15 minutes after practice and have your athletes lie down and visualize their performances and the different scenarios they could encounter during their performances. They can include these visualizations as part of their preperformance routine. Instead of visualizing, some athletes prefer to think about the scenarios and remind themselves of the appropriate responses associated with each scenario.

Learn to Ignore Hardwired Responses

Being successful in the long run often comes down to being emotionally even-keeled. To attain this emotional balance, athletes have to learn to be immune to antecedents that elicit negative emotional responses, particularly **hardwired emotional responses**, which are deeply embedded and easily and unconsciously activated emotional reactions brought about by specific stimuli. Successful athletes must have the ability to ignore responses to thoughts such as "I might win!" or "I might lose!" or "My dad is upset." if these thoughts lead to negative emotions. When momentum suddenly shifts during the contest, your athletes must have the ability to say, "So what," and continue to feel confident, emotionally balanced, mentally focused, and physically ready to perform.

Of course, learning to ignore or become immune to antecedents that engender hardwired responses is difficult because these responses are, well, hardwired. Many of the preventive strategies outlined in this section can help athletes *un*wire (ignore, alter, combat, or eliminate) their reactions to stimuli that activate hardwired emotional responses. Other strategies for ignoring hardwired responses include self-talk, cognitive restructuring, systematic desensitization, avoidance techniques, relaxation, mental imagery, and self-monitoring.

Coping Strategies

Coping strategies are necessary when it's too late for preventive strategies or when preventive strategies are ineffective. In other words, athletes and, yes, even coaches, find themselves in an emotional mess. The 2000-pound gorilla is on their back. So now what can they do? Every athlete has been in this type of situation before. At this point the question is *How can they get out of this emotional mess?*

Deal With Burnout

Maslach and Jackson (1986) have assessed burnout in coaches and athletes using the Maslach burnout inventory (MBI). The MBI measures three characteristics of burnout: emotional exhaustion, depersonalization (detachment from others and possibly oneself), and a perceived decrease in personal accomplishment. To more clearly define burnout Freudenberger (1974) has proposed that it is comprised of three symptoms:

- *Biological and physical symptoms*—such as exhaustion, fatigue, predisposition to catching a cold, stomach complaints.
- *Behavioral and emotional symptoms*—such as irritability, depression, tendency to cry and shout, paranoid symptoms, enhanced risk behavior, cynicism.
- *Cognitive, social, and performance deficits*—such as inflexibility of thinking, ineffective prolonged working hours, social isolation.

Since your athletes feed off of your energy, it is important that you deal with burnout before your effectiveness and ability to lead your program diminishes. Some coping strategies for coaches include taking short breaks, doing things differently, getting a colleague to take practice occasionally, making time for vacations, talking with other coaches, learning new ideas on coaching, finding appropriate ways to vent emotions, learning stress management strategies, and finding ways to make practice more fun, not just for the athletes, but for the coach as well.

Kallus and Kellmann (2000) suggest a formula for calculating overtraining and burnout:

Prolonged stress + Insufficient recovery + Deficient coping = Burnout

Based on this formula and Maslach's characterization of burnout, some coping strategies for athletes include learning stress management strategies, getting more rest, shortening practices, taking a break once in a while, finding ways to have more fun in practice, putting their sport in perspective so that they feel less pressure from themselves and others, talking with teammates and friends, changing practice routines, having more input into their training, and learning additional individualized coping strategies.

Use Coping Strategies for MFS

In addition to the preceding strategies, coping with MFS includes taking an extended rest period accompanied by regular light exercise as well as incorporating intellectual challenges at approximate intervals and psychological stimulation to offset boredom and encourage mental revitalization (Henschen, 2000). Also, athletes should be encouraged to look for the good in their performances and training program and notice the improvements they have made at different points during the season.

Use Cognitive Monitoring and Restructuring

Sometimes athletes do things cognitively, which cause them to be emotionally imbalanced. For example, ruminating on negative aspects and thoughts eventually leads to depression and other dysfunctional emotions. Also, athletes can unconsciously connect with other dysfunctional emotions such as sorrow, distress, fear, and fatigue that impair their ability to perform. Consequently, athletes should monitor their cognition and employ a **stop technique**: When they find themselves ruminating, listening to negative thoughts, or plugging into negative emotions, they tell themselves to stop, recognize, and respond to negative thoughts and talk to themselves in strong and forceful terms until they redirect their focus on appropriate thoughts and emotions.

Also, cognitive restructuring is an important coping skill. **Cognitive restructuring** is the process of refuting cognitive distortions and faulty thinking that generate dysfunctional emotions and replacing them with rational thoughts and clear thinking that leads to healthier thoughts and functional emotions. For example, athletes who feel pressure to place well in competition so that other people will admire them should cognitively restructure why they compete, their purpose for participating in the sport, and their outcome goals. Another example is athletes who put their egos on the line. They should restructure their thinking to understand that their self-worth has nothing to do with how well they perform and they should become task oriented rather than ego oriented.

Resolve Inner Conflict

Problems, at least major problems, most often do not go away by simply ignoring them. Athletes should be encouraged to deal with these problems rather than ignore them and let them fester and grow into more virulent problems. Resolving inner conflict is important for sound mental, physical, and emotional health. Inner conflict resolution is important also for athletes becoming responsible, well-adjusted, and autonomous human beings. For example, when an athlete has an issue with another athlete on the team it is important for the athletes to learn to resolve the issue in a mature and responsible manner. If left unresolved the problem will lead to emotional imbalance and debilitating consequences such as fatigue (both physical and emotional), sickness, or impairing emotions (e.g., unhappy, depressed, sad, unmotivated). These consequences, brought about by emotional disequilibrium, can affect not only athlete training and motor performance but also team dynamics, motivation, and morale.

Express Emotions

Encourage your athletes to express their emotions. Expressing emotion has a cathartic healing effect that allows your athletes to feel better and connect with healthy functional emotions. Expressing emotion also lets others know how athletes are feeling. Without this expression, teammates and coaches can only guess. The best teams always seem to have an atmosphere in which athletes and coaches feel comfortable expressing their feelings. Finally, inviting athletes to express their feelings allows them to experience the emotion of empowerment and to grow as human beings.

Use Self-Talk

Sometimes the most persuasive voice you listen to is ultimately the one in your head. People talk to themselves all the time; it's important to tune into what they are telling themselves. Are they telling themselves the right things? Sometimes athletes are unconsciously their own worst enemy because they use destructive self-talk. For example, a former athlete would utter negative comments to herself after each dive. When I listened carefully I could hear her whisper statements such as "That was terrible" and "You dummy." The more she talked to herself, the worse she performed. After a few practices, I explained what she was doing and the impact her statements were having on her emotions and ensuing performances. As we talked, she indicated that this was something she also did outside of practice in other areas of her life. Together we formulated more positive and directive self-statements she could use inside and outside of practice. It wasn't easy for her to change because she tended to dwell on the negative, but she eventually turned things around and the positive effect it had on her performance was dramatic. She used forceful positive self-talk to cope with impairing emotions and generate enhancing emotions. That year she was the walk-on from Dyer, Indiana, made finals in two events at the conference championship, and narrowly missed finals on a third event, winning consolation finals.

Take Care of Body and Injuries

One day during his sophomore year of college, one of my athletes came to practice looking haggard. As we talked, he babbled on about something and then lost his train of thought and began talking about something else. He was an emotional mess and upset about some vague and nebulous problem. I am not sure why, but I finally asked him, "Jon, have you been sleeping all right?" He replied that he had not had a full night's sleep for almost 3 weeks. In fact, he was only getting about 2 or 3 hours of sleep each night. For the next few weeks we worked together to formulate a plan for improving his sleep pattern. The more his sleep pattern improved the more his diving improved.

Emphasize to your athletes the importance of taking care of themselves and the connection between good health and good emotions. Good emotions promote good health and good health promotes good emotions. Athletes who come to practice tired because they stayed up too late, hungry because they skipped breakfast to sleep a little longer, or injured because they didn't see the trainer for rehabilitation—these athletes are likely to experience impairing emotions such as fatigue, confusion, depression, and distress. Encourage your athletes to take personal responsibility for their physical, mental, and emotional wellness.

Practice Determined Coping

Determined coping refers to the ability to move beyond passive acceptance toward proactive channeling of knowledge, skill, and energy into overcoming injury, conflict, and other antecedent problems that affect emotions. Sometimes athletes like complaining about a problem more than they like solving it. Make sure your athletes don't carry problems around like excess baggage; it eventually drags them down. The same rule applies to you, too: If a problem exists, practice and model determined coping; use your knowledge, skill, energy, and available resources to resolve it—and leave your emotional baggage by the wayside. Determined coping can also be considered a preventative strategy because it keeps (prevents) the athlete from becoming emotionally stuck.

Filter Emotional Messages

Sport is an interesting social microcosm of the real world. There are always athletes, coaches, spectators, or parents who have an opinion, an idea, a suggestion, or a comment—sometimes a nice comment and sometimes a not-so-nice comment. Often accompanying these comments are emotions that send emotional messages. For example, the emotion can be pity: "Too bad you didn't make finals, but you did a good job anyway." (Emotional message: You don't have the ability to perform any better.) It can be jealousy: "Nice job today. Boy, the competition wasn't very good." (Emotional message: You aren't really that good. The competition was just weak.) Of course, the emotion can be positive. It can be certainty: "You didn't make finals. You need to train harder." (Emotional message: You have the ability to do much better.) It can be positive dissatisfaction: "I know you won but you can still perform better than that." (Emotional message: I believe in your potential for greatness.)

You and your athletes need to filter these emotional messages, listening to the ones that encourage enhancing emotions and ignoring the ones that engender impairing emotions. Avoid, ignore, or dismiss irrelevant emotional messages and tune into the positive and supportive emotional messages sent to you by the people who most care about you and have your best interest at heart.

Some years ago at a NCAA national championship, I observed a collegiate and U.S. Olympic coach verbally tear into one of his swimmers after she swam poorly in her evening finals event. His brutal honesty was shocking. He didn't hold back or sugarcoat a word he said. I thought, *What a jerk; she just lost the race and he should be kinder.* But then I noticed something peculiar: the swimmer's reaction. She wasn't upset. She stood there matter-of-factly, calmly, and patiently listening to her coach's comments. My mistake was that I was listening to her coach's verbal message while she was listening to his emotional message, which said: *I believe in you; you are better than that; you can perform at a higher level.* The next night she won her finals event.

Filter the emotional messages you send to your athletes with the language you use, especially after a big loss, heavy training cycle, setback, or other challenging period throughout the season. Your emotional message is far more potent than your verbal message in communicating what you really mean to say, so make sure your emotional message is indeed conveying what you truly want to tell your athletes. Also, habitually interpret the emotional messages athletes send to you and to each other so you keep your finger on your team's emotional pulse to ensure that all team members are sending and receiving appropriate emotional messages.

Change Body Language

You can often (but not always) sense athletes' emotional states by their walk, head position, shoulder movements, facial expressions, and other telltale signs. Athletes experiencing emotions such as resoluteness and determination have a certain commanding look on their faces that says they are in their emotional zone. Conversely, athletes experiencing emotions such as uncertainty and fear have an unmistakable countenance that says they are out of their emotional zone.

Sometimes, just having your athletes change their body language sends an intuitive appraisal message that can alter their emotions for the better. Lisa was an extremely talented athlete who eventually learned the difficult dives she needed for high-level competition. But even though she performed them easily, she remained uncertain and fearful of them and these emotions were interfering with her ability to execute them at a higher level. I told her that when she walked down the board she had an expression on her face as if she was about to be thrown out of an airplane without a parachute. I asked her to practice replacing this expression with one that communicated determination, confidence, resoluteness, and maybe a pinch of anger thrown in for good measure. Soon afterward, Lisa reached her lifelong goal of becoming an NCAA All-American in not one but two events that year. Changing body language is a surprisingly simple but effective strategy for positively influencing emotions and subsequent motor performance. Athletes easily comprehend and quickly imitate looks such as *resolute* and *determined*.

And what about *your* body language; what emotions do you convey to your athletes through your body language during practice and competition? During practice some coaches walk with slumped shoulders, sit through much of practice, or wear a look of disgust. This type of body language conveys to your athletes that you are bored, unmotivated, and uncaring. In contrast, coaches who are energetic, animated, and smiling convey the emotions enthusiastic, charged, and motivated. During competition body language is even more critical. Coaches with relaxed shoulders, bright eyes, and unhurried walk, for example, convey the emotions alert, confident, and purposeful. These emotions are particularly important during critical moments of competition when athletes must maintain similar emotions. In contrast, coaches who move frantically, yell at players, and wear a look of worry convey the emotions panic, concern, unsure, and distress.

Just like athletes, coaches can change their body language to change their emotional countenance and the emotional message they send their athletes. The three strategies for changing body language are observational learning, body language analysis, and mental imagery. *Observational learning* is the process of simply watching successful coaches and then imitating their body language. Hall of Fame football coach John Robinson's demeanor on the sidelines during a game was a thing of beauty to observe, especially when the game was on the line, there was a turnover, or his quarterback made a mistake. I learned a great deal about the power of body language from watching Coach Robinson. Other successful coaches may have body language that is different but equally worthy of imitation, so choose bits and pieces of body language that match your coaching personality.

Employ *body language analysis* by recording yourself coaching and then analyzing your behavior. Such an analysis can be painfully revealing but highly instructive. When my athletes watched replays of their dives, I would occasionally secretly observe my coaching behavior if I was in the background of the replay. On more than one occasion I observed myself exhibiting embarrassingly sloppy body language—an observation that made me quickly straighten up. You also can employ a coaching coach, someone who observes you coaching and makes recommendations. Atul Gawande (2011) has written an entertaining article about the need for experts such as surgeons to have coaches just as expert singers and professional athletes do. He asks, "So why not surgeons?" The same can be said about coaches of athletes.

Mental training is another strategy for changing body language. Visualize yourself behaving the way you want to behave when you are coaching. See yourself on the sideline, courtside, dugout, or another location and visualize the body language you want to portray to your athletes along with the emotions associated with those physical behaviors. Before competitions that I knew would be highly stressful, such as Olympic trials, Olympic Games, and world championships, I found it helpful preparation to visualize how I wanted to act and feel at the competition pool when coaching and interacting with my athletes and other coaches. I would post a picture of the facility on the wall next to the pool so my athletes and I could better visualize our behaviors at the competition venue.

Avoid Distractions (Focus on What's Important)

It is easy for human beings to get distracted by meaningless minutia. A former athlete liked to walk into my office and talk about everyone on the team. She knew exactly what everyone was doing wrong and what everyone should be doing differently. Her support of the program and her leadership were much appreciated, but to a point. She eventually would work herself into an emotional tizzy that appreciably degraded her ability to train. Sometimes people become preoccupied with the business of other people, insignificant things, or matters over which they have no control. After a while, focusing on all these distractions causes them to lose mental focus and emotional balance. It is much easier to maintain emotional balance when coaches and athletes keep it simple by focusing on what's important and controllable: yourself, your program, your performances, and your responsibilities. Don't become distracted by things outside your control.

THE EMOTIONAL ATHLETE

So, a picture of the emotional athlete comes into sharper focus. The **emotional athlete** is the athlete who is dialed in to enhancing individual emotions and able to keep these emotions in check during the heat of the battle, tough training bouts, episodes of defeat and disappointment, or the final minutes of the game. The emotional athlete takes the time to make objective reflective appraisals of antecedent information, prepares emotionally before competition, sets process goals, is task oriented rather than ego driven, and uses preventive and coping strategies to maintain emotional balance. In sum, the emotional athlete knows how to play the emotion game.

THE EMOTIONAL COACH

This chapter also has been about the emotional coach. The **emotional coach** sets the emotional tone for the team and program and acts as a role model by demonstrating emotional balance, stability, and control. It is difficult for an athlete to maintain emotional balance as the guns are firing during the heat of the battle if the coach is uncontrollably ranting and raving and far outside the individualized zone of optimal functioning for effective coaching. The emotional coach knows her enhancing emotions and the optimal range of functioning for these emotions. This coach practices preventive and coping strategies to keep the gorilla off her back. And this coach is adept at interpreting and sending appropriate emotional messages. Like the emotional athlete, the emotional coach plays the emotion game.

YOUR COACHING TOOLBOX

Emotion theory is another useful tool for your coaching toolbox. How useful is emotion theory? Strategies, game plans, periodization, biomechanics, and the like are all immeasurably important for motor performance success. But sometimes, it all comes down to an emotion like it did for Mike in the story at the beginning of this chapter. After all his hard work, dedication, sweat, and tears, his success came down to a single moment in time during his warm-up when he held his emotions in check just enough to tip the emotional scale in his favor.

Certainly, athletes don't win on emotion alone. When the 1980 U.S. Olympic hockey team defeated the juggernaut Soviet team it wasn't simply emotion that carried them to victory and the gold medal. They worked hard, came together as a team, and earned it. Victories are earned in the gym, weight room, court, track, pool, springboard, and so on. And games are won on the field of play. Still, emotions are part and parcel of the performance process, so understanding and using emotion theory helps coaches help their athletes play the emotion game and perform to their highest level, especially when it matters most.

THE SCIENTIFIC AND ARTFUL COACH

The scientific coach comprehends the significance of emotion theory and uses direct and indirect methods to help athletes establish appropriate performance emotions, zones of optimal functioning, and precompetitive anxiety levels. The scientific coach also teaches preventive and coping strategies for helping athletes stay in the zone.

The artful coach is attuned to athletes' emotional balance and senses when athletes are out of touch with their emotions and moving outside their zone of optimal functioning. Since variance between athletes in their individual zones of optimal functioning is slight, the artful coach keeps a finger on the emotional pulse of each athlete by noticing body language, facial expressions, behavioral changes, emotional messages, state-trait anxiety, and other indicators of emotional state.

Optimal emotions that work best for the individual athlete are mediated by intensity, form, time, and context. The scientific coach includes these dimensions when considering the selection and utilization of optimal emotions. The artful coach is sensitive to these dimensions and senses when one or more of the dimensions is less than optimal for the emotion. For example, an athlete's high emotional intensity might be appropriate for practice but inappropriate or ineffective for competition.

IF YOU REMEMBER ONLY THREE THINGS

1. *Remember to include the emotion factor.* Many factors contribute to successful performance—skill acquisition, endurance, flexibility, periodization, physical conditioning, coach–athlete relationship—but perhaps none contribute more than the emotion factor. The emotion factor matters most because it impacts all other aspects of training and competing. For example, athletes experiencing joy are more likely to bring a high level of energy and enthusiasm to their training, conditioning, competition performances, and interpersonal interactions. So, when you evaluate your program and your athletes, ask yourself, "Do we have the emotional makeup of a successful program?" "Are my athletes using enhancing emotions that work best for them?" "Are my athletes capable of maintaining their optimal range of emotions?" "Through my interpersonal interactions with my players, am I sending the appropriate emotional message?" Remember, it's not all about the Xs and Os. Emotion matters.

2. *Remember that you are the emotional leader of your team.* Your athletes feed off you emotionally. If you are upbeat and enthusiastic about your sport, practices, and competition, they will be also. If you want your athletes to maintain appropriate emotions and stay in their optimal zone, then you need to do likewise. For example, when game momentum

suddenly swings in your opponent's favor, you don't let your emotions get the best of you. You maintain your emotional composure and serve as an appropriate emotional role model for your athletes. When it looks like the ship might go down, you remain calm and steadfast at the helm.

3. *Remember the importance of appraisals in influencing emotion and behavior.* The best coaches and most successful athletes are adept at making accurate and optimistic reflective appraisals that lead to enhancing emotions and positive behavioral consequences. Even in defeat there can be victory—a ray of hope and a hint of promise for the future. Your athlete loses, but after the smoke clears the two of you sit down and see the positives: some small improvements that weren't there before, a slight change in performance and the athlete will be right in the midst of the battle, a lesson learned that improves future performance. Sometimes, it's all in how you look at things. Perhaps more important, these types of appraisals send the athlete a powerful emotional message: You will eventually succeed.

After a disastrous conference championship in which he finished last, I took one of my athletes behind the stands and in no uncertain terms told him his level of performance was unacceptable. I loved the kid like a son but I told him his performance was atrocious and far below his ability level. He would become a conference champion even if I had to strap him to my back and drag him there. The performance appraisal: awful and far below your potential. The emotional message: You will eventually succeed. The following year he was crowned conference champion.

SUGGESTED READINGS

Goleman, D. (1997). *Emotional intelligence: Why it can matter more than IQ*. New York: Bantam Books.

[An interesting read that highlights the impact of emotion on human thought and behaviors.]

Hanin, Y.L. (2000). *Emotions in sport*. Champaign, IL: Human Kinetics.

[A must read for any coach in any sport. This should be in your library.]

Jackson, S.A. & Csikszentmihalyi, M. (1999). *Flow in sports: The keys to optimal experiences and performances*. Champaign, IL: Human Kinetics.

[A wonderful guide for achieving emotional richness through engagement in sport.]

Marshall, P. (director). (1992). *A League of Their Own* [motion picture]. USA: Sony Pictures Home Entertainment.

[Manager Jimmy Dugan (Tom Hanks) barks at Evelyn, "There's no crying in baseball." Well, there is crying (emotion) in baseball—and every other sport. In a subsequent scene Jimmy is ready to again rip into Evelyn but thinks better of it. He controls his emotions and talks to her with more restraint resulting in her controlling her emotions and playing better. A number of scenes throughout the movie include emotional control (or lack of control) and development.]

Developing Your Coaching Skills and Philosophy

The final two chapters in part V discuss sometimes overlooked, but critical, considerations and applications for determining coaching effectiveness, success, and satisfaction. Chapter 10 examines how the *principled coach* can use an understanding of the three learning theories—behaviorism, cognitivism, and humanism—to apply preventive and corrective strategies for managing practice and athlete behaviors. The chapter offers some simple but effective applications for keeping the herd moving in the right direction as well as some techniques for dealing with athlete misbehaviors and disseminating punishment—something all coaches, even the most effective ones, must occasionally confront.

Chapter 11 concludes the book with a discussion of the *philosophical coach* and the importance of having a well-thought-out philosophy that guides you and every aspect of your program, such aspects as personal values, career goals, athlete development, decision making, team and athlete goal setting, and much more. The chapter offers some suggestions for creating your personal coaching philosophy and developing ethics within your philosophy. The chapter also considers another stage of cognitive development and how you can become the *wise coach*. The chapter concludes with a discussion of some values you may want to consider including in your philosophy.

CHAPTER 10

The Principled Coach

Applying Principles of Practice Management and Discipline

Key Terms

behavior modification	individualized practice plan	overlapping
dangles	jerky transitions	Premack principle
desist	lesson interruptions	principled coach
discipline	logical consequences	stimulus boundedness
flip-flops	management	three Rs
four Fs	natural consequences	thrusts
fragmentation	overdwelling	truncations
Grandma's rule		with-it-ness

Legendary UCLA basketball coach John Wooden spent as much time scripting his practices as he did running them (Gilbert et al., 2010). His practices ran like clockwork; every second mapped out and accounted for. This is not the case for basketball practice at Club Chaotic.

Club Chaotic is an East Coast club with talented high school students and plenty of potential. However, as its name suggests, practice at this club is chaotic and disorganized. It is filled with energy and activity, but it isn't going in any specific direction, like a windup car that races in random circles. Practice gets off to a slow start and many of the athletes don't seem to know what they are supposed to do. There is a confrontation between two upset teammates. Rather than coaching, the coach is trying to separate the two athletes while simultaneously trying to answer another athlete's question: "Coach, what do you want me to do for practice today?" The coach yells at a player and tells him to get busy. The coach does not look happy.

The next program you visit is Club Cool, a club in the Midwest, also with talented high school athletes and plenty of potential. At first glance, Club Cool looks just like Club Chaotic—same number of athletes, same number of coaches, same sport, same ages, same equipment, and lots of energy and activity. But something is different. In this program, all the energy and activity seems to be going somewhere specific, like a train on a track. It has a sense of order and underlying organization. Practice begins on time and the athletes have been divided into four groups; each group works on specific skills and drills. The head coach moves smoothly between groups, stopping briefly to observe, provide feedback, offer praise, and joke with players. Even though only two coaches are there for that day's practice, all players are busily engaged. Club Cool's practice has an atmosphere of joy and cooperation. Instead of yelling, the coach is quietly focused on the flow of practice activities and happy with the amount of learning that is occurring.

The flow of practice activities and the behavior of your athletes, especially if you have a large number of them, can be unpredictable and a wild ride, much like riding a bucking bronco. At every practice you are confronted with unpredictable variables and you must control these variables so that practice runs smoothly, efficiently, and productively. If you manage these variables, you tame the beast and a great deal of learning occurs. If you don't tame the beast, well, it's going to be a long day—and perhaps a long career.

Dealing with discipline problems is the least enjoyable part of coaching. It is the main reason teachers cite for teaching dissatisfaction and early retirement. Constantly yelling at athletes and being upset like the coach with Club Chaotic is definitely no fun. In fact, a lack of practice management skills keeps coaches from doing what they most likely entered the profession to do first and foremost: teach the sport they love and have fun working with young people.

It is especially unfortunate when an experienced coach quits the profession because of dissatisfaction in dealing with discipline problems. It is unfortunate because it is a loss for everyone involved: the sport, the athletes, and the coach. The sport loses a coach who recruited and developed new athletes. The athletes lose an accomplished coach who could impart knowledge based on experience, expertise, and wisdom gained from years of coaching. And the coach loses a profession that he or she once loved.

However, many coaches have learned to successfully bridle the beast. These coaches, like the coach with Club Cool, spend practice time providing instruction, doling out praise, directing the flow of practice, and generally enjoying the coaching process and the practice experience. This chapter is the story of the *principled coach*. It teaches you to use specific skills to bridle your athletes—to manage practice and effectively deal with inappropriate behaviors so that your practices run smoothly and enjoyably and you spend most of your time doing what you do best—coaching.

CHAPTER OVERVIEW

The chapter first defines the terms *management* and *discipline*. The terms are often used interchangeably but they are actually different. Then the chapter briefly examines some considerations for using management and discipline strategies. Next, it considers specific preventive strategies for managing your athletes and corrective strategies for dealing with athletes who misbehave. These strategies are associated with the three learning theories of humanism, cognitivism, and behaviorism. Along the way scenarios are inserted within the text to demonstrate how to apply specific strategies to real-life situations. The chapter concludes with some simple but effective cognitivistic and humanistic corrective strategies that are good rules to remember when it becomes necessary to administer punishment.

MANAGEMENT AND DISCIPLINE

People often use *management* as a euphemism for the term *discipline*. When you hear that a coach is a real disciplinarian, you might think that coach is good at managing the flow of practice activity. However, the two concepts have a distinct difference. **Management** is the arrangement of practice activities in order to facilitate teaching and learning. The coach from Club Cool ran smooth practices because of good management strategies. **Discipline** means coach actions made necessary by athlete behaviors that disrupt or threaten to disrupt practice activity. The coach from Club Chaotic spent most of practice time disciplining athlete misbehaviors. This chapter will help you learn how to spend most of your time managing your athletes rather than disciplining them.

I still remember my first day of student teaching: It was a sophomore class of all boys. My supervising teacher was more than excited, almost giddy, to let me take over the class for the remainder of the semester. Her parting words to me were "If you need anything, I'll be in the teachers' lounge." Need anything? I needed everything. I didn't have a clue about what I was doing or what I was in for. The minute I began speaking to the class a boy in the back started talking out loud to a friend. After some time, a few of the other boys in the back started talking so loud that the rest of the class couldn't hear what I was saying. And every time I asked them to be quiet, they got louder. Need anything? Yeah, I needed something—a gigantic ring buoy—because I was drowning in desperation.

At some point I gave the class a lame in-seat assignment so I could come up for air and have time to think. Well, maybe it wasn't think; it was more like *react*. I went over to the boy, who was obviously leader of the pack, and whispered in his ear, "If you don't shut up, I am going to beat the living daylights out of you after class!" My words had their desired effect. The boy never said another word in class that day. In fact, he never said another word the entire semester.

My actions were ethically inappropriate and morally and philosophically opposed to what I believe. And I terminated something very sacred that day—the student–teacher relationship. I entered the classroom prepared to teach a unit of curriculum. When the problem arose, I simply didn't know how to respond because I was ill-prepared emotionally and pedagogically to deal with misbehavior. Later, when I became a coach, there came a point in my career where I seriously reconsidered whether or not to continue coaching because of athlete behavioral problems. I stuck it out, and I'm glad I did, but I can see why some coaches choose not to.

All coaches eventually confront difficult athletes and inappropriate behaviors. How you deal with these athletes and their behaviors and how you learn to avoid these problems ultimately determines your coaching happiness and coaching effectiveness and perhaps whether or not you remain in the profession. This chapter provides some proven strategies for correcting inappropriate behaviors and surefire strategies for preventing inappropriate behaviors. Most people know the saying: *An ounce of prevention is worth a pound of cure.* The same can apply to practice management and discipline: *An ounce of preventive strategies is worth a pound of corrective strategies.* Prevention is a far easier and more effective approach for encouraging good behavior. These strategies will help you nurture the coach–athlete relationship and make your coaching experience successful, enjoyable, and rewarding; thereby keeping you for years to come in the sport you love.

Before examining preventive strategies, it is important to briefly examine some moral, ethical, philosophical, and educational aspects of practice management and discipline.

Ethical considerations refer to what is allowed by state laws, school policies, national governing body codes of conduct, club bylaws, and the like. Before you embark on a coaching career, or even if you have been coaching for some time, it is important that you familiarize yourself with these considerations.

Moral considerations are the things that you believe are acceptable and right. You need to ask yourself what you believe are right and wrong approaches to managing and disciplining your athletes. For this reason, it is important to have a well-thought-out coaching philosophy. Don't make the mistake I made my first day of teaching.

Philosophical considerations refer to what is appropriate within your philosophical approach to coaching, sport, competition, and working with athletes. Your philosophy should include the concept that athletics is a means to helping athletes grow and reach their greatest potential as both athletes and as human beings.

Finally, make *educational considerations*. It is important to remember the results of research conducted by Thorndike (1932, 1933). Based on his research, Thorndike asserted that reinforcement is more effective in stamping in a behavior than punishment is in eliminating a behavior. Punishment leads to suppression, not elimination, of a behavior and often negative feelings toward the person administering the punishing. For example, when I punished the boy on my first day of student teaching, he suppressed the inappropriate behavior and learned to hate me.

THE PRACTICE ENVIRONMENT

The practice environment is made up of many variables. At any one time you are required to manage athletes who are different from each other in many ways, such as their backgrounds, personalities, moods, perspectives, goals, and abilities. These athletes often interpret and react differently to different things at different times. You also are required to monitor and control the different drills, sets, rotations, scrimmages, interactions, and the like that occur during practice. Therefore, the key word to remember is *unpredictable* to describe the flow of practice events. From moment to moment anything can happen; both management and discipline are part of the ongoing coaching process.

Part of your job (challenge) as coach is to tame—bridle—your athletes by teaching them to elicit appropriate behaviors and avoid eliciting inappropriate behaviors. With this admonition in mind, the following sections look at two categories of strategies for effective practice management and discipline: preventive strategies and corrective strategies.

APPLYING PREVENTIVE STRATEGIES IN COACHING ATHLETES: HEADING THEM OFF AT THE PASS

So, you have your own team and you are preparing for practice. Maybe it is your first day as a coach. Now what? Head them off at the pass to prevent them from going in the wrong direction. In other words, prepare before practice and manage during practice so that you prevent as much as is humanly possible inappropriate behavior from occurring. Following are some preventive strategies affiliated with the learning theories behaviorism, cognitivism, and humanism along with specific examples of how you can apply these strategies in a practice setting.

Behavioristic Preventive Strategies

You can try several behavioristic strategies for preventing inappropriate behaviors. These strategies mainly use the operant conditioning principle of reinforcement, which was discussed in chapter 4. Perhaps the easiest and most effective way of preventing misbehavior is to reinforce positive behavior.

Reinforce Positive Behavior

A psychologically healthy approach to dealing with misbehavior is to positively reinforce correct behavior when it occurs. In other words, when you see an athlete finally demonstrate the appropriate behavior you have been waiting to see, reinforce that behavior. A positive reinforcer is any stimulus that when administered increases the probability that a response will recur. So, when you reinforce the appropriate behavior, the athlete is likely to elicit that behavior and may ignore the inappropriate behavior in the future. Respected coaches are able to use a number of extrinsic reinforcers such as smiles, praise, attention, scores, and times. Reinforcers are more effective when they are age-related. For very young athletes, tangible reinforcers such as stickers and treats are effective. For older athletes, social recognition reinforcers such as recognition award T-shirts or being named player of the week are more effective.

Set Rules

One of the easiest and most effective ways to prevent inappropriate behavior from occurring and consequently avoid having to administer discipline is to let your athletes know from day 1 of practice what is expected of them. When you communicate expectations, team rules, routines, and procedures, athletes understand what is expected of them and how they should behave. Unfortunately, some coaches do not communicate their expectations and rules for appropriate behavior. Often, athletes learn many rules indirectly after an infraction has occurred. Such a scenario creates bad feelings that are directed from the athlete toward the coach.

Pretend it is the beginning of a new season and you want to avoid the pervasive discipline problems inherent in your program last year. You felt like you did more disciplining than coaching last season and you want this season to be different. So you decide to get off to a better start by calling a team meeting at the first practice. At this meeting, you discuss team rules and ask your players if they would like to clarify or add any rules. Often your more committed players will want even more stringent rules. You then call a second team meeting and disseminate two copies of team rules and policies to each athlete. You ask each player to sign one copy, which you keep, and take the other copy home and post it where they can see it and be reminded of team rules. You also post a copy in the team locker room.

Effective coaches with smooth-running programs let their athletes know precisely what behaviors are acceptable and unacceptable. Perhaps even more important is that these same coaches monitor their players at the beginning of the season to make sure team rules are not only understood but obeyed and enforced. Athletes are more likely to demonstrate good behavior when they know exactly what that behavior is supposed to be and that inappropriate behavior will not be tolerated. Also, if they do misbehave, they are more accepting of the penalties and less likely to direct animosity toward you because they knew beforehand what was expected of them.

Some coaches mistakenly think that if they ignore certain misbehaviors the misbehaviors will disappear, or if they occasionally deal with an infraction that everything will be all right. When you arbitrarily enforce team rules, you send a message to your athletes that team rules don't need to be consistently adhered to. For example, a player is blatantly disrespectful to another team member, which is a violation of the team rule regarding player conduct. A team rule has been overtly broken. If you do nothing, you send a message to your players that team rules don't matter. You must respond and do so swiftly to send an unequivocal message to all team players: Team rules matter and will be consistently enforced. Make your rules clearly understood and consistently enforce them early on. Your effort in the early season will go a long way toward making for smooth-sailing practices and eliminating the need for administering much discipline throughout the season.

Although it is important to enforce rules, enforcement isn't always so simple or clear cut. For example, consider scenario 1. It might be simple to say, "Well, the rule is *this* and your punishment is *that*." On the one hand, the situation is what it is and nothing can be changed. On the other hand, you have a situation in which a senior athlete, who up to this point has been a model athlete, has now broken a rule. Her parents are flying in and it is senior recognition day. What do you do? I am not trying to tell you what you should do, but the point here is that sometimes you have to be *pragmatic* in following team rules and administering punishment.

Scenario 1

Your hardest working athlete, who never misses practice, accidentally oversleeps because she was up late studying for her final exam. You have a team rule that states if an athlete misses practice during the week he or she cannot compete in competition that week. This week's competition is also senior day, where senior athletes and their parents are recognized before the game. Your hardest working athlete who missed practice happens to be a senior and her parents are flying in for the presentation.

I use this scenario because something similar happened to me. I was torn because I thought the athlete made an honest mistake and for a good reason: studying for a final exam. She was an outstanding student and a hardworking and dedicated athlete; maybe not the best athlete on the team but an athlete who made us a better team by her presence. I didn't want to overlook her years of effort and commitment to me and the program and I didn't want to end our relationship on a sour note. However, I also wanted to make sure the team understood that team rules are consistently enforced. In this case, I let the team know that she would have to come in early the next morning to make up the missed practice before she could participate in the competition. I also reminded them of her previous perfect attendance, daily leadership, and academic achievements and that I would make similar exceptions for athletes who demonstrated like behaviors and comparable academic achievements.

Sometimes situations decree that coaches act as King Solomon, making wise decisions by simultaneously enforcing rules while being sensitive to situational nuances—yet another reason why coaching is both an art and a science.

Use Legitimate Praise

A simple way to prevent inappropriate behavior is to praise appropriate behavior. Remember Thorndike's admonition that reinforcement is more effective in stamping in a behavior than punishment is in eliminating a behavior. Therefore, when you observe the kind of behavior you hope to see, take notice and praise the athlete's behavior. It is important, however, to use legitimate praise. In other words, your praise needs to be associated with a specific behavior. For example, instead of saying, "That was good," say, "That was good the way you waited your turn in line." Effective coaches purposefully arrange situations where they can make use of legitimate praise.

In scenario 2 you have an athlete who skips stretching at the end of practice. You can handle this situation in a number of ways, but in this case you decide to wait for the moment when the athlete stretches after practice and then offer legitimate praise by saying, "Hey, good job of stretching. That will really help your performance." This method falls within the category of *catch them being good*. After using this legitimate praise for several practices, the athlete stretches routinely after every practice.

Scenario 2

You have an athlete you really like but he habitually skips stretching at the end of practice even though that is an important time to stretch and stretching is something that will improve his ability to perform. You have talked with him about the advantages of stretching and he has agreed to do it, but he can't seem to include it in his daily routine. You know him well enough to know that he wants to do it.

Use the Premack Principle

Another preventive strategy that uses reinforcement is called the **Premack principle** (Premack, 1965), also sometimes referred to as **Grandma's rule**, which is *Eat your peas and carrots and then you can have dessert.* The Premack principle states that frequently occurring behaviors can be used to reinforce less-frequently occurring behaviors. Parents, teachers, and coaches frequently use this principle. A child is allowed to have dessert after helping with the dishes. A student is allowed to read a favorite book after finishing an assignment. A baseball player is allowed to hit in the batting cage after completing wind sprints.

Cognitivistic Preventive Strategies

Kounin (1970) has identified several teacher behaviors related to successful classroom management that are more likely to encourage appropriate student behaviors. These teacher behaviors can be translated into coach behaviors. They are cognitivistic in their approach because they require the coach to continually cognitively monitor the flow of practice activities and athlete behaviors. These behaviors also encourage athletes to remain cognitively engaged during practice activities.

With-It-Ness

Effective coaches are more aware than less effective coaches of everything that is continually happening during practice. This constant awareness is what Kounin calls **with-it-ness**. For example, these coaches know when it is time for an athlete to move on to a different skill, drill, or set. They detect a small problem before it becomes a major discipline problem. They keep track of what each athlete is doing, which is no easy feat, and direct an athlete when she gets off track. In other words, these coaches are *with it*.

With-it-ness may seem a somewhat vaguely defined term. However, one specific coach behavior associated with the concept is the use of a desist. A **desist** is a verbal command to an athlete to stop engaging in some off-task behavior. Along with this desist, effective coaches also suggest some alternative on-task behavior (rather than simply ask the athlete to stop an off-task behavior), praise on-task behavior while ignoring off-task behavior, and give instructions for desirable behaviors. In contrast, ineffective coaches tend to ask the wrong athlete to desist or they administer the desist either too late, after an inappropriate behavior has been occurring for some time, or too early, before a misbehavior has actually occurred.

In a study conducted by Copeland (1987), the most successful teachers were associated with high teacher vigilance and attentiveness. Consequently, perhaps the best advice for achieving coaching with-it-ness is to remain vigilant and attentive throughout the course of practice. This cognitive effort on your part will deter inappropriate behaviors and allow you to spend most of your time coaching rather than responding to inappropriate behaviors.

Overlapping

Kounin suggests that successful teachers are capable of dealing with several matters occurring at one time, a situation called **overlapping**. Overlapping occurs in two situations. The first situation is when a desist is required in the course of a lesson. The second situation is when something intrudes on the flow of the lesson.

Perhaps one of the greatest management demands on coaches during a practice is simultaneously dealing with several issues. In a sense, overlapping is connected to with-it-ness. A successful coach has to be aware of everything going on during a practice. However, overlapping occurs when the coach simultaneously has to deal with several matters while keeping the flow of practice activity moving in the right direction. Maintaining the flow of practice is particularly important when you have limited practice time, a large team, or different ability levels and ages. Effective coaches want to squeeze as much out of practice time as possible because practice is where athletes get the job done, where they put in the hard work, and where they prove themselves so they can prove it in competition.

As a coach you have probably witnessed or even participated in practices as a former athlete where players weren't doing what they needed to be doing. Things fall apart quickly as they did for the coach of Club Chaotic at the beginning of this chapter. According to the principle of overlapping, the successful coach, like the skilled juggler keeping many balls in the air, has the ability to simultaneously oversee multiple aspects of practice.

Smoothness and Momentum

The flow of practice activity can be rapid and unpredictable, but the successful and prepared coach keeps the pace of practice activity flowing smoothly, which means that besides being with-it and dealing with overlapping issues, the successful coach must make sure that transitions between practice activities occur smoothly. From studying classroom activities, Kounin (1970) has found that a typical day includes an average of more than 33 major changes in learning activities, and these changes do not include nonacademic changes such as going to recess or lunch. Transitions occur in the typical sport practice as well. For example, a coach might begin practice with a stretching session, then transition to a brief lecture, then move on to a demonstration, then skill work, drills, physical practice, team meeting, and more.

As Kounin suggests, effective teachers have smooth transitions that maintain the momentum of classroom activities. Effective coaches do the same thing. In contrast, ineffective coaches tend to be unsure of what should come next in the course of a practice. Most of the time these coaches let the flow of practice activity take its own random and unpredictable course. These coaches are really *managers of practices* rather than *directors of athletes*. They simply react to and manage what serendipitously occurs in practice rather than dictate the direction, pace, and flow of athlete activity.

Kounin reports that slowdowns or interruptions, what he calls **jerky transitions** and **lesson interruptions**, are among the principal causes of students' inattentiveness, restlessness, and misbehavior. It is common for novice coaches to get stuck on one or two activities and never complete the remainder of their intended practice activities. They tell their players at the beginning of practice that practice will consist of six activities but, because of interruptions and late transitions, their players engage in only two or three of the planned activities. For the effective coach, this scenario is the exception; for the ineffective coach, it is the rule.

Kounin describes several slowdowns or interruptions that he noticed in his observations of classroom activities. These same jerky transitions can be identified as slowdowns or interruptions in athletic practices.

- **Stimulus boundedness**. Some outside stimulus interrupts the coach's attention. For example, someone approaches the coach and says there is a phone call. The effective coach says, "Take a message." The ineffective coach takes the call. With some programs, this scenario might occur on a regular basis. Many inferior coaches commonly carry their cell phones during practice, answering phone calls and returning text messages, all the while trying unsuccessfully to keep up with the flow of practice. Institute a no-cell-phone policy during practice for coaches and athletes.

- **Dangles**. The coach interrupts an ongoing activity and then returns to it again. For example, the coach is in the middle of teaching a young basketball player a new skill and unexpectedly walks to the other side of the court and begins talking with an assistant coach. After leaving the athlete dangling, the coach later returns to the player, but the earlier momentum has been lost. The player has lost focus and can't remember exactly what the coach was saying. So the coach has to take valuable practice time to reestablish momentum. Practice activities and interactions with your athletes are sacred. Honor this sacredness by avoiding unnecessary and needless interruptions.

- **Thrusts**. The coach interrupts athletes' activities without prior signal and without consideration for their readiness. For example, a coach gives athletes a drill and asks them to practice it but as they do so the coach begins talking about something disassociated with the drill. Avoid thrusts by being conscious of on-task athlete behaviors.

- **Truncations**. The coach is interrupted and then does not return to the original activity afterward. For example, the soccer coach tells everyone to line up and begin passing drills and then starts conversing with another coach. After her conversation, the coach tells everyone to begin sprint drills. The coach is thinking, *Why don't they do what they are supposed to do?* And the athletes are thinking, *Why doesn't she make up her mind?* Eliminate truncations by avoiding interruptions and following your practice plan.

- **Flip-flops**. These slow-downs occur when the coach makes a transition from one activity to a second activity and then switches back to the first activity, as though he has changed his mind. For example, the gymnastics coach tells his players that Tuesday will be beam and bar day, but when his athletes arrive on Tuesday prepared to practice beam and bar, he tells them they will be working on floor and vault. Then, midway through practice he instructs them to go to beam and bar. The transition not only ruins the flow of practice activity but also conveys to the athletes that the coach is unsure of what to do. It is important to avoid flip-flops. However, if it becomes necessary to make such a reversal, it is prudent to explain to your athletes why the switch is occurring. For example, the gymnastics coach might gather his athletes for a brief meeting and say, "I know I told you yesterday that we would be practicing beam and bar today, however, something has come up and we won't be able to use the spring floor tomorrow so we are going to work on our floor routines today."

• **Overdwelling**. The coach spends an unnecessary and inordinate amount of time opining on something such as an aspect of the sport, a particular motor skill, or an athlete's misbehavior. This overdwelling results in bogging down the pace of practice. Elite athletes hate this momentum killer. Make your point; they get it; get back to practice. A good communicator doesn't need to keep hammering away at a point. Some coaches halt practice and then ramble and repeat themselves until they eventually lose their train of thought. At this point, practice momentum has slowed to a crawl and it is easy for athletes to cool down physically, mentally, and emotionally.

• **Fragmentation**. Fragmentation occurs when the coach breaks down an activity or a group of athletes in such a way that the athletes are required to spend most of their time waiting to do something. Fragmentation is a common coaching error for ineffective coaches. When my son played soccer, 12 players would be placed in 2 groups of 6 and 2 players would dribble the ball back and forth down the field while the other 10 players stood and watched. Because each player brought a ball to practice, the team could easily have been divided into 6 groups of 2 so that each player was engaged for the duration of the activity.

Some coaches unconsciously or perhaps consciously use fragmentation as a means for slowing down the pace of practice and making their job less effortful. It takes much more vigilance, attentiveness, and with-it-ness to coach 12 soccer players simultaneously passing and dribbling the ball than it does to coach 2 players passing and dribbling the ball. Fragmentation is a concern for all coaches, but particularly for those who have large teams or limited practice time. As a coach, maximize your time by keeping your athletes constantly engaged in practice activities. The more they wait in line, the less they accomplish. Avoid fragmentation and maintain smoothness and momentum by breaking down activities and grouping athletes so as many players as possible are simultaneously active.

Maintain Focus

One way to prevent behavior problems is to keep athletes cognitively focused. Maintain focus by providing each athlete with an **individualized practice plan** (IPP) which outlines specific practice activities and goals for these activities. Before each practice (it might be the night before, or when driving to the practice venue, or while your athletes are stretching), review each athlete's previous practice and some of the things he needs to work on for the current practice. Then, before they begin provide each athlete with a written or verbal IPP of what his practice will entail. By providing an IPP, athletes are more likely to maintain focus and less likely to engage in inappropriate behavior. If there are several athletes with similar practice plans, ask them to work as a group and help coach each other. Group work encourages cooperation, team unity, fun, and a break from the daily coach–athlete routine. It also promotes responsibility-taking and a sense of ownership ("This is my team and I take an active role as a member of the team.").

Lay a Solid Foundation

Perhaps the best way to prevent misbehavior and encourage appropriate behavior is to lay a solid foundation from the first day of practice. Grossnickle and Sesko (1990) offer a list of 10 guidelines for establishing classroom management. These guidelines can be translated into relevant guidelines for practice management. The following guidelines include some points already discussed but worth repeating.

- *Establish clear behavior guidelines.* Expectations, standards, and rules should be clear to coaches, athletes, and parents. A parent meeting is useful in answering any questions parents might have regarding rules, expectations, standards, and operating procedures.

- *Adopt a teamwork approach.* The head coach, assistant coach, board members, and parents are a team and should support, follow, and enforce all team rules and regulations.

- *Design a complete discipline ladder.* This ladder is a clear description of corrective disciplinary action and the order in which the actions will be enforced. An example of a discipline ladder might look like this: After two infractions the athlete receives a warning; after the third infraction there is a coach–athlete meeting; after the fourth infraction there is a call and meeting with the parents; after the fifth infraction the athlete is suspended from the team; finally, with the sixth infraction the athlete is dismissed from the team.

- *Teach self-management and self-discipline.* As mentioned in the chapter on humanism, one of your coaching goals should be to help your athletes develop as people. Learning self-management and self-discipline is a part of this development. As athletes develop as people, they become more self-regulatory.

- *Invite good behavior.* As a coach, you invite good discipline in a number of ways: by modeling good behavior, reinforcing good behavior, and creating a climate that engenders good behavior.

- *Focus on athlete successes and self-esteem.* In their zeal to help players improve and reach greater performance heights, coaches often look solely at what their athletes do wrong and not what they do right. Take time to notice and praise what your athletes do right and their successes. Elevate self-esteem by providing positive feedback about them as individual people, offering them challenging but attainable practice goals, and emphasizing effort.

- *Implement firm, fair, and calm enforcement.* Rules and procedures don't mean much to your athletes if they aren't consistently and judiciously enforced but how you implement enforcement says much about you and your approach to working with human beings.

- *Plan and implement specific practice activity.* Much has already been said about this guideline in the preceding sections on smoothness, momentum, and maintaining focus.

- *Continually monitor the practice environment.* This guideline refers to good coaching traits such as with-it-ness and overlapping.

- *Manage problems early.* Essentially, this entire section on preventive strategies is about early detection and intervention. As any experienced coach will tell you, it is infinitely easier to deal with a problem early when it is a small problem, rather than later when it has escalated into a full-blown catastrophe. Unfortunately, inexperienced and unsuccessful coaches often ignore these small problems, hoping the problems will magically disappear. Then, before they know it, the monster has reared its ugly head.

Humanistic Preventive Strategies

Marland (1975) lists a number of specific classroom management strategies and teacher characteristics and behaviors that contribute to a humanistic approach to teaching and help prevent misbehavior in the classroom. These characteristics also can be applied to coaching and preventive measures in the practice setting. These strategies are considered humanistic because they emphasize the individual athlete, affect, athlete self-development, and a supportive environment.

Caring for Athletes

Perhaps the best preventive strategy for deterring inappropriate behavior is genuinely caring for your athletes and communicating and demonstrating your concern and empathy. There are many ways to show that you care about your athletes. Meeting individually with them, getting to know them as individuals, seeking information about them and their families, helping them with problems, being responsive to their questions and concerns, and showing an interest in them and what they do both at practice and outside of practice are all examples of explicitly demonstrating a caring attitude toward your athletes. Perhaps the best form of caring is simply having an attitude of wanting to see your players do well and succeed both as athletes and as human beings.

Take time to listen to your athletes and get to know them. For example, after you conduct your first team meeting, you post a sign-up sheet and have your athletes select a time when they can meet with you. At these meetings, you spend one-on-one time listening to their comments and stories, getting to know them as individuals, understanding their goals and dreams and anything else they want to share with you.

Use Humor

Over the years I have come to believe that humor is one of the most powerful preventive strategies for maintaining good behavior. The best teams seem to have an abundance of it and the worst teams have a dearth of it. There are several compelling reasons for using humor.

Humor helps create a relaxed, friendly, and productive training atmosphere that invites good behavior and promotes learning. The benefits of humor in the practice environment are often overlooked perhaps because some coaches and athletes erroneously believe that seriousness translates into dedication, determination, focus, and success. I am quite convinced that coaches and athletes can laugh and have fun and concomitantly be dedicated, determined, focused, and successful. One effective way to promote humor is for you to learn to laugh at yourself and your mistakes, imperfections, and foibles. When you laugh at your errors you let your athletes know you are imperfect but open, honest, and genuine. You also model the self-deprecating humor and modesty you hope your athletes will imitate.

Consider scenario 3, in which you are caught making the very same mistake you have been railing at your athletes to stop making. You are definitely at fault, busted by one of your own athletes. What do you do? In this situation you decide to use the preventive strategy of humor. You announce to your athletes, "Can you believe I just did that? I can't! I am putting myself in time-out." And then you put a chair in a corner and sit there for 5 minutes while your players laugh at your statement and behavior. Nicely done coach.

Scenario 3

You have been harping at your players for the past 2 weeks to pay more attention to your comments and be better listeners and learners. Oftentimes they remember only half of what you tell them. You are frustrated and have told them that if they forget what you tell them to do you are going to dismiss them from practice. During today's practice one of your better players, who appears agitated and upset, points out that you forgot what correction you gave her earlier and you also forgot to watch her next attempt to see if she made the correction—which she did. She definitely has a point and you definitely made the same mistake your athletes have been making for the past two weeks. So, now what do you do?

Besides keeping practice fun, humor has the added touch of keeping things in perspective. Although goals are important, sometimes people take things— and themselves—far too seriously. Humor has a way of keeping coaches and athletes from hyper-focusing, obsessing, and ruminating on things such as goals, medals, outcomes, and winning. You may want to achieve major breakthroughs in practice, train hard, focus, and win a championship, but don't forget that you coach the game and your athletes play the game for the love of it and for the fun of it. It is a privilege, not a right, to play, so be grateful for the opportunity to participate in the sport. Humor helps maintain this perspective.

Humor also helps coaches and athletes stay loose during practice and competition. Sometimes, a simple joke can help everyone relax and smile. At competitions, especially championships, humor can be in short supply for some teams. You have probably witnessed coaches and athletes who are wound up so tight emotionally, physically, and mentally that they had the deer-in-the-headlights look about them. These coaches often have a serious and stern countenance, pursed face, and arms folded across their chests. One night I was at the finals for the women's 10-meter synchronized event at the USA Diving national championship, which also served as the World Cup trials. My two athletes were ranked first heading into the finals. So besides it being finals, the national championship, and qualification for the world championship (only first place would qualify for the world team), they had the added pressure of being the front runners. Tension was definitely in the air but during warm-up we spontaneously started joking and laughing. They held on to win and qualify for the World Cup (a precursor to the 2012 Olympic Games) in London, England.

When everything goes wrong and things can't possibly get any worse, even then, humor has its place. When defeat, failure, and absolute and utter annihilation are inevitable, you have two choices: laugh or cry. Humor has restorative power, so choose laughter. Often referred to as *gallows humor*, this type of humor is used during stressful and traumatic situations when great loss is unavoidable. (As the condemned prisoner walks toward the electric chair, he asks the warden, "Are you sure this thing is safe?") If athletes (and coaches) can laugh at failure, then failure becomes much less devastating. And if failure loses its sting, then athletes become more emboldened in future competitions.

Finally, humor also serves as a mechanism for diffusing potentially explosive confrontations. A negative situation often can be brought back into emotional and cognitive perspective and a confrontation avoided by finding the lighter side of the situation. It is easy for athletes—and coaches—to lose patience and find themselves in confrontation. Maybe it is an intense practice during your heavy training phase. Your athletes are physically, mentally, and emotionally broken down. Suddenly, things get intense between two of your athletes. Without hesitating, you say something lighthearted and funny and just as suddenly everyone laughs and goes back to practice. Use humor as a preventive strategy.

Shape the Practice Environment

The practice environment and coach–athlete interactions can facilitate or block good practice discipline. Marland (1975) suggests that personalizing the learning environment will encourage good behavior and therefore it will help prevent discipline problems. While these suggestions are aimed at a typical classroom, they can easily be applied to a practice setting.

You can personalize the practice environment in many ways. For example, something as simple as a bulletin board can help create a positive practice environment. Hanging up newspaper articles, photos, letters, and other items about your athletes on the bulletin board personalizes the practice environment. Other ways to personalize the environment include allowing athletes to play their favorite music, displaying motivational quotes, hanging team banners, posting a picture of the athlete of the week, and creating personalized team t-shirts.

The practice environment encompasses more than just the physical properties. The practice environment includes the climate or atmosphere in which athletes practice. This climate should be warm, friendly, positive, and accepting; it should be a climate in which all athletes are seen as capable and are encouraged to reach their greatest potential as athletes and human beings. This type of climate encourages good behavior and thereby helps prevent inappropriate behavior (Glasser, 1969). The converse is also true. A cold, authoritarian climate can impede good behavior and encourage inappropriate behavior.

This climate should also value and encourage cooperation between coach and athlete and among athletes so that everyone associated with the program is supporting and supported. Athletes need to know that if they want supportive teammates, then they themselves need to be supportive teammates in return. Promote cooperation by valuing cooperation and modeling cooperative behavior. For example, have athletes set team goals, and use peer tutoring. The practice climate also should value and encourage athletes to engage in self-management. Encourage self-management by talking about and emphasizing personal responsibility. Engage your athletes in activities such as establishing personal goals, evaluating their performances, and selecting daily practice goals.

Develop Character

From a humanistic perspective, perhaps the best way to prevent bad behavior and encourage good behavior is through the development of character in your athletes. Character has to do with the goodness of people; the values, moral strength, principles, virtues, and ethics that profoundly influence how they make decisions, resolve conflict, interact with others, treat people, and generally behave.

While science might consider character a vague and ill-defined term, the next chapter defines the terms values, morals, and ethics and suggests that the building blocks for success include human characteristics such as loyalty, cooperation, friendship, and self-control and that these blocks are held together with the mortar of integrity, reliability, honesty, and sincerity. Teams that are highly disciplined, consistently exhibit good behavior, and maintain traditions of success are teams with character. This development and maintenance of character doesn't happen by accident, but rather it happens by choice—coaches teaching more than winning; coaches teaching values, principles, and ethics.

The following list summarizes the behavioristic, cognitivistic, and humanistic preventive strategies in coaching athletes.

Preventive Strategies

Behavioristic Preventive Strategies

Reinforce positive behavior

Set rules

Use legitimate praise

Use the Premack principle

Cognitivistic Preventive Strategies

With-it-ness

Overlapping

Smoothness and momentum

Maintain focus

Lay a solid foundation

Humanistic Preventive Strategies

Caring for athletes

Use humor

Shape the practice environment

Develop character

APPLYING CORRECTIVE STRATEGIES IN COACHING ATHLETES: WHEN IT'S TOO LATE TO HEAD THEM OFF AT THE PASS

In a perfect world, all behavior problems would be preventable. Unfortunately, coaches live in the real and imperfect world. In their training environments, coaches must deal with a variety of people who are at different levels of emotional maturity, self-regulation, and self-discipline. Whether you like it or not, you can't always tame or bridle the beast or head them off at the pass. In other words, you can't prevent all bad behavior. You will inevitably have to confront athletes about their inappropriate behaviors, even if you are the most successful and most prepared coach in the world. These problems may vary in their degree of severity, from the simple to the most complex of problems, and how you manage these problems will directly affect the quality of your program, your coaching effectiveness, and your long-term enjoyment of your chosen profession.

So, you are a successful coach and you have done everything possible to prevent misbehavior on your team, but you are suddenly confronted with a misbehavior that for the good of your program simply cannot be ignored. You must act now or you will lose the team's confidence and faith in you and, quite possibly, also lose control of the team. In dealing with these misbehaviors and the athletes involved, there are several guidelines to follow.

- *First, your actions must be within the legal boundaries of your state and in accordance with the regulations and code of your sport.* For example, getting upset and hitting an athlete would not only be inappropriate, unethical, and opposed to your personal coaching philosophy but also would be grounds for a lawsuit and suspension from coaching.

- *Second, whatever actions you take must be done in the best interest of the athlete, with consideration of the athlete's self-esteem and humanity.* For example, you would want to discipline an athlete in a way that would neither embarrass nor humiliate him or her.

- *Third, whatever disciplinary actions you take should be done for the greatest interest of the team.* Sometimes, disciplinary action is necessary to maintain a positive training atmosphere and team cohesiveness. For example, if an athlete does not follow team policies or doesn't give the effort and commitment other teammates give, that athlete may need to be disciplined or dismissed for the betterment of the team, even if it is your top athlete.

The following sections examine different corrective strategies based on the learning theories of behaviorism, cognitivism, and humanism.

Behavioristic Corrective Strategies

Whereas the goal of preventive strategies is to prevent certain behaviors from occurring, the goal of corrective discipline is to change or eliminate an inappropriate behavior that has already occurred. Reinforcement and punishment are the most common strategies for corrective discipline. Consequently, corrective discipline strategies use the principles of operant learning theory outlined in chapter 4. These strategies collectively make up what is called **behavior modification**, which is the use of behavioral learning principles to change human behavior. This section provides a brief recap of the behavioristic tools at a coach's disposal for reshaping athlete behavior and taking disciplinary action.

Shape Behavior

Reinforcement is an effective corrective strategy because it rewards athletes when they elicit appropriate behaviors and encourages them to repeat those behaviors and similar behaviors. Sometimes, however, athletes never elicit the appropriate behavior you are hoping to see. When this occurs, it is necessary to shape behavior. Recall that shaping may be defined as the differential reinforcement of successive approximations. In other words, shaping is the process of reinforcing the individual for every behavior that brings him or her closer to the desired behavior.

Because you may not see the exact desired behavior in the beginning, you shape the athlete's behavior by reinforcing a behavior that is somewhat close to the behavior you hope to ultimately see. You continue to reinforce each behavior that brings the person closer to the desired behavior. For example, assume that one of your athletes habitually arrives late for practice. It is annoying and unfair to all the other team members who arrive on time. You have repeatedly talked with the athlete with little success. You decide to use shaping to change your athlete's behavior. Using the strategy of shaping, you praise the athlete when he arrives 15 minutes late instead of 30 minutes late. Next, you reinforce the athlete when he arrives only 10 minutes late. Then you reinforce for being only 5 minutes late, then being on time, and, finally, when he arrives early for practice. This strategy works well with many athletes, particularly young athletes. It does not, however, work well for an egregious behavior that demands an immediate and forceful response.

Negative Reinforcement

Negative reinforcement is the relief from some sort of aversive stimulus, such as the threat of punishment, failure, ridicule, and other unpleasant consequences. Some coaches use this type of reinforcement like the sword of Damocles: a potentially fatal occurrence hanging constantly over the athlete's head. In some instances negative reinforcement may be necessary to contain an athlete's actions and regain discipline. In the short run this can be an effective tool but in the long run it can create an unproductive learning environment filled with tension, animosity, and mistrust. It also is not an effective corrective response for misbehaviors that necessitate an immediate response.

Extinction

Another concept related to behavior modification and corrective strategies is extinction. According to the principles of behavior modification, responses maintained by reinforcement often can be eliminated through the complete withdrawal of reinforcement (extinction). For example, a coach may be inadvertently reinforcing an athlete's disruptive behavior in practice by paying attention to the athlete each time the behavior occurs. Or, let's say you are conducting a team meeting and an athlete constantly interrupts you when you are talking. Besides distracting the team and you, the behavior is disrespectful and needs to cease. Extinction is an easy and often painless solution for behavior problems. In the case of the interrupting athlete, you may be able to eliminate the athlete's disruptive behavior by simply ignoring it. Even though it is an easy and effective strategy, extinction does not always work. And, sometimes, particularly with highly inappropriate behaviors, more immediate and direct action becomes necessary.

Presentation Punishment (Castigation)

Although there are negative aspects of presentation punishment (castigation), there are occasions when this type of punishment is appropriate, necessary, and effective. Research on punishment suggests three effective forms of punishment that do not carry the disadvantages and side effects of physical punishment. These forms of punishment previously outlined in chapter 4 are reprimands, time-outs, and response cost. When you feel compelled to administer punishment, remember to use these forms. Consider scenario 4, in which an athlete doesn't look at you when you are coaching him.

Scenario 4

One of your athletes performs a skill and then doesn't look at you while you provide feedback. You have asked him to look at you after each attempt but he continues to look away. It makes providing feedback difficult because by the time he does look at you, you have already missed another athlete's performance. Moreover, because he isn't looking at you, you aren't sure if he heard what you said. More important, his behavior is rude and disrespectful and makes you look bad in front of your team. To maintain the respect of your athletes and lead your team you need to discipline the athlete.

You have tried reinforcing the athlete in scenario 4 when he doesn't look at you. You have tried reinforcing another athlete (model) for looking at you. You have reasoned with him. You have tried to shape an appropriate behavior. You have tried ignoring the behavior to extinguish it. You have tried nearly everything. The athlete's behavior is rude and disrespectful and you have a right, not just as a coach, but as a human being, to be treated with dignity—just as your athletes do. Beyond that, either the behavior desists or you lose control of your team. Consequently, you decide to punish him. The next time he displays his rude behavior, you admonish him publicly (reprimand). If he does it again, you tell him to sit out of practice (time-out) for 15 minutes. If it happens again, he is not allowed to travel with the team to the next competition (response cost). This may seem like a strategy for young athletes but I have used it with collegiate divers.

Never Use Your Sport as a Source of Punishment

Never use practice or other sport-related activities as punishment. Recall from chapter 3 that it is never a good idea to connect your sport to an unpleasant stimulus such as punishment. This should go without saying, except that it is an all-too-common practice for some teachers and coaches. Examples of this scenario include the English teacher who punishes a student by making her write, the gym teacher who punishes the student by making him run laps, and the tennis coach who punishes an athlete by making her hit serves after practice. Remember, one of the things coaches want to teach their athletes, besides techniques and good performances, is a passion and love for their sport. When pairing your sport with punishment, you risk conditioning your athletes to dislike your sport.

Removal Punishment (Penalty)

Although there are many objections to the use of presentation punishment, these same objections do not apply to removal punishment. Removal punishment is the loss of a pleasant stimulus (penalty); consequently, it does not carry the negative side effects of presentation punishment and, therefore, is the least objectionable of the two corrective strategies. It is important to note that no research evidence indicates that punishment given by a *loving* parent disrupts the emotional bond between parent and child (Walters & Grusec, 1977). Presumably, the same may be said about the bond between coach and athlete. The key word here, of course, is *loving*.

An example of administering removal punishment would be taking away something the athlete likes to have or do. For example, say that one of your athletes skips an important practice drill and you determine that some sort of punishment is necessary to maintain team discipline. So you decide to punish your athlete by holding her out of scrimmage at the end of practice. In this case, the athlete loses the privilege and fun of participating in the game. The message to your offending athlete and other team members is simple: If you want to play, you have to pay; you have to pay the price during practice and do it all, not some of what is expected of you and every other team member. Removal punishment is one of the most effective corrective strategies available to a coach.

Cognitivistic Corrective Strategies

The following simple but highly effective strategies are cognitivistic because they appeal to an athlete's cognitive processing abilities. Let's begin by considering a corrective strategy from social cognitive learning theory—modeling.

Eliminate the Negative Model

Recall from chapter 5 and the imitating athlete that the modeling effect occurs whenever an observer acquires a new behavior as a result of seeing a model emit that behavior. One of the reasons your team captains are important is that hopefully they model good behavior. In this case, the captains can be used as a preventive strategy for encouraging good behavior in other team members. However, if you choose unwisely and your team captains (or other admired athletes on your team) model inappropriate behavior, team members may imitate similar misbehavior. In this case you need to eliminate the models (get new captains). Eliminating the inappropriate models serves as a corrective strategy.

Use the Inhibitory Effect

The inhibitory-disinhibitory effect involves the suppression or reappearance of previously suppressed deviant behavior as a result of seeing a model either punished or rewarded for similar behavior. As a corrective strategy, you can punish an athlete, especially someone the team admires, for misbehaving, which will have an inhibitory effect on the entire team. For example, suppose you have been struggling to get your athletes to arrive on time for morning practice and this morning your team captain is late. When your team captain finally arrives for practice you remind him of team policy and reprimand him in front of the team. Then, according to team policy, you withhold him from scrimmage that day. You explain to him later that he is the one who has to set an example so that everyone else follows his lead. Without him modeling good behavior the team, particularly the younger athletes, will drift away from the rules, regulations, and expectations necessary to run a championship program.

Remember the Eliciting Effect

The eliciting effect involves the observer engaging in behavior related but not identical to that of the model. This effect can elicit both appropriate and inappropriate behavior and, therefore, can be used as both a preventive and corrective strategy. For example, one of your athletes may befriend a younger teammate by giving him a ride and the next day another athlete decides to imitate similar but not identical Good Samaritan behavior by offering to tutor a younger athlete for an upcoming exam. This is an example of an appropriate modeled behavior eliciting a similar appropriate behavior. Now, consider the example of an athlete on your team who talks derisively about you and is rewarded by teammates with attention, approval, and laughter. The next day another player talks negatively about a teammate and the day after that yet another player trash talks an opposing player. This is an example of an eliciting effect for a negative behavior. Identify not only the elicited negative behavior but also its source (the model) and takes steps to eliminate both.

Coaches, parents, officials, and athletes all serve as models capable of being imitated. How they (we) choose to behave and the ensuing role models they provide will have a major impact on the quality of your program. I have witnessed a number of teams in different sports that could have developed into dynasties except for the fact that they lacked the leaders—the appropriate role models—for passing on champion behaviors to younger athletes. Remember that ultimately it is the coach's responsibility to set the tone for the program and demonstrate behavior worthy of imitation.

The Three Rs

Webster (1968) describes three principles of good discipline referred to as the **three Rs**: reason, respect, and relevance. First, when administering discipline, the discipline should be *reasonable* and interpreted as reasonable by the individual. In other words, if the athlete commits a small indiscretion, the penalty should be equally small. Second, the discipline should also reflect *respect* for the individual. Keep in mind that as a coach you may not like the inappropriate behavior but you must maintain a respect for the athlete as a human being and for the athlete's individual rights. Third, the discipline should be *relevant* to the misbehavior that necessitated the disciplinary action. For example, you may have been irked at some indiscretion earlier in the practice but you waited until the end of practice to invoke a penalty over some behavior disassociated from the original misbehavior.

The strategy of the three Rs is a cognitive corrective strategy because there is a certain amount of mental processing required to determine relevancy and reasonableness. In using the three Rs, a coach must evaluate the severity of the misbehavior, judge the appropriateness of the disciplinary action, and associate the corrective action with the specific misbehavior. Likewise, the athlete must cognitively understand the relevancy and reasonableness connected to the dispensation of the discipline.

In discussing good discipline, Webster (1968) outlines eight principles of non-autocratic order in the classroom. These principles can be translated into principles appropriate for the practice environment and while Webster's advice is neither esoteric nor surprising the principles are still sound advice for coaches making everyday decisions about discipline.

- Coaches must make sure that all athletes understand team rules and standards and the reasons for their existence.
- The first violation of a rule should lead to a warning, a discussion of alternative ways of behaving, and clarification of the consequences of repeated infractions.
- Coaches should endeavor to discover the causes underlying misbehaviors.
- Whenever possible, coaches should address athletes in private regarding their misbehavior.
- Sarcasm, ridicule, and other forms of discipline that lead to public humiliation should be avoided.
- When coaches make mistakes, they should apologize.
- The punishment should fit the crime. Minor infractions should not bring about harsh punishment.
- Extra practice and other sport related activities should never be used as a form of punishment.

The following section offers some examples of team rules. Notice that the sampling of team rules provided takes into consideration the four types of athlete behaviors: social, learning, motor, and champion. If you focus on motor behavior and ignore social, learning, and champion behaviors you won't fully develop the whole athlete. Athletes who lack these behaviors will never reach their greatest potential. Take a holistic approach to coaching your athletes.

Example of Team Rules

Athletes arriving late for practice will be warned. Three warnings will result in demotion.

Athletes must pass the physical readiness test in order to travel and compete.

Athletes must pass the skills and agility test in order to travel and compete.

Athletes with unexcused class absences will not compete that week.

Athletes must wear team apparel to all team functions or they will be asked to leave.

Athletes will be given three warnings per season. A fourth will result in dismissal from the team.

Athletes with a grade lower than a C will attend study table instead of practice until the grade has been improved.

Athletes must call the head coach when they cannot attend practice and arrange a time to make up that practice.

Athletes must make up missed practices or they will not compete in that week's competition.

Athletes being disrespectful to coaches, teammates, or anyone else associated with the program will meet with the coach after practice.

Athletes who cannot attend practice because of an injury must meet with the athletic trainer.

Athletes who don't look the coach in the eyes or are pouty or whiny will be asked to leave practice.

Logical Consequences

According to Dreikurs (Dreikurs & Grey, 1968; Dreikurs, Gunwald, & Pepper, 1982) the consequences of a student's (and presumably an athlete's) misbehaviors can have two types of consequences: natural consequences and logical consequences. **Natural consequences** are the naturally occurring outcomes of behaviors. For example, the natural consequence of an athlete showing up late for the start of a race is missing the race. In contrast, **logical consequences** are the contrived or invented outcomes of behaviors. For example, the logical consequence of an athlete stealing from another athlete on the team might be to have the athlete apologize to the offended athlete, perform community service, and talk with younger athletes about lessons learned.

In the case of logical consequences, the coach and athlete may sit down and agree together what the consequences should entail. In many instances these consequences might not normally occur. The natural consequences for the athlete stealing from another athlete might have been getting arrested by the police. The advantages of logical consequences are several. For one, it appeals to the athlete's cognitive ability. Also, it engages the athlete in the selection of consequences, thereby making it seem less like punishment which in turn makes the coach seem less like a strict authoritarian figure. As a consequence, the athlete is less likely to direct anger toward the coach. Another advantage is that the logical consequences are directly connected to the specific misbehavior.

Humanistic Corrective Strategies

The following corrective strategies are humanistic because they consider the dignity, autonomy, self-worth, and self-growth of the athlete. They recognize and value the humanity of each person as well as the athlete's right and inner need to self-govern. While it isn't always possible or prudent to expect athletes to self-administer corrective strategies (i.e., discipline themselves) it is possible, as made evident by many of the strategies in this chapter, for coaches to administer corrective strategies with a humanistic touch. You can discipline while respecting the rights of the athlete and in a way that protects the athlete's dignity.

Nondirective Approach

Recall from chapter 8 that the nondirective approach to working with athletes means that coaches act as facilitator, helping the athlete define the problem and develop a solution. You can use a nondirective corrective strategy for helping athletes assess the offending behavior and determine the just punishment. In using the nondirective approach the coach acts as facilitator, helping the athlete determine reasonable and appropriate consequences for inappropriate behavior. Consider scenario 5 in which one of your athletes is caught stealing equipment after practice. Using a nondirective approach, you meet privately with him and ask what punishment he thinks is reasonable and appropriate. You remind him that you care about him as both an athlete and person, but according to team rules and the ethical and moral conduct of human beings, some disciplinary action must be taken. You listen, provide feedback, and practice other nondirective habits during your meeting. At the conclusion of the meeting you and your athlete agree on the terms of the discipline.

Scenario 5

An athlete whom you like and believe is a good kid at heart gets caught doing something stupid: stealing. You know the family, parents, and kid well enough to realize that this was just one of those things that many adolescents go through. Rather than report the incident, you decide that this is the perfect learning situation for him to gain insight and growth as a person. You decide to let the athlete determine the severity of the offense and a punishment commensurate with the crime.

The nondirective corrective strategy may perhaps seem naive to some coaches, particularly those who view the role of the coach as autocratic and mute to athlete thoughts, opinions, and input. However, the nondirective corrective strategy is not only effective put also easily implemented. Some coaches might be surprised at how well some (although not all) athletes can determine appropriate consequences for their actions. Besides determining consequences, the nondirective strategy also promotes personal growth because athletes take responsibility for their actions, participate in decision making, and determine the consequences of their actions.

Reasoning

Reasoning involves providing athletes with rational explanations for not engaging in inappropriate behaviors and reasons for engaging in appropriate behaviors. For example, one of your athletes habitually interrupts you when you attempt to provide performance feedback. You can take several approaches to dealing with this problem. You could reprimand the athlete. You could reinforce the athlete when she doesn't say anything. You could reinforce another athlete for modeling the correct behavior, namely to be quiet and listen. But perhaps an easier approach is to use reasoning. You sit down privately with the athlete and explain why it is important for her to listen to your comments. You mention that listening is a sign of respect; that your role as coach is to provide feedback and part of her role as athlete is to listen to your comments; that taking so much time during practice to listen to her numerous comments is unfair to other athletes because it prevents you from coaching them; that you would be happy to listen to her comments after practice when you have more time to listen; and you go on from there. Reasoning is an attractive alternative to other corrective strategies for several reasons.

Reasoning avoids the negative effects of punishment, yet can be an effective corrective strategy. Research (Walters & Grusec, 1977) suggests that effective reasoning for school-age children should use rationales that emphasize the interests of others and, consequently, arouse empathy for others.

Reasoning appeals to an athlete's humanity and cognitive-intellectual ability. Furthermore, the use of reasoning allows coaches to more genuinely relate to their athletes on an equal level, rather than from a position as omnipotent dispenser of rewards and punishments.

Reasoning provides an appropriate model of behavior for athletes to imitate. Using reasoning tells an athlete from a social learning perspective that one strategy for coping with a problem is the use of rational thought.

Reasoning, unlike punishment, makes it possible for coaches to indicate more appropriate and acceptable alternative behaviors for their athletes to model. When reasoning with an athlete, it is natural through the course of the conversation for the coach to discuss alternative behaviors and why these behaviors are more appropriate than other behaviors.

The process of reasoning offers the coach an opportunity to develop the coach–athlete relationship. When a coach and athlete sit down and use reason rather than emotion the by-product of such a meeting is that both individuals get to know each other better and develop an understanding of, respect for, and trust in one another. For all these reasons, reasoning is an effective humanistic corrective strategy.

The Four Fs

Another humanistic corrective strategy is using the **four Fs**: firm, fair, friendly, and forgiving. Like Webster's principles of nonautocratic order, the four Fs are straightforward, simple, and perhaps obvious; however, it is surprising how helpful and effective a little homespun commonsense and a few simple rules can be for helping coaches make sound decisions for administering discipline.

When you must discipline, be *firm* about it. If you are unsure or timid, your athletes will question your decision, your confidence, and your leadership. However, be *fair* in your decision-making. As Webster admonishes, the punishment should be commensurate with the offense. Also, be *friendly* when disciplining. You don't have to like the misbehavior but that doesn't mean you can't still like the athlete as a person. Hate the sin but love the sinner. Sometimes a simple statement, such as, "This hurts me as much as it does you," lets athletes know you care about them as human beings, but your actions are necessary for the good of the program. Finally, be *forgiving* after you have administered the discipline. Don't hold a grudge or continue to discuss the misbehavior. The problem is now in the past and both coach and athlete must look towards the future, maintain a mutual respect for one another, and work toward shared goals.

Praise Publicly, Criticize Privately

This simple admonishment is worth remembering. Athletes in general like praise and in most cases enjoy receiving it in front of their teammates and significant others. These same athletes, however, generally do not like to be reprimanded, punished, or criticized in front of others. In some cases, it may be necessary to administer criticism publicly. For example, it may be necessary to publicly criticize or punish one of your athletes who serves as a team role model in order to achieve an inhibitory effect. But in most cases, out of respect for the individual and to avoid embarrassing or humiliating the athlete in front of the team, it is wise to criticize and punish privately. When you criticize privately, your athletes will gain greater respect for you and appreciate your sensitivity in dealing with them not only as athletes, but also as individuals with the all-too-human characteristics of ego, pride, and feelings.

From a humanistic perspective, praising publicly and criticizing privately means you respect the dignity and rights of your athletes as individuals. Sometimes it is a struggle to follow this maxim. For example, one of your athletes does something inappropriate that really angers you. It has been a long week and an even longer season and your first impulse is to lash out at the offending athlete. Have you ever been in this type of situation? I know I have. You are short on patience, it might be one of your least favorite athletes, and it has been a long and frustrating week. It would be easy to unload on the player. Instead, however, you control your emotions, remember the humanistic corrective adage *praise publicly, criticize privately*, respect the person's dignity and rights, and wait until after practice to confront the athlete.

The following list summarizes the behavioristic, cognitivistic, and humanistic corrective strategies in coaching athletes.

Corrective Strategies

Behavioristic Corrective Strategies

Shape behavior

Negative reinforcement

Extinction

Presentation punishment (castigation)

Never use your sport as a source of punishment

Removal punishment (penalty)

Cognitivistic Corrective Strategies

Eliminate the negative model

Use the inhibitory effect

Remember the eliciting effect

The three Rs

Logical consequences

Humanistic Corrective Strategies

Nondirective approach

Reasoning

The four Fs

Praise publicly, criticize privately

THE BRIDLED ATHLETE

The metaphor of the athlete as *bucking bronco* and *beast* is not meant to imply that athletes are merely beasts of burden and a herd needing to be corralled; it is far from it. Part of the joy of coaching and the electricity of the practice environment comes from the very human traits of youthful enthusiasm, boundless energy, and childlike excitement that athletes, particularly young athletes, bring to their sport. However, the metaphor is somewhat fitting as all this enthusiasm, energy, and excitement must be bridled so that the herd is heading in the right direction; otherwise, chaos is sure to ensue.

Athletes of all ages and all levels of ability require the principled coach. The issues may vary but no matter what age group or skill level of athlete you work with, the strategies described in this chapter help you bridle your athletes and create Club Cool—a program where you spend most of your time coaching, not reining in the herd.

THE PRINCIPLED COACH

When it comes to practice management and discipline, the coach is responsible for making sure team rules, policies, and good behavior are followed by all athletes. Of course, athletes should participate to some degree in determining practice management and discipline, but the ultimate responsibility falls on the shoulders of the coach, not the athletes. The **principled coach** understands the theories of behaviorism, cognitivism, and humanism and their application to preventive and corrective strategies for managing athlete behavior and administering discipline. The principled coach is aware of the guidelines for disseminating discipline as well as the cautionary rules for using punishment. Most important, the principled coach understands that it is easier to prevent misbehaviors than it is to discipline them.

YOUR COACHING TOOLBOX

Here is another tool for your coaching toolbox. Instead of a fly-by-the-seat-of-your-pants approach to maintaining practice management and discipline like I did my first day of student-teaching, you are prepared to apply specific strategies based on the theories of behaviorism, cognitivism, and humanism to help you successfully bridle the beasts and keep the herd moving in the right direction. The strategies you employ focus on the prevention of inappropriate behaviors and the creation and maintenance of appropriate social, learning, motor, and champion behaviors.

Successful coaches like the coach of Club Cool are with-it in practice; they lead the flow of activities rather than simply react to it. Successful coaches deal with problems early; they don't wait until little problems rear their ugly heads and become monster problems. Few coaches like to discipline but sometimes it is unavoidable. In these situations successful coaches take action, but they administer punishment using operant conditioning principles in a way that respects the dignity and rights of the individual athlete. They use cognitivistic and humanistic corrective strategies that rely on reason, relevance, fairness, friendliness and other human characteristics. They don't hold a grudge; they know that everyone makes mistakes—including athletes and coaches.

THE SCIENTIFIC AND ARTFUL COACH

Navigating the tricky and sometimes treacherous waters of practice management and discipline is no easy task and requires you to set a course that uses both science and art. For example, as coaches we want to prevent and correct misbehaviors in a way that bridles the beast yet doesn't kill the spirit. In other words, we want wild animals; we just want them all galloping together in the right direction—a formidable challenge for coaches given the unpredictability of practice and the idiosyncrasy of athletes.

Part of the art of coaching, then, is sensing the *who, what, when, where, and why* factors of a situation when administering preventive and corrective strategies. Some athletes can accept an admonishment and other athletes can't; if you look at them the wrong way they crumble emotionally. As a coach I had moments when I simply ignored the behavior, sensing that it was better to not draw attention and make a big deal out of it. But there were other situations that may have seemed like small indiscretions to some coaches but were huge transgressions and concerns to me, to which I quickly responded because I believed they would have led our team in the wrong direction.

Part of the science of coaching is understanding, valuing, and applying research data and preventive and corrective strategies based on sound learning theories when attempting to maintain practice management and administer disciplinary action. As a result, your decisions will be guided by sound theories and scientific inquiry rather than old wives' tales, folklore, habits, superstitions, bad advice, and the like.

IF YOU REMEMBER ONLY THREE THINGS

1. *Remember to let preventive strategies be your first choice for managing practice and athlete behavior.* This means being proactive by making the effort at the beginning of the season to set rules and procedures, communicate them to your players, and routinely enforce them. It also means taking the time to structure smooth running practices that maintain momentum and athlete focus. Some coaches become lazy and don't take the time or effort to engage in preventive strategies. They expect or hope things will run smoothly without any effort on their part—big mistake. Because of their laziness, these coaches pay the price throughout the season by having to constantly correct misbehaviors. Be smart. Lay a solid foundation early that invites good behavior and creates smooth sailing practices.

2. *Remember the importance of caring for athletes and using humor.* There are perhaps no more effective tools for maintaining a positive athlete–coach relationship and an inviting learning environment than caring for your athletes and using humor. When you let your athletes know that you care for them and want to see them succeed and grow as athletes and human beings, you establish a relationship of trust and mutual respect and invite good behavior. If you don't care about your athletes, you probably need to consider a different profession. Using humor reminds your athletes—and you—that your sport and competition are fun. Humor defuses confrontation, keeps things in perspective, creates a positive learning environment, and lessens the gravity of competition.

Of course, there is a time and place for everything and knowing when to use humor and when to refrain from using it is important. Knowing what type of humor to use is equally important. Although sarcasm is a form of humor, it involves cutting remarks and ridicule directed toward the athlete and it should be avoided.

3. *Remember that if you must use punishment, administer it in a way that respects the dignity and humanity of the athlete and maintains the coach–athlete relationship.* Sometimes this is no easy feat, but by following the guidelines outlined in the section on corrective strategies it is attainable. Whether you want to or not, it is your responsibility to maintain athlete discipline because you are the coach. So be prepared. When administering punishment wisely and judiciously, you help establish good athlete behavior, maintain the coach–athlete relationship, and model behaviors and attitudes you hope your athletes will adopt, such as reasoning, logic, fairness, forgiveness, and respectfulness.

SUGGESTED READINGS

Nater, S. & Gallimore, R. (2010). *You haven't taught until they have learned: John Wooden's teaching principles and practices.* Morgantown,WV: Fitness Information Technology.

[Why is it that outstanding teachers of excellence have few discipline problems? I think it is because these teachers are so busy teaching and their students are so busy learning that no one has spare time for anything else. This book contains timeless bits of wisdom and pedagogy no coach should be without.]

Rich, M. (writer) (2000). *Finding Forrester* [Columbia Pictures].

[A young and gifted aspiring teenage writer Jamal Wallace (Rob Brown) meets reclusive writer William Forrester (Sean Connery). I find it interesting that Jamal is taught by two gruff older teachers. One is effective and one isn't. The main difference between the two is that one cares about him and the other doesn't—an important distinction for all coaches, but especially aspiring coaches, to remember.]

CHAPTER 11

The Philosophical Coach

Applying Wisdom

Key Terms

altruism	means values	pluralism
coaching philosophy	moral calluses	postformal thought
concrete pragmatics	moral compass	satisfactoriness
dialectical thinking	motives	scientific materialism
dualism	natural ties	stability
end values	pedagogy	transparency
ethics	peer resource team	values
holistic ethic (holism)	personality traits	wise coach
introspection	philosophical coach	

Marcus was a young and up-and-coming coach. Everywhere he coached he found immediate success. Because of his successes, he moved quickly from one program to the next, rapidly climbing the coaching ladder, each program more prestigious than the last. He worked hard—as hard as or harder than any coach in the country—and he knew a great deal about his sport, having been more than moderately successful as an athlete himself. But if you asked him why he coached, he was hard pressed to answer. And if you asked him to describe his coaching philosophy, he would stumble to find an answer to that question as well.

At his current position, which would turn out to be his last stop up the coaching ladder, two third-string athletes violated team policy by drinking alcohol. The local police caught the athletes and cited them for underage drinking. Drinking had been a festering problem in the past and the coach was adamant about stopping it, so according to team rules, any athlete caught drinking would be dismissed from the team. Strictly following team policy, the coach summarily dismissed both athletes from the team. Three weeks later and one week before the conference championship, the team's best athlete was caught drinking and the police cited him for underage drinking. In this case, the coach decided to punish the athlete and allow him to remain on the team. The following week the team was crowned conference champions.

After the euphoria of winning dissipated, what followed was the beginning of the end of the program and the coach's rise to higher achievements. Because of his decision to retain rather than dismiss the best athlete on the team—and because of many other similar types of decisions he had made—his players and coaching staff lost respect for him. Disgruntlement and friction rose between the coach and players; no one was ever content. To right the ship the coach returned to his old reliable tools for success—hard work and knowledge of the sport—but they didn't seem to work for him anymore. He continued to find moderate success, winning the occasional conference championship, but like an old jalopy stuck on a muddy back road, the program could advance no further. The lack of a well-defined and clearly thought out philosophy kept the coach, his program, and his athletes from moving forward to greater standards of achievement.

Coaching success is not just about the Xs and Os. At a typical practice coaches, like teachers, are called upon to make a myriad of decisions. The types of decisions coaches make impact factors such as training atmosphere, team morale, athlete discipline, and athlete–coach relationships, all of which are necessary for maintaining the continued success and advancement of the athletes and program.

This chapter is the story of the *philosophical coach*. It shows you how to develop and apply a personal philosophy for guiding your decision making. It also is the story of how you can become a *wise coach* who makes the right decisions and judgments that maintain athlete respect and loyalty and keep your program moving forward on the road to greater and greater achievements.

CHAPTER OVERVIEW

The chapter begins with some considerations for developing a personal coaching philosophy. Next, it offers suggestions for developing ethics within your coaching philosophy and then examines some methods for developing values within your philosophy. The chapter concludes with a discussion of some values associated with sport that you might consider incorporating within your personal coaching philosophy.

CONSIDERATIONS FOR DEVELOPING A COACHING PHILOSOPHY

From the perspective of the artful coach, a coaching philosophy is perhaps the most important tool in your coaching toolbox because a thoughtfully considered and carefully crafted coaching philosophy helps you make prudent decisions, develop and promote personal ethics, prioritize motives and values, and ultimately engender athlete loyalty and respect. Physics, periodization, tactical strategies, and other practical knowledge associated with your sport are important, but to become a coach of excellence, you must know what you value, believe in, and stand for.

What Is a Coaching Philosophy?

Coaching program curriculum requirements often include courses such as anatomy, biology, physiology, biomechanics, motor learning, and motor performance. These fields of study are dominated by an overwhelming emphasis on science and the use of research data, controlled studies, accurate measurement, statistics, and other scientific constructs. In contrast, philosophy does not concern itself with such scientific imperatives. As Kretchmar (2005) notes, "But philosophy is also mystifying because it does not literally measure anything and thus has no need for microscopes, hand dynamometers, or test tubes" (p. 5). Kretchmar goes on to write, "In contrast to the scientist's tendency to gather data, philosophers are not interested in measuring anything empirically. Philosophic study includes intangibles—descriptions of human experiences like hope, trust, and love" (p.11). Science is important for coaching effectiveness, but so too is art. A personal coaching philosophy is a part of the art of coaching.

A **coaching philosophy** is a personal creed, set of beliefs, and knowledge base that guides your thoughts, actions, and coaching style. It helps you live a better life and become a better coach. A coaching philosophy is personal and thus unique to each individual coach, so no two coaches have the exact same philosophies. In your pursuit of becoming an effective and successful coach, you will need to answer some important questions (e.g., *Why do I coach?*) to determine your coaching philosophy. No one can provide you with a blueprint or recipe for answering these questions. These questions include the following:

What is the definition of athletic success?

Why do I coach?

What are my responsibilities to my athletes?

How much control should athletes have over their training?

What are my ultimate coaching goals?

How should I discipline my athletes?

What is the purpose of sport?

What is the purpose of competition?

What are my long range goals for my athletes?

What are my ethical standards?

What are my values?

What types of experiences do I want my athletes to have?

What life lessons do I want my athletes to carry with them when they leave the sport?

No one answer is correct for these questions; their answers are up to you. Your answers to these questions reflect your coaching philosophy and thus profoundly affect your coaching effectiveness and ultimately your coaching career.

An example of a coaching philosophy is reflected in John Wooden's pyramid of success, which he created in 1948 (figure 11.1).

In his pyramid of success, Wooden identifies five personal characteristics—industriousness, friendship, loyalty, cooperation, and enthusiasm—as the foundation for success. Placing these characteristics at the foundation indicates that Wooden's philosophy deems character as primary for success before skill and conditioning. As General H. Norman Schwarztkopf once said, "Leadership is a potent combination of strategy and character. But if you must be without one, be without strategy." What do you think are the necessary building blocks for your philosophy for athletic success?

Here is how Wooden defines success: "Success is peace of mind which is a direct result of self-satisfaction in knowing you made the effort to become the best that you are capable of becoming." Wooden's personal coaching philosophy defines success as giving one's best effort. Some coaches would define success as winning. How do you define success?

Why a Coaching Philosophy Is Necessary

A coaching philosophy is necessary because of its conscious and sometimes unconscious influence on your decisions and the consequences of your decision making. Your coaching philosophy ultimately shapes everything about you, your coaching, and your program. It shapes who you are as a person, your coaching style, your rapport with athletes, your coaching longevity, success, happiness, and more. It affects the direction of your program and the type and level of success your program will achieve. It also shapes the development of your athletes and the types of athletes and human beings they will become. Following are some reasons why a coaching philosophy is important.

• *A philosophy acts as a sounding board for making decisions.* No coaching manual can adequately prepare you to make the right decisions for all the situations you will encounter throughout your coaching career, but a well-developed coaching philosophy is something you can fall back on to make prudent and wise decisions.

• *A coaching philosophy helps you become an effective leader.* With a well-developed philosophy, you react decisively to situations, making sound decisions and good judgments. Rather than appear indecisive and unsure to athletes, staff, and parents, you demonstrate leadership traits.

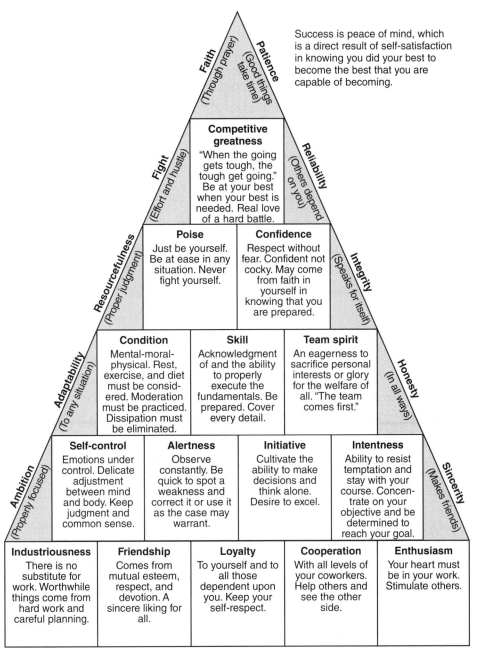

Success is peace of mind, which is a direct result of self-satisfaction in knowing you did your best to become the best that you are capable of becoming.

Faith (Through prayer)

Patience (Good things take time)

Fight (Effort and hustle)

Reliability (Others depend on you)

Resourcefulness (Proper judgment)

Integrity (Speaks for itself)

Adaptability (To any situation)

Honesty (In all ways)

Ambition (Properly focused)

Sincerity (Makes friends)

Competitive greatness
"When the going gets tough, the tough get going." Be at your best when your best is needed. Real love of a hard battle.

Poise
Just be yourself. Be at ease in any situation. Never fight yourself.

Confidence
Respect without fear. Confident not cocky. May come from faith in yourself in knowing that you are prepared.

Condition
Mental-moral-physical. Rest, exercise, and diet must be considered. Moderation must be practiced. Dissipation must be eliminated.

Skill
Acknowledgment of and the ability to properly execute the fundamentals. Be prepared. Cover every detail.

Team spirit
An eagerness to sacrifice personal interests or glory for the welfare of all. "The team comes first."

Self-control
Emotions under control. Delicate adjustment between mind and body. Keep judgment and common sense.

Alertness
Observe constantly. Be quick to spot a weakness and correct it or use it as the case may warrant.

Initiative
Cultivate the ability to make decisions and think alone. Desire to excel.

Intentness
Ability to resist temptation and stay with your course. Concentrate on your objective and be determined to reach your goal.

Industriousness
There is no substitute for work. Worthwhile things come from hard work and careful planning.

Friendship
Comes from mutual esteem, respect, and devotion. A sincere liking for all.

Loyalty
To yourself and to all those dependent upon you. Keep your self-respect.

Cooperation
With all levels of your coworkers. Help others and see the other side.

Enthusiasm
Your heart must be in your work. Stimulate others.

Figure 11.1 The pyramid of success.

Reprinted courtesy of John Wooden and CoachJohnWooden.com.

• *A coaching philosophy ultimately guides your actions, decisions, planning, and interaction with athletes and staff.* In other words, a coaching philosophy permeates every aspect of your program and consequently influences the direction, quality, and overall success of the program. Therefore, the better your coaching philosophy becomes, ultimately the better your program becomes.

• *A coaching philosophy provides greater perspective and insight.* Analytical and logical analyses do not always yield the deepest insight about movement (Kretchmar, 2005). Factors such as motivation, emotion, love for the game, and individual perception, make it impossible to quantify the motor learning and performance experience.

• *A coaching philosophy provides you with a holistic approach to coaching.* A philosophic holistic approach to coaching and problem solving is ultimately more effective than a rigid and logical approach. A philosophic approach to coaching includes a holistic perspective to teaching, relating to athletes, and solving problems. A holistic approach takes into consideration all aspects germane to the athlete: individual differences, emotions, situational factors, personal goals, and much more.

• *A coaching philosophy provides you with a pragmatic approach to coaching.* A philosophic pragmatic approach to coaching and problem solving is also more effective than a rigid and logical approach. A pragmatic approach to coaching means that you don't always do the *right* thing or apply the most logical solution but, rather, you apply the solution most likely to achieve resolution.

What Sources to Consult

As a scientific coach, you want to base much of your thoughts, beliefs, and habits on laws, paradigms, and empirical studies and other conformational data. Therefore, good sources for developing your coaching philosophy are classes and publications in subjects such as motor learning, motor performance, applied sport science, and physiology. Although philosophy does not concern itself with scientific issues, it is nevertheless important to understand certain scientific concepts, theories, or paradigms that are part of the motor learning and performance discussion. After all, you can't philosophize about something you don't know anything about. For example, I could give you my philosophical musings about sumo wrestling but I don't know the first thing about the sport.

As a scientific coach, you also want to base your philosophy on sound teaching and learning principles. Another source, then, is in the area of **pedagogy**, the study of the art and science of teaching. After all, at the heart of the matter you are a teacher. Your classroom just happens to be the pool, court, field, track, mat, or gym. Areas worth reading about and studying include teaching methods, counseling, curriculum development, and, of course, educational psychology.

As an artful coach, observing respected others in your field helps develop your philosophic perspective. Watch, listen, and learn from successful and experienced coaches. Some sports have mentoring programs that pair a novice or young coach with a more seasoned coach. Find a coach you respect and ask that person to be your mentor. Cultivating a relationship with a mentor is important for your development as a coach. This relationship often simply means communicating through telephone and e-mail; talking at clinics, conventions, and competitions; or getting together informally for a meal and talking. On these occasions, take time to pick your mentor's brain and ask probing philosophical questions as well as technical questions and situational questions; in other words, ask what your mentor would do in a specific situation.

Besides a mentor, you also can assemble your own **peer resource team** (PRT), which is a small group of trusted and specialized advisors genuinely interested in your success and that you can call on during difficult times. Your PRT can help clarify problems, suggest potential solutions, listen, offer encouragement, and generally support you through tumultuous and challenging periods during your coaching career. I am grateful to several people in my life who were always there for me when I needed to vent my frustration, question my decision making, overcome self-doubt, solve difficult problems, and find the motivation to rejoin the good fight.

I am grateful also for the opportunity to pay that support forward. For example, I received a phone call from a former athlete who was in his second year of collegiate coaching. He had decided to give his team an ultimatum in practice—do it or get out—and his entire team took the *get out* option. In a panic he gave me a call and we talked about the situation and all of its complexities. He formed a new plan and had a meeting with his team the next day. He called me back a few days later to say that he had regained the trust and control of his team and that they had indeed done what he asked. He is on his way to becoming a coach of excellence.

Your PRT can be a diverse mix of people who bring unique qualities and perspectives to the team. People to consider are colleagues, former coaches, athletic directors, spouses, executive directors, administrators, clergy, sport psychologists, trusted friends, and siblings. Feedback from others is important for maintaining your coaching equilibrium and developing your coaching philosophy. If you do not have a PRT, it is worth the effort to seek out people who will contribute to your coaching philosophy and ultimately to your coaching success.

Another source to consult is yourself. At the end of the day, it is *your* personal philosophy. Some young coaches become philosophical clones of other coaches. These young coaches think and believe exactly like the coaches they studied under or observed. You need to seek your own philosophical identity. Let your coaching philosophy reflect your uniqueness, personality, style, and thinking. Take bits and pieces from people who have influenced you and eventually develop your own coaching philosophy. John Wooden was a great coach and a highly respected person and coaches in any sport can benefit from reading his pyramid of success, but this does not mean he was perfect or his coaching philosophy is perfectly tailored for you.

Be your own coach with your own philosophy.

Who Needs a Coaching Philosophy

The only thing worse than not having a personally customized coaching philosophy is not having a coaching philosophy at all. Anyone who coaches athletes should have a well-established coaching philosophy. This includes the full spectrum of coaches working with novice to elite athletes. No matter what level you coach, you need to have a philosophical sounding board to fall back on when making decisions. As former professional football coach Joe Gibbs put it when discussing the coaching profession, "Have a philosophy and stick with it because you'll be tested."

Your coaching philosophy varies depending on your athletes' personalities and levels. For example, if you are coaching young beginning female athletes, your demeanor and philosophical approach to motivation may be somewhat different than if you are working with young beginning male athletes. Similarly, your philosophy will be somewhat different if you are coaching young athletes in a national training center whose goals are to someday make the Olympic team as opposed to young athletes in a summer recreational league whose goals are simply to have fun, recreate, and make new friends. Your philosophy should reflect the goals and needs of your athletes and program and relate to gender, age, developmental level, and individual differences.

How to Develop a Coaching Philosophy

A coaching philosophy does not simply pop into your head or materialize on a piece of paper with a few quick strokes of a pen. You cultivate it over time. Through personal thought, reflection, and experience you clarify and formalize your philosophy. And as you grow and mature as a coach, like a fine wine your philosophy gets better with age. Following are some considerations for developing your coaching philosophy.

• *Educate yourself in all aspects of your sport.* The first and perhaps most obvious aspect to consider are the Xs and Os of your sport. No matter how badly you want to succeed, you cannot be an effective coach, without knowing the fundamentals, intricacies, and nuances of your sport. As mentioned earlier, a knowledge base is part of building a coaching philosophy. You can't teach what you don't know. Similarly, you can't develop a philosophy about something you don't understand. Uninformed coaches make unenlightened and ineffective teachers, poor leaders, and bad decision makers. Continue to learn more each year about your sport.

• *Know more than the Xs and Os of your sport.* As mentioned throughout this book, effective coaching involves going beyond the Xs and Os. Acquire a knowledge base that includes information on related areas such as effective communication and relationship building, sport psychology, physiology of exercise, team building, and practice management and discipline. This book has contributed to some of these areas of knowledge. The Suggested Readings can help you expand on what you have learned.

• *Use introspection.* **Introspection** is the process of turning your gaze inward for self-examination. It means taking the time to reflect on your past actions, your present behaviors and goals, and your future hopes and desires and asking yourself probing personal questions such as *Am I doing the right thing? Am I staying true to my goals and beliefs? Do I need to reconsider my coaching philosophy?* Genuine and deeply committed coaches are not afraid to be inwardly reflective. Introspection is a necessary part of the continual processes of shaping your coaching philosophy and growing as a coach and human being. Those introspective moments sitting in the dark in a rocking chair at 2 a.m. were perhaps the most defining moments of my coaching career—reflective moments identifying problems and solutions and revealing values and character traits.

• *Use external feedback.* External feedback can come from many valuable sources: colleagues, athletes, formal written evaluations, video analysis, etc. External feedback allows you to better evaluate and understand yourself, your coaching needs and style, your shortcomings and weaknesses, and your strengths and successes. All of this information helps you to better understand yourself and your coaching philosophy.

When to Develop a Personal Coaching Philosophy

A coaching philosophy is a constantly evolving process that starts the day you begin coaching. Over time your coaching philosophy grows and matures just as you grow and mature as a coach—but only if you work on it. As mentioned earlier, the best coaching philosophies are the ones that have been honed through years of effort, education, thought, and self-examination and reflect the depth and breadth of your experience.

According to Piaget's (1961, 1972) cognitive development theory, people have four developmental stages: sensorimotor stage (birth to age 2), preoperational stage—comprised of the preconceptual stage from age 2 to 4 and the intuitive stage from age 4 to 7—concrete operations stage (age 7 to 11), and formal operations stage (after age 11). Piaget and other developmental psychologists considered the formal operations stage to be the final stage of cognitive development achieved during adolescence. It seems a shame to think that our cognitive development as human beings reaches its pinnacle at such an early age and that no further cognitive evolution occurs during adulthood.

Fortunately, researchers suggest a fifth stage of cognitive development called **postformal thought**. For example, Basseches (1984) points out that adults think differently from young children or adolescents and argues that cognitive development continues after adolescence. Rather than become more logical and inflexible and painfully rational, adult thinkers can become more relative—more sensitive to conflict and issues such as moral, ethical, political and individual differences. Basseches calls this type of thinking *dialectical thinking*. **Dialectical thinking** focuses on resolving conflict by creatively finding alternative possibilities and less obvious solutions. Not all adults move toward dialectical thinking; some remain stuck in the formal operations stage. However, the scientific and artful coach continues growing cognitively and achieves postformal thought.

Labouvie-Vief (1980) supports Basseches' contention that another stage of human cognitive development occurs beyond the formal operations stage. According to Labouvie-Vief (1986), mature reasoning requires **concrete pragmatics**. In this pragmatic stage people make decisions based on many factors, not just what is considered the *right* or conventional thing to do because sometimes doing the *right* thing can eventually become the *wrong* thing to do. From a pragmatic point of view, the best solution to a problem might be neither the most logical nor the most commonplace, but it would be the most workable and the most likely solution for solving the problem at hand.

The concepts of dialectical thinking and concrete pragmatics are immensely important for coaches who want to develop postformal thought and reach a higher level of coaching and philosophical effectiveness. It seems to me that coaches who use dialectical thinking and concrete pragmatics are highly effective because they are wise and judicious problem solvers and decision makers. In working with individual athletes, complex situations arise that are neither easily interpreted nor easily solved and often the best approach is a pragmatic problem solving approach: What is the best solution at this time and place for solving this problem? Consider scenario 1.

Scenario 1

The day before competition your best athlete misses practice for the first time all season. Your team policy states that any athlete missing practice during the week will sit out of competition that week. However, the competition that week is the state qualifier. Your team must win the competition to advance to the state championship. What should you do? Here's a review of all the considerations: You have a rule stating that anyone missing practice will not compete in competition that week. You have an athlete who has been a team leader and never missed practice, at least until this week. You have a team that might feel upset and resentful if you play the athlete. Or, you have a team that might feel upset and resentful if you *don't* play the athlete. And you have your best player who might feel upset and resentful if you don't play him.

Now contemplate scenario 1 with these additional considerations: You discover that the athlete's dying father is going to attend the competition. If you lose the competition, you might lose your job. If you lose the competition, your team will not advance to the state finals. And, aside from all this, you truly believe that a team leader who has towed the line, never committed an infraction, and done whatever you have asked should be allowed to play, regardless of the importance of the competition.

Not all coaching situations are so complex, but many of the considerations in scenario 1 have occurred at one time or another. You will confront complex scenarios for which no easy solutions exist. You don't have a problem-solving handbook to consult for a readymade solution. To make the best decision you must ultimately rely on your coaching philosophy.

As people mature and move to a higher level of cognitive development their philosophy matures as well—if they strive to do so. Dyer (2001) wrote, "The rigid never grow old. They tend to do things the same way they've always done them. A colleague of mine who teaches graduate courses for teachers frequently asks the old-timers who have spent thirty years or more in the classroom, 'Have you really been teaching for thirty years or have you been teaching one year, thirty times'" (p. 146)? While Dyer is referring to rigidity of teaching he could also be talking about philosophical rigidity. Coaches whose philosophies are unchanging, unbending, and unforgiving follow the same philosophy 30 times.

Consider the story of a Texas high school football coach who dismissed six players from his team for being late for practice. The reason for their late arrival is that they were giving blood for the school's blood drive (Reilly, 2006). The coach made his rule and the consequence for violating it clear to his players. However, based on the universal bad press and negative responses from athletes, parents, students, and school administrators, consensus would suggest that the Texas high school football coach's personal philosophy was too rigid.

Now contrast the Texas high school football coach's philosophy with UCLA basketball coach John Wooden's philosophy. Coach Wooden's philosophy included the concept of *earned and deserved*. As Nater and Gallimore (2010) write, "Coach Wooden was a stickler for fairness. But for him, that did not mean treating all of his players and students exactly alike. In the 1930's, he came up with an approach he calls 'earned and deserved'" (p. 15). They go on to quote Wooden who said, "I believe, in order to be fair to all students, a teacher must give each individual student the treatment he earns and deserves. The most unfair thing to do is to treat all of them the same" (p. 15).

The dialectical thinking that Basseches describes and the pragmatic stage of cognitive development that Labouvie-Vief outlines are both akin to wisdom. Wisdom requires a certain amount of experience, knowledge, sensitivity, objectivity, compassion, understanding, and commonsense. As a coach, your goal should be to become not only a scientific and artful coach, a disciplined coach, and a philosophical coach, but also a wise coach.

DEVELOPING ETHICS WITHIN YOUR PHILOSOPHY

A wise coach uses pragmatic thinking to develop a coaching philosophy that includes ethics. According to Kretchmar (2005), "Ethics, if nothing else, is about how people ought to live, about preferred values and behaviors" (p.186). **Ethics**, then, is the search for not *how* people live, but how they *ought to* live. The need for ethics really comes from conflict (Midgley, 1994) that arises when you have different choices for responding to situations.

There are many hypothetical approaches to establishing ethical guidelines and personal morality. One approach is to say that ethics is a personal choice developed by each individual. Such an approach makes it difficult to imagine groups of individuals (e.g., athletic teams) being able to coalesce and coexist. Another approach is to say ethics is a group process whereby ethics is established by consensus. This approach makes it difficult for leaders (e.g., coaches) to lead and make quick decisions. Another approach to ethics is grounded in theology in which ethics is determined via the will of God or divine writings. This approach seems untenable when you consider that groups (e.g., athletic teams) might be comprised of individuals with opposing religious convictions.

Other approaches suggest that ethics is a result of reason or that ethics is determined biologically and connected to our evolutionary past. The biological perspective would suggest that human beings are in many ways similar to nonhuman species and, consequently, much of your decision making, values, and behaviors might be seen as predetermined and outside your conscious control. However, much of daily human behavior suggests otherwise; people are not simply controlled by some biological determinant or evolutionary past because much of human behavior is different from that of nonhuman species.

While all of these approaches might lead you to believe there is no way human beings can agree on ethics, Kretchmar (2005) points out that many common human behaviors in daily life suggest some ethical consistency, a sharing of ethical values. Kretchmar goes on to ask, "But what is the foundation for these common experiences and judgments? A holistic, pragmatic ethic can provide at least some partial answers" (p.186).

A **holistic ethic (holism)** considers all the complexities of what it means to be human beings, such as conscious thoughts, perceptions, ideas, and hopes and the effects they have on emotional and physical states. A holistic ethic also embraces pluralistic approaches to ethics. **Pluralism** professes that many choices and combinations exist for solving dilemmas and conflict. And, as previously discussed, pragmatic thinking considers many factors, nuances, sensitivities, and solutions, both unusual and divergent, for making choices and resolving conflict.

Holism and pluralism are commonsense approaches for developing a coaching philosophy and seem more workable than other philosophical approaches such as dualism and scientific materialism. **Dualism** is a position that basically says human beings are composed of two things—mind and body. According to the **scientific materialism** perspective everything in the world can be explained by principles of mathematics and science. Both dualism and scientific materialism have some value for coaching effectiveness and coaches of excellence will combine all three positions into their approach to coaching. However, because coaches work with athletes—complex and often unpredictable human beings—holism seems to be the most effective position for developing an ethical approach to coaching.

Kretchmar suggests several ways for developing moral confidence and sound ethics in professional life. The following sections discuss these suggestions.

Avoid Three Common Pitfalls

Coaches can commonly make three mistakes that undermine what Kretchmar calls the **moral compass**, the instrument that helps you make trustworthy ethical decisions and guides you through your everyday life.

1. *The first mistake is to "look for clear-cut answers to moral dilemmas"* (Kretchmar, 2005, p. 187). Many of life's problems are neither obvious nor simplistic and neither are the answers to these moral dilemmas. The answers may be found through processes such as creativity, compromise, and consideration.

2. *The second mistake is to look for simplistic answers.* As Kretchmar writes, "If we are looking for simple answers to the dilemmas of life, we will be disappointed. Good living is complex, and it can be achieved in countless ways" (p. 188). While many coaches prefer a black and white approach to dealing with athletes, a large area of grey exists. As a coach and as a person you may sometimes prefer the simple and shy away from the complex, but just as no two athletes are alike no two situations are exactly alike.

3. *The third pitfall is to ignore points of consensus.* Holistic ethics recognizes that similarities and agreements indicate commonalities and shared ethics among people. Kidder (1994) conducted interviews with respected leaders throughout the world and noted a consensus of eight common values: love, truthfulness, fairness, freedom, unity, tolerance, responsibility, and respect for life. Such agreement suggests the existence of a uniformity of ethics that human beings can agree on.

Develop Moral Sensitivity

It is important to be sensitive to moral dilemmas. Think of the hard-nosed coach who never shows mercy to his players or opposing teams. Or consider the insensitive athlete who never demonstrates respect or concern for an opposing player. These people have developed what Kretchmar calls **moral calluses**, the inability to function morally, to do the right thing at the right time. According to Kretchmar, these people cope with this ailment by rationalizing their behavior. Some of these rationalizations include *Everyone else does it*, *It's just part of the game*, and *It's just winning strategy*. These rationalizations allow coaches and athletes to maintain their moral calluses and immoral behaviors.

Coaching is a challenging profession that does not come without some amount of heartache, confrontation, and soul searching. Moral calluses, like real calluses of the body, serve a purpose: to keep you from feeling too much. They keep you insulated from feeling all the moral imperatives you encounter throughout your coaching career. Without some moral calluses you would become overwhelmed and lose confidence in your ability to make decisions. On the other hand, you should not become so insensitive that you lose touch with what is important for making good ethical decisions.

Consider scenario 1 again. Say that your third-string player, who has already missed two practices that month, misses practice the same week your best player misses practice. It is important that you be sensitive to the fact that your best athlete also committed the same infraction, but not so sensitive that you ignore past history and patterns of behaviors. Your best athlete has not missed a practice all season whereas your third-string player has missed three practices that month. Should you be as sensitive to the third-string player as you are to the first-string player? Will it look like you are playing favorites if you discipline the third-string player and not the first-string player? We can only speculate, but the Texas high school football coach would most likely sit both players. Coach Wooden would likely sit the third-string player because he deserved to sit, but play the best player because he earned the right to play based on his otherwise flawless practice attendance throughout the season.

Ethical growth is an ongoing natural human process that is engendered in human beings. Watching yourself at your best and worst can help you gain insight into acquiring ethical behavior. Interestingly, some of our best observable human behavior comes from being part of a family and having family ties.

Develop a Family Atmosphere

One way to develop good moral attitudes and habits in your life and program is to connect to natural ties. The term **natural ties** has to do with the biological urge to care deeply about family members. In this regard people are not too unlike animals that care about their offspring. While good ethics should include caring about others, people are more likely to care about those whom they know or are close to in their daily lives (Glover, 2000). Consequently, it is worthwhile to develop familial bonds in your life and in your program. These bonds can be particularly helpful in sports, where a strong sense of family ties can bring together teammates, coaches, and staff and engender good ethics and a high sense of morality.

Some of the best teams and most enduring programs personify the qualities of family. Therefore, foster a sense of family within your program. You can develop a family atmosphere in many ways. Caring for one another is an important quality, and it starts with the coach. When you demonstrate that you genuinely care for your athletes, you send a message to all your players that caring for one another is important. Another way to create a sense of family is to set it as a goal and have team meetings in which everyone talks about how they can demonstrate concern, support, and love for their teammates. Athletes also must learn to trust one another. Many excellent books are available on building a family atmosphere within your team.

Develop Trust

Trust goes a long way in helping to develop good moral attitudes and habits. When trust exists among people, greater ethical behavior is likely to occur. Consequently, it is important to build trust within your entire organization. Singer (1995) suggests five behaviors for fostering trust between individuals:

1. *Begin by cooperating.* As the saying goes, one good turn deserves another. A positive response and cooperative behavior will more likely be followed by a similar behavior from a teammate.

2. *Cooperate as long as your partner cooperates.* Continual cooperation acts as a reinforcer, which helps maintain cooperative behavior and trust.

3. *Defect as soon as your partner defects.* This helps communicate to your teammate that a lack of cooperation comes at a cost. Without this penalty, the other person might perceive no negative consequence for defection and loss of trust.

4. *Be ready to forgive.* Once the individual has shown remorse and a cooperative spirit, the penalty needs to be removed and you need to forgive and resume cooperation, thereby once again reinforcing cooperative behavior.

5. *Emphasize stability and transparency.* Promote stability in relationships and transparency in cooperation and defection. Stability and transparency are important for fostering trust and an ethical environment. **Stability** refers to factors such as commitment, longevity, and devotion. As a coach, are you committed to your program and athletes or are you simply using your position as a stepping stone to another program? Are your athletes committed to one another? **Transparency** has to do with honest and open communication. Are you, your staff, and athletes communicating your real intentions, thoughts, and feelings or are you masking your true intentions? From a humanistic perspective, honest and open communication and being

genuine are important for fostering relationships, trust, and, ultimately, sound ethical behavior.

Promote Altruistic Behavior

Altruism is the unselfish regard for or devotion to the welfare of others. It means doing the right thing even when the right thing is not in your own personal best interest. Besides a feeling of trust, among staff and teammates of the best teams and most enduring programs there exists a strong sense of altruism. Athletes in these programs may be voraciously competitive but they also are capable of noble altruistic behavior. For example, consider a talented basketball player who is accustomed to starting but agrees to come off the bench for the greater good of the team and the chance to win a championship title. Behind hall of fame basketball player Bill Walton, perennial UCLA backup center Swen Nater showed altruistic behavior by playing hard every day in practice even though he knew he would only see mop up duty in the final minutes of each game. Swen is the only player to be selected in the first round of the NBA draft who never started a collegiate game.

You can promote altruistic behaviors in many ways. As a coach, you should model this behavior. When you sacrifice and do what is best for your players and team, your actions communicate your belief in and the importance of altruistic behaviors. Another way to promote altruistic behaviors is to give your athletes the freedom to make their own decisions that will hopefully help them connect with their unique human capacity for putting the needs of others before their own. When they do model altruistic behavior, reward it. Finally, you can promote altruism within your athletes by helping them cognitively work through the concepts of ethics and the importance of altruism and doing the right thing for the greater good.

Develop an Ethics Checklist

It is not always easy as a coach to know the ethically right thing to do. When you are unsure of what is the ethically correct choice for doing the right thing, Gough (1997) has suggested a handy ethics checklist:

- Is it against the rules of the game?
- Is it fair to everyone involved?
- Would my ethical role models do it?
- How will I and those I care about feel about my decision?

Following are three other simple but useful methods for determining what is right. The first is the *newspaper headline test*. How would you feel if what you decided to do was on the front page of the newspaper for everyone to read? Would you be proud of your decision and actions? The next method is the *family test*. Would you be proud to tell members of your family such as your spouse, child, father, or mother of your actions? The other method is the *mirror test*. Would you be able to look yourself in the mirror and say that you are proud of your actions? If the answer is yes to these ethical tests, then your actions are more than likely the appropriate actions.

DEVELOPING VALUES WITHIN YOUR COACHING PHILOSOPHY

Values can be defined as the motives and personality traits people believe are valuable and worth possessing. **Motives** that coaches might value and think worth possessing either for themselves or for their athletes can include many things such as winning, money, competition, fun, knowledge, career advancement, notoriety, health, knowledge, skill, and character development. **Personality traits** that coaches might think worth possessing either for themselves or for their athletes include honesty, conscientiousness, affection, love, patience, courage, perseverance, resoluteness, determination, and resourcefulness. Notice the blocks (personality traits) of industriousness, loyalty, cooperation, and enthusiasm are at the bottom of Wooden's pyramid of success.

Spend time contemplating your motives for coaching. Why do you coach? Is it to win? Is it to enhance your ego? Is it to vicariously achieve, through your athletes, the success you never achieved as an athlete? Or do you take a more holistic view and see the development of the entire person as an athlete and a human being as your motive? And what personality traits do you believe are worth instilling in your athletes? Some coaches give young athletes an exemption from exhibiting certain personality traits if these athletes are talented and can help their teams win. These coaches tend to undervalue and overlook traits such as honesty, fair play, and humility.

With so many motives and traits, how do you prioritize them for your coaching philosophy? For example, kinesiologists generally prioritize the following four values in order of importance: health, knowledge, skill, and fun. The following sections offer some suggestions for developing and prioritizing values in sport.

Prioritize Values

It would be easy to say that all values are important and you have no need to emphasize one value more than another. However, according to Kretchmar (2005), you have three reasons for prioritizing values.

1. *First, value choices make a difference.* What you determine to be of value will inextricably affect your decision making, interactions with athletes, the direction of your program, and many other aspects of your coaching and program. Reconsider the coach at the beginning of this chapter who prioritized winning the conference championship over athlete accountability. His value choice changed his players' attitudes and his relationship with them as well as

how it forever stunted the growth of his program from reaching higher levels of achievement. With a different priority of values, perhaps his team could have gone on to become national champions.

2. *Prioritization of values is unavoidable in life.* Whether we like it or not, we are forced to commit to certain values and emphasize one value over another. Sure, we prefer winning over losing; who in the coaching profession doesn't relish a victory over a defeat, but at what cost? Early in my coaching career I faced the unpleasant and unavoidable task of choosing between the value of winning and the values of coaching enjoyment and coaching autonomy. Although unheralded at the time, my sophomore athlete was clearly destined to become a national champion. There was one problem—the diver was no fun to coach and wanted to call all the shots. I chose to prioritize coaching enjoyment and autonomy over winning. The athlete did go on to win a national title, just not with me. And I went on to an enjoyable and autonomous 37 year coaching career.

Take time to carefully consider your values and which ones are most important to you. Make sure they are motives and personality traits you truly value. As Kretchmar writes, "Have you forfeited your right to make further choices by choosing to follow the crowd? Are your decisions automatic, emotional, and based only on what feels right at the moment? Or are your decisions more deliberate and thoughtful" (p. 217)?

3. *Value choices provide focus.* By prioritizing your values, you bring into focus a clear philosophical picture of who you are as a coach, what you think is important as a coach, and why you coach. Your philosophical clarity makes you a decisive leader, enviable role model, respected professional, and content and autonomous coach. Without philosophical clarity (i.e., clearly prioritized values) you are perceived by others as lacking insight, energy, interest, direction, and courage (Kretchmar, 2005).

The following section will help you come up with a plan for prioritizing your values.

Rank Values

One way to prioritize values is to rank them. According to Baier (1958), there are two processes for effectively ranking values—survey the facts and weigh the reasons.

Survey the Facts

To survey the facts, you need to catalog the characteristics and benefits of each value while paying attention to three factors:

1. Short- and long-term benefits
2. Benefits for yourself and others
3. Benefits as ends in themselves and as means to other ends

To understand the survey process, consider ranking the value of winning. In the short term, winning provides feelings of pleasure, elation, and possibly euphoria, a gold medal, notoriety, and recognition. In the long term, however, the only benefit that remains is generally the medal. A short-term benefit exists for the athlete and possibly the coach, but in the long term the benefit is very little for the athlete and others. The benefit of winning is generally an end in itself. Even for U.S. Olympic gold medalists, little remuneration occurs unless the athlete wins several gold medals. In some cases winning is a means to other ends, such as advancement to a higher level of competition, a job, or entry into another career such as broadcasting. In general, however, most victories are an end in themselves. This realization is often unsettling to many athletes once the thrill of victory has worn off. This reminds me of the lyrics in *Glory Days* by Bruce Springsteen:

> Now I think I'm going down to the well tonight
> and I'm going to drink till I get my fill
> And I hope when I get old I don't sit around thinking about it
> but I probably will
> Yeah, just sitting back trying to recapture
> a little of the glory of, well time slips away
> and leaves you with nothing mister but
> boring stories of glory days
> Glory days well they'll pass you by
> Glory days in the wink of a young girl's eye
> Glory days, glory days

"Glory Days" by Bruce Springsteen. Copyright © 1984 Bruce Springsteen (ASCAP). Reprinted by permission. International copyright secured. All rights reserved.

The United States Olympic Committee (USOC) has a program for athletes after they return from the Olympic Games that helps them make the often difficult transition to retirement. Olympians strive their entire careers to make the Olympic team and win a medal. Once their Olympic experience is over, however, they can experience confusion, disappointment, disillusionment, and depression. Many athletes, not just Olympians, discover afterward that the journey is more meaningful and fulfilling than the destination.

Weigh the Reasons

To weigh the reasons, Baier (1958) suggests using rules of superiority. Kretchmar (2005) proposes three rules for evaluating (weighing) the information gathered in your survey.

• *Values that are good in themselves are superior to values that lead to good things* (Frankena, 1973). In other words, intrinsic values are superior to extrinsic values. For example, as a coach when you have given your all in practice, you feel a sense of pride, accomplishment, and competence, which are all good in and of themselves and therefore need no further justification. For this reason they are called **end values**. However, extrinsic values are intricately tied to intrinsic values. For example, because you value the extrinsic outcome of athlete improvement and success, you work hard in practice and therefore experience intrinsic emotions of pride, accomplishment, and competence. For this reason, extrinsic values are called **means values**, which are good as well because they lead to good things. In other words, the extrinsic value of athlete improvement and success encourages high coaching effort resulting in feelings of pride, accomplishment, and competence.

• *All else being equal, experiences that include satisfaction carry more intrinsic power than those that do not* (Frankena, 1973). We do things many times because they are fun and pleasurable but there is something deeper, more meaningful, and of more value than simple pleasure and fun, something that leads to happiness or what Frankena calls satisfactoriness. **Satisfactoriness** includes experiences that result in contentment and deep satisfaction. These experiences aren't necessarily easy and can be accompanied by discomfort and pain. For example, athletes may remember winning a competition, but they also are likely to remember and value grueling workouts when they left practice exhausted but content, proud, and satisfied in knowing they gave their very best effort.

• *Satisfactory experiences that build a coherent and meaningful life take precedence over those that are isolated moments of pleasure* (MacIntyre, 1984; Bellah et al., 1985, 1991; Singer, 1995). What does it mean to build a coherent and meaningful life? Kretchmar (2005) writes, "A coherent, meaningful life brings with it durable satisfactions. This criterion is about making sense of our lives, of seeing and living a pattern in daily activities that is interesting and worthy. When we say that life has meaning, we are indicating that it is reasonably consistent, has poignancy, has a goal, and is recognizably ours." (p. 227).

Kretchmar suggests that a fundamental experience of a coherent life involves developing and living a story with multiple chapters. When I consider this criterion for ranking values, I am mindful of the different chapters of their stories that athletes play out after their sport experiences. Some successful athletes go on to develop increasingly meaningful and durable satisfactory chapters after their sport careers. They mature, establish new goals, make commitments, and create new patterns of living. Unfortunately, some successful athletes become lost and frozen in time after retiring from their sport. The last chapter to their story is their sport experience. They can't seem to reinvent or rewrite themselves and their lives. Tyson Chandler is an exception.

In an article about 7'1" NBA center Tyson Chandler and his youth basketball experience, Jenkins (2011) writes, "But Chandler vowed that once he was drafted and moved his mother out of the three-bedroom house she shared with eight friends in San Bernardino, he would reject the system that turned him out. 'I hated it,' Chandler says. 'I just felt like I had no options. All I wanted was to make it in the NBA so people would sit down and talk to me and find out who I really am'" (pp. 58-59). Chandler is lucky. He was able to overcome his youth basketball experience and create a new story for himself. In talking about his young son, Chandler says, "I will never let him go through the wringer I did. Men treating kids like they're professionals, like they're properties—it drives me nuts." He goes on to say, "I'm worried about the next kid who is in the same position I was. I want him to know there is a way to get through it all without become something you're not" (p. 59).

To what extent do coaches contribute or steal an athlete's ability to build a coherent and meaningful life? It depends in part on the values we hold and the types of experiences we provide our athletes. When it comes to ranking your values, give considerable weight to satisfactory experiences that help your athletes build coherent and meaningful lives both during and after their sport experiences. Provide experiences that teach them how to write new and wonderful chapters in the stories of their lives.

THE VALUES OF SPORT

I came home from practice one day early in my career and told my wife, "If this is just about winning and losing, then I don't want to coach anymore." I wanted coaching to be about more than that. There has to be a greater good, a higher purpose—a more lasting permanence to what we coaches do. I remember talking to a group of my summer camp divers two years after former Indiana University diver Mark Lenzi won the Olympic gold medal. I was shocked to realize that none of them knew who he was or what he had accomplished. Fame is fleeting, medals tarnish, and champions soon forgotten. So, what lasts?

After finishing my career, I felt a need to give back to the sport of diving and to the young athletes coming up the ranks. My motivation had nothing to do with medals or victories, but rather with a belief that I had come away from my sport experience with something precious that I would carry with me the rest of my life, something that would influence the quality of my life after sport, something that would help me write new, coherent, and meaningful chapters in the story of my life.

Following are some values athletes can learn through their sport experience that are worth considering, modeling, and including in your coaching philosophy.

• *Competition.* Through competition athletes experience the importance of cooperation and mutual gratification. They also enjoy enriched experiences that include joy, tension, drama, excitement, resolution, challenge, and more. They also experience excellence and performing to one's absolute best. Coaches should emphasize these values rather than winning.

- *Positive attitude.* People from all walks of life confront similar universal challenges, the same challenges athletes experience in sport. These challenges include such experiences as failure, defeat, fear, self-doubt, and quitting. What is dissimilar among these people is how they perceive and react to these challenges. Much of this difference can be attributed to attitude. Model and emphasize the value of a positive attitude in your coaching.

- *Failure.* Failure can actually lead to success. Help your athletes learn the value of failure as part of the becoming process. Spanish philosopher George Santayana (1905) wrote, "Those who cannot remember the past are condemned to repeat it" (p. 284). Help your athletes learn that it is okay to make mistakes. Mistakes are enriching learning experiences. Model this value by working harder with your athletes after finding failure.

- *Defeat.* Defeat can be motivating. Teach your athletes the value of defeat and the importance of resiliency and persistence. Help them see defeat today as a temporary setback and a source of motivation for trying harder tomorrow and becoming the unstoppable and resilient athlete. Model persistence and resiliency in your coaching behavior.

- *Courage.* Courage isn't the absence of fear but, rather, the willingness to confront it. With each experience, athletes gain strength, courage, and confidence. Encourage your athletes to value confronting their fears rather than retreating from them. Increase athlete self-efficacy so they believe they have the ability to confront and master the challenge.

- *Self-belief.* Everyone has self-doubt at some time or another and must deal with negative thoughts such as *What if I am not good enough? What if I fail?* and *What if I embarrass myself?* Teach your athletes the value of self-belief for overcoming self-doubt. As former Indiana University swimming coach Doc Councilman said to me, "If you think you can, you will. If you don't, you won't!"

You build athlete self-belief through mastery learning and attainment of success. I once overheard a coach say, "Well, I taught them how to do it; they just aren't doing it right." As Wooden would say, you haven't taught until they have learned (Nater & Gallimore, 2010). Keep coaching it until they get it.

- *Problems.* Teach your athletes to perceive problems as genuine opportunities. Misfortune and temporary setbacks are opportunities to learn and grow. Encourage your athletes to value problems and see them as challenging opportunities not insurmountable obstacles.

- *Responsibility.* Teach your athletes the value of taking responsibility for their actions and failures rather than making excuses for them. Each excuse they make is like a little shovel of dirt digging them deeper and deeper into a hole from which they can never escape.

• *Perseverance*. Sometimes it is not the most talented athlete who wins but the most persistent, just as it is not always the most well-known coach who ultimately wins, but the most persistent. Sometimes the tortoise wins the race. Teach your athletes to value perseverance. Every athlete gets knocked down now and then; the trick is to learn to stand back up and rejoin the good fight. Athletes and coaches alike ponder quitting at times, but successful people find ways to refocus, regroup, and ready themselves for tomorrow. No matter how bad a day you might have, the sun comes up again tomorrow and you receive the precious gift of starting over.

• *Effort*. As English philosopher James Allen (2006) wrote, "In all human affairs there are efforts and there are results. And the strength of the effort is the measure of the result. Chance is not" (p. 41). In other words, what you put into something is what you get out of it. Teach your athletes the value of effort in determining their results. To paraphrase Francis Bacon: The mold of your fortune is in your own hands.

• *Faith*. Faith is the act of believing in something that has yet to happen and has no tangible proof of happening. Without faith, nothing of great consequence is likely to occur. Teach your athletes that along with effort, faith precedes success. Also, model faith to your athletes. Coaches who have faith in themselves also have athletes who believe in their coaches and themselves. The converse is also true.

• *Dream*. Teach your athletes the value of a dream. A dream is important for both athletes and coaches because it gives them a motivational mental image of where they want to go, what they want to accomplish, and who they want to become. A dream sustains and uplifts their spirits during those dark and foreboding days and nights that inevitably come to those who dream.

• *Determination*. When Charlene Westphal, a courageous and strong-willed woman, was asked how she managed to live 5 years with breast cancer after the doctors gave here only 5 months to live, she replied, "Hope starts the dream but determination finishes it." I have witnessed athletes reach their athletic dreams simply because they were so damned determined that they refused to take *no* for an answer and refused to accept anything less than the fulfillment of their dreams. Determined athletes are a combination of the unstoppable athlete, the resilient athlete, and the salivating athlete. When you bundle them into one athlete, that athlete can conquer any challenge and fulfill any dream. Determined athletes—and determined coaches—dream of things that never were and say, *Why not?* And then they make their dreams become reality.

• *Self-discipline*. A dream is important but unobtainable unless athletes and coaches have the self-discipline to put forth the effort to make the dream a reality. Many coaches and athletes talk about greatness in the evening but can't find the self-discipline in the morning to get the job done. Self-discipline is the act of doing what should be done, doing it when it should be done, and doing it all the time, even when no one is watching.

THE PHILOSOPHICAL COACH

As a philosophical coach you begin formulating your philosophy the first day of your coaching career. You use the accumulation of knowledge, past experiences, and the advice of others to develop your philosophy, but ultimately it is your philosophy, reflecting your beliefs, ethics, and values. Your philosophy matures through continued knowledge building, introspection, cognitive development, and experience. With your coaching philosophy you are capable of answering the questions posed earlier in this chapter, such as *What is the purpose of sport?* And *Why do I coach?*

THE WISE COACH

As a wise coach, you carefully and deeply consider your philosophy to the extent that you are capable of articulating it to your athletes, staff, administrators, parents, and others so that your entire program is imbued with your philosophical perspective. You have matured and reached the cognitive stage of postformal thought where you engage in dialectical and concrete pragmatic thinking. You have a holistic and pragmatic philosophy in which you consider all factors when making decisions and look for workable solutions when solving problems. Unlike the coach at the beginning of this chapter, your philosophy helps you make the kinds of decisions that keep your program on track, moving forward, and reaching more distant goals. Your athletes respect you. When they leave your program, they are not only better athletes but better human beings for having been influenced by your coaching and your philosophy.

YOUR COACHING TOOLBOX

A personal coaching philosophy is another important tool for your coaching toolbox. As mentioned at the outset of this chapter, a philosophy that is deeply considered and well thought out guides you along your coaching journey by helping you make good decisions based on clearly defined ethics and values. Your philosophy is what sets you apart from other coaches. It is a statement of who you are as a coach, what you want to accomplish, and how you are going to achieve those accomplishments. It is a reflection of what you believe. To become a coach of excellence, first decide what you believe is right and what is of value for you, your athletes, and your program. Then, make decisions based on those beliefs.

THE SCIENTIFIC AND ARTFUL COACH

We began this book in the introduction by talking about the professional coach and the importance of learning theories, paradigms, and scientific data for becoming a coach of excellence. We end this book looking at something all together different. Philosophy concerns itself with such stuff as moral dilemmas, ethical considerations, and value choices. Unlike science, philosophy doesn't literally measure anything and, therefore, offers no hard scientific data. Nevertheless, philosophy is part of the art of coaching and is as equally important as science for becoming a coach of excellence.

The word *philosophy* is derived from the Greek word *philos* which means love and the Greek word *sophia* which means wisdom. So the word *philosophy* basically means *the love of wisdom*. Philosophy concerns itself with many areas of wisdom including ethics, logic, truth, and genuine knowledge. What is the power that comes from the knowledge of science without the wisdom that comes from the knowledge of philosophy? Becoming a coach of excellence requires becoming both a scientific coach and an artful (wise) coach. May this book help you become both.

IF YOU REMEMBER ONLY THREE THINGS

1. *Remember to have a coaching philosophy.* The importance of a personal coaching philosophy can't be overstated because it is the vehicle for keeping you moving along the winding superhighway of coaching success. As I reflect on my career, I vividly recall several bumps in the road where my coaching philosophy helped guide my way. At the time I didn't truly comprehend the significance of the situations or the monumental impact my decisions would have on my future coaching career. In each case, the decision I made temporarily weakened my team and program, diminished my coaching reputation, and threatened my coaching job. I had misgivings and doubt, but I stuck with my decisions because of my philosophical perspective on coaching, sport, and working with young athletes. In hindsight, they were the two best decisions of my career—for my coaching happiness, longevity, and success.

2. *Remember to let your philosophy reflect holism and pragmatism.* Some situations are black and white, right and wrong; an athlete blatantly breaks specific team rules, and the consequences are unambiguous and the penalties clear. However, not all situations are so neatly simple or clear cut; the best decision may be hiding somewhere in a grey area. A holistic and pragmatic philosophy considers the complexities of human beings who just happen to be athletes. It considers individual differences. It considers alternative solutions for resolving dilemmas and conflict. It considers many factors, both obvious and obscure, and looks to find the most workable and effective resolution within the grey area. Unlike the coach at the outset of this chapter, a holistic and pragmatic coaching philosophy helps you make wise decisions. Part of your philosophy should include providing your athletes with satisfactory experiences that teach them to build coherent and meaningful lives both during and after sport.

3. *Remember to let your coaching philosophy reflect your growth as a coach and human being.* A hardnosed U.S. Olympic coach whom I greatly respect talked about how having children of his own influenced his coaching. Having kids, he said, made him a little more understanding and tolerant. It didn't make him any less tough as a coach, but it did influence his coaching style, persona, and philosophy. When we reflect on them and learn from them, many coaching experiences help us become more effective and wiser. I believe many of the same things I did when I first started coaching, but I am not the same coach I was 30 years ago, 20 years ago, 10 years ago, or even 2 years ago. Let your philosophy reflect the depth and breadth of your experiences and growth as a coach and human being. About a philosophy Santayana (1913) wrote, "A philosophy is not genuine unless it inspires and expresses the life of those who cherish it" (p. 187). Cherish your coaching philosophy and may it indeed inspire and guide you and express the life you choose to lead.

SUGGESTED READINGS

Kretchmar, R.S. (2005). *Practical philosophy of sport and physical activity* (2nd ed.). Champaign, IL: Human Kinetics.

[Much of this chapter is based on ideas, concepts, and suggestions from this well-written book. This book is worth reading for any coach looking to better understand and formalize a coaching philosophy.]   [This book is instructive for developing a coaching philosophy.]

Nater, S. & Gallimore, R. (2010). *You haven't taught until they have learned: John Wooden's teaching principles and practices.* Morgantown, WV: Fitness Information Technology.

[An easy and interesting read and another good book for developing your coaching philosophy.]

Wooden, J. & Carty J. (2010). *Coach Wooden's pyramid of success: Building blocks for a better life.* Ventura, CA: Regal Books.

REFERENCES

Preface

Brunson, D.A. & Vogt, J.F. (1996). Empowering our students and ourselves: A liberal democratic approach to the communication classroom. *Communication Education*, *45*, 73-83.

Buscaglia, L. (Speaker). (1984). "Love." Cassette recording titled *On being fully human*. MCMLXXXIV. Chicago: Nightingale-Conant Corporation.

Chase, W.G. & Simon, H.A. (1973). The mind's eye in chess. In W.G. Chase (ed.), *Visual information processing* (pp. 215-281). San Diego: Academic Press.

Eisner, E.W. (1982). An artistic approach to supervision. In T. J. Sergiovanni (ed.), *Supervision of teaching* (ASCD 1982 Yearbook). Alexandria, VA: Association for Supervision and Curriculum Development.

Kohn, A. (1993). Choices for children: Why and how to let students decide. *Phi Delta Kappa*, *75*, 8-16, 18-21.

Rumelhart, D. & Norman, D. (1981). Analogical processes in learning. In J.R. Anderson (ed.), *Cognitive skills and their acquisition* (pp. 335-360). Hillsdale, NJ: Erlbaum.

Introduction

Brunson, D.A. & Vogt, J.F. (1996). Empowering our students and ourselves: A liberal democratic approach to the communication classroom. *Communication Education*, 45, 73-83.

Counsilman, J.E. (1968). *The science of swimming*. Englewood Cliffs, NJ: Prentice Hall.

Eby, J.W. (1998). *Reflective planning, teaching, and evaluation: K-12* (2nd ed.). Upper Saddle River, NJ: Merrill.

Eggen, P.D. & Kauchak, D. (2008*). Educational psychology: Windows on classrooms*. Upper Saddle River, NJ: Prentice Hall.

Faulkner, W. (1939). *The wild palms*. New York: Random House.

Faulkner, W. (1950). *Nobel prize speech*. Given at the 1950 Nobel Prize banquet at the City Hall in Stockholm, Sweden, December 10.

Kohn, A. (1993). Choices for children: Why and how to let students decide. *Phi Delta Kappa*, 75, 8-16, 18-21.

Leonard, G. (1992). *Mastery: The keys to success and long-term fulfillment*. New York: Penguin Books.

Lortie, D.C. (1975). *Schoolteacher: A sociological study*. Chicago: The University of Chicago Press.

MacKay, A. (1982). *Project Quest: Teaching strategies and pupil achievement*. Occasional Paper Series, Centre for Research in Teaching, Faculty of Education, University of Alberta, Edmonton, Alberta, Canada.

Martens, R. (2004). *Successful coaching* (3rd ed.). Champaign, IL: Human Kinetics.

Moallem, M. (1997). The content and nature of reflective teaching: A case of an expert middle school science teacher. *Clearing House*, 70, 143-150.

Schmidt, R.A., & Wrisberg, C.A. (2008). *Motor learning and performance: A situation-based learning approach* (4th ed.). Champaign, IL: Human Kinetics.

Sellers, C. (2008). 20 years later—What has changed in America's elite coaches? In http://coaching.usolympicteam.com/coaching/kpub.nsf/v/21jan08.

Sternberg, R. J., & Horvath, J.A. (1995). A prototype view of expert teaching. *Educational Researcher*, 24, 9-17.

Chapter 1

Agbor-Baiyee, W. (1997). A cyclical model of student career motivation. *College Student Journal*, *31*, 467-472.

Agne, K., Greenwood, G.E., & Miller, L.D. (1994). Relationships between teacher belief systems and teacher effectiveness. *Journal of Research and Development in Education*, 27, 141-152.

Ashton, P.T., & Webb, R.B. (1986). *Making a difference: Teachers' sense of efficacy and student achievement*. White Plains, NY: Pearson Longman.

Bandura, A. (1962). Social learning through imitation. In N.R. Jones (ed.), *Nebraska Symposium on Motivation*. Lincoln: University of Nebraska Press.

Bandura, A. (1981). Self-referent thought: A developmental analysis of self-efficacy. In Flavell, J.H., & Ross, L. (eds.), *Social cognitive development: Frontiers and possible futures (200-239)*. Cambridge: Cambridge University Press.

Bandura, A. (1986). *Social foundations of thought and action: A social cognitive theory*. Englewood Cliffs, NJ: Prentice-Hall.

Bandura, A. (1993). Perceived self-efficacy in cognitive development and functioning. *Educational Psychologist, 28*, 117-148.

Bandura, A. (1997). *Self-efficacy: The exercise of control*. San Francisco: Freeman.

Callow, N., Hardy, L., & Hall, C. (2001). The effects of a motivational general-mastery imagery intervention on the sport confidence of high-level badminton players. *Research Quarterly for Exercise and Sport, 72*, 389-400.

Covington, M.V. (1984). Motivation for self-worth. In R. Ames & C. Ames (eds.), *Research on motivation in education* (pp. 77-113). New York: Academic Press.

Covington, M.V., & Omelich, C.L. (1984). An empirical examination of Weiner's critique of attribution research. *Journal of Educational Psychology, 76*, 1214-1225.

Covington, M.V., & Omelich, C.L. (1987). "I knew it cold before the exam": A test of the anxiety-blockage hypothesis. *Journal of Educational Psychology, 79*, 393-400.

Cox, R.H. (2002). *Sport psychology: Concepts and applications*. Dubuque, IA: Brown.

Csikszentimichalyi, M. (1990). *Flow: The psychology of optimal experience*. New York: Harper and Row.

Deci, E.; Koestner, R.; Ryan, R. (2001). "The pervasive negative effects of rewards on intrinsic motivation: Response to Cameron (2001)". *Review of Educational Research* 71 (1): 43–51.

Deci, E.L., & Ryan, R.M. (1985). *Intrinsic motivation and self-determination in human behavior*. New York: Plenum.

Deci, E.L., Vallerand, R.J., Pelletier, J.G., & Ryan, R.M. (1991). Motivation and education: The self-determination perspective. *The Educational Psychologist, 26*, 325-346.

Duke, M., Johnson, T.C., & Nowicki, S., Jr. (1977). Effects of sports fitness campus experience on locus of control orientation in children, ages 6 to 14. *Research Quarterly, 48*(2), 280-283.

Eccles, J.S., & Wigfield, A. (2002). Motivational beliefs, values, and goals. *Annual Review of Psychology, 53*, 109-132.

Epstein, J. (1989). Family structures and student motivation: A developmental perspective. In C. Ames & R. Ames (eds.), *Research on motivation in education* (Vol. 3, pp. 259-295). New York: Academic Press.

Feltz, D.L., Chase, M.A., Moritz, S.A., & Sullivan, P.J. (1999). A conceptual model of coaching efficacy: Preliminary investigation and instrument development. *Journal of Educational Psychology, 91*, 765-776.

Feltz, D.L., & Riessinger, C.A. (1990). Effects on in vivo emotive imagery and performance feedback on self-efficacy and muscular endurance. *Journal of Sport and Exercise Psychology, 12*, 132-143.

Feltz, D.L., Short, S.E., & Sullivan, P.J. (2008). *Self-efficacy in sport: Research and strategies for working with athletes, teams, and coaches*. Champaign, IL: Human Kinetics.

Festinger, L.A. (1957). *A theory of cognitive dissonance theory*. Palo Alto, CA: Stanford University Press.

Festinger, L.A. (1962, October). Cognitive dissonance. *Scientific American, 207*, 93-106.

Garza, D.L., & Feltz, D.L. (1998). Effects of selected mental practice techniques on performance ratings, self-efficacy, and competition confidence of competitive figure skaters. *The Sport Psychologist, 12*, 1-15.

George, T.R., & Feltz, D.L. (1995). Motivation in sport from a collective efficacy perspective. *International Journal of Sport Psychology, 26*, 98-116.

Grove, J.R., & Pargmann, D. (1986). Attributions and performance during competition. *Journal of Sport Psychology, 8*, 129-134.

Harter, S. (1978). Effectance motivation reconsidered: Towards a developmental model. *Human Development, 21*, 34-64.

Hitz, R., & Driscoll, A. (1994). Give encouragement, not praise. *Texas Child Care, 17*, 2-11.

Hoffman, E. (1998). Peak experiences in childhood: An exploratory study. *Journal of Humanistic Psychology, 38*, 109-120.

Horn, T.S. (1984). Expectancy effects in the interscholastic athletic setting: Methodological concerns. *Journal of Sport Psychology, 6*, 60-76.

Jackson, S.A. (1992). Athletes in flow: A qualitative investigation of flow states in elite figure skaters. *Journal of Applied Sport Psychology, 4*, 161-180.

Jackson, S.A. (1995). Factors influencing the occurrence of flow state in elite athletes. *Journal of Applied Sport Psychology, 7*, 138-166.

Jackson, S.A., & Csikszentmihalyi, M. (1999). *Flow in sports: The keys to optimal experiences and performances.* Champaign, IL: Human Kinetics.

Jordan, M. (1994). *I can't accept not trying.* New York: Harper Collins.

Joyce, B., Weil, M., & Calhoun, E. (2009). *Models of teaching.* Boston: Allyn & Bacon.

Kimiecik, J.C., & Stein, G.L. (1992). Examining flow experiences in sports contexts: Conceptual issues and methodological concerns. *Journal of Sport Psychology, 4,* 144-160.

Kounin, J.S. (1970). *Discipline and classroom management.* New York: Holt.

Landin, D., & Herbert, E.P. (1999). The influence of self-talk on the performance of skilled female tennis players. *Journal of Applied Sport Psychology, 11,* 263-282.

Lefrançois, G.R. (2000). *Psychological theories and human learning: What the Old Man said* (4th ed.). Belmont, CA: Wadsworth.

Lefrançois, G.R. (2000). *Psychology for teaching.* Belmont, CA: Wadsworth.

Lee, K.S., Malete, L., & Feltz, D.L. (2002). The strength of coaching efficacy between certified and noncertified Singapore coaches. *International Journal of Applied Sport Science, 14,* 55-67.

Maddux, J.E. (1995). Self-efficacy theory: An introduction. In J.E. Maddux (ed.), *Self-efficacy, adaptation, and adjustment: Theory, research, and application* (pp. 3-33). New York: Plenum Press.

Malete, L., & Feltz, D.L. (2000). The effect of a coaching education program on coaching efficacy. *The Sport Psychologist, 14,* 410-417.

Martinek, T. (1981). Pygmalion in the gym. A model for the communication of teacher expectations in physical education. *Research Quarterly for Exercise and Sport, 52,* 58-67.

Maslow, A.H. (1968). Some educational implications of the humanistic psychologies. *Harvard Educational Review, Vol. 38*(4), 685-696.

Maslow, A.H. (1970). *Motivation and personality* (2nd ed.). New York: Harper & Row.

Maslow, A.H.(1971). *The farther reaches of human nature.* Penguin.

Mueller, C.M., & Dweck, C.S. (1998). Praise for intelligence can undermine children's motivation and performance. *Journal of Personality and Social Psychology, 75,* 33-52.

Prapavessis, H., & Carron, A.V. (1988). Learned helplessness in sport. *The Sport Psychologist, 2,* 189-201.

Rogers, C.R., & Freiberg, H.J. (1994). *Freedom to learn* (4th ed.). New York: Merrill.

Rowan, J. (1998). Maslow amended. *Journal of Humanistic Psychology, 38,* 81-92.

Rudisill, M.E. (1988). Sex differences in various cognitive and behavioral parameters in a competitive situation. *International Journal of Sport Psychology, 19,* 296-310.

Seligman, M.E.P. (1995). *The optimistic child.* New York: Houghton Mifflin.

Short, S.E., Bruggeman, J.M., Engel, S.G., Marback, T.L., Wang, L.J., Willadsen, A., Short, M.W. (2002). The effect of imagery function and imagery direction on self-efficacy and performance on a golf putting task. *The Sport Psychologist, 16,* 48-67.

Solomon, G.B. (1998). Coach expectations and differential feedback: Perceptual flexibility revisited. *Journal of Sport Behavior, 21,* issue 3, 298-313.

Solomon, G.B., Striegel, D.A., Eliot, J.E., Heon, S.N., Maas, J.L., & Wayda, V.K. (1996). The self-fulfilling prophecy in college basketball: Implications for effective coaching. *Journal of Applied Sport Psychology, 8,* 44-59.

Stein, G.L., Kimiecik, J.C., Daniels, J., & Jackson, S.A. (1995). Psychological antecedents of flow in recreational sport. *Personality and Social Psychology Bulletin, 21,* 125-135.

Theodorakis, Y., Weinberg, R., Natsis, P., Douma, I., & Kazakas, P. (2000). The effects of motivational versus instructional self-talk on improving motor performance. *The Sport Psychologist, 14,* 253-271.

Vallerand, R.J., & Losier, G.F. (1999). An integrative analysis of intrinsic and extrinsic motivation in sport. *Journal of Applied Sport Psychology, 11,* 142-169.

Weiner, B. (1985). An attributional theory of achievement motivation and emotion. *Psychological Review, 92,* 548-573.

Weiner, B. (1992). *Human motivation: Metaphors, theories, and research.* Newbury Park, CA: Sage.

Weiner, B. (1994). Integrating social and personal theories of achievement striving. *Review of Educational Research, 64,* 557-573.

White, R.W. (1959). Motivation reconsidered: The concept of competence. *Psychological Review, 66,* 297-333.

Wigfield, A., Eccles, J.S., & Rodriguez, D. (1998). The development of children's motivation in school contexts. In P.D. Pearson & A. Iran-Nejad (eds.), *Review of Research in Education, 23,* 73-118.

Woolfolk, A.E. & Hoy, W.K. (1990). Prospective teachers' sense of self-efficacy and belief about control. *Journal of Educational Psychology and Aging, 2,* 3-8.

Woolfolk, A.E., Rosoff, B., & Hoy, W.K. (1990). Teachers' sense of efficacy and their beliefs about managing students. *Teaching and Teacher Education, 6,* 137-148.

Zinsser, N., Bunker, L., & Williams, J.M. (2001). Cognitive techniques for building confidence and enhancing performance. In J.M. Williams (Ed.), *Applied sport psychology: Personal growth to peak performance* (pp. 284-311). Mountain View, CA: Mayfield.

Chapter 2

Atkins, H. (2011). A Nightmare Ends a Dream. *New York Times*, November 13.

Covington, M.V. (1984). Motivation for self-worth. In R. Ames & C. Ames (eds.), *Research on motivation in education* (pp. 77-113). New York: Academic Press.

Covington, M.V., & Omelich, C.L. (1984). An empirical examination of Weiner's critique of attribution research. *Journal of Educational Psychology, 76*, 1214-1225.

Covington, M.V., & Omelich, C.L. (1987). "I knew it cold before the exam": A test of the anxiety-blockage hypothesis. *Journal of Educational Psychology, 79*, 393-400.

Cox, R.H. (2002). *Sport psychology: Concepts and applications*. Dubuque, IA: Brown.

Deci, E.L. & Ryan, R.M. (1985). *Intrinsic motivation and self-determination in human behavior.* New York: Plenum Press.

Deci, E.L. & Ryan, R.M. (2000). The "what" and "why" of goal pursuits: Human needs and self-determination of behavior. *Psychology of Inquiry, 11*, 227-268.

Duke, M., Johnson, T.C., & Nowicki, S., Jr. (1977). Effects of sports fitness campus experience on locus of control orientation in children, ages 6 to 14. *Research Quarterly, 48* (2), 280-283.

Epstein, J. (1989). Family structures and student motivation: A developmental perspective. In C. Ames & R. Ames (eds.), *Research on motivation in education* (Vol. 3, pp. 259-295). New York: Academic Press.

Grove, J.R., & Pargmann, D. (1986). Attributions and performance during competition. *Journal of Sport Psychology, 8*, 129-134.

Heider, F. (1944). Social perception and phenomenal causality. Psychological Review, 51, 358-374.

Heider, F. (1958). The psychology of interpersonal relations. New York: John Wiley and Sons.

Mallett, C., & Hanrahan, S. (2004). Elite athletes: why does the 'fire' burn so brightly? *Psychology of Sport and Exercise, 5*, 183-200.

Prapavessis, H., & Carron, A.V. (1988). Learned helplessness in sport. *The Sport Psychologist, 2*, 189-201.

Rotter, J. B., "Generalized Expectancies for Interpersonal Trust," *American Psychologist*, 1971, 26, pp. 443-452.

Rudisill, M.E. (1988). Sex differences in various cognitive and behavioral parameters in a competitive situation. *International Journal of Sport Psychology, 19*, 296-310.

Seligman, M.E.P. (1995). *The optimistic child*. New York: Houghton Mifflin.

Stallone, S. (1976). *Rocky*.

Vallerand, R.J. (1997). Toward a hierarchical model of intrinsic and extrinsic motivation.

Vallerand, R.J., & Rousseau, F.L. (2001). Intrinsic and extrinsic motivation in sport and exercise: A review using the hierarchical model of intrinsic and extrinsic motivation. In R. Singer, H. Hausenblas, & C. Janelle (eds.), *Handbook of sport psychology* (2nd ed., pp. 389-416). New York: Wiley.

Weinberg, R.S. & Gould, D. (2011). *Foundations of sport and exercise psychology* (5th ed.). Champaign, IL: Human Kinetics.

Weiner, B. (1972). *Theories of motivation: From mechanism to cognition*. Chicago: Rand McNally.

Weiner, B. (1985). An attributional theory of achievement motivation and emotion. *Psychological Review, 92*, 548-573.

Weiner, B. (1992). *Human motivation: Metaphors, theories, and research*. Newbury Park, CA: Sage.

Weiner, B. (1994). Integrating social and personal theories of achievement striving. *Review of Educational Research, 64*, 557-573.

Zanna, M.P. (2004). *Advances in experimental social psychology*. New York: Academic Press.

Chapter 3

Gibbons, T., McConnell, A., Forster, T., Tuffey-Riewald, S., and Peterson, K. (2003). *Reflections on success: U.S. Olympians describe the success factors and obstacles that most influenced their Olympic Development*. Results of the Talent Identification and Development Questionnaire to U.S. Olympians. A USOC 2003 publication.

Grand, D., & Goldberg, A.S. (2011). *This is your brain on sports: Beating blocks, slumps and performance anxiety for good!* Indianapolis: Dog Ear Publishing.

Lefrançois, G.R. (2000). *Psychology for teaching*. Belmont, CA: Wadsworth.

Martens, R. (2004). *Successful coaching*. Champaign, IL: Human Kinetics.

Smith, R.E., & Smoll, F.L. (2001). *Way to go, coach*. Palo Alto, CA: Warde.

Thompson, J. (2003). *The double-goal coach*. New York: Harper-Collins.

Thorndike, E.L. (1898). Animal intelligence: An experimental study of the associative processes in animals. *Psychological Review Monograph Supplement*, 2 (8).

Vallerand, R.J., Blanchard, C., Mageau, C., Koestner, R., Ratelle, C., Leonard, M., et al. (2003). Les passions de l'ame: On obsessive and harmonious passions. *Journal of Personality and Social Psychology*, *85*, 756-767.

Chapter 4

Adams, J.A., (1971). A closed-loop theory of motor learning. *Journal of Motor Behavior, 3*, 111-150.

Ames, C. (1992). Classrooms: Goals, structures and student motivation. *Journal of Educational Psychology, 84*, 261-271.

Brantner, J.P., & Doherty, M.A. (1983). A review of timeout: A conceptual and methodological analysis. In S. Axelrod & J. Apsche (eds.), *The effects of punishment on human behavior*. New York: Academic Press.

Duda, J.L., & Treasure, D.C. (2006). Motivational processes and the facilitation of performance, persistence, and well-being in sport. In J.M. Williams (ed.) *Applied sport psychology: Personal growth to peak performance*. (pp. 57-81). New York: McGraw-Hill.

Gibbons, T., McConnell, A., Forster, T., Tuffey-Riewald, S., and Peterson, K. (2003). *Reflections on success: U.S. Olympians describe the success factors and obstacles that most influenced their Olympic development*. Results of the Talent Identification and Development Questionnaire to U.S. Olympians. A USOC 2003 publication.

Huber, J.J. (2007). *Becoming a champion diver: Striving to reach your greatest potential*. DVD. Ames, IA: Championship Books and Video Productions.

Janelle, C.M., Barba, D.A., Frehlich, S.G., Tennant, L.K., & Cauraugh, J.H. (1997). Maximizing performance feedback effectiveness through videotape replay and a self-controlled learning environment. *Research Quarterly for Exercise and Sport, 68*, 269-279.

Kernodle, M.W., & Carlton, L.G. (1992). Information feedback and the learning of multiple-degree-of-freedom activities. *Journal of Motor Behavior, 24*, 187-196.

Lavery, J.J. (1962). Retention of simple motor skills as a function of the number of trials by which KR is delayed. *Perceptual and Motor Skills, 15*, 231-237.

Lee, D.L., & Belfiore, P.J. (1997). Enhancing classroom performance: A review of reinforcement schedules. *Journal of Behavioral Education, 7*, 205-217.

Lepper, M.R. (1981). Intrinsic and extrinsic motivation in children: Detrimental effects of superfluous social controls. In W.A. Collins (ed.), *Aspects of the development of competence: Minnesota symposium on child psychology* (Vol. 14, pp. 155-213). Hillsdale, NJ: Erlbaum.

Lepper, M.R., & Greene, D. (1975). Turning play into work: Effects of adult surveillance and extrinsic reward on children's intrinsic motivation. *Journal of Personality and Social Psychology, 31*, 479-486.

McFadden, A.C., Marsh, G.E. II, Price, B.J., & Hwang, Y. (1992). A study of race and gender bias in the punishment of school children. *Education and Treatment of Children, 15*, 140-146.

Rothstein, A.L., & Arnold, R.K. (1976). Bridging the gap: Application of videotape feedback and bowling. *Motor Skills: Theory into Practice, 1*, 35-62.

Schembechler, B., & Bacon, J.U. (2007). *Bo's lasting lessons*. New York: Business Plus. Schmidt, R.A., & Lee, T.D. (2011). *Motor control and learning: A behavioral emphasis*. Champaign, IL: Human Kinetics.

Schmidt, R.A., & Wrisberg, C. A. (2008). *Motor learning and performance: A situation-based learning approach*. Champaign, IL: Human Kinetics.

Swinnen, S.P. (1990). Interpolated activities during the knowledge-of-results delay and post-knowledge-of-results interval: Effects on performance and learning. *Journal of Experimental Psychology: Learning, Memory, and Cognition, 16*, 692-705.

Thorndike, E.L. (1931). *Human learning*. New York: Appleton-Century-Crofts.

Van Houten, R., & Doleys, D.M. (1983). Are social reprimands effective? In S. Axelrod & J. Apsche (eds.), *The effects of punishment on human behavior*. New York: Academic Press.

Van Houten, R., Nau, P.A., MacKenzie-Keating, S., Sameoto, D., & Colavecchia, B. (1982). An analysis of some variables influencing the effectiveness of reprimands. *Journal of Applied Behavior Analysis, 15*, 65-83.

Chapter 5

Bandura, A. (1962). Social learning through imitation. In N.R. Jones (ed.), *Nebraska symposium on motivation*. Lincoln: University of Nebraska Press.

Bandura, A. (1977). *Social learning theory.* Morristown, NJ: General Learning.

Bandura, A., & Walters, R. (1963). *Social learning and personality development.* New York: Holt.

Brewer, K.R., & Wann, D.L. (1998). Observational learning effectiveness as a function of model characteristics: Investigating the importance of social power. *Social Behavior and Personality, 26,* 1-10.

Gibbons, T., Hill, R., McConnell, A., Forster, T., & Moore, J. (2002). *The path to excellence: A comprehensive view of development of U.S. Olympians who competed from 1984-1998.* Results of the Talent Identification and Development Questionnaire to U.S. Olympians. A USOC 2002 publication.

Hughes, M., Nowicki, S., & Lohr, B. (1998). Call learning in black-capped chickadees (Parus atricapillus): The role of experience in the development of "chick-a-dee" calls. *Ethology, 104,* 232-249.

Kaiser, D. H., Zentall, T.R., & Galef, B.G. (1997). Can imitation in pigeons be explained by local enhancement together with trial-and-error learning? *Psychological Science, 8,* 459-460.

Masia, C.L., & Chase, P.N. (1997). Vicarious learning revisited: A contemporary behavior analytic interpretation. *Journal of Behavior Therapy and Experimental Psychology, 28,* 41-515.

Chapter 6

Adams, J.A., (1971). A closed-loop theory of motor learning. *Journal of Motor Behavior, 3,* 111-150.

Alba, J.W., & Hasher, L. (1983). Is memory schematic? *Psychological Bulletin, 93,* 203-231.

Allard, F., & Burnett, N. (1985). Skill in sport. *Canadian Journal of Psychology, 39,* 294-312.

Allard, F., Graham, S., & Paarsalu, M.E. (1980). Perception in sport: Basketball. *Journal of Sport Psychology,* 2, 14-21.

Anderson, J.R. (1976). *Language, memory, and thought.* Hillsdale, NJ: Erlbaum.

Anderson, J.R. (1983). *The architecture of cognition.* Cambridge, MA: Harvard University Press.

Anderson, J.R. (1990). *The adaptive character of thought.* Hillsdale, NJ: Erlbaum.

Anderson, J.R. (1993). *Rules of the mind.* Hillsdale, NJ: Erlbaum.

Anderson, J.R. (2007). *How can the human mind occur in the physical Universe?* NY: Oxford University Press.

Anderson, J.R., Kline, P.J., & Beasley, C.M. (1977). *A theory of the acquisition of cognitive skills.* ONR Technical Report 77-1, Yale University.

Anderson, J.R., Kline, P.J., & Beasley, C.M. (1980). Complex learning processes. In R.E. Snow, P.A. Federico, and W.E. Montague (eds.), *Aptitude, learning, and instruction* (Vol. 2). Hillsdale, NJ: Erlbaum Associates.

Armstrong, T.R. (1970). *Training for the production of memorized movement patterns.* (Tech. Rep. No. 26). Ann Arbor: University of Michigan, Human Performance Center.

Atkinson, R., & Shiffrin, R. (1968). Human memory: A proposed system and its control processes. In K. Spence and J. Spence (eds.), *The psychology of learning and motivation* (Vol. 2). New York: Academic Press.

Baars, B.J. (1986). *The cognitive revolution in psychology.* New York: Guilford Press.

Baddeley, A.D. (1997). *Human memory: Theory and practice (Revised edition).* Hove: Psychology Press.

Bard, C., & Fleury, M. (1981). Considering eye movement as a predictor of attainment. In I.M. Cockerill & W.W. MacGillivary (eds.), *Vision and sport* (pp. 28-41). Cheltenham, UK: Stanley Thornes.

Bartlett, F.C. (1932). *Remembering: A study in experimental and social psychology.* Cambridge, England: Cambridge University Press.

Bjork, R.A. (1975). Retrieval as a memory modifier. In R. Solso (ed.), *Information processing and cognition: The Loyola Symposium* (pp. 123-144). Hillsdale, NJ: Erlbaum.

Bjork, R.A. (1979). *Retrieval practice.* Unpublished manuscript, University of California at Los Angeles.

Bruning, R.H., Schraw, G.J., & Ronning, R.R. (1995). *Cognitive psychology and instruction.* Englewood Cliffs, NJ: Prentice-Hall.

Calfee, R.C. (1981). Cognitive psychology and educational practice. In D.C. Berliner (ed.), *Review of research in education* (Vol. 9). Washington, DC: American Educational Research Association.

Catalano, J.F., & Kleiner, B.M. (1984). Distant transfer and practice variability. *Perceptual and Motor Skills, 58,* 851-856.

Chi, M.T.H., Feltovich, P.J., & Glaser, R. (1981). Categorization and representation of physics problems by experts and novices. *Cognitive Science, 5,* 121-152.

Collins, A.M. & Quillian, M.R. (1969). Retrieval time from semantic memory. *Journal of Verbal Learning and Verbal Behavior, 8,* 240-248.

Craik, F.I.M., & Lockhart, R.S. (1986). CHARM is not enough: Comments on Eich's model of cued recall. *Psychological Review, 93*, 360-364.

Dansereau, D.F. (1985). Learning strategy research. In J.W. Segal, S.F. Chipman, & R. Glaser (eds.), *Thinking and learning skills* (pp.1, 209-240). Hillsdale, NJ: Erlbaum.

Easterbrook, J. A. (1959). The effect of emotion on cue utilization and the organization of behavior. *Psychological Review, 66*, 183-201.

Fitts, P.M. (1964). Perceptual-motor skills learning. In A.W. Melton (ed.), *Categories of human learning* (pp. 243-285). New York: Academic Press.

Fitts, P.M. & Posner, M.I. (1967). *Human performance.* Belmont, CA: Brooks Cole.

Gagne, E.D. (1985). *The cognitive psychology of school learning.* Boston: Little, Brown.

Gentile, A.M. (1972). *A working model of skill acquisition with application to teaching.* Quest Monograph XVII, 3-23.

Head, H. (1926). *Aphasia and kindred disorders of speech.* Cambridge: Cambridge University Press.

Huber, J.J. (1997). Differences in problem representation and procedural knowledge between elite and nonelite springboard divers. *The Sport Psychologist, 11*(2), 142-159.

Lee, T.D. & Magill, R.A. (1983b). The locus of contextual interference in motor-skill acquisition. *Journal of Experimental Psychology: Learning, Memory, and Cognition, 9*, 730-746.

Lee, T.D., & Magill, R.A. (1985). Can forgetting facilitate skill acquisition? In D. Goodman, R.B. Wilberg, & I.M. Franks (eds.), *Differing perspectives in motor learning, memory, and control* (pp. 3-22). Amsterdam: Elsevier.

Magill, R.A. (1985). *Motor learning: Concepts and applications.* Dubuque, IA: Brown.

Neisser, U. (1976). *Cognition and reality.* San Francisco: Freeman.

Newell, K.M. (1985). Coordination, control, and skill. In D. Goodman, R.B. Wilberg, & I.M. Franks (eds.), *Differing perspectives in motor learning, memory, and control* (pp. 295-317). Amsterdam: North-Holland.

Paivo, A. (1971). *Imagery and verbal processes.* New York: Holt, Rinehart & Winston.

Paivo, A. (1986a). Dual coding and episodic memory: Subjective and objective sources of memory trace components. In F. Klix & H. Hafgendorf (eds.), *Human memory and cognitive capabilities: Mechanisms and performances* (Part A, pp. 225-236). Amsterdam: North-Holland.

Paivo, A. (1986b). *Mental representations: A dual coding approach.* New York: Oxford University Press.

Pearson, P.D. (1984). Guided reading: A response to Isabel Beck. In R.C. Anderson, J. Osborn, & R.J. Tierney (eds.), *Learning to read in American schools* (pp. 21-28). Hillsdale, NJ: Erlbaum.

Rumelhart, D.E. (1981). Schemata: The building blocks of cognition. In J.T. Guthrie (ed.), *Comprehension and teaching: Research reviews* (pp. 3-26). Newark, DE: International Reading Association.

Rumelhart, D.E. & Norman, D.A. (1978). Accretion, tuning, and restructuring: Three modes of learning. In J.W. Cotton & R. Klatzky (eds.), *Semantic factors in cognition* (pp. 161-184). Hillsdale, NJ: Lawrence Erlbaum.

Schank, R.C. & Abelson, R. (1977). *Scripts, plans, goals, and understanding.* Hillsdale, NJ: Lawrence Erlbaum.

Schmidt, R.A. (1975). A schema theory of discrete motor skill learning. *Psychological Review, 82*, 225-260.

Schmidt, R.A. & Lee, T.D. (2011). *Motor control and learning: A behavioral emphasis* (5th ed.). Champaign, IL: Human Kinetics.

Schmidt, R.A. & Wrisberg, C.A. (2004). *Motor learning and performance: A problem-based learning approach* (3rd ed.). Champaign, IL: Human Kinetics.

Schmidt, R.A. & Wrisberg, C.A. (2008). *Motor learning and performance: A situation-based learning approach (4th ed.).* Champaign, IL: Human Kinetics.

Shaffer, L.H. (1980). Analyzing piano performance: A study of concert pianists. In G.E. Stelmach & J. Relquin (eds.), *Tutorials in motor behavior* (pp. 443-455). Amsterdam: Elsevier.

Shea, C.H., & Kohl, R.M. (1990). Composition of practice: Influence on the retention of motor skills. *Research Quarterly for Exercise and Sport, 62*, 187-195.

Shea, C.H., & Kohl, R.M. (1991). Composition of practice: Influence on the retention of motor skills. *Research Quarterly for Exercise and Sport, 62*, 187-195.

Shea, C.H., Kohl, R.M., & Indermill, C. (1990). Contextual interference: Contributions of practice. *Acta Psychologica, 73*, 145-157.

Shea, C.H. & Zimmy, S.T. (1983). Context effects in memory and learning movement information. In R. A. Magill (ed.), *Memory and control of action* (pp. 345-366). Amsterdam: Elsevier.

Starkes, J.L. & Deakin, J.M. (1984). Perception in sport: A cognitive approach to skilled performance. In W.F. Straub & J.M. Williams (eds.), *Cognitive sport psychology* (pp. 115-128). Lansing, NY: Sport Science Associates.

Ste-Marie, D.M., Clark, S.E., Findlay, L.C., & Latimer, A.E. (2004). High levels of contextual interference enhance handwriting skill acquisition. *Journal of Motor Behavior, 36,* 115-126.

Thorndike, E.L. (1913). *Educational psychology: The psychology of learning.* New York: Teachers College Press.

Tulving, E. (1983). *Elements of episodic memory.* Oxford, England: Oxford University Press.

Tulving, E. (1985). On the classification problem in learning and memory. In L. Nilsson & T. Archer (eds.), *Perspectives on learning and memory* (pp. 73-101). Hillsdale, NJ: Lawrence Erlbaum.

Williams, A.M. & Davids, K. (1998). Visual search strategy, selective attention, and expertise in soccer. *Research Quarterly for Exercise and Sport, 69,* 111-128.

Williams, J.M. & Harris, D.V. (2006). Relaxation and energizing techniques for regulation of arousal. In J.M. Williams (ed.), *Applied sport psychology: Personal growth to peak performance* (5th ed., pp. 285-305). Dubuque, IA: McGraw-Hill.

Wrisberg, C.A. & Mead, B.J. (1983). Developing coincident-timing skill in children: A comparison of training methods. *Research Quarterly for Exercise and Sport, 54,* 67-74.

Chapter 7

Allard, F., Graham, S., & Paarsalu, M.L. (1980). Perception in sport: Basketball. *Journal of Sport Psychology, 2,* 14-21.

Allard, F., & Starkes, J.L. (1980). Perception in sport: Volleyball. *Journal of Sport Psychology, 2,* 22-33.

Arnove, R.F. (2009). *Talent abounds: Profiles of master teachers and peak performers.* Boulder, CO: Paradigm.

Bailey, D.A. & Martin, A.D. (1988). Chapter 9: The growing child and sport: Physiological considerations. In Smoll, Magill, & Ash (eds.), *Children in sport* (3rd. ed.). Champaign, IL: Human Kinetics.

Bloom, B.S. (1984). The 2 sigma problem: The search for methods of group instruction as effective as one-to-one tutoring. *Educational Researcher, 13 (6),* 4-16.

Bloom, B.S. (1985). *Developing talent in young people.* New York: Ballantine.

Book, W.F., & Norvell, L. (1922). The will to learn: An experimental study of incentives in learning. *Pedagogical Seminary, 29,* 305-362.

Bryan, W.L., & Harter, N. (1897). Studies in the physiology and psychology of the telegraphic language. *Psychological Review, 4,* 27-53.

Chi, M.T.H., Feltovich, P.J., & Glaser, R. (1981). Categorization and representation of physics problems by experts and novices. *Cognitive Science, 5,* 121-152.

Cleary, T., & Zimmerman, B.J. (2001). Self-regulation differences during athletic practice by experts, non-experts, and novices. *Journal of Applied Sport Psychology, 13,* 185-206.

Côté, J., & Fraser-Thomas, J. (2008). Play, practice, and athlete development. In Farrow, D., Baker, J., & MacMahon, C. (eds), Developing sport expertise: *Researchers and coaches put theory into practice.* New York: Routledge.

Côté, J., & Gilbert, W. (2009). An integrative definition of coaching effectiveness and expertise. *International Journal of Sports Science & Coaching,* (Vol. 4, no. 3, pp. 307-323).

Côté, J., & Hayes, J. (2002). Children's involvement in sport: A developmental prospective. In J.M. Silva & D. Stevens (eds.), *Psychological foundations of sport* (2nd ed., pp. 484-502. Boston: Merrill.

Csikszentmihalyi, M., Rathunde, K., & Whalen, S. (1993). *Talented teenagers: The roots of success & failure.* Cambridge, UK: Cambridge University Press,

De Groot, A. (1978). *Thought and choice in chess.* The Hague, Netherlands: Mouton. (Original work published 1946.)

Dvorak, A., Merrick, N.L., Dealey, W.L., & Ford, G.C. (1936). Typewriting behavior: Psychology applied to teaching and learning typewriting. New York: American Books.

Ericsson, K.A. (2003). Development of elite performance and deliberate practice: An update from the perspective of the expert performance approach. In J.L. Starkes & K.A Ericsson (eds.), *Expert performance in sports: Advances in research on sport expertise* (pp. 49-84). Champaign, IL: Human Kinetics.

Ericsson, K.A., Krampe, R.T., & Tesch-Romer, C. (1993). The role of deliberate practice in the acquisition of expert performance. *Psychological Review, 100 (3):* 363-406.

French, K.E., & McPherson, S.L. (2004). Development of expertise in sport. In M.R. Weiss (ed.), *Developmental sport and exercise psychology: A lifespan perspective.* Morgantown, WV: Fitness Information.

French, K.E., Spurgeon, J.H., Graham, K.C., Rink, J.E., & McPherson, S.L. (1996). Knowledge representation and problem solving in expert and novice youth baseball performance. *Research Quarterly for Exercise and Sport, 66,* 194-201.

French, K.E., Spurgeon, J.H., & Nevett, M.E. (1995). Expert-novice differences in cognitive and skill execution components of youth baseball performance. *Research Quarterly for Exercise and Sport, 67*, 386-395.

French, K.E. & Thomas, J.R. (1987). The relation of knowledge development to children's basketball performance. *Journal of Sport Psychology, 9*, 15-32.

Grand, D. & Goldberg, A. (2011). *This is your brain on sports: Beating blocks, slumps, and sporting anxiety for good!* Indianapolis, IN: Dog Ear Publishing.

Gustin, W.C. (1985). The development of exceptional research mathematicians. In B.S. Bloom (ed.): *Developing talent in young people* (pp. 139-192). New York: Ballantine.

Hayes, J.R. (1981). *The complete problem solver.* Philadelphia: Franklin Institute Press.

Horton, S. & Deakin, J.M. (2008). Expert coaches in action. In D. Farrow, J. Baker, & C. MacMahon (eds.), *Developing sport expertise: Researchers and coaches put theory into practice* (pp. 75-88). New York: Routledge.

Huber, J.J. (1997). Differences in problem representation and procedural knowledge between elite and nonelite springboard divers. *The Sport Psychologist, 11* (2), 142-159.

Janelle, C.M., & Hillman, C.H., (2003). Expert performance in sport: Current perspective and critical issues. In Starkes, J.L., & Ericsson, K.A. (eds.), *Expert Performance in sports: Advances in research on sport expertise* (pp. 19-48). Champaign, IL: Human Kinetics.

Kalinowski, A.G. (1985). The development of Olympic swimmers. In B.S. Bloom (ed.), *Developing talent in young people* (pp. 139-192). New York: Ballantine.

McCann, S. (2002). So you want to be a great "Big Event Coach"—Three things that can make or break you. USOC publication: http://coaching.usolympicteam.com/coaching/kpub.nsf/v/mind 1.

McDermott, J., & Larkin, J.H. (1978). Re-representing textbook physics problems. *Proceedings of the 2nd National Conference of the Canadian Society for Computational Studies of Intelligence.* Toronto: University of Toronto Press.

McPherson, S.L. (1999). Expert-novice differences in performance skills and problem representation of youth and adults during tennis competition. *Research Quarterly for Exercise and Sport, 70*, 233-251.

Monsaas, J.A. (1985). Learning to be a world-class tennis player. In B.S. Bloom (ed.), *Developing talent in young people* (pp. 211-269). New York: Ballantine.

Pankhurst, A. (2009). *Expert coaches of high performance athletes.* USOC publication: http://coaching.usolympicteam.com/coaching/kpub.nsf/v/21July09.

Pfau, H.D., & Murphy, M.D. (1988). Role of verbal knowledge in chess. *American Journal of Psychology, 101*, 73-86.

Raglin, J.S. & Wilson, G.S. (2000). Overtraining in athletes. In Y.L. Hanin (ed.), *Emotions in sport* (pp.191-207). Champaign, IL: Human Kinetics.

Richman, H.B., Gobet, F., Staszewski, J.J., & Simon, H.A. (1996). Perceptual and memory processes in the acquisition of expert performance: The EPAM model. In Ericsson, K.A. (ed.), *The road to excellence: The acquisition of expert performance in the arts and sciences, sports and games* (pp. 167-188). Mahwah, NJ: Lawrence Erlbaum Associates.

Scanlan, T.K., Russell, D.G., Beals, K.P., & Scanlan, L.A. (2003). Project on elite athlete commitment (PEAK): II. A direct test and expansion of the sport commitment model with elite amateur sportsmen. *Journal of sport and exercise psychology*, 2003, *25*, 377-401.

Silva, J.M. (1990). An analysis of the training stress syndrome in competitive athletes. *Journal of Applied Sport Psychology, 2*, 5-20.

Simon, H.A., & Chase, W.G. (1973). Skill in chess. *American Scientist, 61*, 394-403.

Sloane, K.D. (1985). Home influences on talent development. In Bloom, B.S. (ed.), *Developing talent in young people* (pp. 439-476). New York: Ballantine.

Starkes, J.L., Deakin, J.M., Allard, F., Hodges, N.J., & Hayes, A. (1996). Deliberate practice in sports: What is it anyway? In K.A. Ericsson (ed.), *The road to excellence: The acquisition of expert performance in the arts and sciences, sports and games* (pp. 81-106). Mahwah, NJ: Erlbaum.

Young, B.W., & Medic, N. (2008). The motivation to become an expert athlete: How coaches can promote long-term commitment. In D. Farrow, J. Baker, & C. MacMahon (eds.), *Developing sport expertise: Researchers and coaches put theory into practice* (pp. 43-59). NewYork: Routledge.

Wallingford, R. (1975). Long distance running. In A.W. Taylor, & F. Landry (eds.), *The scientific aspects of sport* training (pp. 118-130). Springfield, IL: Charles C. Thomas.

Webb, N.L. (1975). An exploration of mathematical problem-solving processes. *Dissertation Abstracts International, 36*, 2689A (University Microfilms No. 75-25, 626).

Chapter 8

Bloom, B.S. (1976). *Human characteristics and school learning.* New York: McGraw-Hill.

Buscaglia, L. (Speaker). (1984a). "Love." Cassette recording titled *On being fully human.* MCMLXXXIV. Chicago: Nightingale-Conant.

Buscaglia, L. (Speaker). (1984b). "Love." Cassette recording titled *Teach life.* MCMLXXXIV Chicago: Nightingale-Conant.

Carron, A.V. & Bennett, B.B. (1977). Compatibility in the coach-athlete dyad. *Research Quarterly, 48,* 671-679.

Gilbert, W, Nater, S., Siwik, M, & Gallimore, R. (2010). The pyramid of teaching success in sport: Lessons from applied science and effective coaches. *Journal of Sport Psychology in Action, 1:2,* 86-94.

Heitman, H.M. & Kneer, M. (1976). *Physical education instructional techniques: An individualized humanistic approach.* Englewood Cliffs, NJ: Prentice Hall.

Joyce, B., Weil, M., and Calhoun, E. (2009). *Models of teaching.* Englewood Cliffs, NJ: Prentice Hall.

Lefrançois, G.R. (2012). *Theories of human learning: What the professor said.* Belmont, CA: Wadsworth.

Lombardo, B.J. (1987). *The humanistic coach: From theory to practice.* Springfield, IL: Thomas.

Piaget, J. (1972). Intellectual development from adolescence to adulthood. *Human Development, 15,* 1-12.

Purkey, W.W., & Novak, J.M. (1996). *Inviting school success: A self-concept approach to teaching, learning, and democratic practice* (3rd ed.). Belmont, CA: Wadsworth.

Rogers, C.R. (1951). *Client-centered therapy: Its current practices, implications, and theory.* Boston: Houghton Mifflin.

Rogers, C.R. (1995). *On becoming a person.* New York: Houghton Mifflin.

Simon, S.B., Howe, L.W., & Kirschenbaum, H. (1972). *Values clarification: A handbook of practical strategies for teachers and students.* New York: Hart Publishing Company.

Chapter 9

Alexander, F. (1950). *Psychosomatic medicine: Its principles and applications.* New York: Norton.

Ames, C. (1992). Achievement goals, motivational climate, and motivational processes. In G.C. Robers (ed.), *Motivation in sport and exercise* (pp. 161-176). Champaign, IL: Human Kinetics.

Andersen, M.B. & Williams, J.M. (1988). A model of stress and athletic injury: Prediction and prevention. *Journal of Sport and Exercise Physiology, 10,* 294-306.

Arnold, M.B. (1960). *Emotion and personality* (Vols. 1 & 2). New York: Columbia University Press.

Arnold, M.B. & Gasson, J.A. (1954). *The human person: An approach to an integral theory of personality.* New York: Ronald Press.

Aronson, T. A., Carasiti, I., McBane, D., & Whitaker-Axmitia, P. (1989). Biological correlates of lactate sensitivity in panic-disorder. *Biological Psychiatry, 26,* 463-477.

Bramwell, S.T., Masuda, M., Wagner, N.H., & Holmes, T.H. (1975). Psychological factors in athletic injuries: Development and application of the Social and Athletic-Readjustment Rating Scale (SARRS), *Journal of Human Stress, 1,* 6-20.

Carver, (1996). Cognitive interference and the structure of behavior. In I.G. Sarason, G.R. Pierce, & B.R. Sarason (eds.), *Cognitive interference: Theories, methods, and findings* (pp. 25-45). Mahwah, NJ: Lawrence Erlbaum Associates.

Clore, G.L., Schwarz, N., & Conway, M. (1994). Affective causes and consequences of social information processing. In R.S. Wyer & T.K. Srull (eds.), *Handbook of social cognition* (2nd^d ed., Vol. 1, pp. 323-417). Hillsdale, NJ: Erlbaum.

Cryan, P.O. & Alles, E.F. (1983). The relationship between stress and football injuries. *Journal of Sports Medicine and Physical Fitness, 23,* 52-58.

Dale, J. & Weinberg, R.S. (1990). Burnout in sports: A review and critique. *Journal of Applied Sport Psychology, 2,* 67-83.

Deci, E.L. (1980). *The psychology of self-determination.* Lexington, MA: Heath (Lexington Books).

Duda, J.L. (1992). Motivation in sport settings: A goal perspective approach. In G. C. Roberts (Ed., *Motivation in sport and exercise* (pp. 57-91). Champaign, IL: Human Kinetics.

Duda, J.L., Chi, L., & Newton, M. (1990). *Psychometric characteristics of the TEOSQ.* Paper presented at the annual meeting of the North American Society for the Psychology of Sport and Physical Activity, University of Houston, Houston, TX.

Duda, J.L. & Nichols, J.G. (1992). Dimensions of achievement motivation in school-work and sport. *Journal of Educational Psychology, 84,* 290-299.

Duffy, E. (1957). The psychological significance of the concept of "arousal" or "activation." *Psychological Review, 66,* 183-201.

Easterbrook, J.A. (1959). The effect of emotion on cue utilization and the organization of behavior. *Psychological Review, 66,* 183-201.

Eysenck, H.J. & Calvo, M.G.(1992). Anxiety and performance: The processing efficiency theory. *Cognition and Emotion, 6* (6), 409-434.

Fazey, J., & Hardy, L. (1988). *The inverted-U hypothesis: A catastrophe for sport psychology?* (BASS Monograph 1). Leeds, UK: White Line Press.

Frijda, N.H. (1986). *The emotions.* Cambridge: Cambridge University Press.

Frijda, N.H. (1988). The laws of emotion. *American Psychologist, 43,* 349-358.

Gawande, A. (2011). Personal best: Top athletes and singers have coaches. Should you? *The New Yorker,* October, pp. 1-9.

Goleman, D. (1997). *Emotional intelligence: Why it can matter more than IQ.* New York: Bantam Books.

Gould, D. (1996). Personal motivation gone awry: Burnout in competitive athletes. *Quest, 48,* 275-289.

Gould, D. & Krane, V. (1992). The arousal-athletic performance relationship: Current status and future directions. In T.S. Horn (ed.), *Advances in sport psychology* (pp. 119-141). Champaign, IL: Human Kinetics.

Hackfort, D. (1996). The display of emotions in elite athletes. *American Journal of Sports Medicine, 24,* s80-s84.

Hanin, Y.L. (1978). A study of anxiety in sports. In W. F. Straub (ed.), *Sport psychology: An analysis of athlete behavior* (pp. 236-249). Ithaca, NY: Mouvement.

Hanin, Y.L. (1983a). STAI in sport: Problems and perspectives. In E. Apitzsch (Ed.), *Anxiety in sport* (pp. 129-141). Magglingen, Switzerland: FEPSAC.

Hanin, Y.L. (1986). State-trait anxiety research in the USSR. In C. D. Spielberger & R. Diaz-Guerrero (eds.), *Cross cultural anxiety* (Vol. 3, pp. 45-64). Washington, DC: Hemisphere.

Hanin, Y.L. (1995). Individual zones of optimal functioning (IZOF) model: An idiographic approach to performance anxiety. In K. Henschen & W. Straub (eds.), *Sport psychology: An analysis of athlete behavior* (pp. 103-119). Longmeadow, MA: Mouvement.

Hanin, Y.L. (1997a). Emotions and athletic performance: Individual zones of optimal functioning model. *European Yearbook of Sport Psychology, 1,* 29-72.

Hanin, Y.L. (1997b). Emotions and athletic performance. In *Proceedings, 1st International Meeting on Psychology Applied to Sport and Physical Activity* (pp. 27-48). Braga, Portugal: University of Minho.

Hanin, Y.L. (2000a). Individual zones of optimal functioning (IZOF) model: Emotion-performance relationships in sport. In Y.L. Hanin (ed.), *Emotion in sport* (pp. 65-89). Champaign, IL: Human Kinetics.

Hanin, Y.L. (2000b). Successful and poor performance and emotions. In Y.L. Hanin (ed.), *Emotion in sport* (pp. 157-187). Champaign, IL: Human Kinetics.

Hanson, S.J., McCullagh, P., & Tonymon, P. (1992).The relationship of personality characteristics, life stress, and coping resources to athletic injury. *Journal of Sports and Exercise Psychology, 14,* 262-272.

Hardy, C.J., & Riehl, M.A. (1988). An examination of the life stress-injury relationship among noncontact sport participants. *Behavioral Medicine, 14,* 113-118.

Harger, G.J. & Raglin, J.S. (1994). Correspondence between actual and recalled precompetition anxiety in collegiate track and field athletes. *Journal of Sport and Exercise Psychology, 16,* 206-211.

Heil, J. (2000). The injured athlete. In Y.L. Hanin (ed.), *Emotion in sport* (pp. 245-265). Champaign, IL: Human Kinetics.

Henschen, K. (2000). Maladaptive fatigue syndrome and emotions in sport. In Y.L. Hanin (ed.), *Emotion in sport* (pp. 231-242). Champaign, IL: Human Kinetics.

Izard, C. (1993). Four systems for emotion activation: Cognitive and non-cognitive processes. *Psychological Review, 100,* 68-90.

Jokela, M. & Hanin, Y.L. (1997). Does the IZOF model discriminate between successful and less successful athletes? A meta-analysis. *Annual Congress of the European College of Sports Science. Book of abstracts* (Part II, pp. 637-638). Copenhagen: University of Copenhagen.

Kallus, K.W. & Kellmann, M. (2000). Burnout in athletes and coaches. In Y.L. Hanin (ed.), *Emotion in sport* (pp. 209-230). Champaign, IL: Human Kinetics.

Kelley, B.C. & Gill, D.L. (1993). An examination of personal/situational variables, stress appraisal, and burnout in collegiate teacher-coaches. *Research Quarterly for Exercise and Sport, 64,* 94-102.

Kellman, M., Kallus, K.W., Steinacker, J., & Lormes W. (1997). Monitoring stress and recovery during the training camp for the Junior World Championships in rowing. *Journal of Applied Sport Psychology, 9* (Suppl.), S114.

Kleine, D. (1990). Anxiety and sports performance: A meta-analysis. *Anxiety Research, 2*, 113-131.

Krane, V. (1992). Conceptual and methodological considerations in sport anxiety research: From the inverted-U to catastrophe theory. *Quest, 44*, 72-87.

Kubler-Ross, E. (1969). *On death and dying.* New York: Macmillan.

Landers, D.M. & Boutcher, S.H. (1998). Arousal-performance relationships. In J.M. Williams (ed.), *Applied sport psychology: Personal growth to peak performance* (3rd ed., pp. 197-218). Mountain View, CA: Mayfield.

Lazarus, R.S. (1991a). Cognition and motivation in emotion. *American Psychologist, 46* (4), 352-367.

Lazarus, R.S. (1991b). *Emotion and adaptation.* New York: Oxford University Press.

LeDoux, J.E. (1993). Emotional networks in the brain. In M. Lewis & J. Haviland (eds.), *Handbook of emotions* (pp. 109-118). New York : Guilford Press.

LeDoux, J.E. (1994). Emotion, memory, and the brain. *Scientific American, 270*, 50-57.

LeUnes, A.D. & Nation, J.R. (1996). *Sport psychology: An introduction.* Chicago: Nelson-Hall.

Mandler, G. (1984). *Mind and body: Psychology of emotion and stress.* New York: Norton.

Martens, R., Vealey, R.S., & Burton, D. (1990). *Competitive anxiety in sport.* Champaign, IL: Human Kinetics.

Maslach, C. & Jackson, S.E. (1986). *Maslach Burnout Inventory.* Palo Alto, CA: Consulting Psychologists Press.

Morgan, W.P., Brown, D.R., Raglin, J.S., O'Connor, P.J., & Ellickson, K.A. (1987). Psychological monitoring of overtraining and staleness. *British Journal of Sports Medicine, 21*, 107-114.

Morgan, W.P., O'Connor, P.J., Sparling, P.J., & Pate, R.R. (1987). Psychological characterization of the elite female distance runner. *International Journal of Sports Medicine, 8,* 3124-3131.

Newton, M. & Duda, J.L. (1993). The relationship of task and ego orientation to performance: Cognitive content, affect, and attributions in bowling. *Journal of Sport Behavior, 16*, 209-220.

Nicholls, J. (1984). Achievement motivation: Conceptions of ability, subjective experience, task choice, and performance. *Psychological Review, 91*, 328-346.

Nideffer, R.M. (1989). Anxiety, attention, and performance in sports: Theoretical and practical considerations. In D. Hackfort & C.D. Spielberger (eds.), *Anxiety in sports: An international perspective* (pp. 117-136). New York: Hemisphere.

Niedenthal, P.M. & Setterlund, M.B. (1994). Emotion congruence in perception. *Personality and Social Psychology bulletin, 20*, 401-411.

Oatley, K. & Jenkins, J.M. (1996). *Understanding emotions.* Cambridge, MA: Blackwell Scientific.

Ortony, A., Clore, G.L., & Collins, A. (1988). *The cognitive structure of emotions.* Cambridge: Cambridge University Press.

Oxendine, J.B. (1970). Emotional arousal and motor performance. *Quest, 13*, 23-32.

Pennebaker, J.W. & Beall, S.K. (1986). Confronting a traumatic event: Toward an understanding of inhibition and disease. *Journal of Abnormal Psychology, 95*, 274-281.

Raglin, J.S. (1992). Anxiety and sport performance. In J.O. Holloszy (ed.), *Exercise and sport sciences reviews* (Vol. 20, pp. 243-274). New York: Williams & Wilkins.

Raglin, J.S. & Hannin, Y.L. (2000). Competitive Anxiety. In Y.L. Hannin (ed.), *Emotions in Sport* (pp. 93-111). Champaign, IL: Human Kinetics.

Randle, S. & Weinberg, R. (1997). Multidimensional anxiety and performance: An exploratory examination of the zone of optimal functioning hypothesis. *Sport Psychologist, 11*, 160-174.

Schwarz, N. & Strack, F. (1991). Evaluating one's life: A judgment model of subjective well-being. In F. Strack, M. Argyle, & N. Schwarz (eds.), *Subjective well-being: An interdisciplinary perspective* (pp. 27-47). Oxford: Pergamon Press.

Schwarz, N., Strack, F., Kommer, D., & Wagner, D. (1987). Soccer, rooms and quality of your life: Mood effects on judgments of satisfaction with life in general and with specific life domains. *European Journal of Social Psychology, 17*, 69-79.

Shea, J.B. & Morgan, R.L. (1979). Contextual interference effects on the acquisition, retention, and transfer of a motor skill. *Journal of Experimental Psychology: Human Learning and Memory, 5*, 179-187.

Silva, J.M. (1990). An analysis of the training stress syndrome in competitive athletics. *Journal of Applied Sport Psychology, 2*, 5-20.

Smith, R.E. (1986). Toward a cognitive-affective model of athletic burnout. *Journal of Sports Psychology, 8*, 36-50.

Smith, R.E. (1996). Performance anxiety: Cognitive interference, and concentration enhancement strategies in sports. In I.G. Sarason, G.R. Pierce, & B.R. Sarason (eds.), *Cognitive interference: Theories, methods, and findings* (pp. 261-283). Mahwah, NJ: Lawrence Erlbaum Associates.

Smith, R.E., Smoll, F.L., & Ptacek, S.T. (1990). Conjunctive moderator variables in vulnerability and resiliency: Life stress, social support, coping skills, and adolescent sport injuries. *Journal of Personality and Social Psychology, 58*, 360-370.

Spielberger, C.D. (1972). Anxiety as an emotional state. In C.D. Spielberger (ed.), *Anxiety: Current trends in theory and research* (Vol. 1). New York: Academic Press.

Spielberger, C.D., Gorsuch, R.L., & Lushene, R.E. (1970). *Manual for the state-trait anxiety inventory (STAI)*. Palo Alto, CA: Consulting Psychologist Press.

Spielberger, C.D., Gorsuch, R.L., Lushene, R.E., Vagg, P.R., & Jacobs, G.A. (1983). *Manual for the state trait anxiety inventory: STAI (Form Y)*. Palo Alto, CA: Consulting Psychologist Press.

Taylor, A.H., Daniel, J.V., Leith, L., & Burke, R.J. (1990). Perceived stress, psychological burnout and paths to turnover intentions among sport officials. *Journal of Applied Social Psychology, 2*, 84-97.

Teigen, K.H. (1994). Yerkes-Dodson: A law for all seasons. *Theory & Psychology, 4*, 525-547.

Turner, P.E. & Raglin, J.S. (1996). Variability in precompetition anxiety and performance in college track and field athletes. *Medicine and Science in Sports and Exercise, 28* (3), 378-385.

Vallerand, R.J. (1987). Antecedents of self-related affects in sport: Preliminary evidence on the intuitive-reflective appraisal model. *Journal of Sport Psychology, 9*, 161-182.

Vallerand, R.J. & Blanchard, C.M. (2000). The study of emotion in sport and exercise: Historical, definitional, and conceptual perspectives. In Y. L. Hanin (Ed.), *Emotion in sport* (pp. 3-37). Champaign, IL: Human Kinetics.

Vanden Auweele, Y., Cuyper, B.D., Mele, V.V., & Rzewnicki, R. (1993). Elite performance and personality: From description and prediction to diagnosis and intervention. In R.N. Singer, M. Murphy, & L.K. Tennant (Eds.), *Handbook of research on sport psychology* (pp. 257-289). New York: Macmillan.

Vealey, R.S., Udry, E.M. Zimmerman, V., & Soliday, J. (1992). Intrapersonal and situational predictors of coaching burnout. *Journal of Sports and Exercise Psychology, 14*, 40-58.

Weinberg, R.S. (1990). Anxiety and motor performance: Where do we go from here? *Anxiety Research, 2*, 227-242.

Weiner, B. (1977). Attribution and affect: Comments on Sohn's critique. *Journal of Educational Psychology, 69*, 506-507.

Weiner, B. (1995). *Judgments of responsibility: A foundation for a theory of social conduct*. New York: Guilford.

Williams, J.M. (1986). Psychological characteristics of peak performance. In J. M. Williams (Ed.), *Applied sport psychology: Personal growth to peak performance* (pp. 121-132). Palo Alto, CA: Mayfield.

Winton, W.M. (1987). Do introductory textbooks present the Yerkes-Dodson law correctly? *American Psychologist, 42*, 202-203.

Yerkes, R.M. & Dodson, J.D. (1908). The relation of strength of stimulus to rapidity of habit-formation. *Journal of Comparative Neurology and Psychology, 18*, 459-482.

Zevon, M.A. & Tellegen, A. (1982). The structure of mood change: An idiographic/nomothetic analysis. *Journal of Personality and Social Psychology, 43* (1), 111-122.

Chapter 10

Copeland, W.D. (1987). Classroom management and student teachers' cognitive abilities: A relationship. *American Educational Research Journal, 24*, 219-236.

Dreikurs, R., & Gray, L. (1968). *Logical consequences: A new approach to discipline*. New York: Hawthorne.

Dreikurs, R., Gunwald, B.B., & Pepper, F.C. (1982). *Maintaining sanity in the classroom: Classroom management techniques* (2nd ed.). New York: Harper & Row.

Gilbert, W, Nater, S., Siwik, M, & Gallimore, R. (2010). The pyramid of teaching success in sport: Lessons from applied science and effective coaches. *Journal of Sport Psychology in Action*, 1:2, 86-94.

Glasser, W. (1969). *Schools without failure*. New York: Harper & Row.

Grossnickle, D.R., & Sesko, F.P. (1990). *Preventive discipline for effective teaching and learning*. Reston, VA: National Association of Secondary School Principals.

Kounin, J.S. (1970). *Discipline and classroom management*. New York: Holt, Rinehart & Winston.

Marland, M. (1975). *The craft of the classroom: A survival guide to classroom management at the secondary school*. London: Heinemann Educational Books.

Premack, D. (1965). Reinforcement theory. In D. Levine (Ed.), *Nebraska Symposium on Motivation*. Lincoln, NE: University of Nebraska Press.

Thorndike, E.L. (1932). Rewards and punishment in animal learning. *Comparative Psychology Monographs, 8*, (39).

Thorndike, E.L. (1933). A proof of the law of effect. *Science, 77*, 173-175.

Walters, G.C., & Grusec, J.E. (1977). *Punishment*. San Francisco: Freeman.

Webster, S.W. (1968). *Discipline in the classroom: Basic principles and problems*. New York: Chandler.

Chapter 11

Allen, J. (2006). *As a man thinketh*. New York: Tarcher/Penguin.

Baier, K. (1958). *The moral point of view: A rational basis of ethics*. Ithaca, NY: Cornell University Press.

Basseches, M. (1984). *Dialectical thinking and adult development*. Norwood, NJ: Ablex.

Bellah, R., Madsen, R., Sullivan, W., Swidler, A., & Tipton, S. (1985). *Habits of the heart: Individualism and commitment in American life*. Berkeley: University of California Press.

Bellah, R., Madsen, R., Sullivan, W., Swidler, A., & Tipton, S. (1991). *The good society*. New York: Knopf.

Dyer, W.W. (2001). *Your erroneous zones*. New York: Harper Collins.

Frankena, W. (1973). *Ethics*. (2nd ed.) Englewood Cliffs, NJ: Prentice Hall.

Glover, J. (2000). *Humanity: A moral history of the twentieth century*. New Haven, CT: Yale University Press.

Gough, R. (1997). *Character is everything: Promoting ethical excellence in sport*. Fort Worth, TX: Harcourt Brace.

Jenkins, L. (2011). Big D (finally) gets its big man. *Sports Illustrated*. January, 17, 2011.

Kidder, R. (1994). *Shared values for a troubled world: Conversations with men and women of conscience*. San Francisco: Jossey-Bass.

Kounin, J.S. (1970). *Discipline and classroom management*. New York: Holt.

Kretchmar, R.S. (2005). *Practical philosophy of sport and physical activity*. Champaign, IL: Human Kinetics.

Labouvie-Vief, G. (1980). Beyond formal operations: Uses and limits of pure logic in life-span development. *Human Development*, 23, 141-161.

Labouvie-Vief, G. (1986). Modes of knowledge and the organization of development. In M.L. Commons, L. Kohlberg, F.A. Richards, & J. Sinnott (eds.), *Beyond formal operations. 3: Models and methods in the study of adult and adolescent thought*. New York: Praeger.

McIntyre, A. (1984). *After virtue*. (2nd ed.) Notre Dame, IN: Univ. of Notre Dame Press.

Midgley, M. (1994). *The ethical primate: Humans, freedom, and morality*. New York: Routledge.

Nater, S. & Gallimore, R. (2010). *You haven't taught until they have learned: John Wooden's teaching principles and practices*. Morgantown, WV: Fitness Information Technology.

Piaget, J. (1961). The genetic approach to the psychology of thought. *Journal of Educational Psychology*, 52, 275-281.

Piaget, J. (1972). Intellectual development from adolescence to adulthood. *Human Development*, 15, 1-12.

Reilly, R. (2006). *Dingbats, dodos and doozies*. Sports Illustrated, November 27, 2006.

Santayana, G. (1905). *Life of reason, reason in common sense*. New York: Scribner.

Santayana, G. (1905). *The life of reason, Vol. 1 of 4: The phases of human progress*. New York: Scribner.

Santayana, G. (1913). *Winds of doctrine: Studies in contemporary opinion*. New York: Scribner.

Singer, P. (1995). *The expanding circle: Ethics and sociobiology*. New York: Farrar, Straus & Giroux.

INDEX

Page numbers ending in an *f* or a *t* indicate a figure or a table, respectively.

ABOUT THE AUTHOR

Jeffrey J. Huber, PhD, is head diving coach and an adjunct assistant professor part-time in the department of counseling and educational psychology and the department of kinesiology at Indiana University at Bloomington. As an educational psychologist, Huber has taught courses in educational psychology for both undergraduate and graduate teacher and coach candidates and is a guest lecturer in courses on exercise science, philosophical foundations of coaching, motor learning, and theories of high-level performance.

Huber received his doctorate in educational psychology and master's of education in curriculum and instruction from the University of Nebraska at Lincoln. A collegiate coach for over 35 years, Huber has been the recipient of the Big Ten, NCAA, USA, and USOC National Coach of the Year awards. Huber was named the U.S. National Coach of the Year 11 times and has served as U.S. coach for the Sydney (2000), Athens (2004), and Beijing (2008) Olympic Games.

In his free time, Huber enjoys running, weightlifting, swimming, and writing. He and his wife, Lesa Huber, PhD, reside in Bloomington.